Writers Under Surveillance

The FBI Files

Writers Under Surveillance

THE FBI FILES

EDITED BY

JPat Brown

B. C. D. Lipton

Michael Morisy

FOREWORD BY

Cory Doctorow

AFTERWORD BY

Trevor Timm

This book was set in Expo Serif Pro. Printed and bound in the United States of America.

Library of Congress Cataloging-in-Publication Data is available.

ISBN: 978-0-262-53638-7

10 9 8 7 6 5 4 3 2 1

Contents

Foreword

THE TRADITIONAL JUSTIFICATION FOR open access laws goes like this: "We, the taxpayers, paid these government entities to produce the writings, images, videos and other materials that go into the formation of policy. These documents belong to us. We paid to produce them. We have the right to see them, to use them, to study them and share them. They are our property."

I love this argument, because I love free access to information, and this argument is very powerful. To refute this argument, a secrecy advocate must argue *against* property rights. In the 21st century, where property rights have been elevated to a human right — and even more, to the most important of all human rights — any argument that can only be refuted by denigrating property rights is a winning argument. If you want to win a debate, corner your opponent so they must argue against property rights (this is a lesson that is not lost on both sides of the copyright debate, and is the reason that "intellectual property" was promulgated as an alternative to the once-universal phrase "creators' monopolies").

But the harnessing of government transparency to property rights is fraught with pitfalls. For one, information is almost entirely unlike property. Property is exclusive and excludable — when you leave my house after an evening's socializing, you don't take my house with you; when I tell you my secrets and then take my leave of you, there's no way for me to take the secret back from your knowledge of it.

Information has multiple uses and contexts. Your house is yours. Your phone number is an integer that can be found in the long string of numbers after the decimal in pi, in the ledgers of public companies, and in the software configuration and databases of your phone company's switches. Your phone number is "yours," but not in the same way that your underwear is. Assigning property rights to integers is a fool's errand.

The primacy of property rights at this moment is the reason we talk about information as property: anything valuable must be property. The way we assert value is to assert property rights. We are so trapped in this frame that we are unable to easily perceive it, but think for a moment of how we talk about the most valuable things in our lives: our children.

Kidnapping is not "theft of child." Infanticide is not "deprival of the use of a child." Your child is not your property, and your child is also not *their* property — your child (and you, and me, and all the other humans) are not property, but we are all enmeshed in a web of *interests*, some bidirectional and some unidirectional. My daughter has an interest in herself; I have an interest in her too, as does my wife (who is her mother) and my parents and my wife's parents, and our daughter's godparents, and her teachers, and her friends, and Child Protective Services, and our neighbors. Some of those interests are stronger than others, and some are limited to narrow domains of our child's life and wellbeing, but this blend of overlapping, contesting interests is undeniable, and the fact that none of these are property rights in no way diminishes the value of that human life.

Information, like humans, is not property, but it is incredibly valuable. Hence Steward Brand's horribly misunderstood and brilliant aphorism: "On the one hand, information wants to be free, and on the other hand, information wants to be expensive."

Talking about government information as property is a handy way to win arguments with secrecy advocates who are also property-rights advocates, but it is a gross and ultimately harmful oversimplification. The state is not a business, and taxes are not a customer-loyalty program. If a piece of government information was produced before you paid your first penny in tax, you still have a right to see it. If you are a child who pays no tax, you still have an interest in state documents; if you are a poor person who pays little or no tax, you have the same right to government information as the one percenter who deigns to pay a million dollars in tax rather than hiding it with an offshore financial secrecy vehicle.

The *real* reason we deserve to see the information our governments produce is so that we can understand what our states are doing in our names — not what they're doing with our money. There's no broad consensus on what constitutes good government, of course, but whatever you think of when you think of "good government," you can't know whether you have it unless you can pierce the veil of government secrecy.

Knowledge allows you to observe the workings of the state and form a hypothesis about how to improve things.

Knowledge allows you to recruit others to your cause by revealing the workings of the state and sharing your hypothesis.

Knowledge allows you to evaluate whether your hypothesis was correct, revealing whether you improved things by trying your intervention out.

The freedom to know, in other words, is the foundational freedom that gives us the freedom to *do*.

But knowledge in and of itself is not enough. The right to know without the freedom to act on that knowledge is not empowering, it is a recipe for despair. Indeed, information without agency is a literal tactic of torturers: during the Inquisition, torturers engaged in a practice called "showing the instruments," in which every implement that might be used in the coming torture session was lovingly revealed and shown to the victim, to heighten their anticipation of the horrors to come. Winston Smith knows exactly what's in Room 101 and that is why he dreads it so much. Goldfinger's laser slowly proceeds up the torture table towards James Bond's crotch — rather than simply lancing through his chest-cavity — because Goldfinger wants Bond to suffer before he dies.

But again, knowledge is our necessary precondition for improving even hopeless situations. Knowing what rules the state imposes (that is, which laws are in force and what they say) is the precondition for effecting civil disobedience by skirting the law without breaking it. Knowing how the courts operate, or what procedures the police follow, or which ministries will not reveal their secrets, gives us the raw material for formulating plans to outmaneuver them, to reveal the shape of secrets by exploring the non-secret information that surrounds them: "If you won't tell me the names of everyone who *is* a police informant, then tell me the names of everyone who *isn't* one."

MuckRock's users have remorselessly tugged at every loose thread in the fabric of official secrecy, unraveling schemes and capers, as well as unintentional farces. MuckRock's beautifully simple interface and community features do much to automate the process of not just forming hypotheses about shameful secrets; but also recruiting others to help act on them. Muckrock is the first step in the 21st Century's great experiment in evidence-based rule, in the presumption of transparency, and in the use of transparency to effect change.

This volume you hold now is an extrusion into the physical world of something vast and digital, huge in the way that only digital things can be huge, where adding another zero to an already inconceivably large number is as easy as typing a single keystroke. We have never in our species' history possessed this sort of tool. It is a ferociously exciting prospect. As states move to assert the right to know more and more about our personal business, MuckRock represents the best hope for people knowing more and more about their states.

It's a race we can't afford to lose.

CORY DOCTOROW

Introduction

IN 2010, MUCKROCK WAS started to make it easier for citizens to understand what their government is up to in their name, using public records laws and the Freedom of Information Act. While these laws have existed for decades, they're often complex and challenging for even seasoned reporters to take advantage of, let alone ordinary citizens who find themselves facing off with complex bureaucracy to get answers to basic questions.

You have the right to get information that the government has unless it's specifically exempted (see the latter part of this introduction for a brief overview of some of those exemptions), and MuckRock's goal has been to make that access easier and more collaborative.

Today, we have a large and thriving community of open government watchdogs that share tips, advice, and request ideas, and, we've helped thousands of journalists, researchers, and ordinary people file and share their records requests, publishing millions of pages of previously secret records that rightfully belong to the public. As we're writing this introduction, we've helped file just under 50,000 total requests, covering police surveillance, out of control government spending, and hundreds of other topics.

But no single agency has garnered nearly as much interest — nor as many requests — as the Federal Bureau of Investigation.

Under the federal Freedom of Information Act, you may request the FBI files on deceased individuals. While occasionally there may still be an active investigation or other reason that precludes release, most of the time the FBI will provide the information they collected on that person. The releases often include contradictions, unsubstantiated gossip, intrigue, and, almost always, heavy redactions. They are also often illuminating, though sometimes more about the Bureau or about the politics of the day than the person they portend to be about.

MuckRock published its first FBI file a little under a year after the site was founded in 2010. The file was on actor Leslie Nielsen, whom the Bureau briefly investigated on behalf of the Royal Canadian Mounted Police. A year after that came our first article based on an FBI file, which explored a 1991 background check for Steve Jobs that was released shortly after his death.

By the time we formalized a project to uncover and analyze these files in 2015, MuckRock had already reported on dozens of the Bureau's investigations and released hundreds of other files on our website. To date, we've published over 200 articles on figures ranging from Roger Ailes to Howard Zinn, at a rate of roughly one a week.

Releasing material through FOIA takes time, even in the best cases, and you never know if your request will turn up thousands of heavily-redacted pages or nothing at all. Thanks to a full century of surveillance, however, FBI files are the journalistic equivalent of an infinite resource: the Bureau's not going to run out of dead people it wanted to keep an eye on anytime soon, so even factoring for delays and rejections, it doesn't take that long to build up an collection of material worth reading.

As these things do, the project soon took on a life of its own. Collect enough files, and a hidden history of the 20th century starts to form. One in which unchecked authoritarian power operated in plain sight, ruled for almost fifty years by a single man's belief that his ends justified his means. Did J. Edgar Hoover foil terror plots during his tenure as Director? Certainly. Did he order investigations into people for as little as making fun of his name? Also true. As a man whose ability was only matched by his pettiness, Hoover embodies the institution that could not have existed without him: comical, terrifying, and absolutely everywhere, all at once, even in a pre-digital age where that was prohibitively expensive.

With one exception, every investigation featured in this book was signed off on by Hoover himself. This book, and the larger FBI Files project, is an attempt to understand the world as Hoover saw it, so we may understand the world Hoover left us. For if the 20th century truly was the American century, then it was the Director's century. Join us in bringing that to light.

If you'd like to further explore these files, and thousands more, visit us at MuckRock.com. Maybe you'll even file a request of your own and help uncover some hidden history.

Notes on Selections for this Collection

ACCESS TO THE MATERIALS of the Federal Bureau of Investigation has always been a bit scattershot.

Before the changes to the Freedom of Information Act (FOIA) and federal recordkeeping, not a single Bureau document had been transferred to the National Archives and Records Administration. The change came in 1974, two years after the passing of J. Edgar Hoover, a man who had ruled the agency through its multiple iterations. With these changes came unprecedented access to the reams of materials gathered by the Bureau in the years under his direction, covering the Red Scare and an explosion in FBI resources.

Since then, FBI documents have been routinely destroyed or transferred to NARA. Despite the responsibility to retain historical materials, the application of what counts as important enough to keep has been varied, and, though we imposed our own limitations on those that made it into this collection — based on popularity and provocation — the restrictions of record keeping as they currently exist also made its curatorial contributions.

As mentioned previously, Individual files become public record under FOIA once the subject is deceased; otherwise, that person has to give his or her explicit permission. This excluded any living authors from our collection.

There were a few common causes for authors — or anyone — to end up on the FBI's radar: suspected Communist sympathies, travel to Cuba (Capote, Ginsberg, Hemingway), criticism of Hoover or the FBI (Mailer, Vidal), possible incitement of jaunts in European philosophy (Arendt).

Others we chose based on the effect the Bureau ultimately had on their lives, like Hemingway, whose life in the government got in the way of his writing and may have contributed to his death.

Materials from other agencies do exist, but many have been withheld by the FBI due their initial creation by another department. Newspaper clippings and library cards were removed from this publication, although you can see these clippings in the FBI's original releases on our website. We also removed redundant reports (it's not uncommon for notes to be copied two or three times in one files).

What we've compiled, we hope, is a streamlined look at how our top domestic law enforcement agency kept tabs on some of the greatest leaders in letters, one that can provide anyone some insight into the all-too-human biases and political considerations that gave some authors a place in the FBI's permanent record.

Guide to Exemptions

DESPITE THE AGE OF some of these files, large portions remains redacted under the nine federal exemptions. Wherever there is an excision of the text (usually a white bar, but black marker is not uncommon in the older records) look for a corresponding code in the margins.

b(1) – National security
Material considered classified under an Executive Order. While typically relating to matters of national security, due to the age of these records, it's much more likely they are damaging or embarrassing investigations involving foreign governments.

b(2) – Operational
Material "related solely to the internal personnel rules and practice" which is fairly vague and appears to have been used by the Bureau to exempt the names of some special agents.

b(3) – Specifically exempted by another law
Used in cases where a separate statute or law prohibits disclosure, this exemption is commonly used in conjunction with b(1) and citing the CIA Act of 1949, relating to interagency investigations.

b(4) – Trade secrets/proprietary business information
Used to protect private business information; this exemption doesn't appear in these files.

b(5) – Deliberative process
Another vague exemption that applies to "Inter-agency or intra-agency memorandums or letters that would not be available by law to a party" and has a reputation for abuse, especially with historical records.

b(6) – Privacy
Any information that could reasonably be construed to be an invasion of privacy, used here to redact the names or other identifying material of people the Bureau is not sure are dead.

b(7) – Law enforcement records

Understandably, the exemption most used by the FBI, and broken down into five sub-categories.

(a) Imminent law enforcement proceedings

Related to "open investigations" — due to the historical nature of these files, this exemption is not used.

(b) Imminent trial

Similar to b(7)(a), but for information that would negatively impact a person's right to a fair trial, and similarly not used due to the age of these records.

(c) Privacy

A variation of the b(6) FOIA exemption specifically for law enforcement records, and used fairly interchangeably.

(d) Confidential source

With privacy and law enforcement techniques, probably the most common exemption cited in the files due to the Bureau's extensive network of informants.

(e) Law enforcement technique

Confidential or controversial techniques, such as wiretaps — considering that it is supposed to apply only for such methods still in use, it's reasonable to say this has been overapplied here.

(f) Endanger life or physical safety

Anything that could reasonably be argued puts people at risk through disclosure, which fortunately doesn't apply to decades-old FBI files.

b(8) – Financial records

Materials related to agencies that regulate financial institutions are specifically exempted, which these file are not.

b(9) – Wells

More of a trivia question than a legitimate exemption; there are no wells mentioned within these FBI files.

Glossary

HERE IS A GUIDE to some of the commonly used acronyms from within the FBI's files.

ADEX Administrative Index

AGO Attorney General's Office

ATF Bureau of Alcohol, Tobacco, and Firearms

CIA Central Intelligence Agency

COINTELPRO Counterintelligence Program

CP Communist Party

DEPT Departmental

DOJ Department of Justice

DOKEX Document Examiner

ESP Espionage

EXT Extortion

ELSUR Electronic Surveillance (Wiretaps)

FISUR Physical Surveillance

FOIA Freedom of Information Act

FPC Foreign Police Cooperation

FUG Fugitive

INTD Intelligence Division

IOC Interception of Communication

K&S Known and Suspected

LEGAT Legal Attache

LHM Letterhead Memorandum

MISUR Microphone Surveillance

NSA National Security Agency

OO Office of Origin

PAREN Parenthesis

PCI Priority Case Indicator

REMEMO Reference Is Made to Memo

RELET Reference Is Made to Letter

REREP Reference Is Made To My Report

SA Special Agent

SAC Special Agent in Charge

SED Sedition

SI Security Informant

SM Subversive Matter

SN Serial Number

SPI Special Inquiry

SPIN Conduct Thorough Background Investigation

TOPLEV Top Level Intelligence Program

UNSUBS Unknown Subjects

VIKEX Victim Extortion

WH White House

Writers Under Surveillance

The FBI Files

Hannah Arendt

AS ONE OF THE most prominent political philosophers of the 20th century and the woman who literally wrote the book on totalitarianism and state power, it's not surprising that Hannah Arendt would eventually end up on the FBI's radar. What is surprising, however, is the circumstance that led to the Bureau opening up a file on Arendt — and the decision, signed off by Director J. Edgar Hoover himself, not to pursue the matter any further.

In April of 1956, Hoover received a two-page memo from the FBI's Los Angeles Field Office. A special agent had received a unusually personal tip from a usually reliable informant, whose identity is still redacted in the file. The informant's daughter was currently studying abroad in Europe, a situation with which the informant was very unhappy and for which he blamed Arendt. The informant alleged that Arendt, during her time as a guest professor at the University of California Berkeley, had influenced his daughter's thinking, causing the student to decide to pursue further study abroad. While the informant couldn't say whether Arendt was a Communist, he did claim she was "advocating a totalitarian philosophy," and unless the Bureau did something about it, more fathers across the country might watch their daughters succumb to Arendt's teachings.

The special agent felt the allegation was at least serious enough to warrant more information concerning Arendt, which was provided by the informant or another contact in academia. In addition to outlining her German-Jewish background and a then-current list of degrees and bibliography, the file contains this magnificent description of Arendt: "She is a small, rotund, stoop shouldered woman with a crew-like haircut, masculine voice and a marvelous mind."

Hoover, however, was unimpressed. Another memo, dated a few months later, was in response to a routine inquiry into the case and indicated that no formal investigation had ever begun, as the informant's "non-specific complaint" hadn't warranted the FBI's involvement. Nevertheless, the field office in New York (where Arendt lived) had cross-referenced their files and found that another figure once monitored by the Bureau as a member of the Communist underground had at some point exchanged correspondence with Arendt. For others, that might have been enough to warrant further observation, but it wasn't for Arendt, and her file ends there.

Arendt's file is an example of how what's not in FBI files can often be as mysterious as what is. What was it about Arendt that led Hoover to feel she didn't merit further investigation, despite his, and the Bureau's, demonstrable interest in public intellectuals? Perhaps Hoover counted her reputation as a leading anti-totalitarian sufficient proof of her anti-Communist bona fides? Like Arendt's own work, it's a subject worth a deeper consideration.

STANDARD FORM NO. 64

Office Memorandum • UNITED STATES GOVERNMENT

TO   : DIRECTOR, FBI   DATE: April 30, 1956

FRO[ ]   , LOS ANGELES

SUBJECT: HANNAH ARENDT
         Wa. Hannah Arendt Blucher
         INTERNAL SECURITY - R
         SM - X

       On April 5, 1956, [   ]
Fresno, California, advised SA [   ] that
his daughter, [   ] was presently studying
philosophy under Professor PAUL RICOERUR at Strasbourg,
France. Mr. [   ] advised he felt that HANNAH ARENDT was
very dangerous to the best interests of this country in view
of the fact she is a professor who travels around the United
States instructing at numerous colleges as a visiting professor.
He stated his daughter changed her thinking completely after
taking courses from HANNAH ARENDT at the University of California
at Berkeley, California, in 1955, and feels that it was her
influence which had influenced his daughter to go to Europe
to study under Professor PAUL RICOERUR. Mr. [   ] advised
that from all the information he had been able to gather, he
could not say that HANNAH ARENDT was a Communist, but stated
she was advocating a totalitarian philosophy in her political
courses.

       Mr. [   ] furnished the following information
concerning HANNAH ARENDT, which he obtained from sources in
Berkeley, California. HANNAH ARENDT was born in 1906, educated
in Konigsberg, Germany, and majored in philosophy. She also
studied theology and Greek. She received the degree of
Doctor of Philosophy in Heidelberg, Germany, in the year 1928.
Her first book "The Concept of Love in Augustine" appeared
in 1929 at the publishing house of Springer in Berlin. In 1930,
she began to write a biography of RAHEL VARNHAGEN von ENSE
under the auspices of the Notgemeinschaft der deutschen
Wissenschaft which could never appear since the author had to leave
Germany in 1933 as she is a Jewess. From 1933 until 1940, she
lived in Paris where she was the leader of the Youth Alijah and
also studied European history. She immigrated from Southern
France to the United States in 1941. She became a regular
sponsor of the "Partisan Review", "Commentary," "Review of
Politics" and "Kenyon Review."

2 - Bureau (REGISTERED)
2 - New York (REGISTERED)
2 - San Francisco (REGISTERED)
1 - Los Angeles (105-3361)
[   ]
(7)

RECORDED · 78/45 - 47336

SE 43

MAY 7 1956

b6
b7C

b6
b7C

LA 105-3361

From 1946 to 1948, she was the chief editor of
the "Big Kafka" edition of the Schocken Publishing Company.
In 1949, the publishing company of Lambert Schneider
in Heidelberg published a volume of her essays. In 1951,
this book "The Origins of Totalitarianism," now published
in Germany appeared in America. In 1952, she received a
Guggenheim Fellowship for her works in the field of
political theory and science. She delivered the results of
this study to the public in the autumn of 1953 in a series
of lectures under the auspices of the "Christian Gauss Lecturers"
at Princeton University. In the same year, she gave a second
series of lectures at Notre Dame University. In May, 1954, she
received a prize of the American Acedemy for Arts and Letters
for her literary achievements. In the spring of 1955, she was a
guest professor of Political Science at the University of
California at Berkeley, California. Her maiden name is stated
to be COHEN and she married a man named ARENDT whom she divorced
and later married a man named BLUCHER who is a professor of
philosophy at Bard College on the Upper Hudson. It was described
as a progressive type of institution originally connected with
the Columbia University, according to WOODWARD. She is still
married to Professor BLUCHER and is now residing at 140 Morningside
Drive in New York.

Mr. [   ] stated that the book "Who's Who in
World Jewry" has the following data concerning HANNAH ARENDT.
She was a research fellow at the Kaiser-Leopoldische Museum
in 1931 to 1932; general secretary of the French Branch of the
German Youth Movement in 1935 to 1938; regional director of
Jewish Cultural Reconstruction Committee (US) in 1944 to 1946;
executive secretary of the same committee in 1949 to 1952;
later was on the Board of Directors. At the present time, she is
best described as a writer and visiting professor.

The following is a brief description of the subject
as obtained from information in Mr. [   ] possession:

She is a small, rotund, stoop shouldered woman with
a crew-like haircut, masculine voice and a marvelous mind.
She is described as being very positive, dominating, enthusiastic,
and an eloquent speaker, and as being about fifty years of age.

Information concerning HANNAH ARENDT is being furnished
the Bureau, San Francisco and New York for information purposes.

b6
b7C

- [   ]

- 2 -

STANDARD FORM NO. 64

Office Memorandum · UNITED STATES GOVERNMENT

TO   : SAC, *New York* (Your file ———   DATE: *7-9-56*

FROM   : Director, FBI   (Bufile and Serial *105-47336*

SUBJECT: *Hannah Arendt* *105-0-467* *(+other refs.)* Office of Origin: *ny*
         sm-x

1. ( ) The deadline in this case has passed and the Bureau has not
         received a report. You are instructed to submit a report
         immediately. In the event a report has been submitted, you
         should make a notation of the date on which it was submitted
         on this letter and return it to the Bureau, Room No. *1254*

         Report submitted *CH262396*

         Report will be submitted .... ALL INFORMATION CONTAINED
                                                   HEREIN IS UNCLASSIFIED
         Reason for delay ....   DATE 10-23-86 BY SP-1A6

                        Re L.A. letter dated 4-30-56.

2. (✓) Advise Bureau re status of this case.

3. ( ) Advise Bureau when report may be expected.

4. ( ) Surep immediately.

(Place your reply on this form and return to the Bureau. Note on the
top serial in the case file the receipt and acknowledgment of this communication.)

SEARCHED____ INDEXED____
SERIALIZED____ FILED____
JUL 10 1956
FBI - NEW Y.

105-47336-
ENCLOSURE

b6
b7C

U. S. GOVERNMENT PRINTING OFFICE : 1956—O—377906

Office Memorandum • UNITED STATES GOVERNMENT

TO   :   DIRECTOR, FBI (105-47336)   DATE: 7/11/56

FROM   :   SAC, NEW YORK (105-0-4670A)   CONFIDENTIAL

SUBJECT: HANNAH ARENDT
            SECURITY MATTER -X

Re O-1 form dated 7/9/56, inquiring as to status of this case. O-1 form is attached.

In the opinion of the New York Office, Los Angeles letter of 4/30/56, which carried the character as Internal Security-R, contained a non-specific complaint which did not warrant any active investigation.

Files of the New York Office are negative on HANNAH ARENDT with the following exception:

(U)

Mail cover on [   ] reflected that in October 1946, he received mail from HANNAH ARENDT Schoelen Books, Inc., 342 Madison Avenue, New York City. It will be recalled that [   ] was named by Elizabeth Bentley as a member of the Communist underground group at Washington, D.C.

Los Angeles letter of 4/30/56, has been appropriately indexed and filed in a zero file. No further action is contemplated UACB.

RECORDED

INDEXED-88

2 - Bureau (105-47336)(Att-1) RM   109   105-47336-7
1 - NY 105-0-4670A)

[   ]
   (3)   16 JUL 13 1956

Classified by [   ]
Declassify on: OADR

ALL INFORMATION CONTAINED
HEREIN IS UNCLASSIFIED EXCEPT
WHERE SHOWN OTHERWISE.
CONFIDENTIAL

b6
b7C

James Baldwin

AS AN AUTHOR AND social critic, James Baldwin was known as a powerful voice capturing the racial strife roiling 20th Century America. But to the FBI, Baldwin was something else entirely: a radical danger to the status quo.

The author of *Notes of a Native Son, Giovanni's Room*, and a wealth of other writing instantly checked a whole row of the Bureau's boxes: black, gay, sympathetic to socialist causes, critical of the government. And, in particular, he was critical of FBI Director J. Edgar Hoover.

But as far as the great threat he posed, the FBI's issue with was his ability to articulate, in his words and his speech, an American experience that appeared unfamiliar and dangerous; though it resonated with thousands, it remained perplexing to the establishment.

In one early example, Baldwin appeared to take an active role in turning the Bureau's constant scrutiny to his amusement. In July 1964, the FBI got ahold of a document containing seemingly incontrovertible evidence of a plot against them. Baldwin, in the latest issue of *Playbill*, fresh off his Broadway run of "Blues for Mister Charlie," discussed future projects, which, to the horror of the FBI, included a book about the FBI. Of course, it launched an immediate inquiry into Baldwin's FBI book, even looking into the feasibility of getting advanced copies. Baldwin, however, never wrote the book. And strong evidence suggests he never planned to; he just wanted to the Bureau to think there was a damning exposé waiting around the corner.

Although it's satisfying to think of Baldwin getting some retaliation on the FBI, this incident only encouraged the Bureau. When Hoover himself was informed of the inquiry into Baldwin's purported FBI book, his response was characteristically curt: "Isn't Baldwin a well-known pervert?" No rhetorical question in Hoover's FBI, this comment from the director prompted an additional inquiry into the nature of Baldwin's "perversion," which amounted to a Bureau analysis of Baldwin's writings on an American fear of intimacy and on the psychosexual politics of class and race — the latter of which was a deeply nuanced critique the FBI distilled to "a sympathetic viewpoint on homosexuality."

The Bureau must have forgotten about this report three years later when they received a 1967 letter from someone posing as "Mrs. James Arthur Baldwin," claiming that he was in London. He was, but she certainly wasn't.

Dark comedy such as this, prevalent throughout the file, adds to the horrifying absurdity of a record of Baldwin's surveillance that goes on for decades and stretches for thousands of pages. He was the most dangerous man in America, despite living an ocean away, armed with only a pen.

DECODED COPY

☐ AIRGRAM   ☐ CABLEGRAM   ☐ RADIO   ☒☒ TELETYPE

URGENT 6-6-63   12:40 AM / SAV/DE
TO DIRECTOR   -2-
FROM SAC, NEW YORK   052230

ALL INFORMATION CONTAINED
HEREIN IS UNCLASSIFIED
DATE 5-16-79 BY ...

CONFERENCE WITH ATTORNEY GENERAL, NEW YORK CITY, MAY 24, 1963,
CIVIL RIGHTS MATTERS. MARTIN LUTHER KING, RACIAL MATTERS.
    REFERENCE NEW YORK TELETYPE TO BUREAU DATED MAY 29, 1963
AND NEW YORK AIRTEL TO BUREAU DATED JUNE 4, 1963.
    ON JUNE 4, 1963 NY 3810-S* ADVISED ON ABOVE DATE THAT
STANLEY LEVISON WAS IN CONTACT WITH CLARENCE JONES. LEVISON
INQUIRED WHEN "PHIL" (A. PHILIP RANDOLPH) WAS COMING BACK.
JONES SAID HE WAS AT THE HAMILTON HOTEL IN CHICAGO, COMING
BACK ON THURSDAY. JONES SAID "PHIL'S" REACTION WAS POSITIVE
BUT WANTED TO REFLECT TO WHAT EXTENT THE EMPLOYMENT ISSUE SHOULD
BE PLAYED UP. HE (PHIL) FELT IT WOULD BE "ANTI CLIMATIC TO HAVE
A MARCH IN OCTOBER." JONES SAID THAT "PHIL" WANTS TO TALK TO
MARTIN "LUTHER KING" AND ADDED THAT HE, JONES, HAS BEEN UNABLE
TO REACH MARTIN. JONES FELT THAT MARTIN SHOULD CALL PHIL.
    JONES ALSO STATED THAT HE SPENT ALL DAY SUNDAY AND SUNDAY
EVENING WITH JAMES BALDWIN. HE TOLD LEVISON THAT HE WENT INTO
SOME DETAIL WITH BALDWIN ABOUT SOME OF THE THINKING FOR POLITICAL
ACTION THIS SUMMER. JONES SAID THAT IF MARTIN (KING) ISSUES HIS
STATEMENT THEN BALDWIN WOULD LIKE TO KNOW BECAUSE HE, BALDWIN,
WOULD ALSO ISSUE A STATEMENT SUPPORTING IT, AND BELIEVES IT
MIGHT BE HELPFUL. JONES TOLD LEVISON "I TOLD HIM IT (THE STATE-
MENT) WOULD BE AROUND THE TWELFTH." JONES SAID "HE (BALDWIN)
AGREES WITH IT VERY MUCH WHICH IS THE IMPORTANT THING." JONES
COMMENTED THAT BALDWIN SORT OF GAVE HIM A BLANK CHECK TO DO
WHATEVER HE WANTED IN HIS NAME.
    JONES NEXT INFORMED LEVISON OF A STATEMENT THAT BALDWIN IS
PREPARING. "I HAVE SEEN SOME STATEMENTS OF THE FBI BUT N HAVE

62-108763

NOT RECORDED
199 JUN 20 1963
D JUN

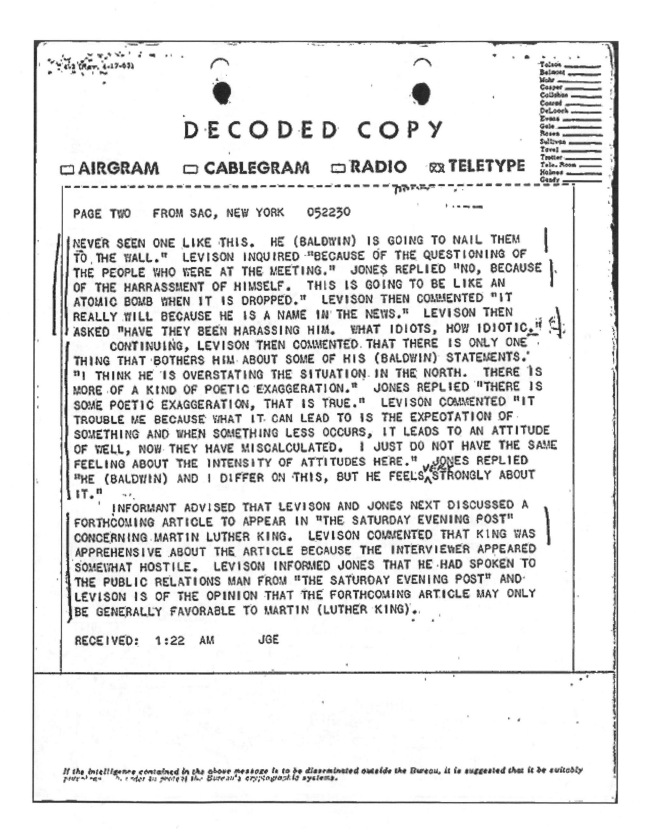

DECODED COPY

☐ AIRGRAM   ☐ CABLEGRAM   ☐ RADIO   ☒ TELETYPE

Tolson _____
Belmont _____
Mohr _____
Casper _____
Callahan _____
Conrad _____
DeLoach _____
Evans _____
Gale _____
Rosen _____
Sullivan _____
Tavel _____
Trotter _____
Tele. Room _____
Holmes _____
Gandy _____

PAGE TWO   FROM SAC, NEW YORK   052230

NEVER SEEN ONE LIKE THIS. HE (BALDWIN) IS GOING TO NAIL THEM
TO THE WALL." LEVISON INQUIRED "BECAUSE OF THE QUESTIONING OF
THE PEOPLE WHO WERE AT THE MEETING." JONES REPLIED "NO, BECAUSE
OF THE HARRASSMENT OF HIMSELF. THIS IS GOING TO BE LIKE AN
ATOMIC BOMB WHEN IT IS DROPPED." LEVISON THEN COMMENTED "IT
REALLY WILL BECAUSE HE IS A NAME IN THE NEWS." LEVISON THEN
ASKED "HAVE THEY BEEN HARASSING HIM. WHAT IDIOTS, HOW IDIOTIC."
    CONTINUING, LEVISON THEN COMMENTED THAT THERE IS ONLY ONE
THING THAT BOTHERS HIM ABOUT SOME OF HIS (BALDWIN) STATEMENTS.
"I THINK HE IS OVERSTATING THE SITUATION IN THE NORTH. THERE IS
MORE OF A KIND OF POETIC EXAGGERATION." JONES REPLIED "THERE IS
SOME POETIC EXAGGERATION, THAT IS TRUE." LEVISON COMMENTED "IT
TROUBLE ME BECAUSE WHAT IT CAN LEAD TO IS THE EXPECTATION OF
SOMETHING AND WHEN SOMETHING LESS OCCURS, IT LEADS TO AN ATTITUDE
OF WELL, NOW THEY HAVE MISCALCULATED. I JUST DO NOT HAVE THE SAME
FEELING ABOUT THE INTENSITY OF ATTITUDES HERE." JONES REPLIED
"HE (BALDWIN) AND I DIFFER ON THIS, BUT HE FEELS VERY STRONGLY ABOUT
IT."
    INFORMANT ADVISED THAT LEVISON AND JONES NEXT DISCUSSED A
FORTHCOMING ARTICLE TO APPEAR IN "THE SATURDAY EVENING POST"
CONCERNING MARTIN LUTHER KING. LEVISON COMMENTED THAT KING WAS
APPREHENSIVE ABOUT THE ARTICLE BECAUSE THE INTERVIEWER APPEARED
SOMEWHAT HOSTILE. LEVISON INFORMED JONES THAT HE HAD SPOKEN TO
THE PUBLIC RELATIONS MAN FROM "THE SATURDAY EVENING POST" AND
LEVISON IS OF THE OPINION THAT THE FORTHCOMING ARTICLE MAY ONLY
BE GENERALLY FAVORABLE TO MARTIN (LUTHER KING).

RECEIVED: 1:22 AM   JGE

If the intelligence contained in the above message is to be disseminated outside the Bureau, it is suggested that it be suitably
paraphrased in order to protect the Bureau's cryptographic systems.

UNITED STATES GOVE

Memorandum

TO   :   Mr. DeLoach   DATE: 6-7-63

FROM   :   M. A. Jones

SUBJECT: JAMES BALDWIN

BACKGROUND:

We have received information to the effect that Baldwin, an author who has been critical of the Bureau and has been connected with communist front and integration activities, is allegedly preparing a statement concerning the FBI which supposedly "is going to nail them to the wall" and "is going to be like an atom bomb when it is dropped." A suggested statement by the Director which can be made in the event Baldwin should make false charges against the Bureau has previously been prepared and will be issued if the circumstances warrant. (WILL, OF COURSE, BE SUBMITTED FOR APPROVAL.)

CURRENT DEVELOPMENT:

A review of today's television listing reflects that a program concerning the "Integration Crisis" will be heard this evening at 9:30 p. m. on local Channel 26. Baldwin will be interviewed by Kenneth Clark of the City College of New York. Also scheduled a statement by Malcolm X, leader of the Black Muslims. Channel 26 is the local educational television station, WETA.

Arrangements have been made for the Laboratory to record this program at 9:30 this evening. A representative of the Crime Research Section will also be present at that time to monitor the program.

CONCERNING KENNETH CLARK

Baldwin and other individuals had a meeting with the Attorney General in New York City on May 24, 1963, at which time racial matters were discussed. One of those attending this meeting was a Dr. Kenneth Clark, who is a psychologist at the City College of New York. Clark has never been investigated by the Bureau. Clark has been very active in the integration movement as well as in the affairs of the National Association for the Advancement of Colored People. In 1959, he was a member of the New York City Board of Education's Commission on Integration in the Schools. In 195__ was reportedly staying at the home of Dr. and Mrs. Clark. _____ in 1958   b6
                                                                                              b7C

RECOMMENDATION:

For information:

1 - Mr. Tolson
1 - Mr. DeLoach   ALL INFORMATION CONTAINED
1 - Mr. Conrad   HEREIN IS UNCLASSIFIED
CJH:jaf   DATE
(7)

62-108763

5 JUN 17 1963   CC MR. TOLSON

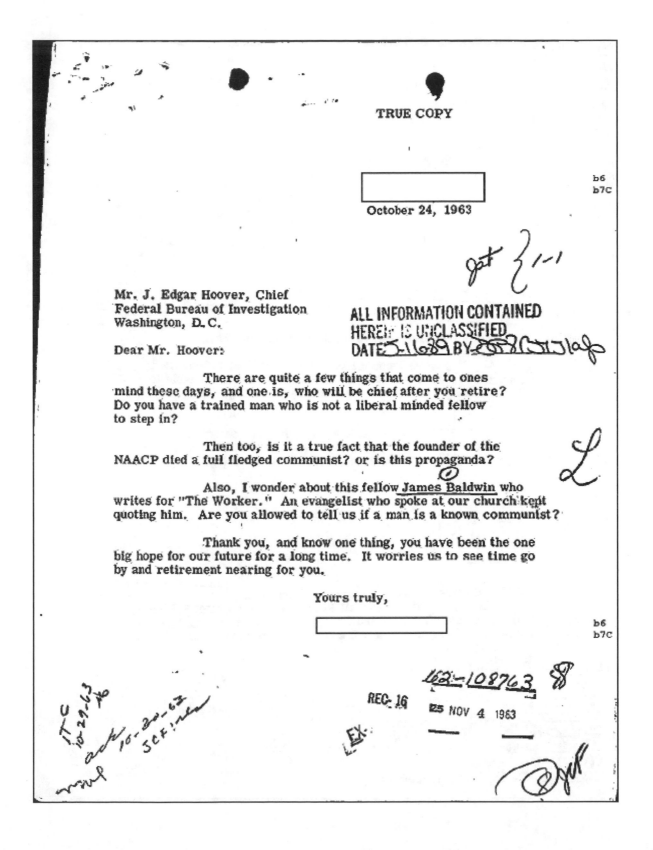

TRUE COPY

b6
b7C

October 24, 1963

ALL INFORMATION CONTAINED
HEREIN IS UNCLASSIFIED
DATE 5-16-89 BY

Mr. J. Edgar Hoover, Chief
Federal Bureau of Investigation
Washington, D.C.

Dear Mr. Hoover:

There are quite a few things that come to ones
mind these days, and one is, who will be chief after you retire?
Do you have a trained man who is not a liberal minded fellow
to step in?

Then too, is it a true fact that the founder of the
NAACP died a full fledged communist? or is this propaganda?

Also, I wonder about this fellow James Baldwin who
writes for "The Worker." An evangelist who spoke at our church kept
quoting him. Are you allowed to tell us if a man is a known communist?

Thank you, and know one thing, you have been the one
big hope for our future for a long time. It worries us to see time go
by and retirement nearing for you.

Yours truly,

b6
b7C

162-108763

REC- 16   25 NOV 4 1963

EX-

REC. 16   62-108763.8

X-101

October 30, 1963

ALL INFORMATION CONTAINED
HEREIN IS UNCLASSIFIED
DATE 5-16-89 BY

FBI

Dear

I have read your letter of October 24th.

While I would like to be of service, information contained in the files of the FBI is confidential and available for official use only pursuant to regulations of the Department of Justice.

You may wish to know, I have made no plans to retire. On the contrary, it is my desire to remain in my present capacity as long as I can be of service to our country.

Sincerely yours,

J. Edgar Hoover

John Edgar Hoover
Director

MAILED 31
OCT 3 0 1963
COMM-FBI

NOTE: Bufiles contain no information concerning
James Baldwin, author, is well-known to the Bureau in connection
with his communist front and integration activities. He has in the
past blamed Mr. Hoover for the racial strife in Alabama.

JCF:rls
(3)

OPTIONAL FORM NO. 10

UNITED STATES GOVERNMENT

Memorandum

TO   : Mr. W. C. Sullivan   DATE: December 10, 1963

FROM   : Mr. J. F. Bland   1 – Mr. Belmont
                                       1 – Mr. Rosen
                                       1 – Mr. Sullivan
                                       1 – Mr. Bland
SUBJECT: JAMES A. BALDWIN   1 – Mr. W. P. Jones
           SECURITY MATTER – C   1 – Mr. Haack
           RACIAL MATTERS

            In connection with a summary of information in
Bureau files on Baldwin the Director inquired, "Is Baldwin
on our Security Index?"

            Baldwin's name is included in the Reserve Index
(special group of individuals who will receive priority
consideration with respect to investigation and/or other
action following apprehension of Security Index subjects).
Although Baldwin's name is not now in the Security Index,
New York has this case under active investigation and,
among other things, his Security Index status will be
evaluated.

ACTION:

            This is submitted in accordance with the
Director's request. New York is being followed closely.

62-108763

ALL INFORMATION CONTAINED
HEREIN IS UNCLASSIFIED
DATE 5-17-89 BY

Included in Security Index
12/19/63

IDH:cad
(7)

EX-102
REC 33   62-108763

12 DEC 20 1963

66 DEC 26 1963

UNITED STATES ~~GOVERNMENT~~ ENT

Memorandum

TO   : Mr. DeLoach   DATE: 6-22-64

FROM : M. A. Jones

SUBJECT: JAMES ARTHUR BALDWIN
          INFORMATION CONCERNING

**ALL INFORMATION CONTAINED
HEREIN IS UNCLASSIFIED
DATE 5-17-89 BY**

The book review section of "The Washington Post" for 6-21-64, contained an article concerning captioned individual. It stated he is contemplating at least four future books, among which will be one "about the F. B. I. in the South." These will be published by Dial Press.

The item goes on to point out that Baldwin's recent books have attracted an enormous response, ringing up best-selling figures all over the Nation. "The Fire Next Time," according to the article, sold 100,000 copies in hardcover; its paperback version, just out, is likely to sell five to ten times that many. "Another Country" is nearing the two million mark in soft cover.

INFORMATION IN BUFILES:

James Arthur Baldwin is a Harlem-born Negro who resides in New York City, and who has become quite well known for his books regarding the relationship of Negroes and whites in our society.

He has been identified as a sponsor for the Fair Play for Cuba Committee and is one of its prominent members.

Baldwin is also listed as one of the sponsors of The Monroe Defense Committee, a group organized as the result of a race riot in Monroe, North Carolina, on 8-27-61. This Committee has received strong support from communist publications such as the "National Guardian."

The "New York Herald Tribune" of 6-17-61, in its "Letters to the Editor" section, contained a communication signed by Baldwin and William Styron which advocated abolishment of capital punishment. This letter said "If there were a shred of proof that the death penalty actually served to inhibit crime, that would be sufficient reason--even from the point of view of 'misguided do-gooders,' as J. Edgar Hoover calls its opponents--to maintain it." It goes on to state Mr. Hoover "is not a lawgiver, nor is there any reason to suppose him to be a particularly

1 - Mr. DeLoach
1 - Mr. Sullivan
HHA:cmk
(6)

@ JUL 16 1964

(Continued, page 2)

M.A. Jones to DeLoach memo
Re: JAMES ARTHUR BALDWIN

profound student of human nature. He is a law-enforcement officer. It is appalling that in this capacity he not only opposes the trend of history among civilized nations, but uses his enormous power and prestige to corroborate the blindest and basest instincts of the retaliatory mob."

On the subject of homosexuality, Baldwin states, "American males are the only people I've ever encountered in the world who are willing to go on the needle before they'll go to bed with each other. Because they're afraid of this, they don't know how to go to bed with women either. I've known people who literally died out of this panic. I don't know what homosexual means any more, and Americans don't either...If you fall in love with a boy, you fall in love with a boy. The fact that Americans consider it a disease says more about them than it says about homosexuality!

In connection with a discussion of why he felt both Attorney General Robert Kennedy, the Justice Department and former President John F. Kennedy were ineffective in dealing with discrimination with the Negroes in the South, Baldwin said he was weary of being told desegregation is legal. He went on to say "... because first of all you have to get Eastland out of Congress and get rid of the power that he wields there. You've got to get rid of J. Edgar Hoover and the power that he wields. If one could get rid of just those two men, or modify their power, there would be a great deal more hope..."

RECOMMENDATION:

None. For information.

ADDENDUM, ECK:amr 6/22/64

In that this book "about the F. B. I. in the South" is one being contemplated by Baldwin, we will follow our sources, and should the book be published, naturally it will be reviewed and you will be advised.

- 2 -

OPTIONAL FORM NO. 10
MAY 1962 EDITION
GSA GEN. REG. NO. 27

UNITED STATES GOVERNMENT

Memorandum

TO   :   Mr. DeLoach   DATE: 7-20-64

FROM   :   M. A. Jones

SUBJECT: JAMES ARTHUR BALDWIN
            INFORMATION CONCERNING

*ALL INFORMATION CONTAINED
HEREIN IS UNCLASSIFIED
DATE 5-17-91 BY [stamp]*

My memorandum dated 7-17-64, which concerned the captioned individual's plans for a future book about the FBI, has been returned by the Director with this question: "Isn't Baldwin a well known pervert?" It is not a matter of official record that he is a pervert; however, the theme of homosexuality has figured prominently in two of his three published novels. Baldwin has stated that it is also "implicit" in his first novel, "Go Tell It on the Mountain." In the past, he has not disputed the description of "autobiographical" being attached to this first book.

The "New York Post" published a series of six articles about Baldwin in January, 1964. Written by Fern Marja Eckman, they were the result of a series of interviews by Mrs. Eckman with the novelist. She asked him why he used homosexuality in two of his novels and he corrected her by pointing out that all three novels contained this theme in one degree or another, using the term "implicit" in connection with the first book.

According to Mrs. Eckman, Baldwin explained the motivation for this recurrent theme in his fiction. He said there are two reasons for it, both of which are similar. He then launched into a diatribe about sex in America and actually never did state these so-called two reasons with any clarity. He says the situation he described in "Another Country" is true, only much worse than he depicted it. (Most of this novel dealt with the carnality of a group of whites and Negroes in Greenwich Village and Harlem. Included in it was one description of the homosexual deeds of a bisexual character in Paris.) Baldwin said he was exposed to all of this when he arrived in Greenwich Village as a Negro adolescent. He criticized American heterosexuality, saying it isn't sex at all but "pure desperation." He claims American homosexuality is primarily a waste which would cease to exist in effect if Americans were not so "frightened of it." He goes on to claim that Americans, Englishmen and Germans--the "Anglo-Saxons"--are the only people who talk about it. It should be noted, however, that he makes a point that it is these people, whom he calls the "Puritans" who speak of homosexuality in a "terrible way."

REC- 33   62-108763-30

1 - Mr. DeLoach
1 - Mr. Sullivan
HHA:jol (7)

Continued on next page.

MORE

6 4 JUL 29 1964   CRIME RESEARCH

M. A. Jones to DeLoach Memo
RE: JAMES ARTHUR BALDWIN

He then contrasts their approach with that of the Italians, stating, "In Italy, you know, men kiss each other and boys go to bed with each other. And no one is marked for life. No one imagines that--and they grow up, you know, and they have children and raise them. And no one ends up going to a psychiatrist or turning into a junkie because he's afraid of being touched."

He continues by saying that is the root of the "American" thing-- "it's not a fear of men going to bed with men. It's a fear of anybody touching anybody." Baldwin concluded this particular discussion with Mrs. Eckman by saying that Negroes were frequent targets of homosexual approaches on the part of whites because they were always looking for somebody to act out their fantasies on, and they seem to believe that Negroes know how to do "dirty things."

During this particular interview, Baldwin intimates that he has had experience in this type of activity, saying, "You wouldn't believe the holocaust that opens over your head...if you are 16 years old..." He ends by stating that they understand in Italy that people "were born to touch each other."

These remarks are similar to others Baldwin has gone on record with regarding homosexuality. While it is not possible to state that he is a pervert, he has expressed a sympathetic viewpoint about homosexuality on several occasions, and a very definite hostility toward the revulsion of the American public regarding it.

RECOMMENDATION:

None. For information.

- 2 -

SIRS:
    TROTZKYITES ARE BEHIND HARLEM RIOTS.
    SOME ARE FOREIGN, IMMIGRANT TROTZKYITES MARRIED TO U.S. CITIZENS.
    A NUMBER OF NEGROID JEWS RESEMBLING CASTRO ARE INVOLVED.
    ALSO, JAS. BALDWIN, FEATURED BY "THE MILITANT" IS RESPONSIBLE. HE INTERVIEWED ATTORNEY GENERAL KENNEDY BEFORE THE ASSASSINATION AND STARTED IT ALL.
                LOYAL CITIZEN

ANONYMOUS COMMUNICATIONS

62 - 108 763 - 32

62 - 108 763 - 30

ALL INFORMATION CONTAINED HEREIN IS UNCLASSIFIED
DATE 5/17/89 BY 203/50

REC 32

JUL 31 1964

CORRESPONDENCE

SECRET

DECLASSIFIED BY AUC 3962735AH/82
ON 1/27/99
CA97-5269

ALL INFORMATION CONTAINED
HEREIN IS UNCLASSIFIED
EXCEPT WHERE SHOWN
OTHERWISE

May 13, 1966

JAMES BALDWIN — Summary

Captioned individual, prominent author and playwright, has been the subject of a security-type investigation conducted by the FBI which has revealed his association with individuals and organizations of a procommunist nature.

In July, 1965, he was the author of a form letter urging the recipients to renew their subscriptions to "Freedomways" magazine which is reportedly staffed by Communist Party (CP) members or sympathizers including _____ of James Jackson, a member of the National Committee of the CPUSA.

b6
b7C

In November, 1965, Baldwin made public appearances in Rome, Italy, at which he stated the United States has no right in Vietnam and that "Western interests" were responsible for events in South Africa and the Cuban "aggression."

In December, 1963, Baldwin spoke before a dinner sponsored by the Emergency Civil Liberties Committee (ECLC), an organization cited by the House Committee on Un-American Activities (HCUA).

An advertisement entitled "What is Really Happening in Cuba" appeared in "The New York Times" of April 6, 1960. This advertisement, placed by The Fair Play for Cuba Committee, was sympathetic to the Castro regime and indicated that the American press had attempted to blacken Castro and his government by reporting untruthful information. The advertisement indicated The Fair Play for Cuba Committee, headquarters in New York, had been formed to furnish the true facts concerning the Cuban revolutionary government. James Baldwin appeared in the advertisement as one of the sponsors of The Fair Play for Cuba Committee.

SECRET

NOTE: Per request of Mrs. Mildred Stegall, White House Staff.

JMM:mjl (8)

Tolson
DeLoach
Mohr
Wick
Casper
Callahan
Conrad
Felt
Gale
Rosen
Sullivan
Tavel
Trotter
Tele. Room
Holmes
Gandy

MAIL ROOM ☐ TELETYPE UNIT ☐

ENCLOSURE
62-108763-39

JAMES BALDWIN

SECRET

        The Washington, D. C., Chapter of the Congress of
Racial Equality held a mass rally for the "Original Freedom Riders"
in Washington on June 11, 1961. Among the speakers at this rally
was James Baldwin. During his talk, Baldwin stated, in substance,
that the West should re-evaluate its international policies in view
of the potential strength of the new Afro-Asian countries. He stated
that the white race had better realize the emerging strength of the
Negro and that he would not care to be in the shoes of the white man
when the African nations become stronger.

        The "New York Herald Tribune" of June 17, 1961, in
its "Letters to the Editor" section, carried a letter by James Baldwin
and William Styron which advocated abolishment of capital punishment. This letter stated in part that "If there were a shred of proof
that the death penalty actually served to inhibit crime, that would
be sufficient reason--even from the point of view of 'misguided
do-gooders,' as J. Edgar Hoover calls its opponents--to maintain
it." It goes on to state that Mr. Hoover "is not a lawgiver, nor is
there any reason to suppose him to be a particularly profound student
of human nature. He is a law enforcement officer. It is appalling
that in this capacity he not only opposes the trend of history among
civilized nations, but uses his enormous power and prestige to
corroborate the blindest and basest instincts of the retaliatory mob."

        On June 2, 1961, the Liberation Committee for
Africa (LCA) held a "first anniversary" celebration at the
Martinique Hotel, New York City. James Baldwin, author, was
listed as one of the principal speakers. During his address,
Baldwin stated that he had spent the past nine years in Paris and
advised that a period of revolution confronted the world and that
America has taken a position throughout the world against revolutions.
Baldwin asserted that only in revolution could the problems of the
United States be solved.

        It is understood that certain local chapters of the
Socialist Workers Party have given support to the Liberation
Committee for Africa. The March 24, 1961, issue of "Young
Socialist Alliance Newsletter," which recognizes the Socialist

SECRET

- 2 -

JAMES BALDWIN

SECRET

Workers Party as the only existing political party capable of
providing the working class with political leadership, has given
strong support to the LCA. The LCA claims to provide a public
forum for African freedom fighters and to re-establish awareness
of the common cultural heritage of Afro-Americans with their
African brothers.

The name of James Baldwin appears as a sponsor on
a news release communication in August, 1961, from the Carl
Braden clemency appeal committee which was being distributed
by the Southern Conference Educational Fund (SCEF). The SCEF
is the successor organization to the Southern Conference for
Human Welfare described by the HCUA as a communist front
organization. It is noted that on May 1, 1961, Carl Braden and
Frank Wilkinson went to prison to begin a one-year sentence for
contempt of the HCUA. The SCEF was endeavoring to obtain
signatures in connection with a petition to President Kennedy for
executive clemency for Braden and Wilkinson.

The April 17, 1961, issue of the "National Guardian"
which the HCUA cites as a virtual official propaganda arm of
Soviet Russia contained an advertisement announcing a rally to
abolish the HCUA on Friday, April 21, 1961, in New York City.
James Baldwin, writer, was listed as a sponsor supporting the
rally.

The April 20, 1962, issue of "New America," an
official publication of "Socialist Party--Social Democratic
Federation," contains a clemency petition for convicted communist
Junius Scales who was serving a six-year sentence in Lewisburg
Penitentiary under the membership clause of the Smith Act. The
petition was sent to President Kennedy on April 3, 1962, and
allegedly contained the signatures of "550 prominent citizens"
among whom was James Baldwin.

- 3 -

SECRET

JAMES BALDWIN

SECRET

Scales, who had a long history of membership and leadership in the CPUSA, was convicted in February, 1958, for violating the Smith Act. He was sentenced to six years in the Federal penitentiary, and after exhausting all appeals, he began serving his sentence on October 2, 1961.

On Christmas Eve, 1962, President Kennedy commuted Scales' sentence which he was serving in Lewisburg, Pennsylvania. During his trial and in connection with appeal motions subsequent to it, Scales endeavored to characterize himself as an ex-communist who had chosen to go to jail rather than name his former associates in the CP.

The cover of the May 17, 1963, issue of "Time" magazine is devoted to author James Baldwin. The cover story describes some of Baldwin's recent efforts in behalf of the American Negro's integration movements. He is described as "a nervous, slight, almost fragile figure, filled with frets and fears. He is effeminate in manner, drinks considerably, smokes cigarettes in chains and he often looses his audience with overblown arguments."

The May, 1963, issue of "Mademoiselle" contains an interview-type article with James Baldwin which was part of a series then currently being carried by the magazine under the caption "Disturber of the Peace."

As indicated by the title of the series, "Disturber of the Peace," James Baldwin gives a lot of gibes to both white and Negroes about the Negro situation in the United States. Baldwin answers many of the questions by introspection. In giving an answer to a question about his father and how he hated him and whether or not his father hated Baldwin in return, he stated "In a way, yes. He didn't like me. But he'd had a terrible time, too. And of course, I was not his son. I was a bastard. What he wanted for his children was what in fact I became...I changed all the diapers and I knew where the kids were, and I could take some of the pressures off my mother and in a way stand between him and her...."

SECRET

- 4 -

JAMES BALDWIN   SECRET

On the subject of homosexuality, Baldwin stated
"American males are the only people I've ever encountered in the
world who are willing to go on the needle before they'll go to bed
with each other. Because they're afraid of this, they don't know
how to go to bed with women either. I've known people who
literally died out of this panic. I don't know what homosexual means
any more, and Americans don't either...If you fall in love with a
boy, you fall in love with a boy. The fact that Americans consider
it a disease says more about them than it says about homosexuality."
(157-6-34-78)

In connection with a discussion of why he feels
Attorney General Robert Kennedy, the Justice Department and
President Kennedy are ineffective in dealing with discrimination
with the Negroes in the South, Baldwin makes the statement that
he is weary of being told that desegregation is legal. He then states
"...because first of all you have to get Eastland out of Congress and
get rid of the power that he wields there. You've got to get rid of
J. Edgar Hoover and the power that he wields. If one could get rid
of just those two men, or modify their power, there would be a
great deal more hope...."

The fingerprint files of the FBI Identification Division
contain no arrest data identifiable with captioned individual based upon
the background information submitted in connection with this name
check request.

SECRET

- 5 -

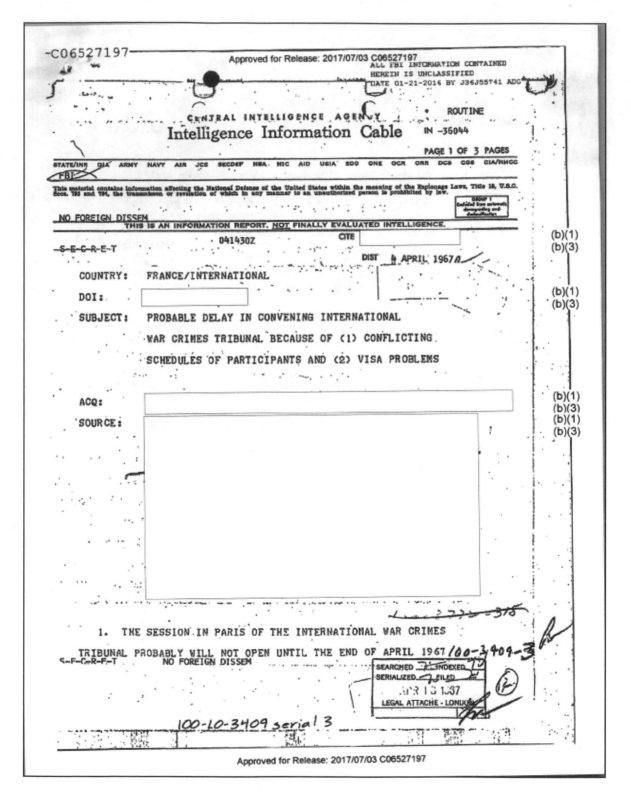

C06527197

Approved for Release: 2017/07/03 C06527197

ALL FBI INFORMATION CONTAINED
HEREIN IS UNCLASSIFIED
DATE 01-21-2016 BY J36J55T41 ADG

CENTRAL INTELLIGENCE AGENCY   • ROUTINE

Intelligence Information Cable   IN -36044

PAGE 1 OF 3 PAGES

STATE/INR DIA ARMY NAVY AIR JCS SECDEF NSA NIC AID USIA SDO ONE OCR ORR DCS CGS CIA/NMCC

FBI

This material contains information affecting the National Defense of the United States within the meaning of the Espionage Laws, Title 18, U.S.C.
Secs. 793 and 794, the transmission or revelation of which in any manner to an unauthorized person is prohibited by law.

GROUP 1
Excluded from automatic
downgrading and
declassification

NO FOREIGN DISSEM

THIS IS AN INFORMATION REPORT, NOT FINALLY EVALUATED INTELLIGENCE.

CITE   (b)(1)
                                            (b)(3)

S-E-C-R-E-T   041430Z

                                        DIST   4 APRIL 1967

COUNTRY: FRANCE/INTERNATIONAL

DOI: (b)(1)
                                                           (b)(3)

SUBJECT: PROBABLE DELAY IN CONVENING INTERNATIONAL

             WAR CRIMES TRIBUNAL BECAUSE OF (1) CONFLICTING

             SCHEDULES OF PARTICIPANTS AND (2) VISA PROBLEMS

ACQ: (b)(1)
                                                           (b)(3)
SOURCE: (b)(1)
                                                           (b)(3)

1. THE SESSION IN PARIS OF THE INTERNATIONAL WAR CRIMES

TRIBUNAL PROBABLY WILL NOT OPEN UNTIL THE END OF APRIL 1967 100-3409-3

S-E-C-R-E-T   NO FOREIGN DISSEM

SEARCHED____INDEXED
SERIALIZED____FILED
APR 13 1967
LEGAL ATTACHE - LONDON

100-10-3409 serial 3

C06527197

36044

(b)(1)
(b)(3)

PAGE 2 OF 3 PAGES

APR 4

S-E-C-R-E-T   NO FOREIGN DISSEM

(classification)   (dissem controls)

BECAUSE OF TRIBUNAL MEMBER JEAN-PAUL SARTRE'S CURRENT TRIP TO   (b)(1)

ISREAL. [ ] COMMENT: [   ]   (b)(3)
(b)(1)
(b)(3)
[ ] MICHEL CONTAT, A SWISS FROM LAUSANNE WHO HAS BEEN   (b)(1)
(b)(3)
COMP[ ]G A BIBLIOGRAPHY ON SARTRE AND WHO IS APPARENTLY CLOSE

TO SARTRE, SAID THAT SARTRE HAS MIXED FEELINGS ABOUT THE

TRIBUNAL AND SOME OF THE PEOPLE ASSOCIATED WITH IT. CONTAT

ADDED HOWEVER THAT SARTRE FELT STRONGLY THAT WORLD PUBLIC

OPINION SHOULD BE MOBILIZED AGAINST THE VIETNAM WAR.) AMERICAN

NEGRO AUTHOR JAMES BALDWIN WILL ALSO BE PARTICIPATING IN THE TRIBUNAL AND WILL

BE COMING FROM TURKEY, WHERE HE IS STAYING,

TO PARIS AT THE END OF APRIL. SINCE THERE ARE MANY PROBLEMS

INVOLVING THE SCHEDULING OF PARTICIPANTS DURING THE SUMMER OF

1967, THE TRIB[ ]L MIGHT NOT END UNTIL SEPTEMBER.   (b)(1)
(b)(3)

2. [ ] COMMENT: [   ]   (b)(1)
(b)(3)
[   ] PAT JORDAN WAS DICTATING A

LETTER OVER THE PHONE TO SOMEONE -- NAME NOT KNOWN -- REGRETTING

THAT NO VISAS HAD BEEN GRANTED TO CERTAIN INDIVIDUALS. [ ]

[ ] WAS UNABLE TO LEARN THE DETAILS ON THE VISA DIFFICULTIES.)   (b)(1)
(b)(3)

3. COGGAN SAID THAT HE AND PAT JORDAN, ALSO OF THE BERTRAND

[RU]SSELL PEACE FOUNDATION, VISITED PARIS ALTERNATELY EVERY TWO

S-E-C-R-E-T   NO FOREIGN DISSEM

(classification)   (dissem controls)

serial 3, p2

-C06527197-

36044

(b)(1)
(b)(3)

PAGE 3 OF 3 PAGES

*S-E-C-R-E-T /   NO FOREIGN DISSEM
  (classification)   (dissem controls)

WEEKS, BUT COGGAN MAINTAINED THAT THE TRIBUNAL'S ADMINISTRA-

TION WOULD CONTINUE TO BE OPERATED FOR THE MOST PART FROM

LONDON.   COMMENT: COGGAN   (b)(1)
                                                             (b)(3)
                                                             (b)(1)
APPEARED TO POSSESS A LARGE SUM OF MONEY IN CASH IN HIS LONDON OFFICE.   (b)(3)

IT IS ASSUMED THAT HE HANDLES THE OFFICE'S PETTY CASH.)

    4.   DISSEM: NONE

REPORT CLASS S E C R E T NO FOREIGN DISSEM   (b)(1)
                                               (b)(3)

serial 3 p3

C06691247

SECRET

CENTRAL INTELLIGENCE AGENCY
WASHINGTON, D.C. 20505

5-2

28 APR 1967

C06527154

MEMORANDUM FOR: Director
Federal Bureau of Investigation
Attention: Mr. S. J. Papich

FROM : Deputy Director for Plans

SUBJECT : James Arthur Baldwin
Security Matter - C

1. Reference is made to your memorandum dated 2 November 1966, your File No. 62-108763 concerning captioned Subject.

(b)(1)
(b)(3)

_____ of the Bertrand Russell Peace Foundation Subject would be traveling from his residence in Turkey to Paris to participate in the International War Crimes Tribunal in April 1967.

3. Subject's address in Turkey, _____ (b)(1)
_____, is Saka House, Meydan Sokak No. 13, Rumeli Hisar, (b)(3)
Istanbul.

(b)(1)
(b)(3)

REC-8   62-108763-47

EX 109

18 MAY 5 1967

Copy to new York
by routing slip for
☐ info ☒ action
date 5-4-67

59 MAY 11 1967

SECRET

C06691248

SECRET

CENTRAL INTELLIGENCE AGENCY
WASHINGTON, D.C. 20505

9 MAY 1967

MEMORANDUM FOR: Director
                  Federal Bureau of Investigation
                  Attention: Mr. S. J. Papich

FROM: Deputy Director for Plans

SUBJECT: James Arthur Baldwin
                  Security Matter C

(b)(1)
(b)(3)

E-2

(b)(1)
(b)(3)

Subject indicated in a letter to the International War Crimes Tribunal that he did not think that he would be able to attend the forthcoming session in Paris, although he promised to attend other sessions of the Tribunal.

(b)(1)
(b)(3)

3. An Associated Press story, dated 26 April 1967 stated that the Trials, banned from France, would be held in Stockholm, and Subject would be attending.

(b)(1)
(b)(3)

Copy to NY
by routing slip for
☒ action
date 5-11-67
by

REC-16   62-108763 - 48

18 MAY 12 1967

5-TGM

62 MAY 18 1967   SECRET

(Rev. 5-22-64)

F B I

Date: 5/24/68

Transmit the following in _____ PLAINTEXT
(Type in plaintext or code)

Via ___ AIRTEL _____
(Priority)

TO   : DIRECTOR, FBI (62-108763)

FROM   : SAC, NEW YORK (100-146553)   (P)

SUBJECT: JAMES ARTHUR BALDWIN
         SM-C
         (00:NY)

ReNYairtel to Bu, 3/14/68; LAlet to Bu, 4/9/68;
NYairtel to SF, 4/30/68.

An annual report in this matter was due at the
Bureau on 5/26/68; however, this report will be held in abey-
ance in effort to further ascertain subject's present residence or address at Palm Springs, California.

On 5/24/68, a pretext telephone call was made by
SA [   ] posing as an American Express Agent and [   ]   b6
[   ] advised that the subject   b7C
was not presently residing at Apt. 1B, 137 W. 71st St., NY,NY.
It was ascertained that the subject does still maintain this
apartment.

For the information of the Bureau, on 4/12/68, [   ]   b7D
[   ] furnished information to the effect that BALDWIN was
to speak in Oakland, California, on 4/12/68, at a memorial
service for BOBBY HUTTON.

LEAD:

    LOS ANGELES

    AT LOS ANGELES AND PALM SPRINGS, CALIFORNIA. Will
contact established sources in further efforts to locate subject's
present residence.   REC 16

(3) Bureau (RM)
2- Los Angeles (100-71381) (RM)
1- San Francisco (INFO) (RM)
1- New York

62-10   5 62

20 MAY 25 1968

CONFIDENTIAL

JDB:amb

31 1968

Approved: _____   Sent _____ M _____
        Special Agent in Charge

NY 100-146763

LEADS: (CONTINUED)

NEW YORK

      AT NEW YORK, NEW YORK. Will prepare report in
this matter as soon as subject's current residence known.

-2-

OPTIONAL FORM NO. 10
MAY 1962 EDITION
GSA GEN. REG. NO. 27

UNITED STATES GOVERNMENT

Memorandum

not

TO   :   DIRECTOR, FBI (62-18763)   DATE: 5/23/68

FROM   :   SAC, LOS ANGELES (100-71381) (P)

SUBJECT :   JAMES ARTHUR BALDWIN
             SM - C

             OO: New York

             Re: New York airtel to Bureau, dated 3/14/68, and
        Los Angeles letter to Bureau dated 4/9/68.

             On 4/1/68, [   ]   b6
        [   ] Palm Springs Spa Hotel, advised that he had   b7C
        asked TRUMAN CAPOTE, the well-known author, if JAMES BALDWIN b7D
        was staying in Palm Springs. He was advised by CAPOTE that
        BALDWIN is staying in some friend's home in Palm Springs while
        he is re-writing some portions of his book, "MALCOLM X".
        CAPOTE could not recall the name of the street but said it
        was some "Circle" approximately one mile from downtown Palm
        Springs.

             On 4/8/68, [   ]   b6
        [   ], advised that JAMES BALDWIN is   b7C
        receiving mail at [   ] He did   b7D
        not know if this BALDWIN was identical with subject.

             On 4/30/68 and 5/13/68, spot checks at [   ]
        [   ] failed to observe BALDWIN residing
        at that address.

        LEAD

             LOS ANGELES

**ALL INFORMATION CONTAINED
HEREIN IS UNCLASSIFIED
DATE 8/5/85 BY** [   ]

             AT PALM SPRINGS, CALIFORNIA: Will continue efforts
        to determine if BALDWIN temporarily residing in Palm Springs.

        2 - Bureau (RM)
        2 - New York (100-146553) (RM)
        2 - Los Angeles
        JWW:gcw
        (6)

        REC-105 62 - 108763 - 63

        MAY 28 1968

        62 JUN 10 1968
             352

FD-263 (Rev. 3-8-67)

FEDERAL BUREAU OF INVESTIGATION

REPORTING OFFICE	OFFICE OF ORIGIN	DATE	INVESTIGATIVE PERIOD
NEW YORK	NEW YORK	JUL 9 1968	6/10/68 - 7/9/68

TITLE OF CASE	REPORT MADE BY	TYPED BY
JAMES ARTHUR BALDWIN		b6 b7C

CHARACTER OF CASE

SM - C

ALL INFORMATION CONTAINED
HEREIN IS UNCLASSIFIED
EXCEPT WHERE SHOWN
OTHERWISE

DECLASSIFIED BY AUG 3697754b
ON 4/21/99

REFERENCES

Report of SA _____ 5/26/67, at New York.
Los Angeles letter, 5/23/68, to Bureau.
New York airtel to Bureau, 5/24/68.
Bureau letter to New York, 7/10/68.
Los Angeles letter to Bureau, 7/12/68.

- P -

Classified by _____
Declassify on: OADR

ADMINISTRATIVE

The pretext on 12/27/67 was a telephone call by
SA _____ posing as a foreign auto sales representative.   b6
                                                                     b7C

The pretext on 7/10/68 was a telephone call to _____
_____ wherein SA posed as a publisher.

ACCOMPLISHMENTS CLAIMED						ACQUIT-TALS	CASE HAS BEEN:		
CONVIC.	AUTO.	FUG.	FINES	SAVINGS	RECOVERIES		PENDING OVER ONE YEAR	☐YES	☐NO
							PENDING PROSECUTION OVER SIX MONTHS	☐YES	☐NO

APPROVED	SPECIAL AGENT IN CHARGE	DO NOT WRITE IN SPACES BELOW

REC-7

COPIES MADE:

5 - Bureau (62-108763) (RM)
1 - Secret Service, New York (RM)
2 - Los Angeles (100-71381) (RM)
3 - New York (100-146553)

62-108763   66

12 JUL 31 1968

Classified by _____
Declassify on: OADR

0 - 1 to NY, 10/9/68
4, PEN/def

Dissemination Record of Attached Report			Notations	
Agency	ACSI RAO SS St		USIA	
Request Recd.			1233	b7E
Date Fwd.	AUG 1 4 1968		FEB 2 1973	
How Fwd.	R/S		Ed DEA	
By	S/CCS			

56 AUG 20 1968

* U.S. GOVERNMENT PRINTING OFFICE (1967) 0—233-877

FD-376 (Rev. 8-1-66)

UNITED STATES DEPARTMENT OF JUSTICE
FEDERAL BUREAU OF INVESTIGATION

CONFIDENTIAL

WASHINGTON, D.C. 20535

In Reply, Please Refer to
File No. NY 100-146553   July 29, 1968

Director
United States Secret Service
Department of the Treasury
Washington, D. C. 20220

Dear Sir: RE: James Arthur Baldwin

The information furnished herewith concerns an individual who is believed to be covered by the agreement between the FBI and Secret Service concerning Presidential protection, and to fall within the category or categories checked.

1. ☐ Has attempted or threatened bodily harm to any government official or employee, including foreign government officials residing in or planning an imminent visit to the U. S., because of his official status.

2. ☐ Has attempted or threatened to redress a grievance against any public official by other than legal means.

3. XX Because of background is potentially dangerous; or has been identified as member or participant in communist movement; or has been under active investigation as member of other group or organization inimical to U. S.

4. ☐ U. S. citizens or residents who defect from the U. S. to countries in the Soviet or Chinese Communist blocs and return.

5. ☐ Subversives, ultrarightists, racists and fascists who meet one or more of the following criteria:

   (a) ☐ Evidence of emotional instability (including unstable residence and employment record) or irrational or suicidal behavior:
   (b) ☐ Expressions of strong or violent anti-U. S. sentiment;
   (c) ☐ Prior acts (including arrests or convictions) or conduct or statements indicating a propensity for violence and antipathy toward good order and government.

6. ☐ Individuals involved in illegal bombing or illegal bomb-making.

Photograph ☒ has been furnished ☐ enclosed ☐ is not available
☐ may be available through _____

Very truly yours,

John Edgar Hoover
Director

1 - Special Agent in Charge (Enclosure(s) (1) (RM)
U. S. Secret Service New York, N.Y.

Enclosure(s) (1)   (Upon removal of classified enclosures, if any, this transmittal form becomes UNCLASSIFIED.) CONFIDENTIAL

FD-323 (Rev. 11-29-61)

UNITED STATES DEPARTMENT OF JUSTICE

FEDERAL BUREAU OF INVESTIGATION

New York, New York

JUL 29 1968

In Reply, Please Refer to
File No.   NY 100-146553

Title   James Arthur Baldwin

Character   Security Matter - C

Reference   Report of SA _____   b6
dated and captioned as above,   b7C
at New York.

All sources (except any listed below) whose identities
are concealed in referenced communication have furnished reliable
information in the past.

NY T-1 is another Government agency with
investigative jurisdiction abroad.

OPTIONAL FORM NO. 10
MAY 1962 EDITION
GSA GEN. REG. NO. 27

UNITED STATES GOVERNMENT

Memorandum

TO   : DIRECTOR, FBI (62-108763)   DATE: 9/26/68

FROM   : SAC, LOS ANGELES (100-71381) (P)

SUBJECT : JAMES ARTHUR BALDWIN
          SM - C
          OO: New York

ALL INFORMATION CONTAINED
HEREIN IS UNCLASSIFIED
DATE 5-19-89 BY

Re Los Angeles letter to Bureau dated 7/12/68
and re New York report of SA [   ] dated
7/29/68.   b6
                                                           b7C

An article entitled "Movie Call Sheet" appeared
in the Los Angeles Times, Los Angeles, California, home
edition of 9/20/68. The article read as follows:

"Stuart Rosenberg will direct 'The
Autobiography of Malcolm X,' Marvin Worth's
production for Columbia Pictures. Arnold
Perl has been signed to corroborate with
previously assigned playwright James Baldwin
on the screen play based on the life of the
slain black leader."

On 9/24/68 [   ]
Columbia Pictures Corporation (conceal established source),
1438 North Gower Street, Los Angeles, advised that JAMES
BALDWIN who is believed in New York City, New York, is   b6
scheduled to return to Columbia Picture Studios, Hollywood,   b7C
California, on 9/30/68 to begin writing the film play on   b7D
the autobiography of MALCOLM X for MARVIN WORTH productions.
He is expected to be in the Los Angeles area for several
weeks. During his stay in Los Angeles, will make several
trips back to New York City, New York. Columbia Studios
presently has no local address on BALDWIN but after he
reports to the studio, he will furnish them his residence
while in Los Angeles, California.

62-108763-68

② - Bureau (RM)
2 - New York (100-146553) (RM)
2 - Los Angeles   18 OCT 2 1968
                          REC- 38
JWW/jem
(6)

LA 100-71381

LEAD

LOS ANGELES

AT LOS ANGELES, CALIFORNIA: Will, continue to follow BALDWIN's activities while in the Los Angeles area.

- 2 -

OPTIONAL FORM NO. 10
MAY 1962 EDITION
GSA FPMR (41 CFR) 101-11.6

UNITED STATES GOVERNMENT

Memorandum

TO   : DIRECTOR, FBI (62-108763)   DATE: 2/14/69

FROM   : SAC, LOS ANGELES (100-71381)

SUBJECT: JAMES ARTHUR BALDWIN
         RM - MISCELLANEOUS
         OO: New York

Re Los Angeles letter to Bureau, 1/13/69.

On 2/11/69, Columbia Picture's Corporation,
1438 North Gower Street, indicated that JAMES BALDWIN
continues to list his address as 137 West 71st Street,
New York City, New York, Apartment 1-B, and his Los
Angeles, California address as 1601 Queens Road, Los
Angeles.

BALDWIN is expected to be in Los Angeles on
2/14/69 and 2/15/69, in order to meet with movie officials.

LEAD

LOS ANGELES

AT LOS ANGELES, CALIFORNIA: Will continue to follow
BALDWIN's activities while in Los Angeles area.

0-1 to NY, 2/26/69
2 & #4 pending

**ALL INFORMATION CONTAINED
HEREIN IS UNCLASSIFIED
DATE 5-19-89 BY**

REC-105   62 - 108763 - 71
ST-101

15 FEB 19 1969

② Bureau (RM)
2 - New York (100-146553)
2 - Los Angeles

JWW/mdm
(6)

MAR - 1 1969

Buy U.S. Savings Bonds Regularly on the Payroll Savings Plan

FC 2/11

OPTIONAL FORM NO. 10
MAY 1962 EDITION
GSA FPMR (41 CFR) 101-11.6

UNITED STATES GOVERNMENT

Memorandum

TO   :   DIRECTOR, FBI (62-1C8763)   DATE: 3/5/69

FROM   :   SAC, NEW YORK (100-146553) (C)

SUBJECT: :   JAMES ARTHUR BALDWIN
                 RM - MISC.
                 (OO: NY)

    A review of subject's file reflects that his permanent and temporary residences are known; permanent at Apt. B, 137 W. 71st Street, NYC, and temporary at 1601 Queens Road, Los Angeles, California, and that his employment (self-employed as a writer) is also known.

    Subject is in Priority III of the Security Index and as a report was written 7/29/68, no report is due.

    In view of the above, New York is closing this case until the next annual report is due. In the event any pertinent information is developed concerning subject's activities the Bureau will be advised by appropriate communication.

ALL INFORMATION CONTAINED
HEREIN IS UNCLASSIFIED
DATE 5-19-89 BY 5883 CTJ/ago

62-105702-72

2 - Bureau (RM)
1 - Los Angeles (100-71381) (INFO) (RM)
1 - New York (43)

TLB:egb
(4)

ST-119   REC-15   12 MAR 6 1969

5 6 MAR 13 1969   RACIAL INT. SECT.

Buy U.S. Savings Bonds Regularly on the Payroll Savings Plan

MAY 1962 EDITION
GSA FPMR (41 CFR) 101-11.6

UNITED STATES GOVERNMENT

Memorandum   CONFIDENTIAL (U)

TO   :   DIRECTOR, FBI (62-108763)   DATE: 12/23/69

FROM   :   SAC, NEW YORK (100-146553) (C)

SUBJECT: JAMES ARTHUR BALDWIN
            RM - MISC.

Enclosed for the Bureau are 11 copies of an LHM dated and captioned as above.

NY T-1 is [ ]   b7E

In the event any pertinent information is developed concerning subject's activities the Bureau will be advised by appropriate communication.

One copy furnished to Secret Service, NYC.

The attached LHM is classified "Secret - No Foreign Dissemination" inasmuch as the information supplied was so classified.

ALL INFORMATION CONTAINED HEREIN IS UNCLASSIFIED DATE 2/12/87 BY SPA/JRM/BCL

CC: USIA
FEB 2 1973
BY: Ed HEH

AGENCY: RAO ATT: ISD, RAO ATT: IDIU
ACSI, SEC SER, CIA (via liaison), STATE
DATE FORW: 1/5/70
HOW FORW: R/S
BY:

CLASS. & EXT. BY 384 JEM/BCC
REASON-FCIM II 1-2, 4.2 Z
DATE OF REVIEW 12/23/89

REC 43

Classified by
Declassify on: OADR

2 - Bureau (ENCL. 11) (RM)   62-108763-78
1 - New York (43)

RTB:egb
(3)

JAN 13 1970

ALL INFORMATION CONTAINED HEREIN IS UNCLASSIFIED
EXCEPT WHERE SHOWN OTHERWISE   CONFIDENTIAL   b7E

Buy U.S. Savings Bonds Regularly on the Payroll Savings Plan

UNITED STATES DEPARTMENT OF JUSTICE

FEDERAL BUREAU OF INVESTIGATION
New York, New York
December 23, 1969

*In Reply, Please Refer to
File No.*

~~SECRET - NO FOREIGN~~
~~DISSEMINATION~~

James Arthur Baldwin
Racial Matter - Miscellaneous

NY T-1, _____ another _____ Government agency which
conducts intelligence investigation advised on July 31,
1969 that James Baldwin arrived at Istanbul, Turkey, from
Athens, Greece via Air France on July 13, 1969.

The following article which appeared in the
August 18, 1969 edition of "Milliyet" a daily newspaper
published in Istanbul, Turkey was furnished by NY T-1 on
October 22, 1969:

"Yasar Kemal, Engin Cezzar, And James Baldwin
Have Formed A Partnership"

"There is a Negro writer whose love for Turkey
is as well-known as his fame on the world scale. He did not
hesitate to frankly state the following on the Paris television: 'I cannot imagine a country in the world as beautiful
as Turkey, a people as nice as the Turks, and another land
where Negroes can live comfortably.' The name of this writer,
who celebrated his 45th birthday two weeks ago, is James
Baldwin."

"Every summer for 5 - 6 years in succession, he
has come to Istanbul, lived here, written a novel, and
departed. His admiration for Istanbul is altogether
different. Originally from the Harlem section of New York,
he says, 'Look here; look there. It's as though one is
drowning amongst the cement blocks without being able to see
the sky and the sea. Its people have been turned into robots.

This document contains neither recommendations
nor conclusions of the FBI. It is the property   ~~SECRET - NO FOREIGN~~
of the FBI and is loaned to your agency; it and
its contents are not to be distributed outside   ~~DISSEMINATION~~
your agency.

GROUP I
Excluded from automatic
downgrading and declassification

DECLASSIFIED BY SP4 JRM/GCL
ON 9/12/80 per LETTER
DTD 11/19/80

62-10970-78

b7E

James Arthur Baldwin

"Whereas here, everyone is friendly and close to one
another.' James Baldwin, who first came to Turkey in 1960,
has many Turkish friends. Every year, he comes, writes
a novel and departs."

    "These are the titles of his novels:"

    "Nobody Knows My Name; Go Tell It To The Mountain;
Another Country; The Fire Next Time; and Giovanni's
Room."

    "These are his plays:"

    "Amen Corner (now playing in Los Angeles) and
Blues For Mr. Charlie."

    "Before coming here, he stayed for 18 months in
Hollywood and prepared a scenario which was taken from a
biography which reflects the white - black problem. So
much so that, because of this, he was a delegate at the
famous meeting between the blacks and Kennedy; he explained
all of the details of this problem to President Kennedy; and
he wanted a remedy to be found for it."

    "Baldwin's method of working is strange. There
are times when he writes continously for 24 hours without
food and drink. Under such circumstances, he does not even
notice if you shout at him or hit him on the shoulder.
Afterwards, he lies down and sleeps. Moreover, he is in a
sound sleep for 48 hours. If you are able to awaken him,
how fortunate you are."

    "Baldwin is here again. This trip is for the
purpose of establishing a new organization. He is establishing this company in order to get his books printed, translated,
and sold, to get his plays produced, and to get his scenarios
filmed. His partners are Yasar Kemal Gokceli, the originator

- 2 -

James Arthur Baldwin

of Ince Memet and his friend Engin Cezzar who had introduced
him to Turkey. The parties have reached an agreement in
principle. They will be in operation soon."

On December 12, 1969, [   ]
137 West 71st Street, New York City, advised that James
Baldwin had returned from his trip to Turkey and resided in
Apartment B at that address but that he is frequently out of
New York on business.

b6
b7C

- 3* -

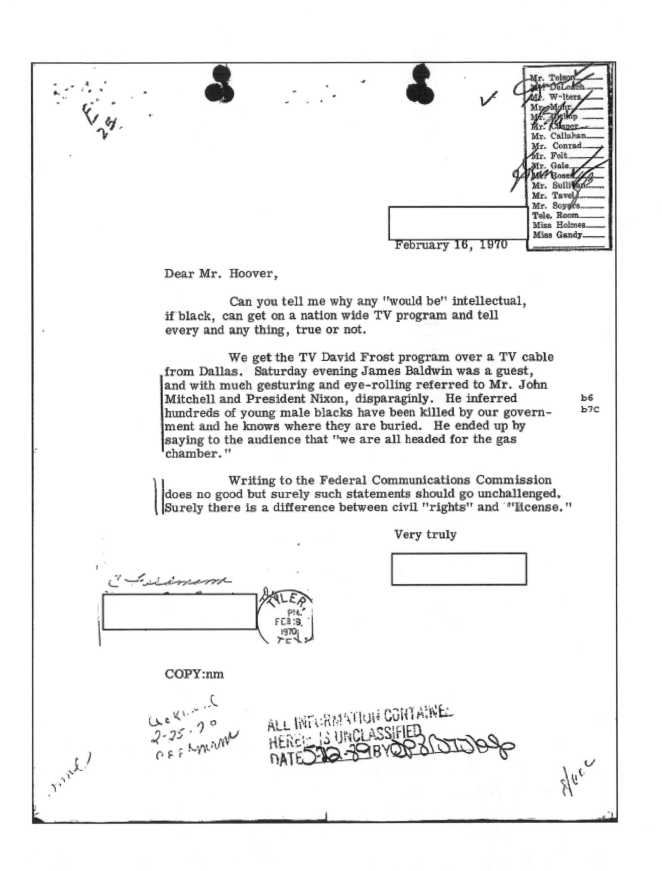

February 16, 1970

Dear Mr. Hoover,

Can you tell me why any "would be" intellectual, if black, can get on a nation wide TV program and tell every and any thing, true or not.

We get the TV David Frost program over a TV cable from Dallas. Saturday evening James Baldwin was a guest, and with much gesturing and eye-rolling referred to Mr. John Mitchell and President Nixon, disparaginly. He inferred hundreds of young male blacks have been killed by our government and he knows where they are buried. He ended up by saying to the audience that "we are all headed for the gas chamber."

b6
b7C

Writing to the Federal Communications Commission does no good but surely such statements should go unchallenged. Surely there is a difference between civil "rights" and "license."

Very truly

COPY:nm

February 25, 1970

BX 110

REC- 120

62 - 108763 - 79

b6
b7C

Dear

Your letter of February 16th has been received

and I certainly understand the concern which prompted you to

write. Since the matter you mentioned is within the purview of

the Federal Communications Commission, I cannot comment as

you desire; however, I am forwarding a copy of your letter to that

agency.

ALL INFORMATION CONTAINED
HEREIN IS UNCLASSIFIED
DATE 5-22-78 BY

Sincerely yours,
J. Edgar Hoover

NOTE: Bufiles contain no information identifiable with correspondent.
Correct spelling of name per telephone directory. Copy of incoming
forwarded to Federal Communications Commission by form referral same
date.

CEE:mrm (3)

Tolson
DeLoach
Walters
Mohr
Bishop
Casper
Callahan
Conrad
Felt
Gale
Rosen
Sullivan
Tavel
Soyars
Tele.
Holmes
Gandy

MAILED 10
FEB 25 1970
COMM-FBI

59 MAR 9 1970

MAIL ROOM   TELETYPE UNIT

~~CONFIDENTIAL~~

UNITED STATES DEPARTMENT OF JUSTICE

FEDERAL BUREAU OF INVESTIGATION
New York, New York
January 21, 1971

In Reply, Please Refer to
File No.

ALL INFORMATION CONTAINED
HEREIN IS UNCLASSIFIED
EXCEPT WHERE SHOWN
OTHERWISE

James Arthur Baldwin
Racial Matters-Black Nationalist

(U)   On November 4, 1970, NY T-1, a confidential source
abroad, advised that the American circles of the extreme
left in Paris, France have been engaging in several
activities to prepare a Press Conference in favor of the
Soledad Brothers and Angela Davis at the American Center
for Students and Artists, 261 Boulevard Raspail, in Paris
on October 12, 1970. As a result of their appeal, they
enlisted the cooperation of several French Circles of
extremists. Source advised that James Arthur Baldwin, an
advocate of black power and a Black Panther Party sympathizer, who was just released from the American Hospital at
Neuilly, France, was in attendance at a meeting held by
one of the extremists on October 9, 1970. Source further
related that Baldwin spoke at the above conference and in his
interpretating statements made by French extremists, he remarked that the United States Prison System was bad and made
other various anti-establishment statements. Following is a
summary of information concerning Baldwin's activities:

Fair Play For Cuba Committee (FPCC)

On May 20, 1961, NY T-2 made available information
indicating that the name and address, JAMES BALDWIN, 81
Horatio Street, New York City, was in the possession of the
FPCC, 799 Broadway, New York City.

On December 10, 1963, [   ]   b6
Bureau of Special Services, New York City Police Department,   b7C
advised that on April 24, 1960, subject was listed as a
sponsor of the FPCC, 799 Broadway, New York City.

CLASSIFIED-DECISIONS FINALIZED BY
DEPARTMENT REVIEW COMMITTEE (DRC)

5|18|99
CLASSIFIED BY Auc 396,775AH/81
DECLASSIFY ON: 25X (4)
CA97-5269

~~CONFIDENTIAL~~
GROUP I
~~Excluded from automatic
downgrading and
declassification~~

Classified by
Declassify on:

This document contains neither recommendations nor conclsuions
of the Federal Bureau of Investigation (FBI). It is the property
of the FBI and is loaned to your agency; it and its contents are
not to be distributed outside your agency.

~~SECRET~~   ENCLOSURE   62-108763-81

CONFIDENTIAL

James Arthur Baldwin

SECRET

A characterization of the FPCC is contained
in the Appendix of this report.

Freedomways Associates, Inc.

On October 25, 1963, NY T-3 advised that ▯▯▯▯▯   b6
▯▯▯▯▯▯ stated she had received a letter from JAMES BALDWIN,   b7C
Negro author, in which BALDWIN wrote that he wanted to
renew his subscription to "Freedomways" for two years.

BALDWIN added that he will give subscriptions to "Freedomways"
as Christmas presents. NY T-3 further advised that ▯▯▯▯
stated that, with BALDWIN's permission, she intends to use
his letter as an advertisement to 25,000 addresses

▯▯▯▯▯▯▯▯▯▯▯▯▯▯▯▯▯ of
the quarterly publication, "Freedomways",
published by Freedomways Associates, Inc.

▯▯▯▯▯▯▯▯▯▯▯▯▯▯▯ of JAMES
JACKSON, who, according to the October 27,
1963 issue of "The Worker", is its Editor.

'The Worker' is an East Coast Communist
newspaper.

A characterization of Freedomways Associates,
Inc. is contained in the Appendix of this
report.

National Lawyers Guild (NLG)

The October 3, 1963 and October 10, 1963 editions
of the "National Guardian" on pages 4 and 8, respectively,
contained an announcement that the New York City Chapter of
the NLG would present an evening with JAMES BALDWIN, author
of "The Fire Next Time", at 8:30 PM, on October 18, 1963,
at Town Hall, New York City. Proceeds will go to the
NLG's committee to assist Southern lawyers.

On October 19, 1963, NY T-4 advised that the NLG
held a public meeting at Town Hall, New York City, on the
evening of October 18, 1963.

Principal speaker of the evening was JAMES BALDWIN,
author, who gave a commentary on the laws concerning Negro
rights. BALDWIN in general statements was critical of the
Attorney General, President JOHN F. KENNEDY, and the Federal
Bureau of Investigation (FBI) for alleged failure to live

-2-

CONFIDENTIAL

SECRET

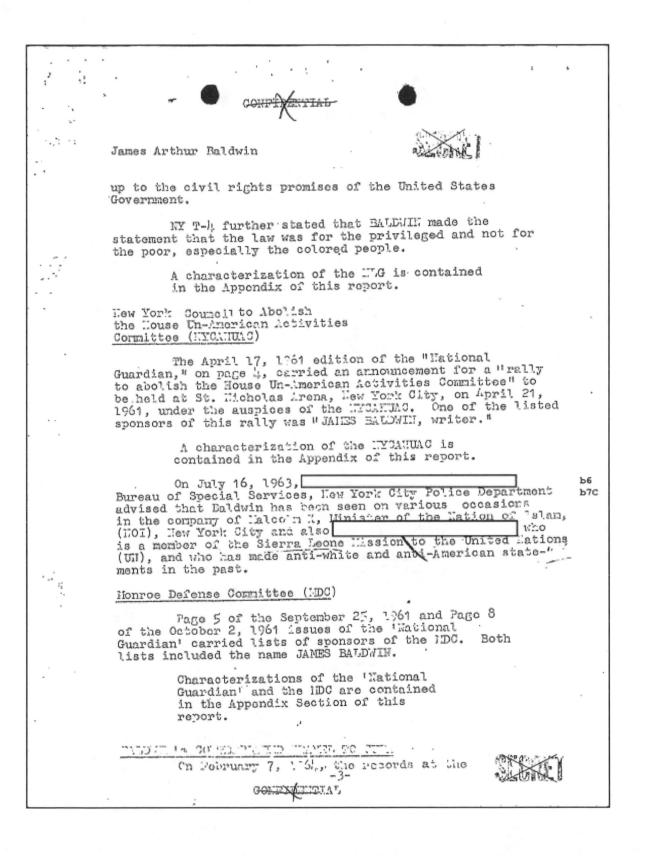

CONFIDENTIAL

James Arthur Baldwin

SECRET

up to the civil rights promises of the United States Government.

NY T-4 further stated that BALDWIN made the statement that the law was for the privileged and not for the poor, especially the colored people.

A characterization of the NYG is contained in the Appendix of this report.

New York Council to Abolish
the House Un-American Activities
Committee (NYCAHUAC)

The April 17, 1961 edition of the "National Guardian," on page 4, carried an announcement for a "rally to abolish the House Un-American Activities Committee" to be held at St. Nicholas Arena, New York City, on April 21, 1961, under the auspices of the NYCAHUAC. One of the listed sponsors of this rally was "JAMES BALDWIN, writer."

A characterization of the NYCAHUAC is contained in the Appendix of this report.

On July 16, 1963, _____ b6
Bureau of Special Services, New York City Police Department b7c
advised that Baldwin has been seen on various occasions in the company of Malcolm X, Minister of the Nation of Islam, (NOI), New York City and also _____ who is a member of the Sierra Leone Mission to the United Nations (UN), and who has made anti-white and anti-American statements in the past.

Monroe Defense Committee (MDC)

Page 5 of the September 25, 1961 and Page 8 of the October 2, 1961 issues of the 'National Guardian' carried lists of sponsors of the MDC. Both lists included the name JAMES BALDWIN.

Characterizations of the 'National Guardian' and the MDC are contained in the Appendix Section of this report.

BALDWIN's CONTACTS WITH THE

On February 7, 1964, the records at the
-3-

CONFIDENTIAL

CONFIDENTIAL

James Arthur Baldwin

Department of State, Passport Office, Washington, D.C.
reflected that JAMES ARTHUR BALDWIN on July 29, 1963, submitted
an application for renewal of passport number 2365037, which
had been issued to him on August 4, 1960. This application
indicated that on June 25, 1963, BALDWIN had received a cablegram invitation to visit Cuba in connection with the 10th
anniversary of the "26th of July Movement", and as a result of
this invitation, the "New Yorker" magazine had requested
BALDWIN to undertake a specific writing assignment in connection
with such a trip to Cuba. Attached to BALDWIN's renewal
application was a letter to the Passport Office, dated July 12,
1963, from Rabell, Rabell and Jones, Attorneys-at-Law, 165
Broadway, New York, New York, which advised they were attorneys
for BALDWIN and which requested that BALDWIN be issued a special
permit for travel to Cuba.

Also attached to the renewal application
was a Passport Office memorandum, dated August 1, 1963,
indicating that ⬛⬛⬛⬛⬛⬛⬛⬛ of the law firm of Rabell,   b6
Rabell and Jones, had informed that BALDWIN was not going to   b7C
Cuba at that time but was going to France. The memorandum
further indicated that if BALDWIN decided to go to Cuba at a
later date he would reapply for validation of his passport for
such travel.

A charaterization of the July 26th
Movement is contained in the Appendix
Section of this report.

EMERGENCY CIVIL LIBERTIES COMMITTEE

A characterization of the Emergency Civil
Liberties Committee is contained in the
Appendix attached hereto.

On April 16, 1964, NY T-5 made available a copy
of the February-March, 1964 issue of "Rights" distributed
by the Emergency Civil Liberties Committee (ECLC)

-4-
CONFIDENTIAL

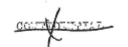

James Arthur Baldwin

which contained portions of a speech given by BALDWIN   at
an SCLC Bill of Rights dinner held in December, 1963,
in New York City.

"Freedomways"

        The Spring, 1964, issue of "Freedomways", Volume 4
Number 2, self-described as "a quarterly review of the Negro
freedom movement", published by Freedomways Associates,
Incorporated, 799 Broadway, New York, New York, contains
an article entitled, "What Price Freedom" by JAMES BALDWIN.

The New York School for Marxist Studies

        A characterization of the New York School
        for Marxist Studies is contained in the
        Appendix attached hereto.

        On March 19, 1964, NY T-6 advised that at a forum
sponsored by the New York School for Marxist Studies, held on
March 17, 1964, at 853 Broadway, New York City, JOE NORTH, who
spoke on the topic "Where Is American Literature Going?", remarked that there should be more writers like JAMES BALDWIN.

        "The Worker" dated March 15, 1964, in
        its masthead identified JOSEPH NORTH as
        being a member of the Editorial Staff
        of that publication.

        "The Worker" is an east coast Communist
        newspaper.

-5-

James Arthur Baldwin

The "National Guardian", dated July 17, 1965
page 7, contains an article captioned, " A magazine for
peace: The Seeds of Liberation".

This article states that "Liberation" magazine
is one of the most important magazine in this country
for those concerned with peace, civil rights and freedom.
"Seeds of Liberation" is a compilation of 67 of the best
articles that have appeared in "Liberation" during its
nine-year history. Among the writers included in "Seeds
of Liberation" was JAMES BALDWIN, who was the author of
an article captioned, "The Artist's Struggle for Integrity."

On April 15, 1965, NY T-7 advised that in the
masthead of the April, 1965, issue of "Liberation" magazine,
JAMES BALDWIN is listed as one of the contributors to
"Liberation".

On May 17, 1965, NY T-8 advised that a Student
Committee on Progressive Education (SCOPE) class was held
at the New York School for Marxist Studies (NYSMS).

During this class, a committee speaker made his final
lecture on "The Struggle for Negro Freedom in the United
States." During this lecture, the speaker made references to
JAMES BALDWIN and MARTIN LUTHER KING, President of the
Southern Christian Leadership Conference, and stated that
these two individuals were moving to the left in their view-
points in connection with social and economic changes.

On December 27, 1965, by use of a pretext,
it was ascertained from ▮▮▮▮▮▮▮▮▮▮▮▮▮▮▮   b6
▮▮▮▮▮▮▮▮▮▮▮ of JAMES ARTHUR BALDWIN, Apartment B,   b7C
137 West 71st Street, New York, New York, that ▮▮▮▮▮▮▮
is currently residing in London, England, the Chelsea Section.

CONFIDENTIAL

James Arthur Baldwin

Mrs. BALDWIN advised that she and her husband
maintain a permanent residence of Apartment D, 137 West
71st Street, New York, New York; however, her husband
is now in London while he completes work on his current
book about MALCOLM X, deceased leader of the Organization
of Afro-American Unity (OAAU).

A characterization of the OAAU, as well
as the Muslim Mosque, Inc. (MMI) and the
Nation of Islam (NOI), is in the Appendix.

On 10/14/68,   NY T-12   indicated that
in July, 1968, Negro author JAMES BALDWIN contributed
$285.00 to the Malcolm X organization of Afro-American
Unity, formerly known as the Malcolm X Foundation.

The Malcolm X Foundation is a
fund raising organization headed
by HAKIM JAMAL. The principal
purpose of the organization is to
enshrine Malcolm X (See Appendix)
in the minds of black people in
America.

The following article appeared in the August 18,
1969 edition of "Milliyet" a daily newspaper published
in Istanbul, Turkey,

"Yasar Kemal, Engin Cezzar, And James Baldwin
Have Formed a Partnership."

"There is a Negro writer whose love for Turkey
is as well-known as his fame on the world scale. He did not
hesitate to frankly state the following on the Paris television: 'I cannot imagine a country in the world as beautiful
as Turkey, a people as nice as the Turks, and another land
where Negroes can live comfortably.' The name of this writer,
who celebrated his 45th birthday two weeks ago, is James
Baldwin."

-7-
CONFIDENTIAL

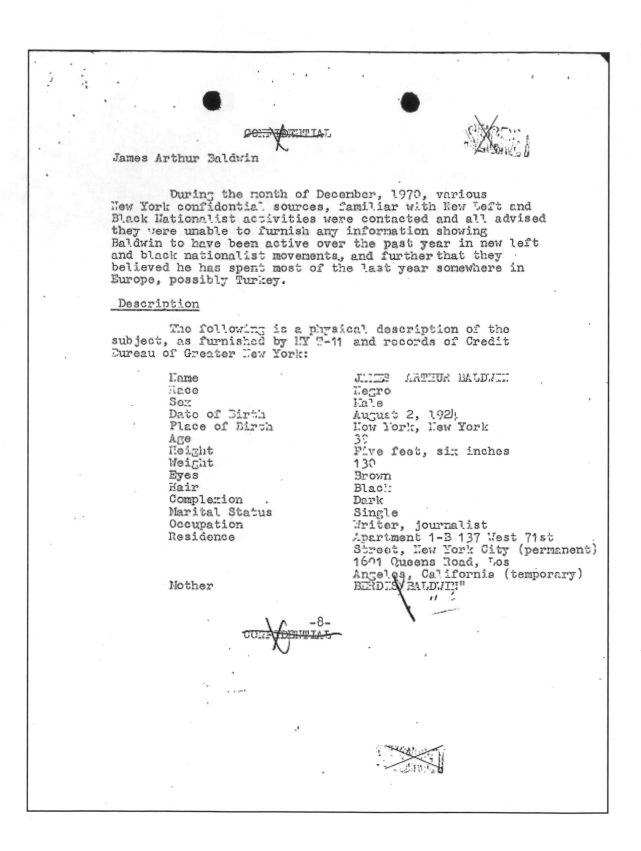

CONFIDENTIAL

James Arthur Baldwin

During the month of December, 1970, various
New York confidential sources, familiar with New Left and
Black Nationalist activities were contacted and all advised
they were unable to furnish any information showing
Baldwin to have been active over the past year in new left
and black nationalist movements, and further that they
believed he has spent most of the last year somewhere in
Europe, possibly Turkey.

Description

The following is a physical description of the
subject, as furnished by NY T-11 and records of Credit
Bureau of Greater New York:

Name	JAMES ARTHUR BALDWIN
Race	Negro
Sex	Male
Date of Birth	August 2, 1924
Place of Birth	New York, New York
Age	39
Height	Five feet, six inches
Weight	130
Eyes	Brown
Hair	Black
Complexion	Dark
Marital Status	Single
Occupation	Writer, journalist
Residence	Apartment 1-B 137 West 71st Street, New York City (permanent) 1601 Queens Road, Los Angeles, California (temporary)
Mother	BERDIS BALDWIN"

-8-

CONFIDENTIAL

SECRET

UNITED STATES DEPARTMENT OF JUSTICE

FEDERAL BUREAU OF INVESTIGATION

WASHINGTON, D.C. 20535

Reply, Please Refer to
File No.

March 24, 1971

ALL INFORMATION CONTAINED
HEREIN IS UNCLASSIFIED
EXCEPT WHERE SHOWN
OTHERWISE

JAMES ARTHUR BALDWIN

On February 5, 1971, a confidential source abroad, advised that James Arthur Baldwin, the well-known American negro author, born February 8, 1924, at New York City, arrived at Orly Airport, Paris, on January 25, 1971, enroute from Amsterdam. Source described Baldwin as a former member of the Bertrand Russell War Crimes Tribunal and a known advocate of Black Power movements in the United States.

On February 23, 1971, a second confidential source abroad, advised Baldwin, subsequent to his arrival in Paris on January 25, 1971, resided temporarily with

b6
b7C

This source noted that Baldwin spent a considerable amount of time in the southern part of France during this visit for health reasons.

The second source indicated that Baldwin, in spite of the vitriolic and violence-prone statements contained in his book, "The Fire Next Time," is apparently more moderate in his attitude, which is possibly attributable to an improved financial situation. Source described Baldwin as a militant whose revolutionary zeal has lessened considerably and who is presently far removed from the mainstream of Black Panther Party and other Black Power organizations activity. Source indicated there is no indication Baldwin has been actively engaged in Black Power activities during his recent trip to France.

On March 10, 1971, the first confidential source abroad advised that Baldwin arrived at Orly Airport on March 3, 1971, enroute from Amsterdam.

This document contains neither recommendations nor conclusions of the FBI. It is the property of the FBI and is loaned to your agency; it and its contents are not to be distributed outside your agency.

SECRET

OPTIONAL FORM NO. 10
MAY 1962 EDITION
GSA FPMR (41 CFR) 101-11.6

UNITED STATES GOVERNMENT

Memorandum

~~SECRET~~

TO   : DIRECTOR, FBI (62-108763)   DATE: 6-16-71

FROM : LEGAT, PARIS (100-2660)(RUC)

SUBJECT: JAMES ARTHUR BALDWIN
         RM - BN

ALL INFORMATION CONTAINED
HEREIN IS UNCLASSIFIED
EXCEPT WHERE SHOWN
OTHERWISE

Remylet 4-23-71 captioned "Black Panther Party (BPP),
International Relations, mylet and LHM 3-24-71 captioned as
above.

No information has been received from Paris sources
which would indicate current involvement or activity by subject
in connection with the BPP or other Black Power organizations
in France. As noted in referenced letter dated 4-23-71, the
"International Herald Tribune" issue of 4-20-71 reported
BALDWIN had participated in a rally held in London on 4-18-71
on behalf of ANGELA DAVIS.

Paris sources have advised previously that BALDWIN
is currently far less militant than in the past and apparently
is considerably removed from the mainstream of Black Power
activities. Sources indicated BALDWIN's poor health and considerable prosperity may have contributed to his withdrawal from
these activities.

Sources are aware of our continuing interest in
the activities of subject and will furnish any information
developed upon receipt. All logical investigation at this
time has been completed and captioned matter is being RUCed.

4 - Bureau
    (1 - Foreign Liaison Desk)
    (1 - New York, 100-146553)
1 - Paris
MGZ:jmw
    (5)

62-108763-83

ST-105

61 JUL 6 1971

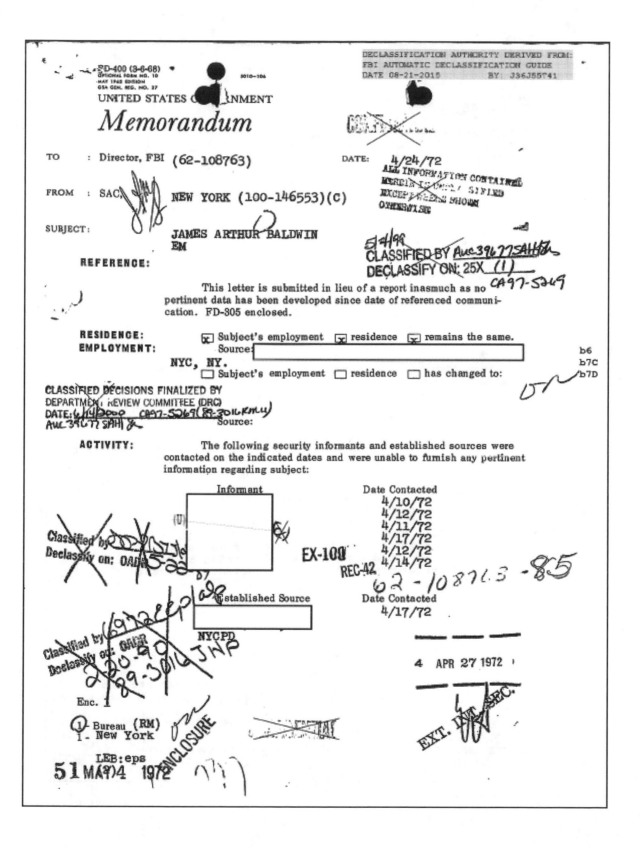

FD-400 (3-6-68)
OPTIONAL FORM NO. 10
MAY 1962 EDITION
GSA GEN. REG. NO. 27
5010-106

UNITED STATES GOVERNMENT

Memorandum

TO   : Director, FBI (62-108763)   DATE: 4/24/72

FROM   : SAC, NEW YORK (100-146553)(C)

SUBJECT: JAMES ARTHUR BALDWIN
         EM

REFERENCE:
        This letter is submitted in lieu of a report inasmuch as no
pertinent data has been developed since date of referenced communication. FD-305 enclosed.

RESIDENCE: ☒ Subject's employment ☒ residence ☒ remains the same.
EMPLOYMENT: Source: b6
        NYC, NY.   b7C
                ☐ Subject's employment ☐ residence ☐ has changed to: b7D

ACTIVITY: The following security informants and established sources were
        contacted on the indicated dates and were unable to furnish any pertinent
        information regarding subject:

Informant	Date Contacted
	4/10/72
	4/12/72
	4/11/72
	4/17/72
	4/12/72
	4/14/72

Established Source	Date Contacted
NYCPD	4/17/72

EX-100
REC-42

62-108763-85

4 APR 27 1972

Enc. 1

① Bureau (RM)
1 - New York

LEB:eps

51 MAY 4 1972

DECLASSIFICATION AUTHORITY DERIVED FROM:
FBI AUTOMATIC DECLASSIFICATION GUIDE
DATE 08-21-2015   BY: J36J55T41

ALL INFORMATION CONTAINED
HEREIN IS UNCLASSIFIED
EXCEPT WHERE SHOWN
OTHERWISE

CLASSIFIED BY
DECLASSIFY ON: 25X (1)

FD-305 (Rev. 11-22-71)

NY 100-146553

1. [X] Subject's name is included in the ADEX.
2. [ ] The data appearing on the ADEX Card are current.
3. [ ] Changes on the ADEX Card are necessary and Form FD-122 submitted to the Bureau.
4. [X] A suitable photograph [X] is [ ] is not available.
   Date photograph was taken _____ 1963 _____
5. [ ] Subject is employed in a key facility and ____ ____ is
   charged with security responsibility. Interested agencies are _____
   _____
6. [ ] This report is classified _____ because
   (state reason)

7. [ ] Subject previously interviewed (dates) _____
   [X] Subject was not reinterviewed because (state reason)
      **Subject is a well-known Negro author and it is
      almost certain that he would use such an attempt
      to embarrass the Bureau.**

ALL INFORMATION CONTAINED
HEREIN IS UNCLASSIFIED
DATE 5-22-8? BY _____

8. [ ] This case no longer meets the ADEX criteria and a
   letter has been directed to the Bureau recommending cancellation.
9. [X] This case has been reevaluated in the light of the ADEX
   criteria and it continues to fall within such criteria because (state reason)
      **of subject's past outspoken stand in the civil
      rights issue, and his prominence as an author,
      subject could again in time of national emergency
      be dangerous to the national defense interests.**

10. [X] Subject's ADEX card is tabbed Category [ ] I   [ ] II   [X] III   [ ] IV
    [ ] Subject's activities warrant such tabbing because (state reasons)
       **NY and French confidential sources have reported no
       black extremist activity on subject's past in over a year.**
11. [ ] Security Flash Notice (FD-165) to Identification Division:

    [ ] Submitted _____   Placed [ ] Yes   [ ] No
                (date)

12. [ ] Subject is Extremist in Category I of ADEX and Stop Notice has been placed
    with NCIC.

ENCLOSURE 62-108763-85

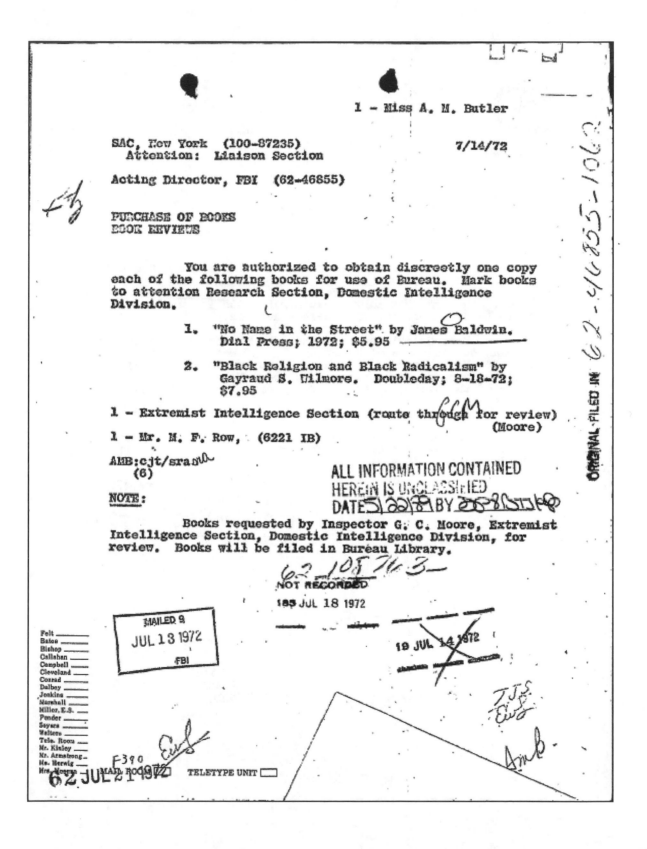

1 - Miss A. M. Butler

SAC, New York (100-87235)   7/14/72
   Attention: Liaison Section

Acting Director, FBI (62-46855)

PURCHASE OF BOOKS
BOOK REVIEWS

        You are authorized to obtain discreetly one copy
each of the following books for use of Bureau. Mark books
to attention Research Section, Domestic Intelligence
Division.

        1. "No Name in the Street" by James Baldwin.
            Dial Press; 1972; $5.95

        2. "Black Religion and Black Radicalism" by
            Gayraud S. Wilmore. Doubleday; 8-18-72;
            $7.95

1 - Extremist Intelligence Section (route through for review)
                                            (Moore)
1 - Mr. M. F. Row, (6221 IB)

AMB:cjt/sram
   (6)

NOTE:

ALL INFORMATION CONTAINED
HEREIN IS UNCLASSIFIED
DATE 5/22/81 BY

        Books requested by Inspector G. C. Moore, Extremist
Intelligence Section, Domestic Intelligence Division, for
review. Books will be filed in Bureau Library.

62-108763

NOT RECORDED

185 JUL 18 1972

MAILED 9
JUL 13 1972
FBI

19 JUL 14 1972

Felt
Bates
Bishop
Callahan
Campbell
Cleveland
Conrad
Dalbey
Jenkins
Marshall
Miller, E.S.
Ponder
Soyars
Walters
Tele. Room
Mr. Kinley
Mr. Armstrong
Ms. Herwig
Mrs. Neenan

F-390

62 JUL 21 1972   MAIL ROOM   TELETYPE UNIT

UNITED STATES DEPARTMENT OF JUSTICE

FEDERAL BUREAU OF INVESTIGATION

New York, New York

December 28, 1967

In Reply, Please Refer to
File No.

Bufile 62-108763
NY file 100-146553

M R S James Arthur Baldwin

On December 27, 1967, by use of a suitable pretext,
it was ascertained from ⬛⬛⬛⬛⬛⬛⬛⬛⬛⬛⬛⬛⬛⬛⬛⬛⬛⬛⬛⬛⬛⬛
⬛⬛⬛⬛⬛⬛⬛⬛⬛⬛⬛ James Arthur Baldwin, Apartment B, 137 West 71st
Street, New York, New York, that her husband is currently residing in London, England, the Chelsea section.

        b6
        b7C

Mrs. Baldwin advised that she and her husband maintain
a permanent residence of Apartment B, 137 West 71st Street, New
York, New York; however, her husband is now in London while he
completes work on his current book about Malcolm X, deceased
leader of the Organization of Afro-American Unity (OAAU).

A characterization of the OAAU is attached hereto.

Mrs. Baldwin further advised that her husband departed
for London a few days ago and she expects his return to New York
City during the month of January, 1968, exact date unknown.

ALL INFORMATION CONTAINED
HEREIN IS UNCLASSIFIED
DATE 5-19-8 BY ⬛⬛⬛⬛⬛⬛⬛

THIS DOCUMENT CONTAINS NEITHER
RECOMM... ... N... C N LUSIONS
OF T... ... ... TY
AGE... ... O YOUR
NOT TO ... ...IBUTED OUTSIDE
YOUR AGENCY.

62-108763-57

ENCLOSURE

UNITED STATES DEPARTMENT OF JUSTICE
FEDERAL BUREAU OF INVESTIGATION
New York, New York

In Reply, Please Refer to
File No. Bufile 62-108763
NYfile 100-146553

February 12, 1968

James Arthur Baldwin

Reference is made to the previous memorandum on this matter dated December 28, 1967.

On January 10, 1968, a search of the records of the Bureau of Vital Statistics (Marriage Records) for the Borough of Manhattan, by Special Agent Frank J. Meyers, failed to reveal any record of marriage for James Arthur Baldwin [   ] for the period of August 18, 1967 to January 9, 1968.

On February 1, 1968, [   ] [   ] 137 West 71st Street, New York, New York, advised that James Arthur Baldwin still resides in London, England. Mrs. Maher further stated that [   ] apartment B, 137 West 71st Street, New York, New York, is [   ] James Arthur Baldwin.

b6
b7C

ALL INFORMATION CONTAINED
HEREIN IS UNCLASSIFIED
DATE 3-19-89 BY [   ]

This document contains neither recommendations nor conclusions of the Federal Bureau of Investigation (FBI). It is the property of the FBI and is loaned to your agency: it and its contents are not to be distributed outside your agency.

62-108763. 58

-1*-

Ray Bradbury

SCIENCE FICTION GRAND MASTER Ray Bradbury's impressive career spanned eight decades, with hundreds of short stories and dozens of books across multiple genres. *Fahrenheit 451*, arguably his most famous work, is a dystopian vision of an American police state where books are burned and the populace is ruled by fear and ignorance. While it's easy to imagine this clear-cut commentary on the evils of censorship would attract the Bureau's interest, that book, under its original title, *The Fireman*, is only mentioned in passing in Bradbury's file, and even then in the context of having been banned in Russia. In fact, despite having being denounced by the Soviet Union, the bulk of the file concerns the FBI's investigation into whether Bradbury himself was a Communist sympathizer and was using his position as a freelance writer to disseminate his dangerous, defeatist ideas to the American public.

The Bureau first became interested in Bradbury in January of 1968, when he was named among the American literary figures potentially involved in the Cultural Congress of Havana in Cuba. While the associated memos remain heavily redacted, what was in them — combined with Bradbury's public criticism of the House Un-American Activities Commission — was enough for the FBI's Los Angeles Field Office to open a security investigation a few months later to determine if Bradbury was part of the "Communist efforts to infiltrate Hollywood." Unable to find direct evidence of Communist Party membership, the investigation turned to Bradbury's writing and what the special agent perceived to be an anti-capitalist bias contained therein — "the repeated theme of that earthmen are despoilers and not developers."

One of the Bureau's informants, Martin Berkeley, who would later gain notoriety for his role as the HUAC's "number one friendly witness," took this odd form of literary criticism even further. Citing an alleged incident in which Bradbury called other members of the Screen Writers Guild "cowards and McCarthyites" for proposing to bar members who refused to swear under oath they weren't members of the Communist Party, Berkeley observed that science fiction authors as whole have a tendency to be Communists and that the ideology found fertile ground in that genre.

Berkeley painted a lurid picture of science fiction authors, including Bradbury, as fifth columnists bent on using their stories to paralyze the American public with fear, allowing the Soviets to win the Third World War before it even began.

While the FBI, or at the very least the special agent in charge of the investigation, took these allegations seriously enough to write them down, it didn't take them seriously enough to act. The Bureau's interest in Bradbury waned after it was determined that he *hadn't* attended the conference in Cuba, and owing to his background as a "known liberal writer," an interview was deemed unadvisable. The case was put on permanent hiatus and Bradbury's work was left to speak for itself.

FD-204 (Rev 9-23-58)

UNITED STATES DEPARTMENT OF JUSTICE
FEDERAL BUREAU OF INVESTIGATION

CONFIDENTIAL

Copy to:

Report of.
Date:

SA JOHN S. TEMPLE
June 8, 1959

Office: Los Angeles, California

File Number: LA 100-57129

Title: RAYMOND DOUGLAS BRADBURY

Character: SECURITY MATTER - C

Synopsis: RAYMOND DOUGLAS BRADBURY, a free-lance science fiction,
television and motion picture scenario writer, resides
at 10265 Cheviot Drive, Los Angeles. BRADBURY has
been described as being critical of the United States
Government and the HCUA. The works of BRADBURY have
appeared in the California Quarterly. He was scheduled
to speak before the steering committee of the educational
panel, Southern California Chapter of the National
Council of Arts, Sciences and Professions in April,
1953. He was a guest of the 7th Annual Women for Legislative Action in November, 1958. The name of RAY BRADBURY
appeared in a paid advertisement published by the Los
Angeles Times and the Los Angeles Mirror News (1958),
which was a pronouncement in opposition to the HCUA.
Background data and physical description set forth.
Informants who have general knowledge of the CP and
its activities in the area in which BRADBURY resides
advised he is unknown to them.

- C -

CONFIDENTIAL

DECLASSIFIED BY 60267 NLS/DSS/CB
ON 5/9/03   #9667606

*This document contains neither recommendations nor conclusions of any kind. It is the property of the FBI, and is a loan to your agency;
it and/or its contents are not to be distributed outside your agency.*   16—74625-1   GPO

JST:JPA/jei
LA 100-57129

BACKGROUND

Birth

Current Biography,
published by H. W. Wilson Company
New York, 1953

RAY (DOUGLAS) BRADBURY was born on August 22, 1920
at Waukegan, Illinois.

Citizenship

BRADBURY is an American citizen by viture of his birth.

Relatives

Current Biography
(supra)

BRADBURY is the son of LEONARD SPAULDING BRADBURY
and ESTHER BRADBURY, nee MOBERG of Waukegan, Illinois. His
brother, LEONARD BRADBURY, is a writer. Current Biography
disclosed BRADBURY's ancestors arrived in Salisbury, Massachusetts in 1630. His mother's family originated in Stockholm,
Sweden.

EDUCATION

Current Biography
(supra)

BRADBURY attended the Waukegan, Illinois, Public
School System until 1934, at which time the BRADBURY family
moved to Los Angeles, California. He entered the Los
Angeles High School in 1934 graduating in 1938.

Military Service

LA T-1: (4/8/59)

RAYMOND DOUGLAS BRADBURY was registered on
February 15, 1942 at which time his address was given
as 3054½ West 12th Street, Los Angeles. His occupation
was that of a writer and his employer was named as LEONARD
BRADBURY, 3054½ West 12th Street, Los Angeles. He was
classified 1-A and reported for a physical examination in

- 2 -

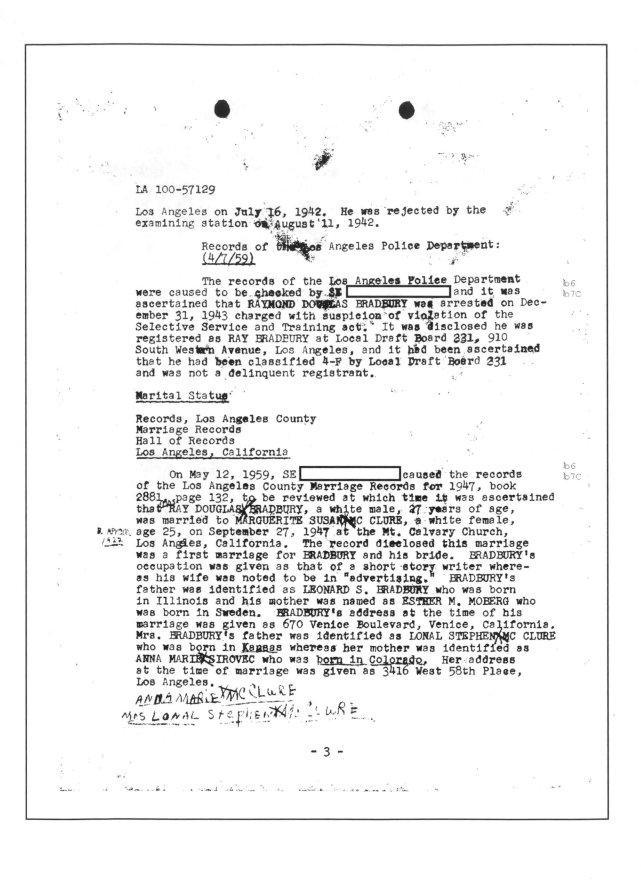

LA 100-57129

Los Angeles on July 16, 1942. He was rejected by the examining station on August 11, 1942.

Records of the Los Angeles Police Department:
(4/7/59)

The records of the Los Angeles Police Department were caused to be checked by SE [   ] and it was ascertained that RAYMOND DOUGLAS BRADBURY was arrested on December 31, 1943 charged with suspicion of violation of the Selective Service and Training act. It was disclosed he was registered as RAY BRADBURY at Local Draft Board 231, 910 South Western Avenue, Los Angeles, and it had been ascertained that he had been classified 4-F by Local Draft Board 231 and was not a delinquent registrant.

Marital Status

Records, Los Angeles County
Marriage Records
Hall of Records
Los Angeles, California

On May 12, 1959, SE [   ] caused the records of the Los Angeles County Marriage Records for 1947, book 2881, page 132, to be reviewed at which time it was ascertained that RAY DOUGLAS BRADBURY, a white male, 27 years of age, was married to MARGUERITE SUSAN MC CLURE, a white female, age 25, on September 27, 1947 at the Mt. Calvary Church, Los Angeles, California. The record disclosed this marriage was a first marriage for BRADBURY and his bride. BRADBURY's occupation was given as that of a short story writer whereas his wife was noted to be in "advertising." BRADBURY's father was identified as LEONARD S. BRADBURY who was born in Illinois and his mother was named as ESTHER M. MOBERG who was born in Sweden. BRADBURY's address at the time of his marriage was given as 670 Venice Boulevard, Venice, California. Mrs. BRADBURY's father was identified as LONAL STEPHEN MC CLURE who was born in Kansas whereas her mother was identified as ANNA MARIE SIROVEC who was born in Colorado. Her address at the time of marriage was given as 3416 West 58th Place, Los Angeles.

- 3 -

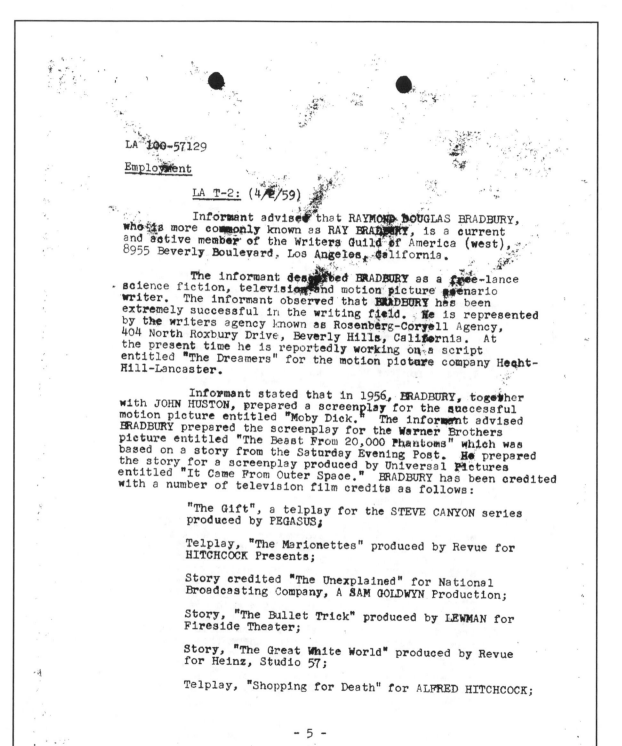

LA 100-57129

Employment

LA T-2: (4/2/59)

Informant advised that RAYMOND DOUGLAS BRADBURY, who is more commonly known as RAY BRADBURY, is a current and active member of the Writers Guild of America (west), 8955 Beverly Boulevard, Los Angeles, California.

The informant described BRADBURY as a free-lance science fiction, television and motion picture scenario writer. The informant observed that BRADBURY has been extremely successful in the writing field. He is represented by the writers agency known as Rosenberg-Coryell Agency, 404 North Roxbury Drive, Beverly Hills, California. At the present time he is reportedly working on a script entitled "The Dreamers" for the motion picture company Hecht-Hill-Lancaster.

Informant stated that in 1956, BRADBURY, together with JOHN HUSTON, prepared a screenplay for the successful motion picture entitled "Moby Dick." The informant advised BRADBURY prepared the screenplay for the Warner Brothers picture entitled "The Beast From 20,000 Phantoms" which was based on a story from the Saturday Evening Post. He prepared the story for a screenplay produced by Universal Pictures entitled "It Came From Outer Space." BRADBURY has been credited with a number of television film credits as follows:

"The Gift", a telplay for the STEVE CANYON series produced by PEGASUS;

Telplay, "The Marionettes" produced by Revue for HITCHCOCK Presents;

Story credited "The Unexplained" for National Broadcasting Company, A SAM GOLDWYN Production;

Story, "The Bullet Trick" produced by LEWMAN for Fireside Theater;

Story, "The Great White World" produced by Revue for Heinz, Studio 57;

Telplay, "Shopping for Death" for ALFRED HITCHCOCK;

- 5 -

LA 100-57129

Story, "And So Died RIABOVCHINSKA" for ALFRED HITCHCOCK;

Story, "Arcade" and "The World Out There" for Columbia Broadcasting System, TV;

Story, "Zero Hour" for the American Broadcasting Company.

The informant advised that BRADBURY is a member of the Screen Writers Branch Board of the Writers Guild of America (west)(WGAw).

Current Biography disclosed that BRADBURY, while a young man, sold papers and did miscellaneous small jobs. In 1942 his writings were beginning to return him a descent livelihood. During World War II he wrote a number of Radio Appeals for the Red Cross and short dramas for blood donor drives. The publication observed that BRADBURY has written the following books, most of which are composed of a number of short stories:

"The Golden Apples of the Sun;"

"Dark Carnival;"
"The Martian Chronicles;"

"The Illustrated Man;"
"Fahrenheit 451."

The publication observed that BRADBURY has done much radio and motion picture writing and was a prime contributor to "Suspense" a Columbia Broadcasting System (CBS) production. His work has been compared to that of EDGAR ALLEN POE, SAKI, SHIRLEY JACKSON and JOHN COLLIER. The publication reported that "The Martian Chronicles," which was published in 1950, afforded BRADBURY national recognition and the second edition of the publication sold over 200,000 books. This book dealt with the development and exploitation of Mars, its effects on mankind and its home world. The stories were connected by the repeated theme that earthmen are despoilers and not developers. The publication disclosed that BRADBURY told the writer of Current Biography "I have often been misquoted as disliking science. I would like to be quoted as saying I think science is a glove, so much depends on what

- 6 -

JST:JPA/jei
LA 100-57129

stories to Collier and McCall magazines and though they
buy his stores they do not employ him. These periodicals
disclosed BRADBURY, in 1950, received $1,250 per short
story and in a period of eight to ten months earned $7,000.

MISCELLANEOUS

MARTIN A. BERKELEY,
1336 North Benedict Canyon Road
Los Angeles, California (4/10/59)

MARTIN A. BERKELEY, a self-admitted former member
of the CP in New York City and Los Angeles, California, and
who has previously testified under oath before the HCUA, on
April 10, 1959, advised that BRADBURY was one of the more
prominent writers of science fiction in the United States.
He also felt BRADBURY was probably sympathetic with certain
pro-Communist elements in the WGAw. He stated BRADBURY,
during a meeting of Screen Writers Guild (SWG), now known as
WGAw, entered into a discussion of a resolution propounded
for the membership as to whether or not to keep CP members and
those writers who had invoked the Fifth Amendment from
becoming members of the SWG.

BERKELEY reported that BRADBURY, during the course
of the discussion, rose to his feet and shouted "Cowards and
Mc Carthyites" when the resolution was discussed. BERKELEY
stated it has been his observation that some of the writers
suspected of having Communist backgrounds have been writing
in the field of science fiction and it appears that science
fiction may be a lucrative field for the introduction of
Communist ideologies. He noted that some of BRADBURY's
stories have been definitely slanted against the United
States and its capitalistic form of Government.

LA T-3:(1/5/59)

Informant observed that Communists have found fertile
opportunities for development; for spreading distrust and
lack of confidence in America institutions in the area of
science fiction writing. Informant declared that a number of
science fiction writers have created illusions with regard
to the impossibility of continuing world affairs in an
organized manner now or in the future through the medium of
futuristic stories concerned with the potentialities of science.

- 8 -

JST:JPA/je¹
LA 100-57129

Informant advised that individuals such as
RAY BRADBURY are in a position to spread poison concerning
political institutions in general and American institutions
in particular. He noted that individuals such as BRADBURY
have reached a large audience through their writings which
are generally published in paper backed volumes in large
quantities. Informant stated that the general aim of these
science fiction writers is to frighten the people into a
state of paralysis or psychological incompetence bordering
on hysteria which would make it very possible to conduct a
Third World War in which the American people would seriously
believe   could not be won since their morale had been
seriously destroyed.

The informant observed that this appeal taken
by the science fiction writers sympathetic to Communist
ideology, is similar to the approach taken by a small number
of scientists who hold that it is impossible to conceive
of war without threatening the isolation of the Universe.

MILTON BUTTREY
901 Hermosa Avenue
Redondo Beach, California
(May 1, 1953)

BUTTREY advised that BRADBURY, during the course of
a talk before the Southwest Manuscriptors, a writers group,
on November 21, 1952, at Clark Stadium, Hermosa Beach, ridi-
culed the United States Government and the HCUA hearings.
Informant described BRADBURY as a science fiction writer, whose
work has appeared in numerous magazines and books.

Daily Variety
(May 23, 1957)

The Daily Variety, a periodical devoted to the
entertainment field, Los Angeles, on May 23, 1957, reported
that RAY BRADBURY had been elected as a new council member
of the WGAw.

American Civil Liberties Union (ACLU)
(See Appendix)

- 9 -

JST:JMA/lei
LA 100-57129

Avenue, Los Angeles, on April 14, 1953. The informant
advised that the affair at which RAYMOND BRADBURY was to
speak had been postponed due to his lack of time at this
time.

Women for Legislative Action (WLA).
(See Appendix)

     LA T-9: (2/2/59):

     The evening chapter of Women for Legislative
Action bulletin dated January 19, 1959, page four, disclosed
that RAY BRADBURY, a well known science fiction writer,
related that he uses "This medium (science fiction) to try
to bring to light some of the current fallacies in human
values today."

     LA T-10: (12/23/58)

     The Women for Legislative Action bulletin, volume
7, number 4, for December, 1958 disclosed that RAY
BRADBURY had been a guest at the 7th annual WLA dinner which
had been held at the Statler Hotel, Los Angeles, California,
November 8, 1958.

"People's World" (PW); "Daily People's World" (until 1957)

     The "Daily People's World" now known as the
"People's World," became a weekly publication in February,
1957, and is a West Coast Communist newspaper.

     The "Daily People's World": (11/13/52)

     The "Daily People's World" on page seven as dated
above, published an article which disclosed that RAY BRADBURY
in a full page advertisement in the trade paper "Daily Variety"
(previously identified) noted:

          "'I have seen too much fear in a country that has no
          right to be afraid. I have seen too many campaigns
          in California, as well as in other states won on the
          issue of fear itself, and not on the facts. I do not
          want to hear any more of this claptrap and nonsense
          from you.
          "'I will not welcome it from McCARTHY or McCARRAN,
          from Mr. NIXON, DONALD JACKSON or a man named SPARKMAN.
          I do not want any more lies, any more prejudice, any

- 11 -

JST:JPA/jei
LA 100-57129

more smears. I do not want intimations, hearsay
or rumor. I do not want unsigned letters or
nameless telephone calls from either side, or
from anyone.'"

<u>PW:</u> (9/6/58)

The PW on page three as dated above, published an
article entitled "UnAmericans Stir Public Ire." The article
observed that 100 eminent citizens among them scientists,
college professors, legislators, religionists of many
denominations, professional leaders and businessmen publicly
proclaimed their objections to the abuses of the UnAmerican
Committee of Congress in a notable document. The article
noted that the pronouncement took the form of an ad published
in the Los Angeles Times and the Los Angeles Mirror News
(Large daily Los Angeles Metropolitan newspapers). The ad
quoted the "opinion of the Board of Governors of the State
Bar of California, that proceedings of the committee were
'improper and lacking in dignity...and such a character as
to pose a threat...to proper independence of the bar!"
Signers of the ad were, according to the PW article, "hailed
as representing probably the broadist and most represented
group yet to challenge the procedures of the UnAmericans."
BRADBURY was named as one of the signers of this pronouncement.

<u>LA T-11:</u> (4/28/59)

Informant advised that BRADBURY appeared before a
small group of people who had gathered at the La Positino Coffee-
house, 19453 West Pacific Coast Highway, Malibu, California
on April 19, 1959. BRADBURY told those present how he wrote
his stories and he discussed in particular a short story
entitled "The Fireman." He stated this story sold over
50,000 copies in Russia until it was banned by the Russian
Government apparently since the Russian Government felt it
slandered their type of government as well as many other
countries.

Informants who have general knowledge of the
CP and its activities in the area in which BRADBURY resides,
advised he is unknown to them.

- 12 -

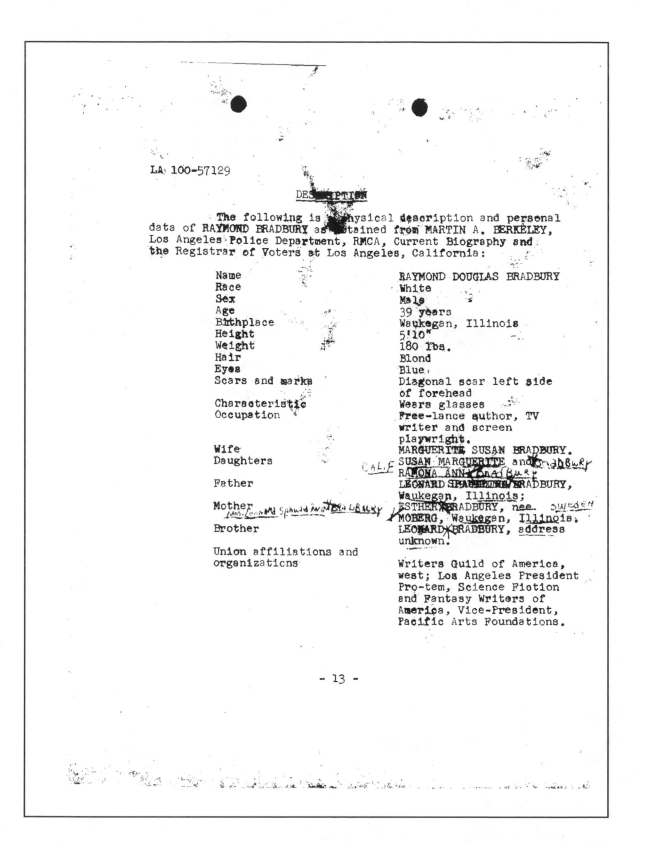

LA 100-57129

DESCRIPTION

The following is a physical description and personal
data of RAYMOND BRADBURY as obtained from MARTIN A. BERKELEY,
Los Angeles Police Department, RMCA, Current Biography and
the Registrar of Voters at Los Angeles, California:

Name	RAYMOND DOUGLAS BRADBURY
Race	White
Sex	Male
Age	39 years
Birthplace	Waukegan, Illinois
Height	5'10"
Weight	180 lbs.
Hair	Blond
Eyes	Blue
Scars and marks	Diagonal scar left side of forehead
Characteristic	Wears glasses
Occupation	Free-lance author, TV writer and screen playwright.
Wife	MARGUERITE SUSAN BRADBURY.
Daughters	SUSAN MARGUERITE and RAMONA ANN BRADBURY
Father	LEONARD SPAULDING BRADBURY, Waukegan, Illinois;
Mother	ESTHER BRADBURY, nee MOBERG, Waukegan, Illinois,
Brother	LEONARD BRADBURY, address unknown.
Union affiliations and organizations	Writers Guild of America, west; Los Angeles President Pro-tem, Science Fiction and Fantasy Writers of America, Vice-President, Pacific Arts Foundations.

- 13 -

UNITED STATES DEPARTMENT OF JUSTICE

FEDERAL BUREAU OF INVESTIGATION
Los Angeles 17, California
June 8, 1959

In Reply, Please Refer to
File No.

RAYMOND DOUGLAS BRADBURY
SECURITY MATTER - C

Confidential informants utilized in the report
of Special Agent John S. Temple dated as above at Los
Angeles, California, have furnished reliable information
in the past.

This document contains neither recommendations
nor conclusions of any kind. It is a loan to your agency,
as it is the property of the FBI, and it and/or its contents
are not to be distributed outside your agency.

UNITED STATES DEPARTMENT OF JUSTICE

FEDERAL BUREAU OF INVESTIGATION

In Reply, Please Refer to
File No.

Washington, D. C.   20535

April 25, 1968

Referral/Consult

RAY DOUGLAS BRADBURY
INTERNAL SECURITY - CU

ALL INFORMATION CONTAINED
HEREIN IS UNCLASSIFIED
DATE 5/9/03   BY 60217NLS/DSS/CE
#966766   /00-431061-X2

INCLOSURE

RAYMOND DOUGLAS BRADBURY

Hair	Blond-brown
Eyes	Blue
Wife	Marguerite Bradbury, nee McClure
Children	Susan Marguerite
	Ramona Ann
Residence	10265 Cheviot Drive
	Los Angeles, California
Employment	Free lance writer, author
Organizational	
Affiliations	Writers Guild of America, West,
	Founder of Help Establish Lasting
	Peace

On March 12, 1968, LA T-2 advised that Bradbury is
an extremely active writer in the science fiction area and
has produced some plays. LA T-2 further stated that Bradbury
is active in opposing United States policy in Vietnam and
has actively participated in local demonstrations for many
causes. LA T-2 could furnish no information on the present
activities or involvement of Bradbury.

On March 21, 1968, LA T-3 advised that Raymond Douglas
Bradbury was a member of the Writers Guild of America, West
and that he is currently residing at 10265 Cheviot Drive,
Los Angeles, California. LA T-3 advised he was unable to
furnish any information on the current activities of Bradbury.

On April 17, 1968, LA T-4 advised that Raymond
Douglas Bradbury resides at 10265 Cheviot Drive, Los Angeles,
California, telephone number VE 9-6530 (unlisted) and is
married to Marguerite Bradbury, nee McClure. According to
LA T-4 Bradbury was one of the founders of HELP (Help Establish
Lasting Peace), a group formed in 1961 in the Los Angeles area
with the purpose of demonstrating for peace.

As of 1964, LA T-4 stated that Bradbury was a member
of the American Civil Liberties Union.

LA T-4 stated that Bradbury was active in the
following groups, which were formed to participate and demon-
strate against the war in Vietnam in the Los Angeles area:

- 2 -

RAYMOND DOUGLAS BRADBURY

　　　　In 1967, he was a sponsor for Assembly of Men and
Women of the Arts concerned with the war in Vietnam; in 1966,
he was a sponsor for the Westside Committee of Concern on
Vietnam; in 1963, he was a sponsor for Southern California
Council for a Sane Nuclear Policy; as of 1960 he was a member
of Los Angeles Committee for a Sane Nuclear Policy.

　　　　LA T-4 stated that Bradbury was observed on October 27,
1962 as a protestor on a picket line sponsored by the Los
Angeles Student Peace Union, a group formed to protest the
blockade of Cuba. In 1963, Bradbury, according to LA T-4,
was active with CORE, a civil rights organization, in planning
strategy of demonstrations.

　　　　On September 29, 1962, LA T-4 stated that the "Daily
People's World", a well known West Coast communist publication,
contained an article on page 12 entitled "Opposition at Home
and Abroad Rises Against U. S. Policy in Cuba." This article
made reference to a public hearing by 44 prominent Americans
against military intervention and an appeal for re-establishing
relations with Cuba. This appeal appeared as an advertisement
in the "New York Times" on September 16, 1962 and Bradbury
was a signer.

　　　　　　On July 19, 1968, LA T-4 was recontacted and he
(U)　advised that he could furnish no further information on Bradbury nor could he furnish any information which would indicate
[why _____ was furnished Bradbury's name.]   b6
                                                                   b7C

　　　　On July 22, 1968, LA T-3 was recontacted and advised
that he could furnish no information concerning Bradbury
which would indicate any possible Cuban connections.

　　　　　　On August 9, 1968, LA T-2 was recontacted and he
(U)　advised that he could furnish no information which would
indicate a connection between Bradbury and _____   b6
_____ He added that Bradbury   b7C
would be a type person who might be invited to attend the
Cultural Congress of Havana because of his liberal view but
that he had no definite information concerning this matter.

- 3 -

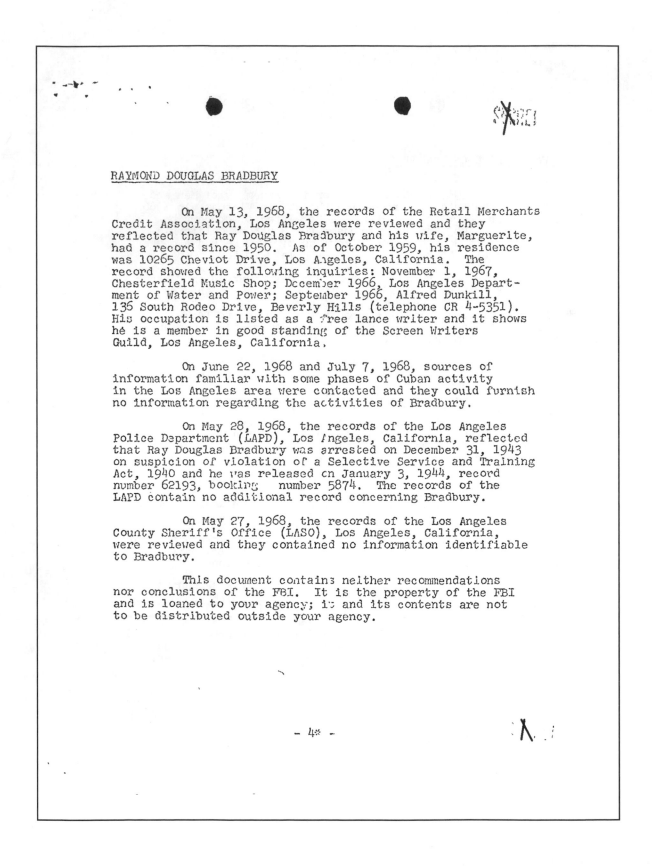

RAYMOND DOUGLAS BRADBURY

On May 13, 1968, the records of the Retail Merchants
Credit Association, Los Angeles were reviewed and they
reflected that Ray Douglas Bradbury and his wife, Marguerite,
had a record since 1950. As of October 1959, his residence
was 10265 Cheviot Drive, Los Angeles, California. The
record showed the following inquiries: November 1, 1967,
Chesterfield Music Shop; December 1966, Los Angeles Department of Water and Power; September 1966, Alfred Dunkill,
136 South Rodeo Drive, Beverly Hills (telephone CR 4-5351).
His occupation is listed as a free lance writer and it shows
he is a member in good standing of the Screen Writers
Guild, Los Angeles, California.

On June 22, 1968 and July 7, 1968, sources of
information familiar with some phases of Cuban activity
in the Los Angeles area were contacted and they could furnish
no information regarding the activities of Bradbury.

On May 28, 1968, the records of the Los Angeles
Police Department (LAPD), Los Angeles, California, reflected
that Ray Douglas Bradbury was arrested on December 31, 1943
on suspicion of violation of a Selective Service and Training
Act, 1940 and he was released on January 3, 1944, record
number 62193, booking number 5874. The records of the
LAPD contain no additional record concerning Bradbury.

On May 27, 1968, the records of the Los Angeles
County Sheriff's Office (LASO), Los Angeles, California,
were reviewed and they contained no information identifiable
to Bradbury.

This document contains neither recommendations
nor conclusions of the FBI. It is the property of the FBI
and is loaned to your agency; it and its contents are not
to be distributed outside your agency.

- 4* -

Truman Capote

TRUMAN CAPOTE, BORN TRUMAN Streckfus Persons in New Orleans, Louisiana, captured a certain downtown decadence with *Breakfast at Tiffany's*, which led to his rise to New York City celebrity status — one he enjoyed in a seemingly uncharacteristically comfortable way as open homosexual during the social period.

Despite his love of scandal, both his own and others', Capote didn't enter the Bureau's files until 1956, and even then as a footnote. The FBI had interviewed members of the American company The Everyman's Opera following their production of "Porgy and Bess" in the Soviet Union, and a member of the troupe mentioned Capote's book depicting the tour, *The Muses are Heard*.

Three years later, Capote's own publisher Bennett Cerf got in touch with the FBI to see if the Agency could help out with what would become *In Cold Blood*. Believing that his reputation preceded him, the author was surprised to find that the local police of Garden City, Kansas hadn't heard of him, putting a bit of a snag in his plans to investigate the Clutter family murders that had captivated the state a month before. The investigator on the case happened to be a former special agent for the FBI, leading Cerf to hope that the boys back at headquarters might have some sway. Unfortunately for Cerf, the Bureau hadn't heard of Capote, either.

Famously, Capote's friend, Harper Lee, herself the author of *To Kill a Mockingbird*, assisted with the research, later publishing a piece in the FBI's Grapevine on the very agent who wouldn't speak with Capote. Curiously, the FBI claims that Lee doesn't have her own file.

Soon thereafter, Capote joined a series of other prominent authors and thinkers in signing a letter in support of Fair Play for Cuba Committee, which appeared as a full page ad in the *New York Times*. "Let me have summaries on each of the above under-lined," wrote J. Edgar Hoover when he saw the news release listing Capote alongside Waldo Frank, Simone de Beauvoir, Kenneth Tynan, and Jean Paul Sartre.

That association earned Capote the majority of the pages in his file, as the FPCC became the subject of Congressional investigation — first for its ties to Communism and later for its connection to the JFK assassination (Lee Harvey Oswald was at one point associated with the group).

Capote's later run-in with an impersonator didn't end up warranting FBI attention, and none of his previous interactions prohibited him from attending White House events, invitations which triggered a check of Bureau files.

STANDARD FORM NO. 64

Office Memorandum • UNITED STATES GOVERNMENT

TO   :   Mr. DeLoach

FROM   :   M. A. Jones

DATE: December 21, 1959

ALL INFORMATION CONTAINED
HEREIN IS UNCLASSIFIED
DATE 8/5/85   BY SP6D/all mjb
      ⌐   33.034

Tolson _____
Belmont _____
DeLoach _____
McGuire _____
Mohr _____
Parsons _____
Rosen _____
Tamm _____
Trotter _____
W.C. Sullivan _____
Tele. Room _____
Holloman _____
Gandy _____

SUBJECT: CALL FROM ▮▮▮▮▮▮▮▮▮
            OF RANDOM HOUSE

Today at 1:05 p.m ▮▮▮▮▮▮▮▮▮▮▮▮▮▮▮▮▮▮▮▮▮ Random House,
called Inspector Suttler from New York and said "Bernie, I want the FBI to do
me a favor." Suttler told him we would if it was within our jurisdiction.

▮▮▮▮▮▮▮▮▮▮▮▮▮▮ stated a close friend of his by the name of Truman
Capote, who had written several fine books and was a nationally-known writer,
was at this moment in Garden City, Kansas, to do a story on the Clutter murder
mystery for "The New Yorker" magazine.   *New York*   *Born 1927*

He stated it is the story of a wealthy man, his wife and 2 children
who were apparently murdered for no reason whatsoever. Mr. Capote stated that
the ▮▮▮▮▮ at Garden City, Kansas, is named ▮▮▮▮▮ and that ▮▮▮▮▮ is a former
Special Agent of the FBI. Capote called ▮▮▮ from Garden City, Kansas, and stated
▮▮▮▮ would not give him any information on the Clutter case, as he,
▮▮▮ took no credentials to Garden City with him and ▮▮▮ does not believe he
is a writer assigned to do a story for "The New Yorker" magazine ▮▮▮▮▮▮▮▮▮
stated that Capote did not take any credentials, as he felt his many articles in "The
New Yorker" had given him a national stand as a writer and he is quite crushed to
think that the ▮▮▮▮▮ of Garden City, Kansas, has never heard of him.

▮▮▮▮▮▮▮▮▮▮▮▮▮ stated Capote had written many splendid articles and books
and has a fine, national reputation as a writer and he ▮▮▮▮▮ would appreciate the
FBI sending a wire to ▮▮▮▮▮▮▮▮▮ identifying Truman Capote as a legitimate
writer assigned to do a story for "The New Yorker" magazine. Suttler asked
▮▮▮▮▮ why Mr. Capote did not request "The New Yorker" magazine to identify him
and further why didn't ▮▮▮▮▮ merely pick up the phone and call ▮▮▮▮▮▮▮▮
and identify Mr. Capote as a friend of his of many years standing ▮▮▮▮ stated the
▮▮▮▮▮ would not accept any telephonic identification according to Capote, so it
would do no good for "The New Yorker" magazine or for him to try to identify Capote
by phone.

Suttler told ▮▮▮▮▮▮▮ that as much as we would like to do him a favor,
some checking would have to be done, as he was not personally acquainted with
either Truman Capote or ▮▮▮▮▮▮▮▮▮▮▮ nor could he see why the FBI *should* enter the
picture ▮▮▮ then stated "See what can be done, Bernie, and call me back at

BMS
(4)   53 JAN 6 1960   EX. - 124   100-369422   42
                               REC- 24   1 (continued) 1959

ALL (b)(7)(C), (D)

Jones to DeLoach memo (continued)

████████████ probably called Suttler in view of the fact that
Suttler took ████ and his family through the Bureau on a tour some time ago and
████ has written him several times since, the last time inviting him to lunch with
him at any time he might be in the New York area.

BUREAU FILES:

████████████████████ EOD 1-21-41 as a Special Agent. He
served in the New Orleans, San Diego, RA at Waco, Texas, Miami, RA at
Tallahassee, and his last office was Denver, Colorado. He resigned on 11-15-45.
Our last correspondence with him was on 9-21-53 when he requested a booklet on
the qualifications of a Special Agent and other Bureau pamphlets and signed himself
as ██████ of Garden City, Kansas. Our correspondence with him since his resigna-
tion has been cordial.

The only reference in Bureau files on Truman Capote is in a file
titled ████████████████ Internal Security-R ████████████████████
████████ exhibited a new book he had purchased titled "The Muses
are Heard," a novel by Truman Capote, which is a story covering the 8-day period
between the Berlin departure and the Leningrad premiere of "Porgy and Bess" group.
The ██ had
violated restrictions in Russia by taking some photographs which he should not
have taken and his name was mentioned in Capote's book on page 57. (100-398446-28)

Truman Capote is not listed in "Who's Who In America," but Time
Magazine of November 3, 1958, contained a review of his novel, "Breakfast at
Tiffany's" published by Random House. Other reference sources show he was born
in 1924, now 35 years old; that he has written several books, all of which have been
published by Random House, thus showing why ████████████ is interested in helping
Capote now.

No reference source shows Capote's connection with "The New Yorker,"
so he might be used for special assignments only.

RECOMMENDATION:

That Mr. DeLoach or someone in his office call ████████████████
New York and explain the FBI's position; that we should not intercede in this matter,
as we are not acquainted with Mr. Truman Capote, nor are we familiar with his
connection with "The New Yorker" magazine, and the Clutter case is not a Federal
case under our jurisdiction.

*Suttler called and told not.
book and could not in ??? are
this FBI could ??? understood
insert itself in
local ??? ???
BmS
12-22-59*

FD-263 (Rev. 5-1-59)

FEDERAL BUREAU OF INVESTIGATION

REPORTING OFFICE	OFFICE OF ORIGIN	DATE	INVESTIGATIVE PERIOD
NEW YORK	NEW YORK	2/17/61	11/28/60 - 1/12,

TITLE OF CASE	REPORT MADE BY	TYPED BY
STUDENT COUNCIL, FAIR PLAY FOR CUBA COMMITTEE		CONFIDENTIAL

ALL INFORMATION CONTAINED
HEREIN IS UNCLASSIFIED
EXCEPT WHERE SHOWN
OTHERWISE

CHARACTER OF CASE

RA - CUBA
IS - CUBA

(per release 190-1596) portions relating to
Carl Sandau reviewed

Classified by _____
Declassify on: OADR 10/30/84
250,747

Classified by _____
Exempt from GDS Category _____
Date of Declassification Indefinite
Date of Declassification Indefinite

REFERENCE

Bulet 12/22/60.

- P -

ADMINISTRATIVE

Attached is an initial report on the Student Council,
Fair Play for Cuba Committee (SC, FPCC).

For the information of offices which did not
receive copies of the referenced letter, the Bureau has
instituted an investigation on the SC, FPCC to deal with
campus activities of the Fair Play for Cuba Committee (FPCC).
The Bureau instructed that information concerning the FPCC and
its chapters which are not affiliated with students should
continue to be reported under the FPCC caption, Bureau File
97-4196, NY File 97-1792. FPCC activity which relates to
students or campus matters is to be reported under the
SC, FPCC caption, Bureau File 97-4428, NY File 97-1890. NY
is office of origin in both cases.

APPROVED	SPECIAL AGENT IN CHARGE	DO NOT WRITE IN SPACES BELOW

COPIES MADE:

9 - Bureau (97-4428) (RM)
1 - Baltimore (Information) (RM)
1 - Boston (Information) (RM)
1 - Charlotte (Information) (RM)
1 - Chicago (Information) (RM)
1 - Cleveland (Information) (RM)
3 - New York (97-1890)
Copies Cont'd on next page.

97-4428-15   REC

25 FEB 23 1961

EX-10

Dissemination Record of Attached Report		Notations
Agency	Copy to: CIA/State/ARB/ ONI/OSI/G2/ UCIA	APPROPRIATE AGENCIES AND FIELD OFFICES ADVISED BY ROUTING SLIP(S) OF
Request Recd.	by routing slip for info	
Date Fwd.	Date 8-22-61 by _____	
How Fwd.		
By	5 9 MAR 3 1961	DATE 8-22-61

CONFIDENTIAL

ALL (b)(2), (b)(7)(C), (D)

NY 97-1890

SECRET

[On November 18, 1960 _____ observed] a letter
in the offices of the national headquarters of the Socialist
Workers Party, 116 University Place, New York City, which was
intended   for circulation by the Socialist Workers
Party. This letter reads as follows:

"Dear Friend:

     "A grave crisis is at hand for the Cuban people ...
and for the sweeping social and economic revolution that
has given them their first real hope since the founding of
the Republic.

     "This week's State Department bulletin warning
U.S. citizens to get out of Cuba ... to stay away from Cuba ...
can only be interpreted as an ominous portent of what is
intended.

     "To quote United Press International: 'The last
time such advice was given was in July when American
missionaries were urged to leave the strife-torn Congo.
Americans were also evacuated from Suez during the
1956 crisis there, and from Lebanon in 1958.'

     "In other words, U.S. citizens are evacuated in
the event of civil war or imminent invasion! Which will it be
in Cuba? One indication is the renewed talk of a possible
Cuban 'grab' at the U.S. naval base at Guantanamo Bay ... an
insistent newspaper theme despite the energetic protests
of the Cuban leaders that no such action is intended.

-7-

SECRET

NY 97-1890

"Other indications: reports of Cuban 'warplanes' said to be 'buzzing' U.S. aircraft ... a new U.S. ban on exports of petroleum refining machinery replacement parts and catalysts ... the harassment of the Cuban delegation to the U.N. and of intellectuals like drama critic Kenneth Tynan who have voiced their support of the Cuban Revolution.

"For these and other reasons we consider it URGENT to establish, at once, student chapters of The Fair Play for Cuba Committee on every college campus in the United States. Purpose: to propagate and rally the sentiment of thinking Americans behind a firm policy of HANDS OFF CUBA!

"What is the Fair Play for Cuba Committee? The Fair Play for Cuba Committee was established last April by a group of distinguished writers, artists, journalists, professionals (James Baldwin, Simone de Beauvoir, Truman Capote, John Killens, Sidney Lens, Jean Paul Sarte, Kenneth Tynan, Norman Mailer, John Henrik Clarke, Frank London Brown, et al) for the following purpose:

'To disseminate truth, to combat untruth, to publish factual information which the U.S. mass media suppress, which the American public has a right to know, and in the process to combat the ignorance, the inadequate leadership, the blatantly distorted reporting which we believe constitute not merely a grave injustice to the Cuban people and a serious threat to their dream of a better life, but a serious threat, as well, to the free traditions of our own people, our nation, our Hemisphere.'

"Prominent members include Columbia University professor C. Wright Mills, author of 'The Power Elite,' Crusader editor, Robert F. Williams, literary critic Maxwell Geismar, Waldo Frank, Carleton Beals, Dr. Samuel Shapiro, I. F. Stone and economists Leo Huberman and Paul Sweezy, co-authors of 'Cuba: Anatomy of a Revolution', and many others.
-8-

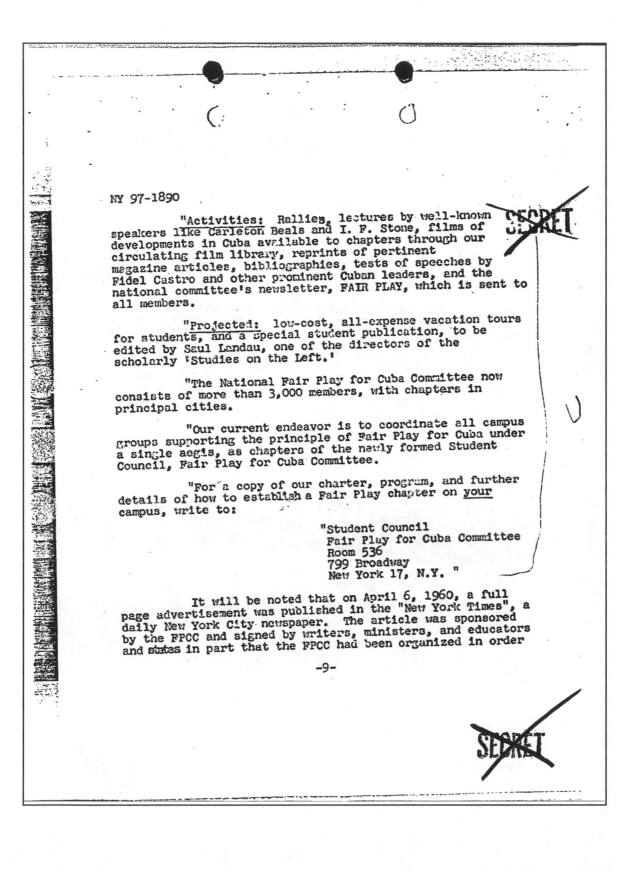

NY 97-1890

"Activities: Rallies, lectures by well-known speakers like Carleton Beals and I. F. Stone, films of developments in Cuba available to chapters through our circulating film library, reprints of pertinent magazine articles, bibliographies, tests of speeches by Fidel Castro and other prominent Cuban leaders, and the national committee's newsletter, FAIR PLAY, which is sent to all members.

"Projected: low-cost, all-expense vacation tours for students, and a special student publication, to be edited by Saul Landau, one of the directors of the scholarly 'Studies on the Left.'

"The National Fair Play for Cuba Committee now consists of more than 3,000 members, with chapters in principal cities.

"Our current endeavor is to coordinate all campus groups supporting the principle of Fair Play for Cuba under a single aegis, as chapters of the newly formed Student Council, Fair Play for Cuba Committee.

"For a copy of our charter, program, and further details of how to establish a Fair Play chapter on your campus, write to:

> "Student Council
> Fair Play for Cuba Committee
> Room 536
> 799 Broadway
> New York 17, N.Y. "

It will be noted that on April 6, 1960, a full page advertisement was published in the "New York Times", a daily New York City newspaper. The article was sponsored by the FPCC and signed by writers, ministers, and educators and states in part that the FPCC had been organized in order

-9-

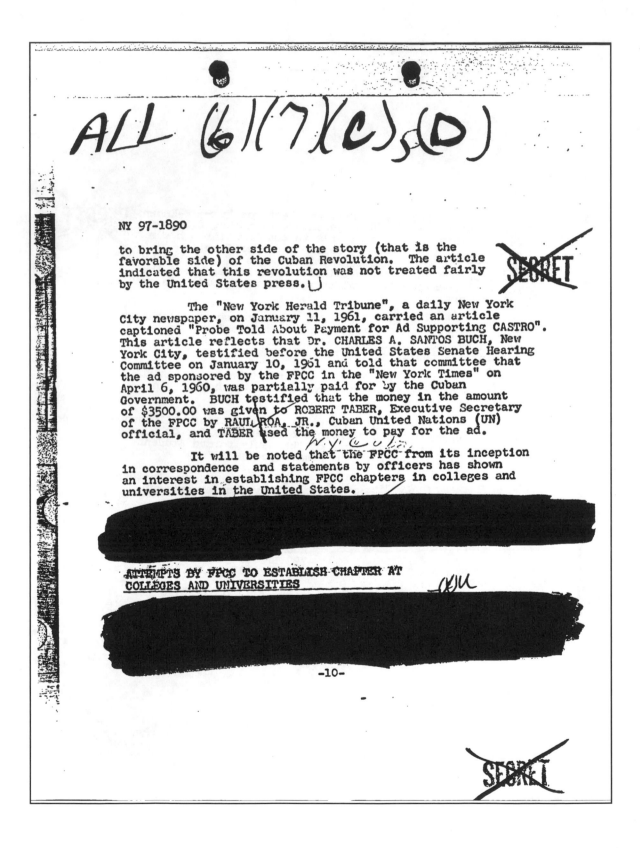

ALL (6)(7)(C),(D)

NY 97-1890

to bring the other side of the story (that is the
favorable side) of the Cuban Revolution. The article
indicated that this revolution was not treated fairly
by the United States press.

SECRET

The "New York Herald Tribune", a daily New York
City newspaper, on January 11, 1961, carried an article
captioned "Probe Told About Payment for Ad Supporting CASTRO".
This article reflects that Dr. CHARLES A. SANTOS BUCH, New
York City, testified before the United States Senate Hearing
Committee on January 10, 1961 and told that committee that
the ad sponsored by the FPCC in the "New York Times" on
April 6, 1960, was partially paid for by the Cuban
Government. BUCH testified that the money in the amount
of $3500.00 was given to ROBERT TABER, Executive Secretary
of the FPCC by RAUL ROA, JR., Cuban United Nations (UN)
official, and TABER used the money to pay for the ad.

It will be noted that the FPCC from its inception
in correspondence and statements by officers has shown
an interest in establishing FPCC chapters in colleges and
universities in the United States.

ATTEMPTS BY FPCC TO ESTABLISH CHAPTER AT
COLLEGES AND UNIVERSITIES

-10-

SECRET

ALL (6)(7)(C),(D)

SECRET

CORNELL UNIVERSITY
ITHACA, NEW YORK

The November 28, 1960 issue of the "Cornell Daily"
a campus publication of Cornell University, Ithaca, New
York, carried the following article:

"GROUP PLANS TRIP TO CUBA

"The National Student Council of the Fair Play for
Cuba Committee will sponsor a low-cost vacation in Cuba for
American students from Dec. 23 to Jan.2.

"The tour is part of the committee's program designed
to acquaint students with the Cuban situation.

"The committee was established in April by a group
of distinguished writers, artists, journalists and profess-
ionals. Among the prominent members are C. WRIGHT MILLS,
SIMONE DE BEAUVOIR, TRUMAN CAPOTE, JOHN KILLENS, I.F. STONE,
LEO HUBERMAN, KENNETH TYNAN, NORMAN MAILER and JEAN PAUL
SARTRE."

"Students who wish to make the trip to Cuba have
been requested to make reservations with the Student Council,
Fair Play for Cuba Committee, Room 536, 799 Broadway, New
York 3, N.Y."

- 32 -

SECRET

OPTIONAL FORM NO. 10
MAY 1962 EDITION
GSA GEN. REG. NO. 27

3010-106

UNITED STATES ~~~~~~~~ MENT

Memoranaum

DATE: October 3, 1963

TO : Mr. Mohr

FROM : C. D. DeLoach

SUBJECT: "CASTRO'S NETWORK IN THE UNITED STATES
(Fair Play For Cuba Committee)" - Part 6
SENATE INTERNAL SECURITY SUBCOMMITTEE

Tolson
Belmont
Mohr
Casper
Callahan
Conrad
DeLoach
Evans
Gale
Rosen
Sullivan
Trotter
Tele. Room
Holmes
Gandy

There is attached one copy of a proposed press release to
be issued by the Senate Internal Security Subcommittee (SISS) on Monday,
October 7, 1963. The release announces the release of testimony given
before the SISS on February 8, 1963, by Lyle Stuart, a New York publisher
whose book lists are dominated by earthy novels, sex-technique manuals
and pro-Castro works. In his testimony, Stuart tells about his connection
with the Fair Play for Cuba Committee but added he is no longer a member
of the Committee. There is also attached one copy of the printed testimony,
captioned as above.

ALL INFORMATION CONTAINED
HEREIN IS UNCLASSIFIED
DATE ____ BY ____

ACTION:

For record purposes.

ALL (6)(7)(C)

Enclosures
1 - Mr. Belmont
1 - Mr. Sullivan, Att: Miss Lewis
1 - Mr. J. F. Condon, 635 RB
1 - Mr. George Medler, 7266
1 - ▮▮▮▮▮▮▮▮▮▮▮▮ Rm. 635 RB
1 - Mr. M. A. Jones

**Additional copies of the printed
testimony will be furnished upon
receipt from Committee.

REC-89   97-4196-81

CDD
(8)

DEC 6 1963

ENCL. BEHIND FILE
DEC 10 1963

FOR RELEASE IN F. S OF MONDAY, OCTOBER 7, 1 3
FROM THE SENATE INTERNAL SECURITY SUBCOMMITTEE

WASHINGTON, D. C.--A New York publisher whose book lists are dominated by earthy novels, sex-technique manuals, and pro-Castro works, gives testimony about his connection with the Fair Play for Cuba Committee in a previously closed hearing released today by Chairman James O. Eastland (D-Miss.) of the Senate Internal Security Subcommittee.

The witness, Lyle Stuart, said he is no longer a member of the Fair Play for Cuba Committee, but maintained that while he was a member his presence was the main reason that Communists were not able to get control of the organization.

Subcommittee Counsel J. G. Sourwine asked Stuart if his withdrawal from Fair Play "permitted it to become Communist controlled since you left?" Stuart replied, "I am not that egotistical that my walking out would have done it, but I would assume this had something to do with it, yes." However, he said he had no present knowledge which would enable him to determine if the FPCC is Communist-dominated.

Senator Thomas J. Dodd (D-Conn.), Vice-Chairman of the Subcommittee, presided over the hearing.

Stuart published three widely-known books on Latin America: "History Will Absolve Me," by Fidel Castro; "M-26, the Biography of a Revolution," by Robert Taber, founder of the FPCC who was fired by CBS News because of pro-Castro activities; and "The Shark and the Sardines," a violently anti-American book written by a former president of Guatemala, Dr. Juan Jose Arevalo. Stuart has written numerous articles about Cuba in the Independent, a monthly publication he owns and edits. (more)

Stuart said he agreed to become the first treasurer of the New York Chapter of the Fair Play for Cuba Committee when he recognized an effort by Communists to move into the leadership. Material Stuart furnished the Subcommittee showed that Attorney Victor Rabinowitz asked Joanne Grant to be secretary of the New York Chapter.

"My own feeling was that no one should be barred from membership on political grounds," Stuart said in an article. "But, at a time when the Committee had already started to be red-baited, it was quite destructive of its chance to have as an officer a woman known far and wide for her Communist-oriented activities."

The witness said he quit as an officer of the New York Chapter after Richard Gibson, who had become head of Fair Play following disclosures about Fair Play by the Senate Internal Security Subcommittee, burned the records of FPCC.

"I was treasurer of the New York Chapter," Stuart wrote in an article in the Independent. "As treasurer I was a member of the executive board. But the destruction of the records had taken place without any meeting. Gibson had talked with an attorney nemed Stanley Faulkner and then gone into action. Only after the act, was I informed."

The Subcommittee introduced into the record advertisements for a number of Stuart's publications, including such titles as "Pleasure Was My Business," "Diary of a Nymph," "The Art and Science of Love," "The Fair Sex, a gallery of female nudes. "Transvestism," "The Marriage Cage" and others.

# # # #

FEDERAL BUREAU OF INVESTIGATION

~~CONFIDENTIAL~~

REPORTING OFFICE	OFFICE OF ORIGIN	DATE	INVESTIGATIVE PERIOD
NEW YORK	NEW YORK	4/27/64	11/26/63-4/14/64

TITLE OF CASE

THE FAIR PLAY FOR CUBA
COMMITTEE OF THE INSTITUTE
FOR THE IMPROVEMENT OF
INTER-AMERICAN RELATIONS,
INCORPORATED aka Fair Play
for Cuba Committee (FPCC)

REPORT MADE BY ▮▮▮▮

CHARACTER OF CASE

RA-CUBA
IS-CUBA
IS-C
IS-SWP

APPROPRIATE AGENCIES
AND FIELD OFFICES
ADVISED BY ROUTING
SLIP (S) BY _____ MLK
DATE 10/13/78

REFERENCE

Report of SA ▮▮▮▮ dated 11/29/63,
at NY.

ADMINISTRATIVE

It is to be noted that the FPCC is merely a
committee of the Institute for the Improvement of Inter-
American Relations, Inc., and that the FPCC was in a
position to declare or consider itself disbanded without
taking any positive legal steps.

Copies of this report are being designated for
the offices indicated and to INS, G-2, ONI and OSI, locally,
because of their interest in this matter.

ALL INFORMATION CONTAINED
HEREIN IS UNCLASSIFIED
EXCEPT WHERE SHOWN
OTHERWISE

COPIES MADE:

9-Bureau (97-4196) (RM)
1-INS, NYC (RM) (RRR)
1-G-2, NYC (RM) (RRR)
1-ONI, NYC (RM) (RRR)
1-OSI, NYC (RM) (RRR)
1-New York (97-1798)
COPIES CONTINUED

97-4196-902

25 APR 30 1964

ALL (6)(7)(c)

February 17, 1966

BY LIAISON

Name Checks

Honorable Marvin Watson
Special Assistant to the President
The White House
Washington, D. C.

Dear Mr. Watson:

Reference is made to a name check request from Mrs. Mildred Stegall relative to individuals who are to be invited to a White House affair.

The central files of the FBI were checked and found to contain either no derogatory data or no identifiable information concerning the individuals listed below:

The files of the Identification Division of the FBI were also checked and no arrest data was located concerning the above individuals based upon the background information submitted in connection with these name check requests.

Attached are separate memoranda on each of the following individuals included in these name check requests:

Truman Capote

Sincerely yours,

ENCLOSURE
1 - Mr. DeLoach(sent direct) - Enclosures   1 - Mr. Rosen - Enclosures
1 - Mr. Gale - Enclosures
NOTE: Per request Mrs. Mildred Stegall, White House Staff. Names furnished b
Mrs. Stegall were to be checked for invitations to a dinner honoring Prime
Minister Shastri but, with Shastri's death the affair was cancelled, Mrs. Stega
has requested, however, that the names still be checked as the individuals will
Enclosures (3)   included as guests at another dinner later on.

Tolson
DeLoach
Mohr
Wick
Casper
Callahan
Conrad
Felt
Gale
Rosen
Sullivan
Tavel
Trotter
Tele. Room
Holmes
Gandy

MAIL ROOM ☐ TELETYPE UNIT ☐

Delivered to Mildred Stegall
on 2-17-66

February 17, 1966

TRUMAN CAPOTE — Summary

FBI files reflect that "The New York Times" published a full-page advertisement concerning the formation of the Fair Play for Cuba Committee in its April 6, 1960, issue. This advertisement carried a list of sponsors for the new organization and the name Truman Capote appeared on this list. This advertisement indicated that the Fair Play for Cuba Committee was being formed to promulgate "the truth about revolutionary Cuba" to neutralize the distortions being printed by the American press.

The central files of the FBI contain no additional pertinent information relating to Truman Capote.

The fingerprint files of the Identification Division of the FBI contain no arrest data identifiable with Mr. Capote based upon background information submitted in connection with this name check request.

It is to be noted that Mr. Capote is the author of a recently released book entitled "In Cold Blood," which is currently a nonfiction best sel

NOTE: Per request Mrs. Mildred Stegall, White House Staff.

(8)

Tolson _____
DeLoach _____
Mohr _____
Wick _____
Casper _____
Callahan _____
Conrad _____
Felt _____
Gale _____
Rosen _____
Sullivan _____
Tavel _____
Trotter _____
Tele. Room _____
Holmes _____
Gandy _____

MAIL ROOM ☐ TELETYPE UNIT ☐ ENCLOSURE

MAILED
AUG 9 1966
NAME CHECKS

August 8, 1966

Summary

TRUMAN CAPOTE
Born: September 30, 1924
New Orleans, Louisiana

No investigation has been conducted by the FBI concerning the captioned individual. However, the files of this Bureau reveal the following information which may relate to the subject of your name check request.

The April 6, 1960, issue of "The New York Times" published a full-page advertisement concerning the formation of the Fair Play for Cuba Committee. Included in a list of sponsors for the new organization was the name Truman Capote. This advertisement indicated that the Fair Play for Cuba Committee was being formed to promulgate "the truth about revolutionary Cuba" to neutralize the distortions being printed by the American press.

(62-5-24789)

Original and 1 - State (CU/ECS)
Request received - July 13, 1966

(4)   61 7 (c)

NOTE: Mr. Capote is the author of the book "In Cold Blood," which is currently a nonfiction best seller.

EX-103

REC 30 62-5-26119

19 AUG 10 1966

56 AUG 16 1966

OPTIONAL FORM NO. 10
MAY 1962 EDITION
GSA GEN. REG. NO. 27

UNITED STATES GOVERNMENT

Memorandum

TO   :   DIRECTOR, FBI (62-18763)   DATE: 5/23/68

FROM   :   SAC, LOS ANGELES (100-71381) (P)

SUBJECT :   ▓▓▓▓▓▓▓▓▓▓▓▓▓▓▓▓▓▓▓▓▓
              SM - C

              OO: New York

              Re: New York airtel to Bureau, dated 3/14/68, and
Los Angeles letter to Bureau dated 4/9/68.

              On 4/1/68 ▓▓▓▓▓▓▓▓▓▓▓▓ (conceal) ▓▓▓▓▓▓▓▓▓▓▓
▓▓▓▓ Palm Springs Spa Hotel, advised that he had
asked TRUMAN CAPOTE, the well-known author, if ▓▓▓▓
was staying in Palm Springs. He was advised by CAPOTE that
▓▓▓▓▓▓ is staying in some friend's home in Palm Springs while
he is re-writing some portions of his book ▓▓▓▓▓▓▓▓▓▓▓▓▓▓
CAPOTE could not recall the name of the street but said it
was some "Circle" approximately one mile from downtown Palm
Springs.

              On 4/8/68 ▓▓▓▓▓▓▓▓▓▓▓▓▓▓▓▓▓▓▓▓▓▓▓▓
Palm Springs (conceal), advised that ▓▓▓▓▓▓▓▓▓▓▓▓ is
receiving mail at ▓▓▓▓▓▓▓▓▓▓▓▓▓▓▓▓ Palm Springs. He did
not know if this ▓▓▓▓▓▓▓ was identical with subject.

              On 4/30/68 and 5/13/68, spot checks at ▓▓▓▓▓▓▓▓
▓▓▓▓▓ Palm Springs, failed to observe ▓▓▓▓▓▓ residing
at that address.

ALL INFORMATION CONTAINED
HEREIN IS UNCLASSIFIED
DATE 8/5/85 BY SP6 bja/lmw

<u>LEAD</u>

     <u>LOS ANGELES</u>

              AT PALM SPRINGS, CALIFORNIA: Will continue efforts
to determine if ▓▓▓▓▓▓▓ temporarily residing in Palm Springs.

2 - Bureau (RM)
2 - New York (100-146553) (RM)
2 - Los Angeles ▓▓▓▓▓
(6)

REC-105 62-108763-63

11 MAY 28 1968

62 JUN 10 1968

GREENBAUM, WOLFF & ERNST

212-PLAZA 8-4010   437 MADISON AVENUE   NEW YORK 10022

CABLES
"GREWOLFERN" "MORERNST"
—
TELEX 423007

March 27, 1969

Mr. Cartha D. deLoach
F.B.I. Inspector
Department of Justice
Washington, D. C.

Dear Mr. deLoach:

I believe we met some time ago with Morris Ernst and I
am bothering you directly now because I really don't
know who would be the proper party to deal with what
follows. I would be most obliged if you would channel
this matter to the appropriate party in the Bureau.

We represent Truman Capote. On March 6 and 7 there was
broadcast on two radio stations in Chicago, WCFL and WGN,
a statement allegedly written by Mr. Capote, indicating
that the late President, John F. Kennedy, is still alive,
in a vegetable-like state and that the marriage of the
former Mrs. Kennedy to Mr. Onassis was a sham. Obviously
this statement was not written by Mr. Capote and he knew
nothing of it until the broadcast was brought to his attention.

I am enclosing three tapes, one of which I received from
WCFL and two from WGN. These tapes contain the complete
statement as well as certain indications of where the
material came from.

Because of the public nature of the allegations about the
late President I thought it appropriate to bring this
matter to the attention of the Bureau so that they could
try to track down the source of the statement. You will
note from the second WGN tape that the statement which is

GREENBAUM, WOLFF & ERNST

Mr. Cartha D. deLoach   -2-   March 27, 1969

now attributed to Mr. Capote apparently has been circulating for some time in the Illinois area and indeed was
published by a national "scandal" newspaper.

If this matter is of concern to the Bureau I would appreciate it very much if you could advise me of what is
finally uncovered. At any rate I would like to get the
tapes back when you are finished with them.

Kind regards.

Yours sincerely,

Alan U. Schwartz

AUS/tr
encs.

cc: Mr. Truman Capote

AL (b)(7)(c)

April 3, 1969

REC-33 62- *109060—6828*

INET ATTORNEY

Mr. Alan U. Schwartz
437 Madison Avenue
New York, New York 10022

Dear Mr. Schwartz:

Your letter of March 27, 1969, directed to Mr. DeLoach
has been brought to my attention.

The subject matter of your inquiry, namely the false
statements attributed to Mr. Capote, does not violate a Federal
law over which this Bureau has jurisdiction. I am, therefore,
returning the three tapes transmitted with your letter since it
appears this matter can best be handled through civil litigation.

Sincerely yours,

J. Edgar Hoover

MAILED 22
APR 4 - 1969
COMM-FBI

Enclosures (3)

NOTE: Mr. Schwartz is an attorney with the law firm of Greenbaum,
Wolff & Ernst, New York City, which represents Truman Capote, well-known
author and playwright. Schwartz transmitted tapes from two Chicago radio
stations which allege Mr. Capote as stating that the late President Kennedy
is still alive in a vegetable-like state and that the marriage of the former
Mrs. Kennedy to Mr. Onassis was a sham. No violation of Federal law
is apparent and the tapes are being returned in view of Mr. Schwartz's
summarization of the contents as set forth in his letter, and are, therefore,
not being reviewed.

Tolson _____
DeLoach _____
Mohr _____
Bishop _____
Casper _____
Callahan _____
Conrad _____
Felt _____
Gale _____
Rosen _____
Sullivan _____
Tavel _____
Trotter _____
Tele. Room _____
Holmes _____
Gandy _____

(3)

56 APR 15 1969

MAILED

MAY 21 1975

NAME CHECK

MAY 20 1975

TRUMAN CAPOTE *Summary*

Captioned individual, who you advised is an author and can be contacted in care of Random House, Inc., 201 East 50th Street, New York, New York, is not known to have been a subject of an investigation conducted by this Bureau.

Our files, however, reveal that the April 6, 1960, issue of "The New York Times" newspaper published a full-page advertisement concerning the formation of the Fair Play for Cuba Committee, an organization cited as a communist front. Included in a list of the sponsors for the new organization was the name Truman Capote. The advertisement indicated that the Fair Play for Cuba Committee was being formed to promulgate "the truth about revolutionary Cuba" to neutralize the distortions being printed by the American press.
(62-5-24789; 62-5-26119)

The central files of the FBI, including the files of the Identification Division, contain no additional pertinent information concerning captioned individual based upon background information submitted in connection with this name check request.

REC-88 62-5-41863

☑4 MAY 22 1975

(6)(7)(c)

NOTE: Per request of Miss Jane Dannenhauer, Staff Assistant (Security), the White House.

Assoc. Dir. ___
Dep. AD Adm. ___
Dep. AD Inv. ___
Asst. Dir.:
Admin. ___
Comp. Syst. ___
Ext. Affairs ___
Files & Com. ___
Gen. Inv. ___
Ident. ___
Inspection ___
Intell. ___
Laboratory ___
Plan. & Eval. ___
Spec. Inv. ___
Training ___
Legal Coun. ___
Telephone Rm. ___
Director Sec'y ___

DELIVERED BY LIAISON
ON 5/20/75

JUN 05 1975
366
MAIL ROOM ☐   TELETYPE UNIT ☐

GPO 954-54

Tom Clancy

ONE OF THE BEST-SELLING authors of all time, Tom Clancy's Jack Ryan novels pioneered the modern military thriller. In a notable departure from most of the other writers featured here, Clancy's depiction of hyper-competent spies using cutting-edge tech to take out the bad guys on the global stage endeared him to many in the U.S. government — his first novel *The Hunt for the Red October*, received a ringing endorsement from no less than President Ronald Reagan — and as his file shows, that included the FBI.

Clancy's file begins in 1989 and is broken into two parts, the first and longest of which consists of a Bureau background check after Vice President Dan Quayle nominated him for a position within the White House's National Space Council. The "investigation" mostly consisted of asking Clancy's friends if he was the right guy for the job, and the interviewees were universally positive, the closest thing to a criticism being one friend's caveat that having a job tended to cut into Clancy's thriller-writing time.

Clancy himself was interviewed (he gave himself a ringing endorsement), and mentioned that the only contact he'd had with a foreign government was a personal invite by the Soviet Embassy to view Russian ships visiting the Norfolk Navy Yard — apparently Mikhail Gorbachev was also a fan.

Other than an unflattering college transcript (he had graduated near the bottom of his class), the Bureau found nothing objectionable, and Clancy joined the Council. He would later go on to take credit for the controversial firing of NASA head Richard Harrison Truly, claiming that during his time on the NSC he had loudly and repeatedly urged Quayle to do so.

The second section is far shorter, but arguably more interesting, consisting of correspondence between Clancy and FBI director William S. Sessions. Clancy and Sessions appeared to have struck up a friendship during the course of the the background check; later, Sessions attended the premier for the film adaption of *The Hunt for Red October*, and Clancy was invited to speak at the FBI academy on more than one occasion. Early in their relationship, Clancy had gifted Sessions with a copy of a rather colorful death sentence (included in the file) allegedly handed down by infamous Texas judge Roy Bean in 1881.

According to a letter to Clancy, Sessions spent a not-inconsiderable amount of time and energy (not to mention Justice Department resources) to determine its veracity, and with the help of legal librarians and Wild West historians, was able to declare it a forgery.

Four years later, Sessions was dismissed amid numerous allegations of ethics violations, including using FBI resources for personal use. Sessions' successor apparently wasn't as close with Clancy, and the file ends there.

AIRTEL

July 18, 1989

Director, FBI (161-21821)

SACS,   Washington Metropolitan Field - Enc. (3)
        Baltimore - Enc. (4)
        Miami - Enc. (2)

THOMAS LEO CLANCY
SPIN (C)
BUDED: AUGUST 14, 1989

    Bureau has been requested to conduct investigation of
Clancy who is being considered for a consultant position with the
White House Space Council. Appointee was born 4-12-47, in
Baltimore, Maryland, and resides at 5000 Camp Kaufmann Road,
Huntingtown, Maryland.

    Baltimore will interview captioned individual in
accordance with MIOG, Part II, Section 17-5.6, as set forth in
Bureau airtel to all offices dated April 22, 1988.

    Baltimore will insure that at least 20 persons
knowledgeable concerning the appointee are interviewed. Check
appropriate state insurance regulatory agency.

    WMFO: Check White House, US Secret Service.

    Receiving offices should telephonically advise FBIHQ of
any derogatory information, confirm by teletype, and record
pertinent interviews on FD-302's.

    SF 86 and records release enclosed.

    All Offices: Direct results to the attention of
    SPIN Unit, Room 4371.

(7)

WMFO copy forwarded   7/18/89

            RETURN TO MR   ROOM 4371   NOV 8 1989

161-21821-1

MAILED 40
JUL 19 1989

Exec AD Adm. ____
Exec AD Inv. ____
Exec AD LES ____
Asst. Dir.:
  Adm. Servs. ____
  Crim. Inv. ____
  Ident. ____
  Insp. ____
  Intell. ____
  Lab. ____
  Legal Coun. ____
  Off. Cong. &
    Public Affs. ____
  Rec. Mgnt. ____
  Tech. Servs. ____
  Training ____
Off. Liaison &
  Int. Affs. ____
Telephone Rm. ____
Director's Sec'y ____   MAIL R

b6
b7C

Standard Form 86
Revised October 1987
U.S. Office of Personnel Management
FPM Chapter 736

**QUESTIONNAIRE FOR
SENSITIVE POSITIONS**

Form Approved:
O.M.B. No. 3206-0007
Expires: 8-31-90
NSN 7540-00-634-4036

Part 1 OPM USE ONLY

Codes   Case Number

Agency Use Only (Complete items A through P using instructions in FPM Supplement 296-33.)

A Type of Investigation	B Extra Coverage	C Sensitivity Level	D Access	E Nature of Action Code	F Date of Action	Month	Day	Year

G Geographic Location
H Position Code
I Position Title

J SON	K Location of Official Personnel Folder	None / NPRC / At SON	Other Address		ZIP Code b6 b7C

L SOI	M Location of Security Folder	None / At SOI / NPI	Other Address		ZIP Code

N SIBAC Number
O Accounting Data and/or Agency Case Number

P Requesting Official — Name and Title   Signature   Telephone Number (including Area Code)   Date   b6 b7C

Persons completing this form should begin with the questions below. Please type or print your answers.

1 FULL NAME
- If you have only initials in your name, use them.
- If you have no middle name, enter "NMN".
- If you are a "Jr.","Sr.", "II", etc., enter the abbreviation in the box after your middle name.

Last Name	First Name	Middle Name	Abbrv.
CLANCY 1-25	Thomas	Leo	(Jr.)

2 DATE OF BIRTH

Month	Day	Year
04	12	47

3 PLACE OF BIRTH • Use the two letter code for the state.

City	County	State	Country (if not in the United States)
Baltimore	(N/A)	MD	

4 SOCIAL SECURITY NUMBER 217 - 50 - 3929

5 OTHER NAMES USED • Give other names you used and the period of time you used them (for example: your maiden name, name[s] by a former marriage, former name[s], alias[es], or nickname[s]). If the other name is your maiden name, put "nee" in front of it.

Name	Month/Year From	Month/Year To	Name	Month/Year From	Month/Year To
N/A					
Name	Month/Year From	Month/Year To	Name	Month/Year From	Month/Year To

6 OTHER IDENTIFYING INFORMATION

Height (feet and inches)	Weight (pounds)	Hair Color	Eye Color	Sex (mark one box)
6' 2"	180 lbs	Brown	Blue	☐ Female ☒ Male

7 TELEPHONE NUMBERS

Work (include Area Code and extension)	Home (include Area Code)
(301) 535-2721	(301) 535-2721

8a CITIZENSHIP Mark the box at the right that applies to you and follow the instructions next to the box you marked.

I am a U.S. citizen by birth in the U.S.	XX Go to 8c
I am a U.S. citizen, but I was NOT born in the U.S.	Go to 8b
I am not a U.S. citizen.	Go to 8d

8b UNITED STATES CITIZENSHIP If you are a U.S. Citizen, but were not born in the U.S., enter your mother's maiden name in the box to the right and provide information about one or more of the following proofs of your citizenship. Then go to Item 8c.

Mother's Maiden Name

Naturalization Certificate (Where were you naturalized?)

Court	City	State	Certificate Number	Month/Day/Year Issued

Citizenship Certificate (Where was the certificate issued?)

City	State	Certificate Number	Month/Day/Year Issued

State Department Form 240–Report of Birth Abroad of a Citizen of the United States

Give the date the form was prepared and give an explanation if needed.	Month/Day/Year	Explanation

BASED UPON INFORMATION FURNISHED
A SEARCH OF THE IDENTIFICATION
DIVISION FILES FAILED TO DISCLOSE
ANY IDENTIFIABLE INFORMATION.

U.S. Passport This may be either a current or previous U.S. passport.

Passport Number	Month/Day/Year Issued

8c DUAL CITIZENSHIP If you are (or were) a dual citizen of the United States and another country, provide the name of that country in the space to the right.

Country

8d ALIEN • If you are an alien, provide the following information:

Place You Entered the United States:	City	State	Date You Entered U.S. Month / Day / Year	Alien Registration Number	Country of Citizenship

86-108

ENCLOSURE

Page 1

16c. ACTIVE SERVICE   Show each period of active service (includes active military reserve service). Use one of the following in the box for Code. Mark "O" for Officer or "E" for Enlisted.

1 - Air Force	4 - Marine Corps	7 - National Guard
2 - Army	5 - Coast Guard	
3 - Navy	6 - Merchant Marine	

Month/Year Month/Year To	Code	Service or Certificate Number	O	E	Month/Year Month/Year To	Code	Service or Certificate Number	O	E
		N/A							

17   YOUR RELATIVES   Give full names and enter the correct code for all relatives, living or dead, specified below:

1 - Mother	4 - Stepfather	7 - Stepchild	10 - Stepbrother	13 - Half-sister	16 - Guardian
2 - Father	5 - Foster parent	8 - Brother	11 - Stepsister	14 - Father-in-law	b6
3 - Stepmother	6 - Child (adopted also)	9 - Sister	12 - Half-brother	15 - Mother-in-law	b7C

Full Name (if deceased, check box on the left before ent	Code	Date of Birth Month/Day/Year	Country of Birth	Country of Citizenship	Current Street Address and City (country) of Living Relatives	State
Catherine M. Clancy	1	07/28/18	U.S.A.	U.S.A.	7300 20th St. Lot611 Vero Beach,	FL
Thomas L. Clancy, Sr.	2	10/06/18	U.S.A.	U.S.A.	7300 20th St. Lot 611 Vero Beach	FL

18   YOUR MARITAL STATUS   Mark one of the following boxes to show your current marital status:

| ☐ 1 - Never married (go to question 19) | ☐ 3 - Separated | ☐ 5 - Divorced | b6 |
| ☒ 2 - Married | ☐ 4 - Legally separated | ☐ 6 - Widowed | b7C |

Current Spouse. Complete the following about your current spouse.

Maiden name

Country of Citizenship   Date Married   Place Married (Include country if outside the U.S.)   State M D

If Separated, Date of Separation (Mo./Day/Yr.)   If Legally Separated, Where is the Record Located? City (Country)   State

Address of Current Spouse (Street, city, and country if outside the U.S.)   State ZIP Code

UNABLE TO IDENTIFY UNIT ARREST RECORD ON BASIS OF INFORMATION FURNISHED. FBI IDENTIFICATION DIVISION.

JUL 26 1969

Former Spouse(s) Complete the following about your former spouse(s).

Full Name	Date of Birth	Place of Birth (Include country if outside the U.S.)	State
n/a/			
Country of Citizenship	Date Married	Place Married (Include country if outside the U.S.)	State
Check One, Then Give Date ☐ Divorced ☐ Widowed	Month/Day/Year	If Divorced, Where is the Record Located? City (Country)	State
Address of Former Spouse (Street, city, and country if outside the U.S.)			State ZIP Code

19   Does the citizen of another country, or a United States citizen by other than birth, live at your residence? If "Yes", provide the information required below. If a United States citizen by other than birth lives with you, show both "United States" and prior country of citizenship below. Don't list your spouse or other relatives you provided in question 17.

Yes | No: X

Name of Person	Country of Citizenship	Relationship

Enter your Social Security Number before going to the next page.   21 7 - 5 0 - 3 9 2 9

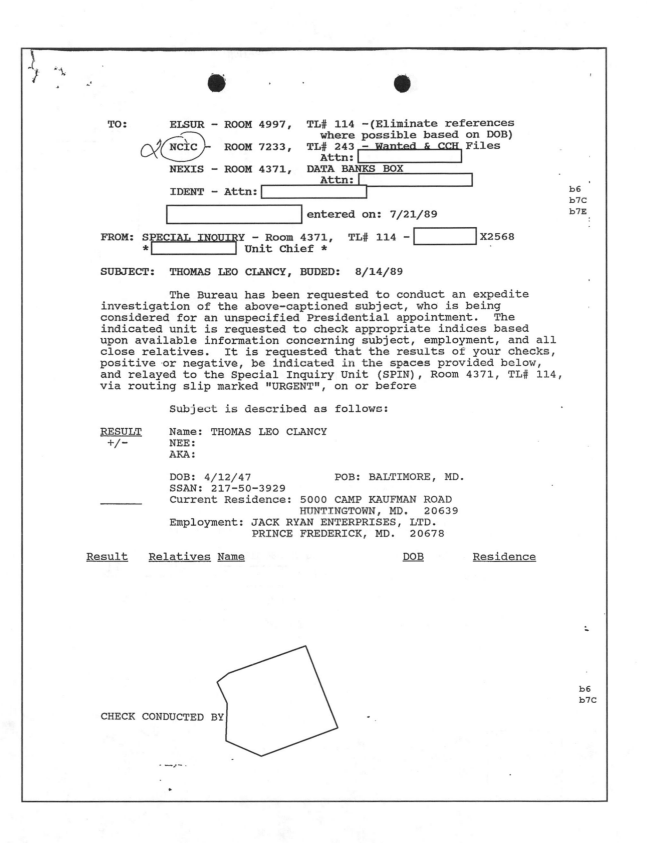

TO: ELSUR – ROOM 4997, TL# 114 –(Eliminate references
                                        where possible based on DOB)
      NCIC – ROOM 7233,   TL# 243 – Wanted & CCH Files
                                  Attn: [   ]
      NEXIS – ROOM 4371, DATA BANKS BOX
                                  Attn: [   ]

      IDENT – Attn: [   ]   b6
                                                                   b7C
      [   ] entered on: 7/21/89   b7E

FROM: SPECIAL INQUIRY – Room 4371, TL# 114 – [   ] X2568
      * [   ] Unit Chief *

SUBJECT: THOMAS LEO CLANCY, BUDED: 8/14/89

        The Bureau has been requested to conduct an expedite
investigation of the above-captioned subject, who is being
considered for an unspecified Presidential appointment. The
indicated unit is requested to check appropriate indices based
upon available information concerning subject, employment, and all
close relatives. It is requested that the results of your checks,
positive or negative, be indicated in the spaces provided below,
and relayed to the Special Inquiry Unit (SPIN), Room 4371, TL# 114,
via routing slip marked "URGENT", on or before

        Subject is described as follows:

RESULT   Name: THOMAS LEO CLANCY
 +/-   NEE:
         AKA:

         DOB: 4/12/47   POB: BALTIMORE, MD.
         SSAN: 217-50-3929
_____   Current Residence: 5000 CAMP KAUFMAN ROAD
                              HUNTINGTOWN, MD. 20639
         Employment: JACK RYAN ENTERPRISES, LTD.
                     PRINCE FREDERICK, MD. 20678

Result   Relatives Name   DOB   Residence

                                                                   b6
                                                                   b7C

CHECK CONDUCTED BY

RECEIVED
TELETYPE UNIT

28 JUL 89   U 2 5 6B

FEDERAL BUREAU
OF INVESTIGATION

INBOX.31 (#10770)

TEXT:

VZCZCMM0012

RR HQ

DE MM #0012 2082237

ZNR UUUUU

R 272127Z JUL 89

FM FBI MIAMI (161C-HQ-R-21821) (RUC)

TO DIRECTOR FBI/ROUTINE/

BT

UNCLAS

CITE: //3460//

PASS: [   ] SPIN UNIT, ROOM 4371.

b6
b7C

SUBJECT: THOMAS LEO CLANCY; SPIN (C); BUDED: AUGUST 14, 1989.

     RE BUREAU AIRTEL TO MIAMI, DATED JULY 18, 1989.

     MIAMI GENERAL INDICES WERE CHECKED BY [   ]   161-21821-3

CONFIDENTIAL INDICES BY [   ]; AND ELSUR INDICES BY   NOV 8 1989

[   ] ALL NEGATIVE RE: CANDIDATE AND CLOSE FAMILY ON

JULY 26 - 27, 1989.

     MIAMI INVESTIGATION COMPLETE.

BT

#0012

SSP
FD-263 (Rev. 4-30-63)
CLASS
REC'D
SER
REC

FEDERAL BUREAU OF INVESTIGATION

REPORTING OFFICE	OFFICE OF ORIGIN	DATE	INVESTIGATIVE PERIOD
BALTIMORE	BUREAU	8/11/89	7/27/89 – 8/10/89

TITLE OF CASE	REPORT MADE BY	TYPED BY:	
THOMAS LEO CLANCY	SA		b6 b7C
	CHARACTER OF CASE		
	SPECIAL INQUIRY		

REFERENCE:

Bureau airtel to WMFO, July 18, 1989.

- RUC -

ADMINISTRATIVE DATA: BUDED: 8/14/89

None of the individuals contacted requested confidentiality under the provisions of the Privacy Act.

Baltimore indices, consisting of general, confidential and ELSUR, were negative regarding the appointee and other pertinent individuals.

b6
b7C

APPROVED	SPECIAL AGENT IN CHARGE	DO NOT WRITE IN SPACES BELOW

COPIES MADE:

② - Bureau (Attn: [ ] Unit, Room 4371)
1 - Baltimore (161C-HQ-21821) (SQ 9)

SPIN 161-21821-5

NOV 8 1989

CC DESTROYED

DISSEMINATION RECORD OF ATTACHED REPORT				Notations	
Agency					
Request Recd.					
Date Fwd.					
How Fwd.					
By					

A*
COVER PAGE

FD-204 (Rev. 3-3-59)

UNITED STATES DEPARTMENT OF JUSTICE
Federal Bureau of Investigation

Copy to:

Report of: SA _____   Office: BALTIMORE DIVISION   b6
Date: August 11, 1989   b7C

Field Office File #: 161C-HQ-21821   Bureau File #:

Title: THOMAS LEO CLANCY

Character: SPECIAL INQUIRY

Synopsis:

    Appointee interviewed and advised that information contained on SS-86 is true and correct to the best of his knowledge. He advised that he has had no contact with representatives of a foreign government except for visit by invitation to Soviet ships at Norfolk, Virginia, and to the Soviet Embassy. Appointee's education at Loyola College verified. Appointee's employment at and ownership of O.F. Bowen Agency, Inc., verified favorable. References favorably recommends. Former neighbors recommend. Credit check satisfactory. Arrest check negative.

- RUC -

DETAILS:

INTERVIEW OF APPOINTEE:

FD-302 (REV. 3-10-82)

FEDERAL BUREAU OF INVESTIGATION

Date of transcription   8/7/89

THOMAS LEO CLANCY, 5000 Camp Kaufmann Road, Huntington, Maryland, advised that the information contained on standard form 86 is true and correct to the best of his knowledge.

CLANCY advised that JACK RYAN Enterprises, LTD., is the name that he uses for his occupation, which is a self-employed author. He advised that his present residence is located at the end of a quarter mile lane at the end of Camp Kaufmann Road. He stated that he has had no contact with any of his neighbors to date and therefore, none of them would be acquainted with him.

CLANCY stated that he has never used illegal drugs or abused alcoholic beverages and has never had to participate in any counseling regarding same. He said that he has never had any debts that have been placed for collection, no repossessions and no bankruptcy proceedings. He has never been a plaintiff or defendant in any civil suits or divorces. He advised that he has never been involved in any criminal matter as a suspect or subject and has never been arrested. He has never been denied employment or dismissed from any employment. He stated that he has had no contact with any representatives of a foreign Government except for a visit by invitation to the Soviet Embassy and two Soviet ships at Norfolk, Virginia. He advised that there are no details regarding his personal life that could be used to coerce him. He advised that to his knowledge there has never been any professional complaints or nonjudicial disciplinary action taken against him. He advised that he could think of no business or investment circumstances that could involve a conflict of interest. He stated that he has never had any psychological counseling or been counseled by psychiatrists or other counselors. He advised that he does not belong to any organization that restricts its membership on a basis of sex, race, color, religion or national origin.

Investigation on 8/3/89   at Huntingtown, Maryland   File # BA
161C-HQ-21821

by ___ SA[   ]_ _ _ _ _ _ _ _ _ _ ·   Date dictated 8/7/89   b6
b7C

161C-HQ-21821

EDUCATION:

Loyola College, Baltimore, Maryland:

On July 28, 1989, the following investigation was
conducted by SA [   ]   b6
                                                                         b7C
[   ] Supervisor, Records Office, Loyola
College, provided the official Academic Record of the appointee.
The record contained the following information:

Name:	THOMAS LEO CLANCY, JR.
Date of Birth:	April 12, 1947
Place of Birth:	Baltimore, Maryland
Residence:	1530 Glen Eagle Road, Baltimore, MD
Date of Attendance:	Fall of 1965 to June 8, 1969
Date of Graduation:	June 8, 1969
Degree:	Bachelor of Arts
Major:	English
GPA:	1.93 on a 4.0 scale
Rank:	220 out of 224

The record contained no information as to who the
appointee's instructors or counselors may have been.

EMPLOYMENT:

O. F. Bowen Agency, Inc., Owings, Maryland:

On August 10, 1989, [   ]   b6
[   ] advised that she [   ] the O. F. Bowen   b7C
Agency, Inc. She stated that this company is an insurance agency
and that she [   ] She
stated that she [   ]
She advised that she hired the appointee as an insurance agent in
July, 1973, and he remained with her company as an agent and
manager until he purchased the company [   ] in August, 1980.
She advised that he performed his duties in an excellent manner.
She described him as a very efficient, honest, trustworthy and
dependable individual, whose character, loyalty, associates and
reputation are above reproach. She advised that she saw no
indication that the appointee has ever used illegal drugs or
abused alcoholic beverages and stated that he is a very
financially responsible person. She advised that the appointee

3

161C-HQ-21821

has sold the agency [   ] b6
She stated that [   ] and the [   ] and b7C
that [   ] the agency. She stated that she
would highly recommend the appointee for a position of trust with
the United States Government.

On August 10, 1989, [   ] O. F. Bowen b6
Agency, Inc., advised that he has been acquainted with the b7C
appointee since 1966. He stated that he is [   ]
[   ] and that [   ] the
agency. He advised that he was first employed with the agency in
March, 1987, and [   ] in May,
or June, 1989. He advised that the appointee found it difficult
to attempt to run the agency and write books at the same time.
He stated that he has found the appointee to be a totally honest,
trustworthy and dependable individual, whose character, loyalty,
and reputation are above reproach. He advised that he has never
known the appointee to use illegal drugs or abuse alcoholic
beverages and considers him to be a financially responsible
person. He stated that the appointee is a very good family man
and he would not hesitate to highly recommend him for a position
of trust with the United States Government.

On August 10, 1989, [   ] O.F. b6
Bowen Agency, Inc., advised that she has been employed wit the b7C
agency for about 13 years. She stated that she worked with the
appointee while he was both manager and owner of the agency. She
described him as a hard working individual. She stated that she
is [   ] the
appointee. She stated that she has found him to be an honest and
trustworthy person and she advised that she would not question
his character, loyalty, associates or reputation. She stated
that she has never known him to use illegal drugs or abuse
alcoholic beverages and believes him to be financially
responsible. She advised that she could favorably recommend him
for a position of trust and confidence with the United States
Government.

REFERENCES:

On August 2, 1989, LCDR [   ], USN, b6
Security Department, Patuxent River Naval Air Station, Patuxent b7C
River, Maryland, telephone number [   ], advised he has
known the appointee for approximately twenty four years. [   ]

4

161C-HQ-21821

advised he first met the appointee in high school and they have
maintained their friendship since, with several lapses due to
being in different parts of the country. [   ] advised that
they have been close friends for the last six years continuously
since they have both been back in Maryland.

[   ] advised that the appointee is friendly, down to
earth, very intelligent, and resourceful. He further advised
that the appointee is very honest, dependable, and a good friend
who has not let his financial success change him. [   ]
advised he has the highest regard for the appointee's character
and his reputation is spotless. [   ] advised that the
appointee has a wide circle of friends and associates, all of
which are, to the best of his knowledge, of high character.
[   ] advised that he considers the appointee to be a very
loyal U.S. Citizen and an individual who has never used illegal
drugs or abused alcohol. [   ] advised that the appointee
appears to live a lifestyle well within his financial means and
he would highly recommend him for a position of trust and
responsibility with the United States Government.

On August 10, 1989, [   ]
[   ] advised that she was the appointee's
[   ] Instructor and [   ] while he was attending
Loyola College, Baltimore, Maryland. She advised that she has
remained in contact with the appointee through the years and that
she and her husband are [   ] of the appointee's
[   ] She stated that she considers the appointee to be a loyal
citizen and an honest, trustworthy and dependable person. She
stated that she believes that he associates only with people of
good reputation and to her knowledge, has never used illegal
drugs or abused alcoholic beverages. She advised that he is a
financially responsible individual and she would highly recommend
him for a position of trust with the United States Government.

On August 10, 1989, [   ]
[   ] advised that he has been acquainted with the
appointee and his family since 1976. [   ] stated that he
opened [   ] and the
appointee's spouse was [   ] at this time. He stated
that the appointee has an excellent reputation and he considers
him to be an honest trustworthy and dependable person. He
advised that he has found the appointee to be a loyal citizen,
and has never known him to use illegal drugs or abuse alcoholic

b6
b7C

b6
b7C

b6
b7C

b6
b7C

5

161C-HQ-21821

beverages, and stated that he lives well within his financial
means. He advised that he would not hesitate to give the
appointee his highest recommendation for a position of trust with
the United States Government.

NEIGHBORHOOD:

⬚ M. F. Bowen Road, Huntington,
Maryland ⬚:

On August 3, 1989, ⬚ M. F. Bowen
Road, Huntington, Maryland, advised that the appointee and his
family were neighbors of his for 11 or 12 years, ending in
October, 1985. He stated that the appointee had an excellent
reputation in the neighborhood and that he considered him to be a
very good neighbor. He described him as an honest and
trustworthy person and stated that he would not question his
character, loyalty, or associates. He advised that he never had
any indication that the appointee ever used illegal drugs or
abused alcoholic beverages and believed him to be a financially
responsible person. He stated that he could favorably recommend
the appointee for a position of trust with the United States
Government.

On August 3, 1989, ⬚ M. F. Bowen Road,
advised that the appointee was the neighbor of hers for about 10
to 12 years, ending in the fall of 1985. She stated that she
considered him to be a very good neighbor and she knew nothing of
an unsatisfactory nature regarding him. She advised that she had
no reason to question the appointee's character, loyalty or
reputation. She advised that she never knew him to use illegal
drugs or to abuse alcoholic beverages, and believed him to be a
financially responsible person. She stated that she could
favorably recommend him for employment with the United States
Government.

On August 3, 1989, ⬚ M. F. Bowen Road,
advised that the appointee was the neighbor of hers from the
early 1970's to the fall of 1985. She stated that she was not
well acquainted with him. She advised that he had a good
reputation in the neighborhood and that she knows of nothing of
an unsatisfactory nature regarding him. She advised that she
never had any reason to doubt the appointee's character,
loyalty, or reputation. She stated that she never knew of him to

6

161C-HQ-21821

use illegal drugs or abuse alcoholic beverages, and stated that
she could not comment regarding his financial status. She stated
that she could favorably recommend him for employment with the
United States Government.

1625 Twirly Court, Prince Frederick, Maryland:

On August 10, 1989, [   ]   b6
Twirly Court, advised that they were neighbors of the appointee   b7C
for approximately 3 years. They advised the appointee moved from
the neighborhood in March, 1989. They stated that they
considered the appointee to be a very good neighbor and they
advised that they would not question his character, loyalty or
reputation. They stated that they never knew the appointee to
use illegal drugs or abuse alcoholic beverages and believed him
to be a financially responsible person. They advised that they
could favorably recommend the appointee for a position of trust
with the United States Government.

On August 3, 1989, [   ]Cedar   b6
Point Lane, advised that the appointee was the neighbor of theirs   b7C
for approximately 4 years. They stated that they considered the
appointee and his family to be very good neighbors and they knew
of nothing of an unsatisfactory nature regarding him. They
advised that the appointee is an honest, trustworthy and
dependable person, whose character, loyalty, and reputation are
above reproach. They stated that they never had any indication
that the appointee has ever used illegal drugs or abused
alcoholic beverages and believed him to be financially
responsible. They stated they would highly recommend the
appointee for a position of trust with the United States
Government.

On August 10, 1989, [   ]   b6
Twirly Court, advised that they were neighbors of the appointee   b7C
for approximately 8 months. They stated the appointee moved from
the neighborhood in March, 1989. They advised that they
considered him to be a very good neighbor and would not question
his character, loyalty or reputation. They stated they never
knew the appointee to use illegal drugs or abuse alcoholic
beverages and believed him to be financially responsible. They
stated they could favorably recommend the appointee for a
position of trust with the United States Government.

7

161C-HQ-21821

On August 10, 1989, [   ]
Twirly Court, stated that the appointee and his family resided
across the street from them for approximately 4 years. They
advised that the appointee had a very good reputation in the
neighborhood and that they knew nothing of an unsatisfactory
nature regarding him. They stated that they would not question
the appointee's character, loyalty, or reputation. The stated
that they never knew him to use illegal drugs or abuse alcoholic
beverages, and believed him to live within his financial means.
They stated they could favorably recommend the appointee for a
position of trust with the United States Government.

b6
b7C

On August 10, 1989, [   ] Cedar
Point Lane, advised that they were neighbors of the appointee
from July, 1986, to May, 1989. They stated that they found the
appointee and his family to be very good neighbors and they would
not question his character, loyalty or reputation. They advised
that they never knew the appointee to use illegal drugs or abuse
alcoholic beverages and believed him to live within his financial
means. They stated that they knew nothing of an unsatisfactory
nature regarding the appointee and highly recommended him for a
position of trust with the United States Government.

b6
b7C

On August 10, 1989, [   ] Twirly
Court, advised that they were neighbors of the appointee from
October, 1986, to May, 1989. They advised that they found the
appointee and his family to be very nice neighbors and they had
a good reputation in the neighborhood. They stated they could
think of no reason to question the appointee's character, loyalty
or reputation. They stated that they never knew of him to use
illegal drugs or abuse alcoholic beverages, and believed him to
be a financially responsible person. They stated that they could
favorably recommend the appointee for a position of trust with
the United States Government.

b6
b7C

<u>5000 Camp Kauffmann Road, Huntington, Maryland</u>:

A canvas of the neighbors near the above address
revealed that they are aware that the appointee resides at a new
house, constructed at the end of Camp Kauffmann Road. They
advised that they have not had any personal contact with the
appointee and therefore, they could not furnish any further
information regarding him.

8

1 - [redacted]   b6
                                                                   b7C

AUG 18 1989
BY COURIER

Honorable C. Boyden Gray
Counsel to the President
The White House
Washington, D.C.

Dear Mr. Gray:

        In accordance with a request received from your office
dated July 6, 1989, a background investigation has been conducted
concerning Mr. Thomas Leo Clancy, Jr. Transmitted herewith are
three copies of a summary memorandum containing the results of this
investigation.

                                Sincerely yours,

                                WHB/[initials]
                                William M. Baker
                                Assistant Director
                                Criminal Investigative Division

Enclosures (3)

NOTE: This case was opened on July 18, 1989. Mr. Clancy is
currently self-employed as an author, doing business as Jack Ryan
Enterprises, Limited. He is being investigated for a consultant
position with the Office of the Space Council. Investigation is
favorable. Investigation is complete.

Exec AD Adm. _____
Exec AD Inv. _____
Exec AD LES _____
Asst. Dir.:
   Adm. Servs. _____
   Crim. Inv. _____
   Ident. _____
   Insp. _____
   Intell. _____
   Lab. _____
   Legal Coun. _____
   Off. Cong. &
     Public Affs. _____
   Rec. Mgnt. _____
   Tech. Servs. _____
   Training _____
Off. Liaison &
   Int. Affs. _____
   [Tel]ephone Rm. _____
   [Direc]tor's Sec'y _____

2 - ENCLOSURE

(3)

Closed
MAIL ROOM ☑ WHB/[initials]

NOV 8 1989   b6
                                                                   b7C

RETURN TO [redacted] ROOM 4371

AUG 1 8 1989

THOMAS LEO CLANCY, JR.

THE INVESTIGATION OF MR. CLANCY COVERED INQUIRIES AS TO HIS CHARACTER, LOYALTY, AND GENERAL STANDING, BUT NO INQUIRIES WERE MADE AS TO THE SOURCES OF HIS INCOME.

Birth

Mr. Clancy was born on April 12, 1947, in Baltimore, Maryland.

Education

Mr. Clancy attended Loyola College, Baltimore, Maryland, from September, 1965, to June, 1969, receiving a B.A. degree in English.

Military Service

Mr. Clancy has indicated no prior military service.

Employment

Since July, 1973, Mr. Clancy has been employed by the O.F. Bowen Agency, Owings, Maryland, initially as manager, subsequently as vice president, and currently as president.

Since December, 1985, Mr. Clancy has been self-employed as an author in Prince Frederick, Maryland, and doing business as Jack Ryan Enterprises, Limited.

Family Status

Mr. Clancy is married to the former [ ] b6
who he has indicated is a United States citizen. They and their b7C
children, [ ], reside
at 1625 Twirly Court, Prince Frederick, Maryland.

In addition to his wife and children, Mr. Clancy has listed the following close relatives:

Mother   Catherine M. Clancy

Exec AD Adm. ____
Exec AD Inv. ____
Exec AD LES ____
Asst. Dir.:
  Adm. Servs. ____
  Crim. Inv. ____
  Ident. ____
  Insp. ____
  Intell. ____
  Lab. ____
  Legal Coun. ____
  Off. Cong. &
    Public Affs. ____
  Rec. Mgnt. ____
  Tech. Servs. ____
  Training ____
  Off. Liaison &
    Int. Affs. ____
  'ephone Rm. ____
  'or's Sec'y ____   MAIL ROOM ☐

(2)

161-21821-7

RETURN TO [ ] , ROOM 4371   b6
b7C

U.S. Department of Justice

Federal Bureau of Investigation

Washington, D.C. 20535

THOMAS LEO CLANCY, JR.

THE INVESTIGATION OF MR. CLANCY COVERED INQUIRIES AS TO HIS CHARACTER, LOYALTY, AND GENERAL STANDING, BUT NO INQUIRIES WERE MADE AS TO THE SOURCES OF HIS INCOME.

<u>Birth</u>

Mr. Clancy was born on April 12, 1947, in Baltimore, Maryland.

<u>Education</u>

Mr. Clancy attended Loyola College, Baltimore, Maryland, from September, 1965, to June, 1969, receiving a B.A. degree in English.

<u>Military Service</u>

Mr. Clancy has indicated no prior military service.

<u>Employment</u>

Since July, 1973, Mr. Clancy has been employed by the O.F. Bowen Agency, Owings, Maryland, initially as manager, subsequently as vice president, and currently as president.

Since December, 1985, Mr. Clancy has been self-employed as an author in Prince Frederick, Maryland and doing business as Jack Ryan Enterprises, Limited.

<u>Family Status</u>

Mr. Clancy is married to the former ⬛⬛⬛⬛⬛⬛⬛⬛⬛   b6
who he has indicated is a United States citizen. They and their   b7C
children,⬛⬛⬛⬛⬛⬛⬛⬛⬛⬛⬛⬛⬛⬛⬛, reside
at 1625 Twirly Court, Prince Frederick, Maryland.

In addition to his wife and children, Mr. Clancy has listed the following close relatives:

Mother   Catherine M. Clancy
                                Vero Beach, Florida

FBI/DOJ

Thomas Lee Clancy, Jr.

Father   Thomas Leo Clancy
                                Vero Beach, Florida

Brother   b6
                                                                    b7C

Sister

     Based on the background information furnished by
Mr. Clancy, he has no close relatives residing in communist-
controlled countries.

Interviews

     Twenty persons, consisting of current and former
colleagues, present and former neighbors, references, professional
associates, and social acquaintances, were interviewed. They
provided favorable comments concerning Mr. Clancy's character,
associates, reputation, and loyalty. They stated they are unaware
of any illegal drug use or alcohol abuse by Mr. Clancy, nor have
they ever known him to exhibit any type of bias or prejudice
against any class of citizen or any type of religious, racial or
ethnic group. They also commented that they believe Mr. Clancy
lives within his financial means. All persons interviewed
recommended him for a position of trust and responsibility.

Credit and Arrest Checks

     A review of appropriate credit records revealed either no
record or no pertinent information concerning Mr. Clancy.

     Information has been received from appropriate law
enforcement agencies indicating their files contain no record
concerning Mr. Clancy.

Agency Checks

     Information has been received from the following
governmental agencies indicating their files contain either no
record or no additional pertinent information concerning
Mr. Clancy:

          Office of Personnel Management;
          United States Secret Service;
          and the White House Office.

- 2 -

Thomas Lee Clancy, Jr.

Searches of the various indices of the FBI, including but
not limited to the central index maintained at FBI Headquarters,
the index of the Identification Division, the indices of
appropriate field offices and other appropriate computer data
bases, did not identify any documents that contain pertinent
information identifiable with Mr. Clancy or his close relatives.

It should be noted that the currency of the data input
into the various indices can vary from days to even months from the
date of the document as a result of existing clerical backlogs
throughout the FBI.

- 3 -

November 3, 1989

Mr. Tom Clancy
Post Office Box 800
Huntingtown, Maryland   20639-0800

Dear Tom:

This letter is to provide you with what research I was able to have done concerning the "Death Sentence--1881," which you gave me when I visited with you at your residence. I am enclosing a copy of that sentence, together with a copy of a Baltimore Sun news article in their October 7, 1989, edition concerning this same death sentence, for your reference.

Although the copy you gave me indicates that it was handed down by the Honorable Judge Roy Bean, the news article indicates it was handed down by Judge Isaac Parker in 1882 (instead of the 1881 sentence attributed to Judge Bean). I did not initially believe that it was something Judge Roy Bean would have done, and it seemed more logical to me that it might have been done by Judge Parker who was referred to as the "hanging judge" from Fort Smith, Arkansas. I indicated that we might check this with the law clerk of Judge Morris Arnold, U.S. District Judge in Fort Smith, Arkansas, who is an expert on Judge Parker.

In the interim, I am advised that research was done through the Department of Justice Law Library, and their librarians were very interested in the opinion and made every effort possible to try to locate it. They, however, were not able to locate the opinion in any of their computers, data bases, or old law books. They then called ▮▮▮▮▮▮ historian with the New Mexico Archival Library, to see if ▮▮▮▮▮▮ had any information on the opinion as it was allegedly written in the U.S. District Court for the New Mexico Territorial Sessions, Taos, New Mexico.

b6
b7C

JAH:aeb

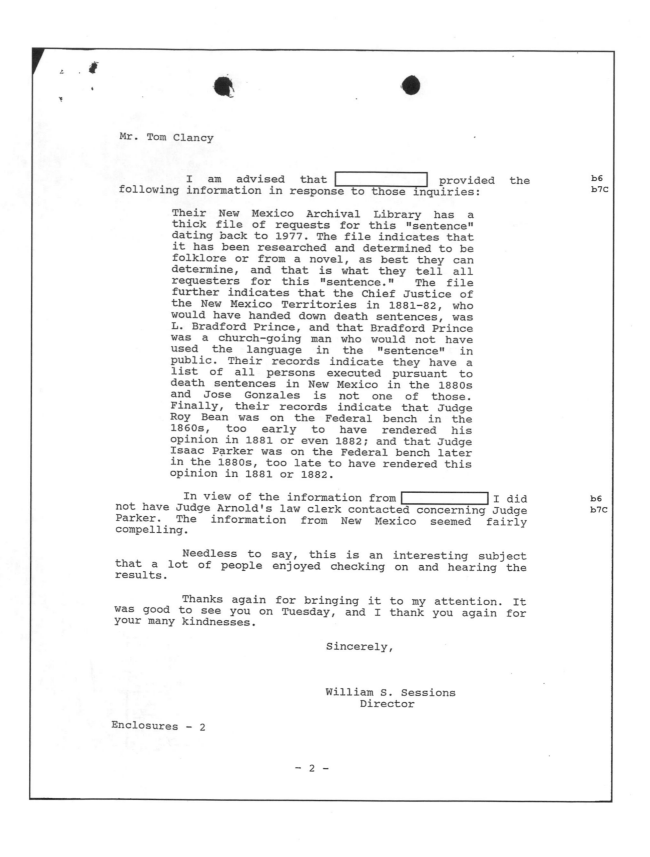

Mr. Tom Clancy

I am advised that [   ] provided the   b6
following information in response to those inquiries: b7C

Their New Mexico Archival Library has a
thick file of requests for this "sentence"
dating back to 1977. The file indicates that
it has been researched and determined to be
folklore or from a novel, as best they can
determine, and that is what they tell all
requesters for this "sentence." The file
further indicates that the Chief Justice of
the New Mexico Territories in 1881-82, who
would have handed down death sentences, was
L. Bradford Prince, and that Bradford Prince
was a church-going man who would not have
used the language in the "sentence" in
public. Their records indicate they have a
list of all persons executed pursuant to
death sentences in New Mexico in the 1880s
and Jose Gonzales is not one of those.
Finally, their records indicate that Judge
Roy Bean was on the Federal bench in the
1860s, too early to have rendered his
opinion in 1881 or even 1882; and that Judge
Isaac Parker was on the Federal bench later
in the 1880s, too late to have rendered this
opinion in 1881 or 1882.

In view of the information from [   ] I did   b6
not have Judge Arnold's law clerk contacted concerning Judge   b7C
Parker. The information from New Mexico seemed fairly
compelling.

Needless to say, this is an interesting subject
that a lot of people enjoyed checking on and hearing the
results.

Thanks again for bringing it to my attention. It
was good to see you on Tuesday, and I thank you again for
your many kindnesses.

Sincerely,

William S. Sessions
Director

Enclosures - 2

- 2 -

Death Sentence -- 1881

"José Manuel Miguel Xavier Gonzales, in a few short weeks it will be spring, the snows of winter will flee away, the ice will vanish, and the air will become soft and balmy, in short, José Manuel Miguel Xavier Gonzales, the annual miracle of the years will awaken and come to pass, but you won't be there.

"The rivulet will run its soaring course to the sea, the timid desert flowers will put forth their tender shoots, the glorious valleys of this imperial domain will blossom as the rose, still, you won't be there to see.

"From every treetop some wild woods songster will carol his mating song, butterflies will sport in the sunshine, the busy bee will hum happily as it pursues its accustomed vocation. The gentle breeze will tease the tassels of the wild grasses, and all nature, José Manuel Miguel Xavier Gonzales, will be glad, but you, you won't be here to enjoy it because I command the sheriff or some other officers of this country to lead you to some remote spot, swing you by the neck from a knotting bough of some sturdy oak; and let you hang until you are dead.

"And then, José Manuel Miguel Xavier Gonzales, I further command that such officer or officers retire quickly from your dangling corpse, that vultures may descend from the heavens upon your filthy body until nothing shall remain but bare, bleached bones of a cold-blooded, copper-colored, blood-thirsty, throat-cutting, chili-eating, sheep-herding, murdering son-of-a-bitch."

United States of America v. Gonzales (1881), United States District Court, New Mexico Territorial Sessions, Taos, New Mexico.

The Honorable Judge Roy Bean
United States Judge

SSP

CLASS
SRC'D
S R
REC

March 1, 1990

Mr. Tom Clancy
Post Office Box 800
Huntington, Maryland 20639-0800

Dear Tom:

I thoroughly enjoyed talking with you at dinner and at the premiere of "The Hunt for Red October."

I am also very pleased you can speak as part of our Distinguished Lecturer Series on May 7 at 11 a.m. at the J. Edgar Hoover F.B.I. Building. As [   ] may have told you, our series is designed to broaden the Headquarters' tour of duty of Special Agents in the senior and executive ranks of the Bureau.

Following your remarks, I do hope you can join me for lunch.

Sincerely,

William S. Sessions
Director

62-122745-2

1 - Mr. Clarke
1 - Mr. Revell
1 - Mr. Otto
1 - Mr. Baker
1 - Mr. Davenport
1 - Mr. W. Johnson
1 - Mr. Nelson
1 - Mr. Moran
1 - Mr. Carter
1 -
1 - [   ]
1 - Mr. McCarron

APPROVED:

Director
Dep. Dir. _____
ADD-Adm. _____
ADD-Inv. _____

Adm. Servs. _____
Crim. Inv. _____
Ident. _____
Inspection _____
Intell. _____
Laboratory _____

Legal Coun. _____
Rec. Mgmt. _____
Tech. Servs. _____
Training _____
Cong. Aff. Off. _____
EEO _____

Off. of Liaison
& Int. Affs. _____
Off. of
Public Affs. _____

Note: The Director approved Mr. CLANCY as guest, and this letter coordinated with SSA [   ] CID, and [   ] SSA [   ] knows him and will coordinate with OPA arranging Mr. CLANCY's visit.

DJM:dpm (14)

Dep. Dir. _____
ADD Adm. _____
ADD Inv. _____
Asst. Dir.:
  Adm. Servs. _____
  Crim. Inv. _____
  Ident. _____
  Insp. _____
  Intell. _____
  Lab. _____
  Legal Coun. _____
  Rec. Mgmt. _____
  Tech. Servs. _____
  Training _____
Cong. Affs. Off. _____
Off. of EEO _____
Off. Liaison &
  Int. Affs. _____
Off. of Public Affs. _____
Telephone Rm. _____
Director's Sec'y _____ MAIL ROOM ☐

Return to Rd [   ]

b6
b7C

b6
b7C

b6
FBI/DOJ b7C

SSP
CLASS
SEC'D
SER
REC

June 7, 1991

Mr. Tom Clancy
Post Office Box 800
Huntingtown, Maryland 20639-0800

Dear Tom:

At the end of this month I will have the pleasure of
hosting the Federal Bureau of Investigation[   ]   b7D
[   ] Senior Executive Retreat. This conference is held
every two years and offers a relaxed environment in which the
senior executives of both agencies may discuss common issues and
forge cooperative directives for future law enforcement
initiatives.

I would like to invite you to participate in the retreat
by joining us for dinner at the FBI Training Academy, Quantico,
Virginia, on the evening of June 26, 1991, in the Executive Dining
Room at 7:00 p.m. My guests and I would be most appreciative if
you could give an informal talk following dinner.

Many thanks for your continued friendship and support of
the FBI.

Sincerely,

62-122725-3

William S. Sessions
Director

Dep. Dir. _____ 1 - Mr. Clarke
ADD Adm. _____ 1 - Mr. Gow
ADD Inv. _____
Asst. Dir.: ____ 1 - Mr. Guido
Adm. Servs. ___ 1 - Mr. Pimentel
Crim. Inv. _____
Ident. _____ 1 -
Insp. _____ 1 - OLIA (FBI/   Sr. Executive Retreat)
Intell. _____
Lab. _____ CKM:SWM/
Legal Coun. ____
Rec. Mgnt. _____   b6
Tech. Servs. ___   b7C
Training _____   Original ...   b7D
Cong. Affs. Off.   Sent direct 6/7/21 by DO.
Off. of EEO ____
Off. Liaison &
   Int. Affs. ____
Off. of Public Affs.
Telephone Rm. __
Director's Sec'y   MAIL ROOM

W. E. B. Du Bois

W. E. B. DU BOIS HAD just passed his 74th birthday when a letter showed up at the FBI's Atlanta Field Office talking about his most recent trip to Japan.

The year was 1942, and the United States had just entered World War II, though it had been keeping tabs on the conflict that had already been waging in Europe for four years against Germany, Italy, and Japan. The message discussed the well-known and well-regarded African-American writer's recent trip to the island Axis nation, where he reportedly stated, among other things, "that in the Japanese he saw the liberation of the negroes in America." With that, a new file was opened on "William Edward Burghardt DuBois (Colored)."

Right away, interviews and engagement with the author's own published works revealed that Du Bois had no Communist allegiances. The investigation into his subversiveness was closed — and then opened after the war, with rumors of his Communist sympathies and his appearance on a list of "Concealed Communists." The Department of Justice soon indicted Du Bois and fellow leaders of the Peace Information Center for failing to register their organization, and though those charges were dropped, the Bureau continued to keep note of his awards, speaking engagements, and travel — which was limited for most of the '50s due to restrictions the DOJ placed on his on his passport.

The final remaining entries of his file see Du Bois leaving for Ghana, where he would eventually die, after the U.S. rejected his petition to renew his passport, forcing him to become a citizen of the newly-formed African country. He was 94.

FEDERAL BUREAU OF INVESTIGATION CONFIDENTIAL

FORM No. 1
THIS CASE ORIGINATED AT   ATLANTA, GEORGIA   FILE NO.

REPORT MADE AT	DATE WHEN MADE	PERIOD FOR WHICH MADE	REPORT MADE BY
ATLANTA, GEORGIA	11-12-42	8-4;9-10,11,12; 15,18,28;10-26-42	

TITLE

WILLIAM EDWARD BUREHARDT DUBOIS

ALL INFORMATION CONTAINED
HEREIN IS UNCLASSIFIED
EXCEPT WHERE SHOWN
OTHERWISE

CHARACTER OF CASE

INTERNAL SECURITY - J
CUSTODIAL DETENTION.

SYNOPSIS OF FACTS: advised subject is Professor
at Atlanta University and considered to be one of most out-
standing and competent negroes in Atlanta, that several talks
were heard to be made by the subject but he did not say anything to indicate he was subversive, that while not a member
of the Communist Party he was in sympathy with the Southern
Negro Congress. Writings of subject in book "Dusk of Dawn",
edited 1940, reflect mention of Japan's defeat of Russia as
giving rise to fear of colored revolt against white exploitation. In this book he writes that he is not a Communist but
that the basic American negro creed is the ultimate triumph
of some form of socialism the world over. Subject's aim is
to improve the status of the whole negro group. In this book
he wrote "I tried to say to the American negro.......'you must
put behind your demands, not simply American negroes, but west
Indians and Africans and all the colored races in the world.

- P -

REFERENCE: Report of   dated July 29,
              1942, at Charlotte, North Carolina.

DETAILS: AT ATLANTA, GEORGIA:

                        disclosed that the subject's address in Atlanta is 223 Chestnut
Street, SW and that he has another property address at 2302 Montebello
Terrace, Baltimore, Maryland.   he
is 71 years of age; married with his wife as dependent. His social and
economic characteristics are good. His employment is said to be Atlanta

APPROVED
FORWARDED

AGENT IN
CHARGE

DO NOT WRITE IN THESE SPACES

100-99729-3

COPIES OF THIS REPORT

5 Bureau

CONFIDENTIAL

U. S. GOVERNMENT PRINTING OFFICE—O—   7—2034

->3

CONFID*X*NTIAL

University where he has been a professor of Sociology for six years. His income is approximately $4500 per year and his net worth is estimated to be several thousands of dollars. ▮▮▮▮▮
the information was obtained that the subject was formerly employed by a newspaper in New York City for several years and returned to Atlanta six years ago. In June, 1936 he was appointed editor of the Encyclopedia "Negro" and since that time has been devoting a part of his time to compiling this encyclopedia. He has some income from that source but informants however do not know the amount.

He is highly recommended by his employers and is considered to be respectable and is said to own a home in Baltimore, Maryland at the address stated above.

▮▮▮▮▮ was contacted as to further information but was unable to offer same. He stated that he believed the subject to be a radical in his attitude on the racial and negro question. He also said that he had heard that the subject may have played a prominent part in the riot in Tulsa, Oklahoma several years ago in which a number of negroes were killed. He stated that it was discovered that the subject was headed to New York from Tulsa, Oklahoma the day after the riot occurred. He was unable to offer any information as to the subversive activities of the subject in Atlanta.

The following investigation was conducted by ▮▮▮▮▮ in a memorandum submitted by him on September 18, 1942

- 2 -

CONF*X*ENTIAL

CONFIDᴇᴺTIAL

Atlanta, ▓▓▓▓▓▓▓▓

in which he stated that he had contacted ▓▓▓▓▓▓▓▓▓▓▓▓▓▓▓▓▓▓
▓▓▓▓▓▓▓▓▓▓▓▓▓▓▓▓▓▓▓▓▓▓▓▓▓▓▓▓▓ and ▓▓▓▓▓▓▓▓▓▓▓▓ had stated that
the subject is a Professor at Atlanta University and is considered to be
one of the most outstanding and prominent negroes in Atlanta.
▓▓▓
▓▓▓▓▓▓▓▓▓▓▓▓▓▓ This informant also advised that the subject is frequently
called upon by negro lodges and Civic organizations to make addresses,
that he had heard him make several talks but had never heard him say anything which would indicate that he is subversive.

5   The subject according to this informant, while not a member
of the Communist Party was one who was known to be in sympathy with the
Southern Negro Youth Congress and who had contributed money to this Congress. The informant added that she had no definite information which
would indicate that the subject knew the Southern Negro Youth Congress
was dominated by Communists but she believed he would have such knowledge
inasmuch as he is an intelligent man. This informant concluded that she
would make a special effort to find out when the subject was to speak
next and would be in attendance at his talk in an effort to ascertain
whether he was spreading propaganda through his speeches.

            In order to obtain some indication of the subject's attitude
and tendencies in foreign sympathies the writer read parts of "Dusk of
Dawn", a book edited by the writer in 1940. This book was copyrighted
in 1940 by Harcourt, Brace and Company, Incorporated and is an essay
toward an autobiography of a race concept. It also contains the writer's
autobiography.

            Information was contained in this book that the subject was
born February 23, 1868 at Great Barrington, Massachusetts and that his
ancestral family was divided into whites, blacks and mulattoes, most of
them being mulattoes. The subject wrote and published a number of books
from 1899 through 1940 most of which dealt with the problems of the negro
race.

            The following are quotations from the book, "Dusk of Dawn"
edited by the subject on the date mentioned above:

            On Page 232,"It is evident too that the defeat of Russia by
Japan had given rise to a fear of colored revolt against white exploitation."

            On Page 245, referring to the first World War, "Then came the
refusal to allow colored soldiers to volunteer into the army; but we are

- 3 -

Atlanta, ▮

consoled by saying 'Why should we want to fight for America or America's
friends and how sure could we be that America's enemies were our enemies
too?' ".

Page 255, "Today I do not know; and I doubt if the triumph
of Germany in 1918 could have had worse results than the triumph of the
Allies. Possibly passive resistance of my twelve millions to any war activity might have saved the world for black and white. Almost certainly
such a proposal on my part would have fallen short and perhaps slaughtered
the American negro body and soul. I do not know. I am puzzled."

Page 256, referring to JOEL SPINGARN, of the NAACP, "It was
due to his advice and influence that I became during the World War nearer
to feeling myself a real and full American than ever before or since."

Page 266, Anti-Lynching bill, 1924, died with the filibuster
in the United States Senate, "It was not until years after that I knew
what killed that anti-lynching bill. It was a bargain between the South
and the West. By the bargain, lynching was let to go on uncurbed by
federal Law, on condition that the Japanese be excluded from the United
States."

Page 52, "Europe was determined to dominate China and all but
succeeded in dividing it between the chief white nations, when Japan stopped
the process."

Page 301, speaking of program for assisting negroes economically,
"I stood, as it seemed to me, between paths diverging to extreme Communism
and violence on the one hand and extreme reaction toward plutocracy on the
other."

Page 302, "I am not and was not a Communist. I do not believe
in the dogma of inevitable revolution in order to right economic wrong. On
the other hand I believed and still believe that KARL MARX was one of the greatest men of modern times and that he put his fingers squarely upon our difficulties when he said that economic foundations , the way in which men earn
their living, are the determining factors in the development of civilization
and the basic pattern of culture.

Page 304, "The whole set of the White world in America, in
Europe and in the World was too determinedly against racial equality to
give power and persuasiveness to our agitation. I tried to say to the
American negro ...... 'You must put your demands not simply to American
negroes but West Indians, Africans and all the colored races in the world.'"

Page 320, referring to the basic negro creed, "We believe in
the ultimate triumph of some form of socialism the world over; that is,
common ownership and control of the means of production and equality of income.'

- 4 -

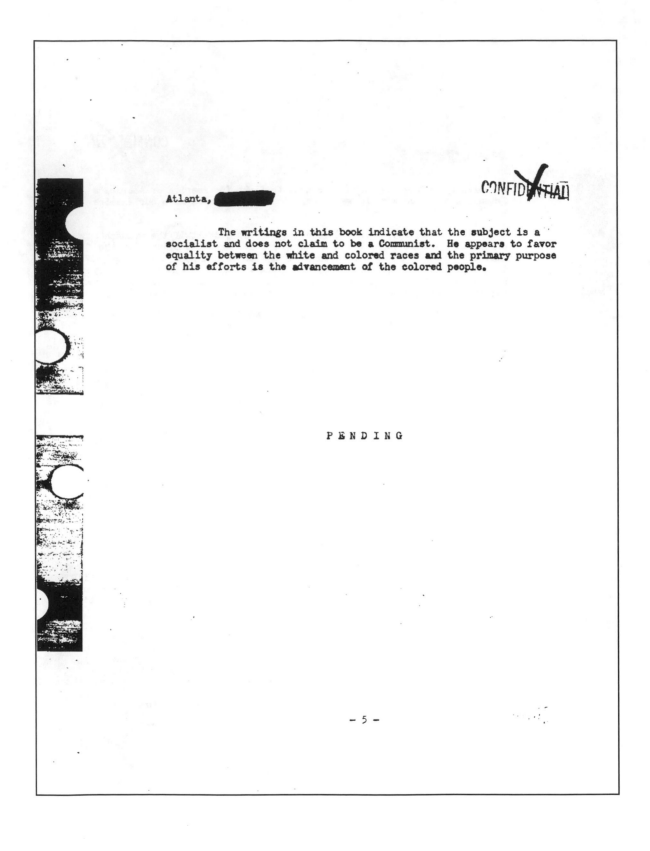

Atlanta, ▮▮▮▮   CONFID̶E̶N̶TIAL

     The writings in this book indicate that the subject is a
socialist and does not claim to be a Communist. He appears to favor
equality between the white and colored races and the primary purpose
of his efforts is the advancement of the colored people.

P E N D I N G

- 5 -

Atlanta, ▮▮▮▮▮

CONFID╳NTIAL

UNDEVELOPED LEADS:

▮▮▮▮▮▮▮▮▮▮▮▮▮▮▮▮▮▮▮▮

Will determine the occupants of the premises of ▮▮▮▮
▮▮▮▮▮▮▮▮ and conduct an investigation to determine
if they are engaged in subversive activities with the subject in this
country if at all.

▮▮▮ Will make appropriate discreet inquiries at the resident and
business addresses of subject to ascertain whether he is engaged in any
subversive activities.

THE BALTIMORE FIELD DIVISION at Baltimore, Maryland will determine if the subject has been engaged in subversive activities while a
resident at 2302 Montebello Terrace, that city.

THE ATLANTA FIELD DIVISION at Atlanta, Georgia will re-contact
▮▮▮▮▮▮▮▮▮▮ to determine if she has attempted to attend
any meetings at which the subject has spoken for the purpose of ascertaining whether or not he is spreading propaganda.

P E N D I N G

CON╳DENTIAL

6

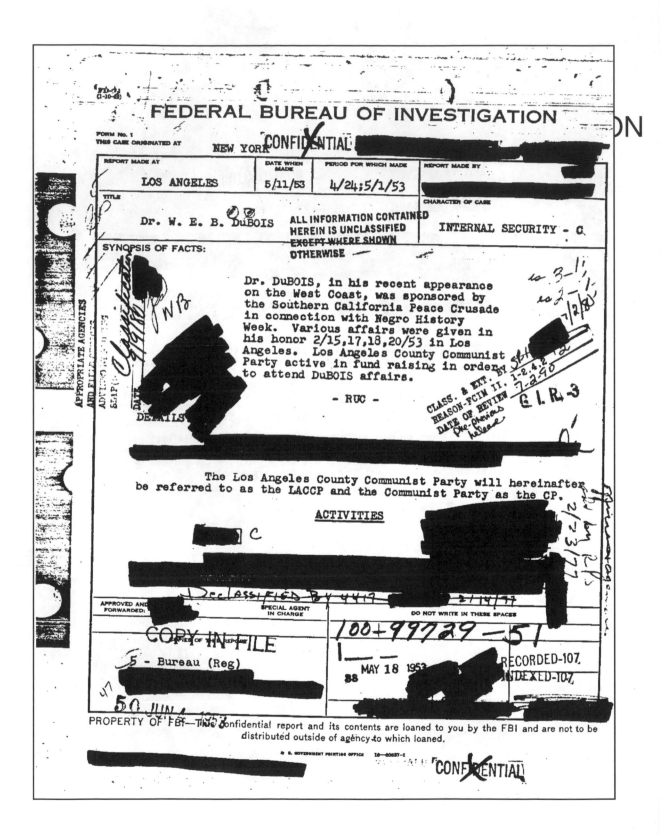

FEDERAL BUREAU OF INVESTIGATION

FORM No. 1
THIS CASE ORIGINATED AT   NEW YORK   CONFIDENTIAL

REPORT MADE AT	DATE WHEN MADE	PERIOD FOR WHICH MADE	REPORT MADE BY
LOS ANGELES	5/11/53	4/24;5/1/53	

TITLE	CHARACTER OF CASE
Dr. W. E. B. DuBOIS ALL INFORMATION CONTAINED HEREIN IS UNCLASSIFIED EXCEPT WHERE SHOWN OTHERWISE	INTERNAL SECURITY - C

SYNOPSIS OF FACTS:

Dr. DuBOIS, in his recent appearance on the West Coast, was sponsored by the Southern California Peace Crusade in connection with Negro History Week. Various affairs were given in his honor 2/15,17,18,20/53 in Los Angeles. Los Angeles County Communist Party active in fund raising in order to attend DuBOIS affairs.

- RUC -

DETAILS

The Los Angeles County Communist Party will hereinafter be referred to as the LACCP and the Communist Party as the CP.

ACTIVITIES

APPROVED AND FORWARDED: SPECIAL AGENT IN CHARGE   DO NOT WRITE IN THESE SPACES

COPIES OF THIS REPORT

5 - Bureau (Reg)

100+99729-51

MAY 18 1953

RECORDED-107
INDEXED-107

PROPERTY OF FBI—This confidential report and its contents are loaned to you by the FBI and are not to be distributed outside of agency to which loaned.

U. S. GOVERNMENT PRINTING OFFICE   16—60837-1

CONFIDENTIAL

CONFIDENTIAL

in March, 1952, advised that the launching of the American Peace Crusade was announced at a meeting of the Executive Committee of the National Labor Peace Conference in Chicago, Illinois, on January 28, 1951. further advised that in the Los Angeles area, the major policies and the orientation of the American Peace Crusade (APC) are determined by CP members and that the CP exercises control of the APC by the assignment of CP members to work within the organization. The Southern California Peace Crusade, which has replaced the Southern California Peace Council, is the Los Angeles chapter of the APC.

In December, 1952, made available a "peace bulletin" issued by the Southern California Peace Crusade, which stated that Dr. W. E. B. DuBOIS, accompanied by his wife, SHIRLEY GRAHAM, would arrive in the Los Angeles area on or about February 11, 1953, which would be their first stop on an extended tour of the West Coast under the auspices of the Southern California Peace Crusade.

This bulletin also pointed out that his visit in the Los Angeles area was timed to coincide with Negro History Week, and his activities in this area would begin with a testimonial dinner in the honor of Dr. DuBOIS for his lifetime contributions to the cause of peace.

- 2 -

CONFIDENTIAL

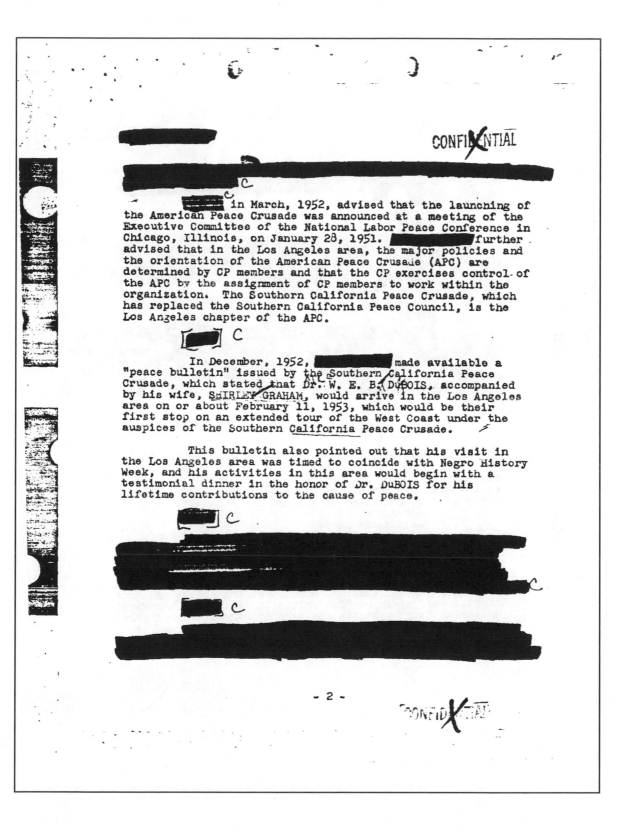

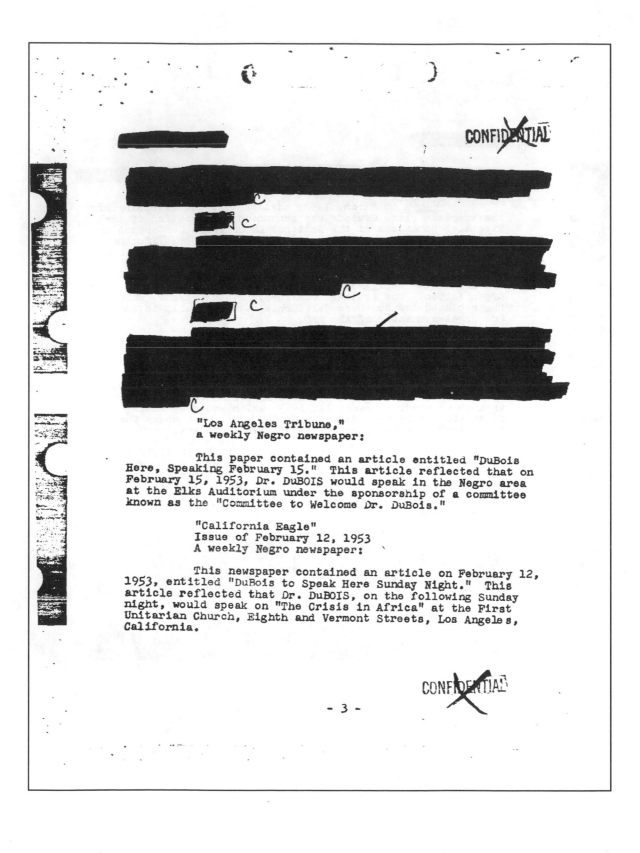

CONFIDENTIAL

"Los Angeles Tribune,"
a weekly Negro newspaper:

This paper contained an article entitled "DuBois
Here, Speaking February 15." This article reflected that on
February 15, 1953, Dr. DuBOIS would speak in the Negro area
at the Elks Auditorium under the sponsorship of a committee
known as the "Committee to Welcome Dr. DuBois."

"California Eagle"
Issue of February 12, 1953
A weekly Negro newspaper:

This newspaper contained an article on February 12,
1953, entitled "DuBois to Speak Here Sunday Night." This
article reflected that Dr. DuBOIS, on the following Sunday
night, would speak on "The Crisis in Africa" at the First
Unitarian Church, Eighth and Vermont Streets, Los Angeles,
California.

CONFIDENTIAL

- 3 -

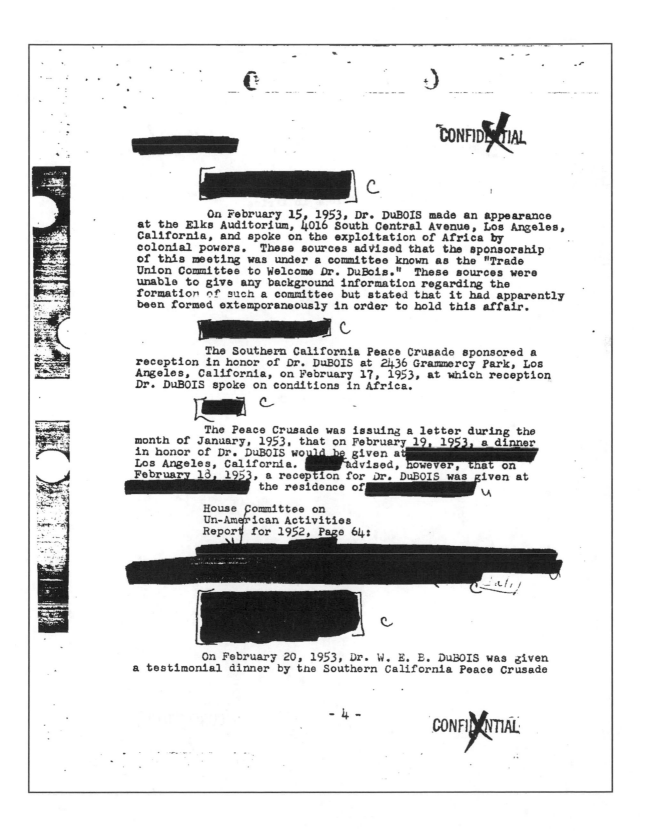

CONFIDENTIAL

On February 15, 1953, Dr. DuBOIS made an appearance
at the Elks Auditorium, 4016 South Central Avenue, Los Angeles,
California, and spoke on the exploitation of Africa by
colonial powers. These sources advised that the sponsorship
of this meeting was under a committee known as the "Trade
Union Committee to Welcome Dr. DuBois." These sources were
unable to give any background information regarding the
formation of such a committee but stated that it had apparently
been formed extemporaneously in order to hold this affair.

The Southern California Peace Crusade sponsored a
reception in honor of Dr. DuBOIS at 2436 Grammercy Park, Los
Angeles, California, on February 17, 1953, at which reception
Dr. DuBOIS spoke on conditions in Africa.

The Peace Crusade was issuing a letter during the
month of January, 1953, that on February 19, 1953, a dinner
in honor of Dr. DuBOIS would be given at ▓▓▓▓▓▓▓
Los Angeles, California. ▓▓▓▓▓ advised, however, that on
February 18, 1953, a reception for Dr. DuBOIS was given at
▓▓▓▓▓▓▓ the residence of ▓▓▓▓▓▓▓

House Committee on
Un-American Activities
Report for 1952, Page 64:

On February 20, 1953, Dr. W. E. B. DuBOIS was given
a testimonial dinner by the Southern California Peace Crusade

- 4 -

CONFIDENTIAL

CONFIDENTIAL

at Park Manor, 607 South Western Avenue, at which dinner he
spoke concerning conditions in Africa.

- RUC -

CONFIDENTIAL

- 5 -

UNITED STATES DEPARTMENT OF JUSTICE
FEDERAL BUREAU OF INVESTIGATION

In Reply, Please Refer to
File No.

Washington 25, D. C.
JUL 25 1960

WILLIAM EDWARD BURGHARDT DU BOIS
LOLA GRAHAM DU BOIS
Also Known As
SHIRLEY GRAHAM DU BOIS
SECURITY MATTER - C

The files of the Passport Office, United States
Department of State (USDS), Washington, D. C., were reviewed
on July 18, 1960, and the following information was contained
in the passport folders for William Edward Burghardt Du Bois
and his wife, Shirley Graham Du Bois: W

Name:	William E. Burghardt Du Bois
Date of Birth:	February 23, 1868 at Great Barrington, Massachusetts
Passport Application Dated:	May 11, 1960, at New York, New York.
Passport Number:	2285216 issued June 7, 1960
Permanent Residence:	31 Grace Court, Brooklyn 1, New York.
Parents:	
Father:	Alfred Du Bois, born 1825, Haiti, United States citizen, deceased.
Mother:	Mary S. Burghardt, born Massachusetts, 1831, deceased.
Spouse:	Shirley Graham Du Bois, born November 11, 1899, Indianapolis, Indiana.
Date of Marriage:	February 14, 1958
Travel Plans:	
Port of Departure:	New York City
Approximate Date of Departure:	June 20, 1960
Mode of Travel:	Air
Intended Stay Abroad:	Three months
Proposed Itinerary:	Ghana
Purpose of Trip:	Inaugural of the Republic of Ghana.
Description:	
Height:	Five feet, six and a half inches
Hair:	Bald
Eyes:	Brown
Occupation:	Retired

Declassified by 4417
1/2/17

ALL INFORMATION CONTAINED
HEREIN IS UNCLASSIFIED
DATE 7/25/80 BY SP

100-991729-154

CONFIDENTIAL

ENCLOSURE

WILLIAM EDWARD BURGHARDT DU BOIS
LOLA GRAHAM DU BOIS

A notation appears on this passport application that subject's last passport, number 1103544, issued June 30, 1958, had been canceled because of subject's travel to Communist China in violation of the geographical restrictions contained in that passport.

Dr. William E. Burghardt Du Bois submitted a sworn affidavit to the Passport Office, USDS, Washington, D. C., dated May 11, 1960, in which he stated that in any future travel he would not use his passport in violation of the restrictions contained therein or of any similar restrictions subsequently promulgated by the United States Government.

This affidavit further stated that Dr. Du Bois and his wife have been officially invited by the Government of Ghana to come to Ghana as its guests to participate in the ceremonies to take place June 29, 1960, to July 4, 1960.

The following information was obtained from the passport folder of Shirley Graham Du Bois, wife of Dr. Du Bois:

Name:	Shirley Graham Du Bois
Born:	November 11, 1899, Indianapolis, Indiana
Passport Application Dated:	May 11, 1960, at New York, New York
Passport Number:	2285215 issued June 7, 1960
Permanent Residence:	31 Grace Court, Brooklyn 1, New York
Parents:	
Father:	David Andrew Graham, born Evanston, Indiana, 1860, deceased.
Mother:	Lizzie Etta Bell, born Missouri, 1873, deceased.
Spouse:	William E. Burghardt Du Bois, born February 23, 1868, Great Barrington, Massachusetts
Travel Plans:	
Port of Departure:	New York
Approximate Date of Departure:	June 20, 1960
Mode of Travel:	Air
Intended Stay Abroad:	Three months
Proposed Itinerary:	Republic of Ghana
Purpose of Trip:	To accompany husband to inaugural of Republic of Ghana.
Description:	
Height:	Five feet, four inches.
Hair:	Black-grey
Eyes:	Brown

- 2 -

WILLIAM EDWARD BURGHARDT DU BOIS
LOLA GRAHAM DU BOIS

Identifying Marks: Scar on neck
Occupation: Writer

Passport number 1103545 issued to Shirley Graham
Du Bois on June 30, 1958, was withdrawn because of her travel to
Communist China in violation of the geographical restrictions
contained in that passport.(U)

Shirley Graham Du Bois submitted a sworn affidavit to the
Passport Office, USDS, dated May 11, 1960, in which she stated
that in any future travel she would not use her passport in
violation of the restrictions contained therein or of any similar
restrictions subsequently promulgated by the United States
Government. (U)

A review of the entries in passport number 1103545
issued June 30, 1958, to Shirley Graham Du Bois, reflects travel
by this individual to the following places in 1958-1959: (U)

London, South Hampton, Harwick, England; Accra and
Adoba, Ghana; Kiev, Moscow Russia; Holland; Paris, France;
Brussels, Belgium; Prague, Czechoslovakia; Cairo, Egypt; East
German Republic; Berlin, Germany; Bromma, Sweden; Khartoum,
United Arab Republic; and Belgrade, Yugoslavia. (U)

Passport number 1103545 issued to Shirley Graham Du Bois
on page twelve contains a stamp which reflects entry of the
bearer of this passport at Tirana, Albania, on December 18, 1958.
This stamp also carries the caption of "R.-P. Shqiperise"
(the People's Republic of Albania) P.K.K.(U)

This passport does not reflect the length of stay for
Shirley Graham Du Bois in Albania. Page five of this passport
contains a restriction against travel to Albania.(U)

A review of the entries in passport number 1103544
issued June 30, 1958, to William Edward Burghardt Du Bois,
reflects travel by this individual to the following places in
1958-1959: (W)

London, South Hampton, Harwick, England; Moscow, Russia;
Holland; Prague, Czechoslovakia; Brussels, Belgium; Paris, France;
East German Republic; Berlin, Germany; and Bromma, Sweden. (V)

Passport number 1103544 issued to Dr. Du Bois on
June 30, 1958, does not reflect travel by this individual to
Albania.(U)

- 3 -

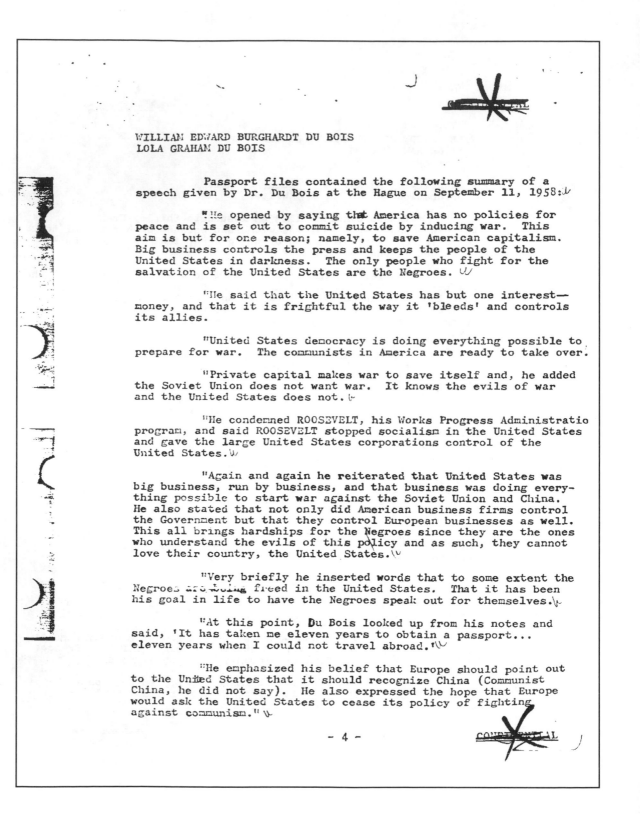

WILLIAM EDWARD BURGHARDT DU BOIS
LOLA GRAHAM DU BOIS

Passport files contained the following summary of a
speech given by Dr. Du Bois at the Hague on September 11, 1958:

"He opened by saying that America has no policies for
peace and is set out to commit suicide by inducing war. This
aim is but for one reason; namely, to save American capitalism.
Big business controls the press and keeps the people of the
United States in darkness. The only people who fight for the
salvation of the United States are the Negroes.

"He said that the United States has but one interest—
money, and that it is frightful the way it 'bleeds' and controls
its allies.

"United States democracy is doing everything possible to
prepare for war. The communists in America are ready to take over.

"Private capital makes war to save itself and, he added
the Soviet Union does not want war. It knows the evils of war
and the United States does not.

"He condemned ROOSEVELT, his Works Progress Administratio
program, and said ROOSEVELT stopped socialism in the United States
and gave the large United States corporations control of the
United States.

"Again and again he reiterated that United States was
big business, run by business, and that business was doing everything possible to start war against the Soviet Union and China.
He also stated that not only did American business firms control
the Government but that they control European businesses as well.
This all brings hardships for the Negroes since they are the ones
who understand the evils of this policy and as such, they cannot
love their country, the United States.

"Very briefly he inserted words that to some extent the
Negroes are being freed in the United States. That it has been
his goal in life to have the Negroes speak out for themselves.

"At this point, Du Bois looked up from his notes and
said, 'It has taken me eleven years to obtain a passport...
eleven years when I could not travel abroad.'

"He emphasized his belief that Europe should point out
to the United States that it should recognize China (Communist
China, he did not say). He also expressed the hope that Europe
would ask the United States to cease its policy of fighting
against communism."

- 4 -

CONFIDENTIAL

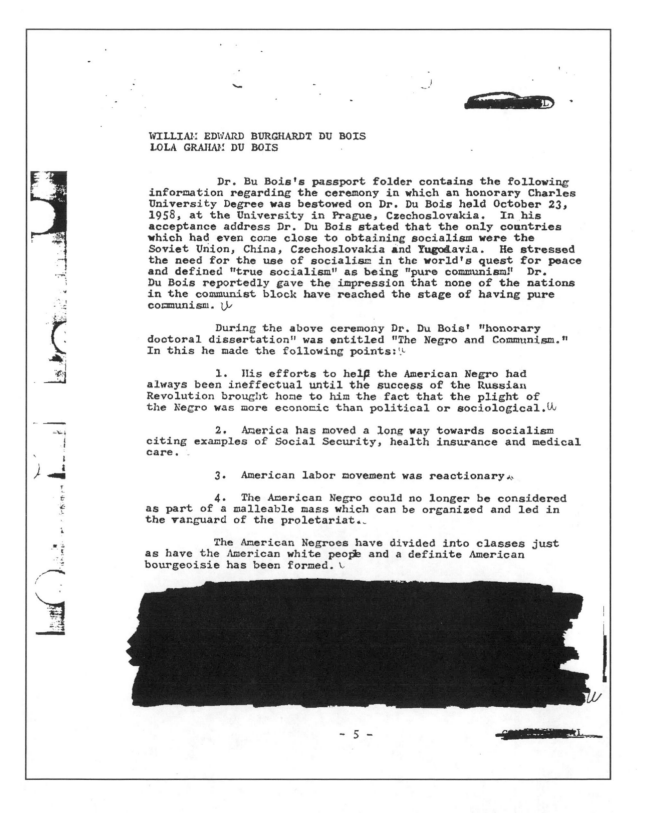

WILLIAM EDWARD BURGHARDT DU BOIS
LOLA GRAHAM DU BOIS

        Dr. Bu Bois's passport folder contains the following
information regarding the ceremony in which an honorary Charles
University Degree was bestowed on Dr. Du Bois held October 23,
1958, at the University in Prague, Czechoslovakia. In his
acceptance address Dr. Du Bois stated that the only countries
which had even come close to obtaining socialism were the
Soviet Union, China, Czechoslovakia and Yugoslavia. He stressed
the need for the use of socialism in the world's quest for peace
and defined "true socialism" as being "pure communism!" Dr.
Du Bois reportedly gave the impression that none of the nations
in the communist block have reached the stage of having pure
communism.

        During the above ceremony Dr. Du Bois' "honorary
doctoral dissertation" was entitled "The Negro and Communism."
In this he made the following points:

        1. His efforts to help the American Negro had
always been ineffectual until the success of the Russian
Revolution brought home to him the fact that the plight of
the Negro was more economic than political or sociological.

        2. America has moved a long way towards socialism
citing examples of Social Security, health insurance and medical
care.

        3. American labor movement was reactionary.

        4. The American Negro could no longer be considered
as part of a malleable mass which can be organized and led in
the vanguard of the proletariat.

        The American Negroes have divided into classes just
as have the American white people and a definite American
bourgeoisie has been formed.

Allen Ginsberg

BEST KNOWN FOR THE rhythmic and profane nature of his poetry — most notably, "Howl," which inspired obscenity charges from the San Francisco Police Department in 1957 — the FBI wasn't completely off base when they described Allen Ginsberg, one of the progenitors of the Beat Generation, as "beatnik in appearance."

However, the man's writing, homosexuality, and marijuana activism make only brief appearances in his file, which is primarily interested in his association with and advocacy for Cuba, a recurring concern for the Bureau in the '60s. The FBI's interest began in earnest with a letterhead memorandum regarding economist Leo Huberman, composer Paul Bowles, and Ginsberg. In January 1965, the Foreign Broadcast Information Service, the Central Intelligence Agency's open source news outlet, reported that Ginsberg had arrived in Cuba to judge an international poetry competition.

By the next month, J. Edgar Hoover had ordered the New York Field Office to "ascertain whether he is engaged in any activities which would be considered inimical to the interest of the U.S.," indicating that extra circumspection should be had given his association with the literary magazine Evergreen Review (its publisher, Barney Rosset, was also extensively surveilled by the Bureau).

A letter soon went to the Secret Service as part of an agreement "concerning Presidential protection" related to certain types of dangerous individuals identified by the Bureau. Ginsberg checked all three boxes under the label "Subversives, ultrarightists, racists and fascists."

The Bureau's assessment from that same day, however, states that Ginsberg's "activities, while bizarre, have not indicated any direction or being inimical to the interests of the U.S." Nevertheless, the file contains multiple summaries of articles written about or by Ginsberg and description of his travel during the late '60s, including his expulsions from both Cuba and Czechoslovakia.

Three years later, the Bureau echoed its earlier sentiments: "His activities, while extremely eccentric, apparently lack any specific direction." Though the FBI continued to monitor Ginsberg's activities through the end of the decade, the file ends abruptly in 1971, their interest in him apparently dying with Hoover.

MAILED
SEP · 6 1963
NAME CHECK

1 -   b6
                                 b7C

September 26, 196░

ALLEN GINSBERG
416 East 34th Street   ALL INFORMATION CONTAINED
Paterson, New Jersey   HEREIN IS UNCLASSIFIED
                             DATE 2-22-2004 BY 60227 uc/Nls/prv

#984876

        No investigation pertinent to your inquiry has been
conducted by the FBI concerning the captioned individual.
However, the files of this Bureau reveal the following
information which may relate to the subject of your name
check request.

        The "San Francisco Examiner" for October 4, 1957,
carried an article stating that Lawrence Ferlinghetti,
38 year old poet who was proprietor of the "City Lights
Pocket Book Shop," 261 Columbus Avenue, San Francisco,
California, and Shigeyoshi Murao, a nisei art student and
clerk in the store, had been acquitted on charges of dealing
in obscene literature. The article went on to explain that
Ferlinghetti was the publisher of a 44-page booklet that
contained a poem entitled "Howl," written by Allen Ginsberg.
The article stated that Municipal Court Judge Clayton Horn
found at least some "redeeming social importance" in "Howl."

        Records of the San Francisco Police Department
reveal an arrest of _____ on June 6, 1957,
when he was charged with violation of Section 311.3, in that   b6
he "writes or prints or publishes or sells or exhibits any   b7C
obscene or indecent writing...." The dispositionn of the
charge was given as "not guilty," on October 3, 1957.

                              (105-73929-1 page 9)

ORIGINAL & 1 - USIA
Request Received: 9-10-63   REC- 84
BVG:bep
D(4)   105-137059-X
NOTE: Subject of name check described as a "Beat" poet who
         was author of "Howl and Other Poems."

57 OCT 4 1963
256   Deleted Copy Sent
                              by Letter
                              Per FOIA Request

U.S. POET--The U.S. poet Allen Ginsberg arrived in Cuba to participate as a
poetry judge in this year's international contest of the Cuban cultural
organization, House of the Americas. He will be part of the jury that is
made up of outstanding poets from different countries. (Havana Spanish
Americas 1600 GMT 19 January 1965--E)

DAILY REPORT.....LATIN AMERICA
NO. 14, Friday 22, 1965
FOREIGN BROADCAST INFORMATION SERVICE

NOT RECORDED

9 FEB 26 1965

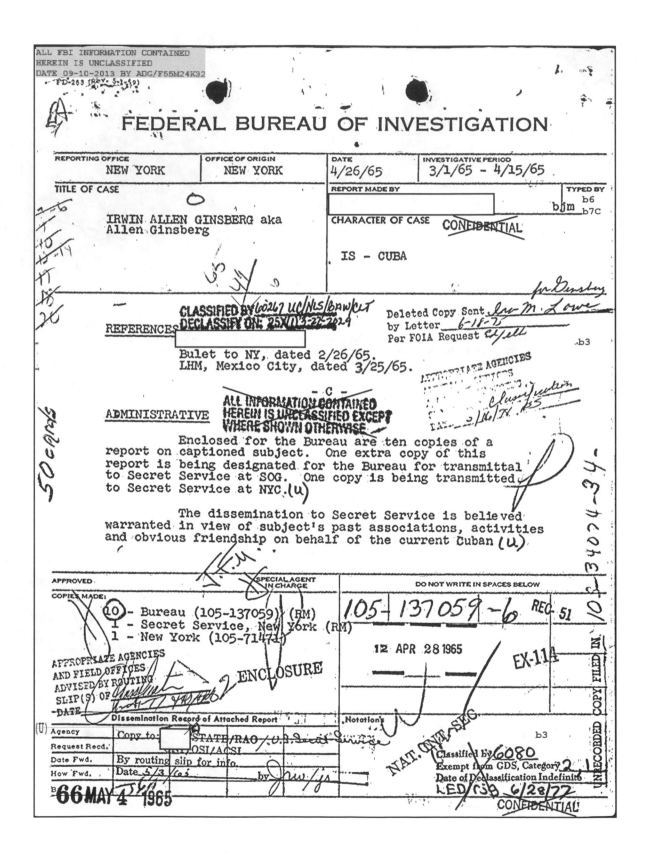

ALL FBI INFORMATION CONTAINED
HEREIN IS UNCLASSIFIED
DATE 09-10-2013 BY ADG/F55M24K32

FD-263 (REV. 3-1-59)

FEDERAL BUREAU OF INVESTIGATION

REPORTING OFFICE	OFFICE OF ORIGIN	DATE	INVESTIGATIVE PERIOD
NEW YORK	NEW YORK	4/26/65	3/1/65 - 4/15/65

TITLE OF CASE	REPORT MADE BY	TYPED BY
IRWIN ALLEN GINSBERG aka Allen Ginsberg		bjm

CHARACTER OF CASE   ~~CONFIDENTIAL~~

IS - CUBA

CLASSIFIED BY 60267 UC/NLS/BAW/CLT
DECLASSIFY ON: 25X(1)3-27-2029

Deleted Copy Sent
by Letter 6-18-75
Per FOIA Request

REFERENCES
Bulet to NY, dated 2/26/65.
LHM, Mexico City, dated 3/25/65.

- C -

ADMINISTRATIVE   ALL INFORMATION CONTAINED
HEREIN IS UNCLASSIFIED EXCEPT
WHERE SHOWN OTHERWISE

Enclosed for the Bureau are ten copies of a
report on captioned subject. One extra copy of this
report is being designated for the Bureau for transmittal
to Secret Service at SOG. One copy is being transmitted
to Secret Service at NYC. (U)

The dissemination to Secret Service is believed
warranted in view of subject's past associations, activities
and obvious friendship on behalf of the current Cuban (U)

APPROVED	SPECIAL AGENT IN CHARGE	DO NOT WRITE IN SPACES BELOW

COPIES MADE:

10 - Bureau (105-137059) (RM)
1 - Secret Service, New York (RM)
1 - New York (105-71471)

105-137059-6   REC 51

12 APR 28 1965   EX-114

2 ENCLOSURE

APPROPRIATE AGENCIES
AND FIELD OFFICES
ADVISED BY ROUTING
SLIP(S) OF
DATE

Dissemination Record of Attached Report   Notations

Agency	Copy to: STATE/RAO
Request Recd.	OSI/ACSI
Date Fwd.	By routing slip for info.
How Fwd.	Date 5/3/65

Classified by 6080
Exempt from GDS, Category 2
Date of Declassification Indefinite

LED/rsb 6/28/77

66 MAY 4 1965   CONFIDENTIAL

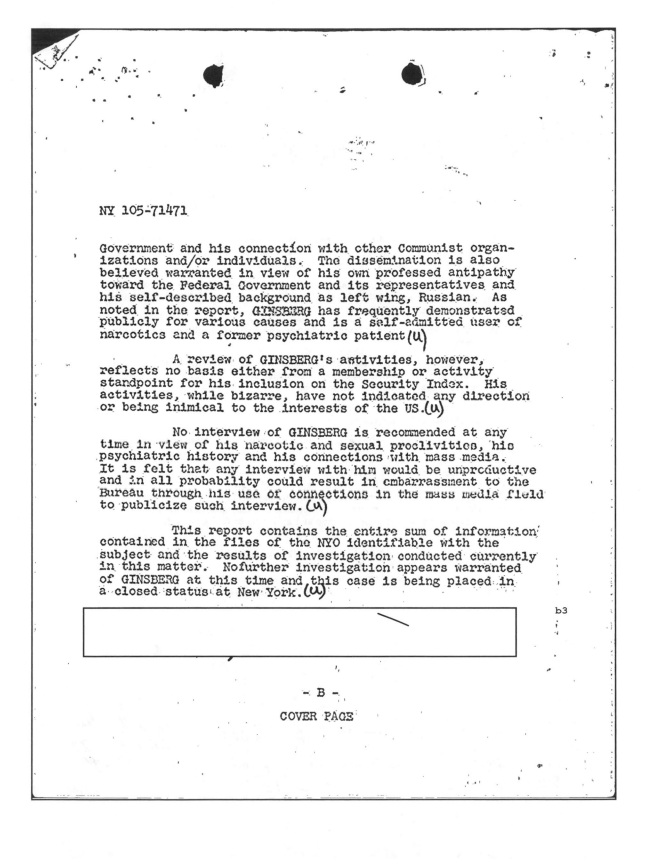

NY 105-71471

Government and his connection with other Communist organizations and/or individuals. The dissemination is also
believed warranted in view of his own professed antipathy
toward the Federal Government and its representatives and
his self-described background as left wing, Russian. As
noted in the report, GINSBERG has frequently demonstrated
publicly for various causes and is a self-admitted user of
narcotics and a former psychiatric patient (U)

A review of GINSBERG's activities, however,
reflects no basis either from a membership or activity
standpoint for his inclusion on the Security Index. His
activities, while bizarre, have not indicated any direction
or being inimical to the interests of the US. (U)

No interview of GINSBERG is recommended at any
time in view of his narcotic and sexual proclivities, his
psychiatric history and his connections with mass media.
It is felt that any interview with him would be unproductive
and in all probability could result in embarrassment to the
Bureau through his use of connections in the mass media field
to publicize such interview. (U)

This report contains the entire sum of information
contained in the files of the NYO identifiable with the
subject and the results of investigation conducted currently
in this matter. No further investigation appears warranted
of GINSBERG at this time and this case is being placed in
a closed status at New York. (U)

b3

- B -

COVER PAGE

FD-376 (3-8-65)

UNITED STATES DEPARTMENT OF JUSTICE

FEDERAL BUREAU OF INVESTIGATION

SECRET

WASHINGTON, D.C. 20535
April 26, 1965

In Reply, Please Refer to
File No.

Bureau file 105-137059
New York file 105-71471

Chief
United States Secret Service
Department of the Treasury
Washington, D. C. 20220

Re: Irwin Allen Ginsberg
      Internal Security - Cuba

Dear Sir:

The information furnished herewith concerns an individual who is believed to be covered by the agreement between the FBI and Secret Service concerning Presidential protection, and to fall within the category or categories checked.

1. ☐ Has attempted or threatened bodily harm to any government official or employee, including foreign government officials residing in or planning an imminent visit to the U. S., because of his official status.

2. ☐ Has attempted or threatened to redress a grievance against any public official by other than legal means.

3. ☒ Because of background is potentially dangerous; or has been identified as member or participant in communist movement; or has been under active investigation as member of other group or organization inimical to U. S.

4. ☐ U. S. citizens or residents who defect from the U. S. to countries in the Soviet or Chinese Communist blocs and return.

5. ☒ Subversives, ultrarightists, racists and fascists who meet one or more of the following criteria:

    (a) ☒ Evidence of emotional instability (including unstable residence and employment record) or irrational or suicidal behavior:

    (b) ☒ Expressions of strong or violent anti-U. S. sentiment;

    (c) ☒ Prior acts (including arrests or convictions) or conduct or statements indicating a propensity for violence and antipathy toward good order and government.

6. ☐ Individuals involved in illegal bombing or illegal bomb-making.

Photograph ☐ has been furnished ☒ enclosed ☐ is not available
☒ may be available through *U. S. Secret Service, New York, New York*

DECLASSIFIED BY 60216 uc/NLG/BAIO/CLT
ON 3-22-2004

Very truly yours,

SECRET

John Edgar Hoover
Director

1 - Special Agent in Charge (Enclosure(s) (2)
   U. S. Secret Service, New York, New York

ENCLOSURE

*1 copy to Secret
Service 5/3/65*

Enclosure(s) (1)
Registered Mail

(Upon removal of classified enclosures, if any, this transmittal form becomes UNCLASSIFIED.)

105-137059

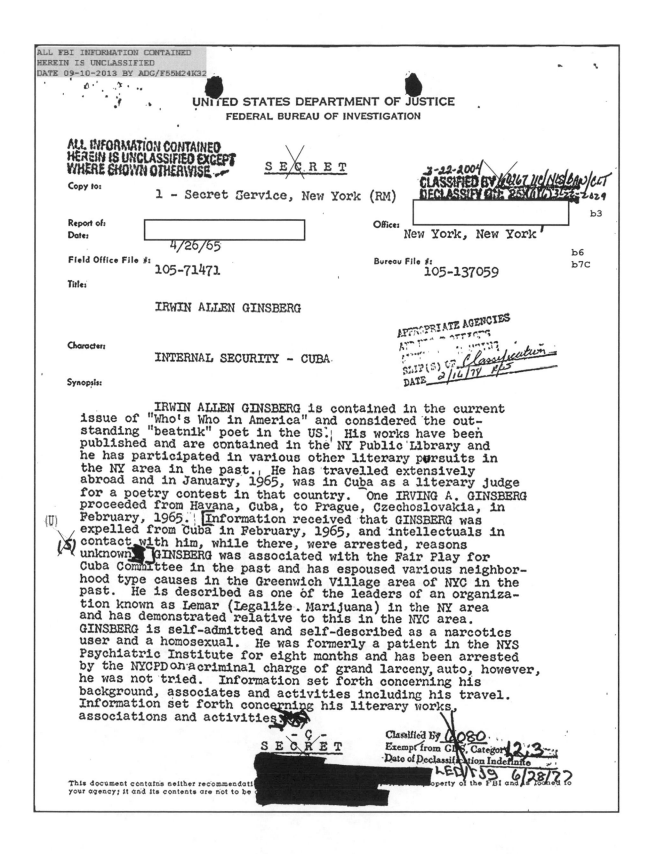

ALL FBI INFORMATION CONTAINED
HEREIN IS UNCLASSIFIED
DATE 09-10-2013 BY ADG/F55M24K32

UNITED STATES DEPARTMENT OF JUSTICE
FEDERAL BUREAU OF INVESTIGATION

ALL INFORMATION CONTAINED
HEREIN IS UNCLASSIFIED EXCEPT
WHERE SHOWN OTHERWISE

S E C R E T

3-22-2004
CLASSIFIED BY 60467 UC/NIS/baw/CLT
DECLASSIFY ON 25X(0)03522-2629

Copy to:

    1 - Secret Service, New York (RM)

Office: New York, New York   b3

Report of:
Date: 4/26/65

Field Office File #:   105-71471

Bureau File #:   105-137059   b6
                                                             b7C

Title:

    IRWIN ALLEN GINSBERG

Character:

    INTERNAL SECURITY - CUBA

APPROPRIATE AGENCIES
AND FIELD OFFICES
SLIP(S) OF _Classification_
DATE _2/16/74_ RLS

Synopsis:

        IRWIN ALLEN GINSBERG is contained in the current
issue of "Who's Who in America" and considered the outstanding "beatnik" poet in the US. His works have been
published and are contained in the NY Public Library and
he has participated in various other literary pursuits in
the NY area in the past. He has travelled extensively
abroad and in January, 1965, was in Cuba as a literary judge
for a poetry contest in that country. One IRVING A. GINSBERG
proceeded from Havana, Cuba, to Prague, Czechoslovakia, in
February, 1965. Information received that GINSBERG was
expelled from Cuba in February, 1965, and intellectuals in
contact with him, while there, were arrested, reasons
unknown. GINSBERG was associated with the Fair Play for
Cuba Committee in the past and has espoused various neighborhood type causes in the Greenwich Village area of NYC in the
past. He is described as one of the leaders of an organization known as Lemar (Legalize Marijuana) in the NY area
and has demonstrated relative to this in the NYC area.
GINSBERG is self-admitted and self-described as a narcotics
user and a homosexual. He was formerly a patient in the NYS
Psychiatric Institute for eight months and has been arrested
by the NYCPD on a criminal charge of grand larceny, auto, however,
he was not tried. Information set forth concerning his
background, associates and activities including his travel.
Information set forth concerning his literary works,
associations and activities.

- C -
S E C R E T

Classified By 6080
Exempt from GDS, Category 12,3
Date of Declassification Indefinite
LED/59 6/28/72

This document contains neither recommendati.... .....operty of the FBI and is loaned to
your agency; it and its contents are not to be d....

NY 105-71471

DETAILS:

I.   INFORMATION RELATIVE TO SUBJECT'S
      TRAVEL AND ACTIVITIES IN FOREIGN
      COUNTRIES

The Foreign Broadcast Information Service for January 22, 1965, in daily report – Latin America Number 14, reflected the following transmittal in Spanish from Havana, Cuba, on January 19, 1965: (u)

"The United States poet ALLEN GINSBERG arrived in Cuba to participate as a poetry judge in this year's contest of the Cuban Cultural Organization, House of the Americas. He will be part of the jury that is made up of outstanding poets from different countries." (u)

On February 15, 1965, NY T-1 made available a photograph which appeared in "Hoy", the official organ of the Communist Party (CP) Cuban, Havana, Cuba, on January 20, 1965. This photograph with its caption translated from the Spanish is as follows: (u)

"AMERICAN POET ALLEN GINSBERG ARRIVES IN CUBA

"The American poet ALLEN GINSBERG arrived here from Mexico. He will be one of the judges for the Casa de las Americas Prize for Literature for 1965. He was met by officials of the Casa de las Americas." (u)

On the same date NY T-1 also made available the February 5, 1965 issue of "Bohemia", weekly magazine published in Havana, Cuba, under the control and direction of the FIDEL CASTRO Government of Cuba. (u)

- 2 -

NY 105-71471

Summary translation of an article which appeared on Page 24 of this magazine is as follows:(u)

"CONTEST BY CASA DE LAS AMERICAS

"The 'Casa de las Americas' of Cuba, which is directed by HAYDEE SANTAMARIA, has held a contest during the last five years in the course of which literary works in various categories are judged. This year, the contest will be held as usual.(u)

"Since the early part of January, the judges for this contest have been arriving in Cuba.(u)

"The judges for poetry this year are the following: ALLEN GINSBERG, JAIME SABINES, CARLOS BARRAL, NICANOR PARRA, J. H. COHEN and JOSE LEZAMA DIMA.(u)

"Born in Newark in 1926, ALLEN GINSBERG, along with JACK KEROUAC, GREGORY CORZO and LAWRENCE FERLINGHETTI, is one of the most important figures in the beatnik movement in North American literature. GINSBERG studied at Columbia University and worked in the Merchant Marine. He has lived in different parts of the world, from Mexico to Tangiers, passing through Venice, London and Paris. In 1945, he published his famous poem, HOWL."(u)

On Page 68 of the February 5, 1965 issue of "Bohemia" is a photograph with the following caption:(u)

"The groups of judges for the literary prize of the Casa de las Americas is officially formed. It is composed of well-known Cuban and foreign literary figures, among them the following: VICENTINA ANTUNA, JOSE LEZAMA, HUMBERTO ARENAL, JAIME SARUSKI, ABELARDO ESTORINO, CAMILO JOSE CEIA, ALLEN GINSBERG, ABELARDO ZALAMEA and BERNARDO CANAL REIJOO. The directress of this institution, HAYDEE SANTAMARIA, presided over the meeting."(u)

- 3 -

NY 105-71471

(U)

ALLEN GINSBERG, the American poet, arrived in
Cuba in January, 1965, and served on the panel of judges
which awarded the 1965 Casa de las Americas literary prize.
After approximately one months stay on the island, GINSBERG
was reportedly expelled from Cuba. Numerous young Cuban
intellectuals who had come into contact with GINSBERG were
arrested after his expulsion from Cuba but no explanation
(U)   was given for the arrest. (S)

On March 23, 1965, NY T-3 advised that one IRVING
A. GINSBERG was a passenger on a Czechoslovakia Airlines
flight, number 524, from Havana, Cuba, to Prague, Czechoslovakia,
(U)   on February 18, 1965. (S)

II.   CONNECTIONS WITH COMMUNIST DOMINATED
ORGANIZATIONS, OTHER ACTIVITIES AND
ASSOCIATIONS

On September 24, 1960
New York City Police Department (NYCPD), Bureau of Special
Services, provided a list of persons invited to a reception
sponsored by the Fair Play For Cuba Committee (FPCC) on
September 22, 1960, in the Skylight Room of the Hotel Theresa
in New York City to honor the arrival of Cuban Prime Minister
FIDEL CASTRO. The name ALLEN GINSBERG was contained on this
list. (u)

- 4 -

NY 105-71471

On May 21 and 22, 1961, NY T-4 made available names and addresses of individuals maintained on addressograph plates at the headquarters of the FPCC, Room 329, 799 Broadway, New York City. The name ALLEN GINSBERG, 170 East Second Street, Apartment 16, New York City, appeared thereon. (U)

On September 24 and 25, 1961, NY.T-4 made available a list of names and addresses maintained at FPCC headquarters, Room 329, 799 Broadway, New York City, at that time. On this list was the name ALLEN GINSBERG, 170 East Second Street, Apartment 16, New York City. (U)

A characterization of the FPCC is appended hereto. (U)

On July 25, 1950, ⬜⬜⬜⬜⬜ was arrested by the Philadelphia Police Department and found in his possession was a personal notebook which had a list captioned "Our Peoples Chorus". Under the heading was a list of names, addresses and phone numbers. Included therein was the name ALLAN GINSBERG, 226 West Hudson, LB 1484. (U)

b6
b7C

The "Morning Freiheit" issue of September 20, 1949, stated that DITCHIK was the leader of the American Delegation Chorus at the World Youth Festival held in Budapest, Hungary, in September, 1949. (U)

A characterization of the "Morning Freiheit" is appended hereto. (U)

"The Worker" issue of July 1, 1962, Page 15, Column 1, contained an advertisement for a magazine titled "Pa'Lante". This advertisement reflected that a prose contribution by ALLEN GINSBERG would appear in their next issue. (U)

- 5 -

NY 105-71471

"The Worker" is an east coast
Communist weekly newspaper.(u)

"Jewish Currents" issue of December, 1964, on
Page 45, in a column captioned "Letters to the Editor",
had a sub-title "Poet Defends LEROI JONES". Following
this was a letter signed by ALLEN GINSBERG defending JONES
treatment of a Jewish girl from Yonkers, New York, a
character in JONES' play "Dutchman". The last sentence of
this letter stated,"Besides LEROI JONES once kissed me on
my lips".(u)

A characterization of "Jewish
Currents" is appended hereto.(u)

In a passport application filed April 21, 1961,
by ⬛⬛⬛⬛⬛⬛⬛⬛⬛⬛⬛⬛⬛⬛⬛ listed ALLEN GINSBERG, a friend,
170 East Second Street, New York City, as the person to be
notified in the event of death or accident to ⬛⬛⬛⬛⬛⬛(u)

b6
b7C

On December 6, 1961, NY T-5 advised
that ⬛⬛⬛⬛⬛⬛⬛⬛ was one of the
speakers at a forum of the New York
Chapter of the FPCC held December 4,
1961, at Adelphi Hall, 74 Fifth
Avenue, New York City. The forum
dealt with a Cultural Congress held
in Cuba in 1961.(u)

On February 11, 1964, the Office of the United
States Attorney, Southern District of New York, United States
Court House, Foley Square, New York City, made available a
letter addressed to Mr. ROBERT M. MORGENTHAU, United States
Attorney for the Southern District of New York, dated
January 30, 1963, over the name ALLEN GINSBERG, care of
Eighth Street Book Store, 32 West Eighth Street, New York City(u)

- 6 -

NY 105-71471

In this letter GINSBERG was protesting the
Government's prosecution of an income tax case against
the Living Theater, JULIAN BECK and JUDITH MOLINA. In
this letter he indicated that he had furnished material
for use in this theater. In the letter he stated that he
had assignments or requests to write for various publications
including "Playboy" and "Esquire" as well as access to
letter columns in the "New York Times" and "London Times".
He stated he maintained correspondence with large magazines
in India, Russia, France and England. He said he felt it would
be his duty to go all out and start screaming through these
media if he judges that the Government policy decision in the
Living Theater matter ultimately amounts to political and/or
cultural confusion. (U)

The following is a summary translation of an item
in Spanish which appeared in "Bohemia" issue of February 28,
1965, published in Venezuela. This item was furnished by
NY T-1 on March 8, 1965: (U)

MISERIES OF CIVILIZATION

The Permanent Central Board on Opium in the
United Nations has just declared that it considers the
war on the illegal drug traffic lost. (U)

In view of this statement, and bearing in mind
the experience of the English, the New York Medical
Association has requested that physicians be authorized
to furnish drugs to addicts in limited quantities.
Judge BERNARD BOTEIN of the New York Court of Appeals has
proposed that special treatment be afforded to alcoholics,
drug addicts and homosexuals, and stated that society
should revise its opinions concerning the "social vices". (U)

"At the same time that this news was made public,
groups of 'beatniks' of Greenwich Village, headed by the
existentialist poet, ALLEN GINSBERG, marched through the (U)

- 7 -

NY 105-71471

streets of New York's Bohemian district in a demonstration,
requesting the authorities to legalize the consumption of
marijuana which they say is less dangerous than alcohol."(u)

The newspaper "Marcha" of Montevideo, Uruguay,
issue of December 1, 1961, contained a "Declaration of
Conscience" signed by several people which is as follows:(u)

"The people of Revolutionary Cuba have the right
to determine their own destiny without intervention from
the United States Government.(u)

"We consider that in financing, arming and training
exiled Cubans and in planning and participating in the
invasion of April 17, 1961, the United States Government
has intervened and has committed an act of aggression
against the Cuban people.(u)

"We understand that the invasion of April 17 and
the continued aggressive attitude of our Government places
in danger not only the people of Cuba and the cause of
world peace but also our own liberty as North Americans.
The request by President KENNEDY that the Press install
a system of self-censore does nothing but continue the
process of suppression and regimentation of North American
life under the pretext of 'the struggle in the cold war'.
It is not a coincidence that the acts of hostility against
Revolutionary Cuba which culminated in the April invasion
have been enthusiastically seized by the 'official liberals'
of the regime as well as by the militarists, the 'big
businessmen' and their Press, the southern racists and
the McCarthyites.(u)

"If we want to safeguard liberty in the United States,
we must do everything in our reach to oppose and avoid all
ulterior aggression against the people of Revolutionary Cuba."(u)

- 8 -

NY 105-71471

The newspaper article, which was from the December 1, 1961, edition, contained the names of the following persons who signed the declaration: ELAINE DE KOONING, DIANE DI PRIMA, EDWARD DORN, LAWRENCE FERLINGHETTI, ALLEN GINSBERG, PAUL GOODMAN, LE ROI JONES, NORMAN MAILER, JONAS MEKAS, WARREN MILLER, MARGARET RANDALL, MAX SCHLEIFER, ESTABAN VINCENTE, ATHOS ZACHARIAS. (U)

The "New York Herald Tribune" edition of December 28, 1964, on Page 13, contained an article by BILL WHITWORTH of the Herald Tribune staff captioned "With Cymbals and Symbols". (U)

This article reflected that in the East Village area of New York City on the preceeding day a demonstration was held by a group called Lemar. This name is a contraction of "Legalize Marijuana". The article stated, however, that the group has no officers, no formal organization and no firm plan of action beyond distributing leaflets and staging demonstrations. (U)

The demonstrators on this occasion demonstrating in front of theDepartment of Welfare Building on East Ninth Street and Avenue C carried signs reading "Smoke pot, it is cheaper and healthier than liquor", and "Pot is a Reality Kick". Pot is a term for marijuana. (U)

Among the demonstrators were ALLEN GINSBERG and PETER ORLOVSKY, poets, who carried little Japanese finger cymbals and chanted Hindu prayer formulas   directed to Shiva, one of the Hindu principle deities. GINSBERG described Shiva as the god of meditation, yoga and marijuana. GINSBERG predicted that marijuana will be recognized in the United States within five years. (U)

The "New York Times" issue of January 4, 1965, Page 24, column 3, contained an article about an organization known as Lemar founded in San Francisco to fight legislation against marijuana. It identified ALLEN GINSBERG, the poet, as a leading New York member of Lemar. (U)

- 9 -

NY 105-71471

The "New York Times" issue of December 28, 1964, identified ALLEN GINSBERG, the poet, as one of the leaders of the group, Lemar, which demonstrated at East Ninth Street and Avenue C in New York City, on December 27, 1964. This article was similar to the article contained in the "New York Herald Tribune" mentioned above. (U)

The "New York Times" issue of January 28, 1963, identified ALLEN GINSBERG with Lemar. It stated that he and PETER ORLOVSKY donned Japanese finger cymbals and showed up outside the New York Department of Welfare carrying a sign reading "Smoke Pot, It is Cheaper and Healthier than Liquor" on the previous day. (U)

The "New York Times" issue of July 29, 1964, contained an article reflecting that GINSBERG spoke at a meeting to form a neighborhood association in the McDougal Street area of Greenwich Village, New York. He spoke for the right of young people to read poetry in the coffee houses and put on dramatic performances without charge. (U)

The "New York Times" issue of May 24, 1964, contained an article concerning the Cafe Le Metro which had recently been cited by a license inspector of the New York City Department of Licenses for conducting dramatic performances without the necessary licenses. The article stated that GINSBERG has read poetry there along with other individuals such as PETER ORLOVSKY, LEROI JONES, PAUL BLACKBURN, et cetera. The article stated that when the inspector arrived at the Cafe, GINSBERG was not present. He had just returned to New York after a three year stay in Europe, North Africa and India. GINSBERG became incensed at the citation and was one of the leaders in the protest against it. In this connection the article stated that GINSBERG worked with Manhattan Borough President HENRY STERN and the leader of the East Village Council SAUL SHERRISON, who were sympathetic to GINSBERG's cause. It (U)

- 10 -

NY 105-71471

stated that he also worked with the Village Independent
Democrats in this cause.   STERN went with GINSBERG to the
Department of Licenses of New York City and the American Civil
Liberties Union aided GINSBERG by assigning a lawyer to work
with him in the matter. The article also stated that
GINSBERG carried his protest to the New York City Office of
Cultural Affairs. (U)

III.   SUBJECT'S LITERARY WORK, ACTIVITIES AND ASSOCIATES

        The New York Public Library Card Index under the
name ALLEN GINSBERG, born 1926, reflects the following published works contained in their files: (U)

        Empty Mirror
        Totem Press, 1961,
        New York, New York

        Howl and Other Poems
        City Lights Books,
        San Francisco, California,
        1959

        America Luna
        Taller de Artes Graficas, 1961,
        Los Angeles, California,
        Copy number 108 of 300 copies

        Kaddish and Other Poems 1958 - 1960
        City Lights Books, 1961

- 11 -

NY 105-71471

Reality Sandwiches 1953 - 1960 (u)

City Lights Books, 1963   (u)

There is nothing listed under the name IRWIN
GINSBERG or under the spelling GINSBURG.(u)

The "New York Times" edition of January 20, 1957,
identified ALLEN GINSBERG as one of the leaders of an avant
garde group of writers from San Francisco, California. It
identified him as a friend of JACK KEROUAC and WILLIAM
BURROUGHS. It stated that he was in New York until February 1,
1957, when he planned to go to Paris with KEROUAC to publish
a novel by BURROUGHS in that city. His address was listed at
that time as 416 East 34th Street, Paterson, New Jersey.(u)

The "New York Times" issue of February 29, 1964,
contained a review of a play "Guns of the Trees" by JONAS
MEKAS, which was narrated by ALLEN GINSBERG.(u)

"New York Times" issues have contained reviews of
GINSBERG's works, Kaddish and Howl.(u)

The "New York Times" issue of March 15, 1960,
identified ALLEN GINSBERG as one of the cast of the film,
"Pull My Daisy", which was a twenty-nine minute film based on
a JACK KEROUAC play. In addition to GINSBERG, PETER ORLOVSKY,
GREGORY CORSO, and LARRY RIVERS are also in the cast. The
movie was produced by ROBERT FRANK and directed by ALFRED
LESLIE.(u)

The "New York Times" issue of December 6, 1964,
contained an article about a translation of a poem by the
Lithuanian poet, EDUARDOS B. MEZHELAYTIS titled Howl Above
Brooklyn Bridge. The article reflected that this poem was (u)

Russia

- 12 -

NY 105-71471

influenced by GINSBERG's poem Howl. GINSBERG on interview
said that he had met a group of Soviet writers in 1960,
and that MEZHEL may have been one of them at a club here
in New York City where the meeting occurred. GINSBERG
disclaimed any politics for himself and stated "Howl had
been an affirmation of man's feeling and glory and tenderness
above and beyond the mechanistic, capitalist brain wash, insanity
and war mongering poured out of Washington."(u)

    The "New York Times" issue of March 15, 1960, con-
tained an article reflecting that in Prague, Czechoslovakia,
there is a Cafe called Viola, which is a Greenwich Village
type. The article stated that works of GINSBERG were read
there to jazz accompaniment.(u)

    The "New York Times" issue of June 9, 1963, under
the heading "A Week's Miscellany" stated that spokesmen for
South Viet Nam Buddhists had felt sure that the man was a spy
"tall, long beard, hair very long in back and curly. He
said he was a poet and a little crazy and liked Buddhists. They
did not know what else he was and decided he was a spy." The
article humorously identified this individual as ALLEN
GINSBERG, the beatnik poet, passing through South Viet Nam
after a stay in India. It should be noted that another article
in the "New York Times" of January 6, 1963, indicated that
GINSBERG had spent several days in South Viet Nam on his way
to British Columbia.(u)

    The "New York Post" issue of March 13, 1959, con-
tained a several page article captioned "The Beat Generation"
by ALFRED G. ARONOWITZ. This article was entirely on ALLEN
GINSBERG. The article identified his father as LOUIS GINSBERG,
age 63, an English teacher and poet in Paterson, New Jersey.
It described his mother as a psychotic and a Communist who had
been in and out of mental institutions and was at that time in
the New York State Psychiatric Hospital. (u)   B. APPROX.   1886

- 13 -

NY 105-71471

GINSBERG in the interview stated that his poem Howl had been written for his mother and had sold more than 20,000 copies to date. It was a manifesto of the beat generation like JACK KEROUAC's novel, "On The Road". (U)

The article gave an example of the type of fan telegrams that GINSBERG receives in the following: (U)

"The pregnant angel and the white centipede are hot to make orange duck real tonight". (U)

It was pointed out that GINSBERG has many disciples among the beat generation and has himself been cast as a character in other beatnik literary works. He has been invited to read his works at various colleges and has read at the Library of Congress in Washington, D.C. (U)

In his past he has worked as a baggage clerk for Greyhound Bus Lines, a seaman, and wrote speeches for a candidate for United States Congress. (U)

The article covered a period in GINSBERG's early life when he was involved with an individual named HERBERT HUNCKE! They were arrested by the NYCPD on an auto theft charge and the article indicated that HUNCKE and GINSBERG had been close friends and living together during the period of the arrest. As a result of this arrest GINSBERG was committed to the New York State Psychiatric Hospital for a period of eight months. (U)   H.E.

The article contained a story about when GINSBERG was a student at Columbia and was suspended on charges of sleeping with another male student. To this story GINSBERG stated with some anger that at the time of the suspension the charges were not yet true. (U)

- 14 -

NY 105-71471

The article commenced with the statement that
in the recent past when GINSBERG was in Chicago he was
approached by a woman there who asked him,"Why is there
so much homosexuality in your poetry?" His reply was,
"Because madam I'm queer. I sleep with men and women.
I am neither queer nor not queer nor am I bisexual. My
name is ALLEN GINSBERG and I sleep with whoever I want."(u)

The "New York Times" issue of May 3, 1964, contains an article about the new edition of "Who's Who in
America" for 1964-1965. ALLEN GINSBERG is contained therein
for the first time.(u)

The magazine "Pa'Lante" published by the League
of Militant Poets, Post Office Box 88, Peter Stuyvesant
Station, New York City, printed in New York City, May 19,
1962, contains a letter, dated October 16, 1961, at Athens,
Greece, from ALLEN GINSBERG. This letter is titled "Prose
Contribution to Cuban Revolution". In the letter GINSBERG
admits using narcotics, having homosexual experiences and
homosexual love affairs. He describes himself as a person
who desired to be a laboring peoples hero. He described
his background as Jewish, left wing, atheist, Russian.(u)

In this letter he mentions various individuals
such as VAN DOREN, KEROUAC, NEIL, BILL, HUNCKE, PETER, and
TRILLING. An editors note identified these individuals
as MARK VAN DOREN, Columbia University Professor, American
writers PETER ORLOVSKY, NEIL CASSIDY, WILLIAM BURROUGHS and
HERBERT HUNCKE, and Columbia University Professor, LIONEL
TRILLING.(u)

- 15 -

NY 105-71471

IV.   MISCELLANEOUS BACKGROUND INFORMATION,
      SOURCE CHECKS AND CRIMINAL RECORD

On March 4, 1965, Investigative Clerk [   ] reviewed the files of the New York Board of Elections for Manhattan. They reflected that ALLEN GINSBERG, residing at 704 East Fifth Street, Apartment 5A, New York City, has been registered in New York State and New York City for ten years and is in the 8th Manhattan Congressional District. His date of birth is listed as June 3, 1926, in the United States. He is described as a male, single, five feet ten inches, brown eyes, brown hair. He last voted in 1960, at which time his address was 170 East Second Street, New York City, apartment 16, and his employment was listed as City Lights, 261 Columbus Avenue, San Francisco, California. He indicated a party preference for one of the major parties. (U)

b6
b7C

On March 15, 1965, NY T-6 advised that his files reflect a listing for ALLEN GINSBERG, 206 East 7th Street, New York City, under number 9127324. His date of birth is listed in these files as June 2, 1926, and his marital status as single. In 1953, he was a copyboy for the "New York World Telegram", 125 Barcley Street, New York City, however, his connection with NY T-6 was severed many years ago. (U)

On March 4, 1965, NY T-7 advised that his files reflect only the information that ALLEN GINSBERG can be reached at Grove Press, 64 University Place, New York City, OR 4-7200. (U)

On March 15, 1965, [   ] Security Supervisor, New York Telephone Company, 104 Broad Street, New York City, advised SA JAMES M. ANDERSON that telephone number OR 3-3638 formerly listed at 704 East Fifth Street, (U)

b6
b7C

- 16 -

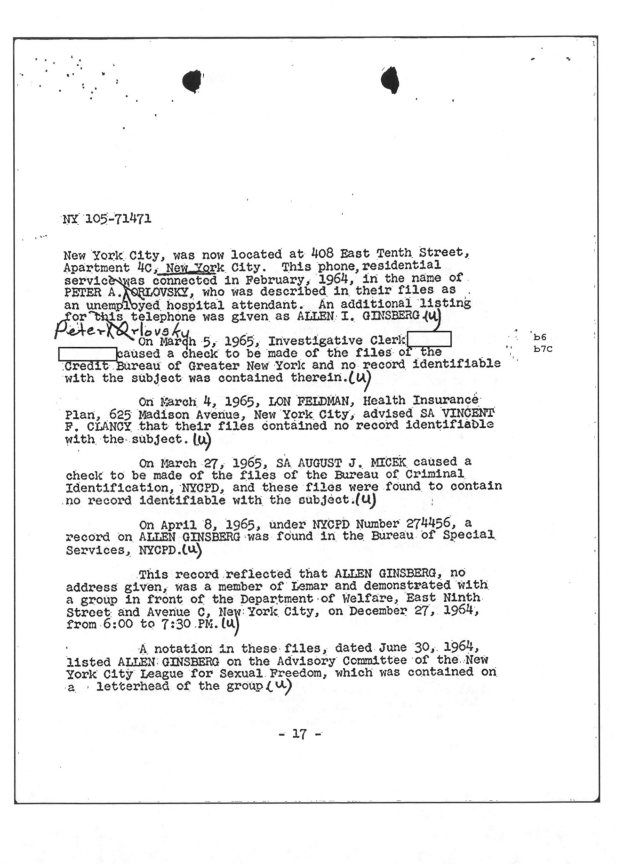

NY 105-71471

New York City, was now located at 408 East Tenth Street, Apartment 4C, New York City. This phone, residential service was connected in February, 1964, in the name of PETER A. ORLOVSKY, who was described in their files as an unemployed hospital attendant. An additional listing for this telephone was given as ALLEN I. GINSBERG (u)

Peter Orlovsky

On March 5, 1965, Investigative Clerk [   ] caused a check to be made of the files of the Credit Bureau of Greater New York and no record identifiable with the subject was contained therein. (u)

b6
b7C

On March 4, 1965, LON FELDMAN, Health Insurance Plan, 625 Madison Avenue, New York City, advised SA VINCENT F. CLANCY that their files contained no record identifiable with the subject. (u)

On March 27, 1965, SA AUGUST J. MICEK caused a check to be made of the files of the Bureau of Criminal Identification, NYCPD, and these files were found to contain no record identifiable with the subject. (u)

On April 8, 1965, under NYCPD Number 274456, a record on ALLEN GINSBERG was found in the Bureau of Special Services, NYCPD. (u)

This record reflected that ALLEN GINSBERG, no address given, was a member of Lemar and demonstrated with a group in front of the Department of Welfare, East Ninth Street and Avenue C, New York City, on December 27, 1964, from 6:00 to 7:30 PM. (u)

A notation in these files, dated June 30, 1964, listed ALLEN GINSBERG on the Advisory Committee of the New York City League for Sexual Freedom, which was contained on a letterhead of the group. (u)

- 17 -

NY 105-71471

In November, 1949, three letters addressed to BILL and signed ALLEN were taken from the possession of WILLIAM STEWARD BURROUGHS, Federal Bureau of Investigation Number 4578739, by Federal Bureau of Narcotics Agents in New Orleans, Louisianna. These letters contained references to the use of narcotics, criminal activities in the New York City area and homosexual activity. (U)

In December, 1949, ▓▓▓▓▓▓▓▓ who was at that time in the Queens City Prison, identified the BILL of these letters as WILLIAM BURROUGHS and the ALLEN as ALLEN GINSBERG. He described GINSBERG as a graduate of Columbia University, an intellectual who aspired to be a writer and who wanted to gather material by association with criminal types. He stated that GINSBERG was a homosexual and a user of narcotics. He described BURROUGHS as a narcotics addict. (U)

He, at this time, advised that ▓▓▓▓▓▓▓▓ was a literary friend of GINSBERG's; ▓▓▓▓▓▓▓▓ a friend of GINSBERG's at Columbia University, as was ▓▓▓▓▓▓▓▓ who was then studying in Denver, Colorado. He described ▓▓▓▓▓▓▓▓ as a school friend of GINSBERG's, who lived with him at 1401 York Avenue, New York City, and was believed to be a homosexual. (U)

On April 9, 1949, a burglary was committed at the home of ▓▓▓▓▓▓▓▓ and approximately $18,000 worth of valuables and personal property and $18,000 worth of United States bonds were stolen. (U)

In June, 1949, Detective ▓▓▓▓▓▓▓▓ of the 110th Squad of the NYCPD advised that ▓▓▓▓▓▓▓▓, NYCPD number ▓▓▓▓▓▓▓▓ ALLEN GINSBERG, NYCPD number 274456, ▓▓▓▓▓▓▓▓ NYCPD number ▓▓▓▓▓▓▓▓ and ▓▓▓▓▓▓▓▓ NYCPD number ▓▓▓▓▓▓▓▓ were the principal suspects in this burglary. He said that these four individuals were arrested by the NYCPD on April 22 and 23, 1949, when the stolen car in which they were attempting to (U)

- 18 -

NY 105-71471

escape overturned at Bayside, New York.   In the car at the
time of the arrest was found loot from the burglary of the
home of [   ]   b6
[   ] on April 20, 1949. (U)   b7C

On May 27, 1949, [   ] denied the burglary of
the [   ] home but admitted to the burglary of the [   ]
home. He did not implicate GINSBERG and stated that he had
previously served sixty days in prison, Rikers Island, New
York City, from December, 1948, until February, 1949, on a   b6
narcotics charge of illegal possession of a hypodermic   b7C
needle. After his release he went to live with ALLEN GINSBERG,
a former acquaintance, at 1401 York Avenue, New York City.
Subsequently [   ] moved in with her boyfriend,
[   ] on May 27, 1949. (U)

Detective [   ] in May of 1949, advised that GINSBERG
was at that time being held in the Queens County Jail without   b6
bail pending a local grand jury indictment. He was described   b7C
by [   ] as follows: (U)

Residence	1401 York Avenue, New York City
Race	White
Age	21
Height	5 feet 9 inches
Weight	140 pounds
Hair	Black
Eyes	Hazel
Occupation	Student at Columbia University

In September, 1949, subject's father, LOUIS GINSBERG,
324 Hamilton Avenue, Paterson, New Jersey, advised that the
subject was then in the New York State Psychiatric Institute,
722 West 168th Street, New York City, however, he was permitted to visit his home on weekends, which he did. LOUIS (U)

NY 105-71471

GINSBERG stated that his other son,⬚ was in ✗Ginsberg
much closer contact with ALLEN GINSBERG and⬚ could ✗Ginsberg
at that time be reached through⬚
N.Y. (u)

b6
b7C

NYCPD files reflect that ALLEN GINSBERG was
fingerprinted by them on April 22, 1949, under the name
ALLEN GINSBERG, charged with grand larceny auto by Officer
⬚of the 111th Squad, Queens.(u)

b6
b7C

On September 8, 1949, the subject denied any
participation or knowledge of the burglary of the⬚
residence. He advised that in January, 1949, he was working
with the Associated Press at Rockefeller Center as a copyboy and resided at 1401 York Avenue, New York City. In
February, 1949, he took in⬚upon
release from jail. About the first part of April, 1949,
⬚moved into his room since
they intended to sublet it when he left.(u)

b6
b7C

He advised that he was in the car with⬚and
⬚when it overturned, when⬚was fleeing from a
NYCPD patrol car. He also denied any knowledge of the
burglary of the⬚residence.(u)

b6
b7C

At the time of the interview GINSBERG was then in
the New York State Psychiatric Institute. The NYCPD prosecution of GINSBERG was discontinued when the Queens County
Grand Jury failed to return a true bill against him on charges
of grand larceny auto and receiving stolen property.(u)

In the months of March and April, 1965, confidential
informants all of whom have some knowledge of Cuban and/or
Communist dominated organizations and their activities were
contacted and advised that they had no knowledge concerning
the subject.(u)

- 20 -

UNITED STATES DEPARTMENT OF JUSTICE

FEDERAL BUREAU OF INVESTIGATION

In Reply, Please Refer to
File No.

WASHINGTON 25, D. C.   20535

MAY 20 1965

IRWIN ALLEN GINSBERG
Also Known As Allen Ginsberg

It will be noted information has been set forth
previously in this case concerning planned travel to Cuba
by Irwin Allen Ginsberg early in 1965, for which his current
passport, Z-126223, issued June 19, 1962, at Calcutta,
India, was specifically validated by the Department of State.
This validation was approved January 8, 1965, and his
passport was so stamped January 11, 1965, at the Boston
Passport Agency.

A representative of the FBI reviewed the passport
file of Ginsberg on May 11, 1965, at the Passport Office,
Department of State, and the following information was
obtained:

The passport file was noted to contain a news
clipping from the January 8, 1965, issue of "Time" magazine.
The news item made reference to Allen Ginsberg and it is
being set out here:

> "The name of the group is LEMAR, for
> legalized marijuana, and the activist
> San Francisco branch has even held
> puff-ins to protest the laws that forbid
> its use. Beat Poet Allen Ginsberg, 38,
> concedes that puff-ins might be fool-
> hardy but he's all for protests. So
> together with Fellow LEMARite Peter
> Orlovsky, he donned Japanese finger cymbals
> and showed up outside New York's
> Department of Welfare carrying a sign
> which read; SMOKE POT it's cheaper and
> healthier than liquor. New York's narcotic
> experts were contemplating a demonstration
> of their own for Ginsberg & Company.
> 'They should be picked up by the scruff of
> their necks', said Harlem's Dr. Robert
> Baird, 'and scrubbed down with Tide and
> Lestoil.'"

ALL INFORMATION CONTAINED
HEREIN IS UNCLASSIFIED
DATE 3/23/04 BY 60367N15uc/cr7/BL

105-137059-7
ENCLOSURE

IRWIN ALLEN GINSBERG

On April 15, 1965, at the American Embassy,
Warsaw, Poland, Irwin Allen Ginsberg, showing local address
as Hotel Europejski, Warsaw, presented Passport No. Z126223
for renewal. On his Application for Renewal, Ginsberg
listed his permanent residence in the United States as
416 E. 34th Street, Paterson, New Jersey; named persons to
notify in event of death or accident as Eugene Brooks and
Louis Ginsberg (father), at the same address, in Paterson,
New Jersey. Ginsberg stated he intended to return to the
United States within three months; that his purpose in
continuing to reside abroad during that period was "tourism."

"The Washington Evening Star" newspaper, Friday,
May 14, 1965, carried an article captioned, "East Europe
Ferment, CZECHS TRYING 'NEW MODEL'", under the byline of
George Sherman, European Correspondent of "The Star". This
article was datelined at Prague, Czechoslovakia. In this
lengthy article, Sherman related the changes going on
currently in Czechoslovakia and at one point discussed culture
and the tastes of the so called younger set. Specifically,
the article stated, "For the more sophisticated university
set, there is the combination bar and poetry-reading room at
the 'Viola' in central Prague. In March Allen Ginsberg drew
full houses to readings of his American 'beat' poetry."

"The Washington Post" on Monday, May 17, 1965,
on Page 1, carried a small article datelined Prague, May 16,
by Associated Press, captioned "Czechs Expell Allen Ginsberg"
and it is quoted as follows:

"American beat poet Allen Ginsberg has
been expelled from Czechoslovakia, the
Czechoslovak youth newspaper Mlada
Fronta reported today.

"Ginsberg was briefly detained and his
diary seized before his expulsion
May 7. The diary contained details
about Ginsberg's conduct while in
Czechoslovakia, the paper said.

"He came to Prague to reign as king of
a May Day weekend youth festival. He
was voted the title by student admirers
in Prague."

- 2 -

(3-22-64)

F B I

Date: 3/16/70

Transmit the following in _____
                                    (Type in plaintext or code)

Via   AIRTEL   AIRMAIL
                              (Priority)

TO: DIRECTOR, FBI (100-446997-Sub-52)

FROM: SAC, SPRINGFIELD (100-11185) (P)

SUBJECT: APPEARANCE OF ALLEN GINSBERG
         AT QUINCY COLLEGE
         QUINCY, ILLINOIS
         MARCH 18, 1970
         IS - MISCELLANEOUS

[   ] Quincy College,
Quincy, Illinois, a retired SA and an established source,
advised that ALLEN GINSBERG, billed as the "Hippie Poet"
is scheduled to read poetry at Social Hall, Quincy College,
Quincy, Illinois, at 8:00 PM on March 18, 1970.

     This appearance is sponsored by the Quincy College
Cultural Affairs Committee, a faculty organization at Quincy
College.

     Since this appearance does not seem to have any
connection with New Left activities, no coverage is being
afforded by Springfield and this is being furnished only
for the Bureau's information.

b6
b7C

ALL INFORMATION CONTAINED
HEREIN IS UNCLASSIFIED
DATE 1-22-2004 BY 60267 UC/NLS/BAW/CLT

REC 107

②- Bureau (100-446997)(Sub 52) (RM)   105-137059-10
2 - Springfield (100-11185)
EHD/es
  (4)   9 MAR 19 1970

Approved: _____ Sent _____ M Per _____
          Special Agent in Charge

EXEMPTED FROM AUTOMATIC
DECLASSIFICATION
AUTHORITY DERIVED FROM:
FBI AUTOMATIC DECLASSIFICATION GUIDE
EXEMPTION CODE: 25X(6)
DATE 09-10-2013

5010-106

...ERNMENT

Memorandum   ~~SECRET~~

ALL INFORMATION CONTAINED
HEREIN IS UNCLASSIFIED EXCEPT
WHERE SHOWN OTHERWISE

Tolson
Sullivan
Mohr
Bishop
Brennan, C.D.
Callahan
Casper
Conrad
Dalbey
Felt
Gale
Rosen
Tavel
Walters
Soyars
Tele. Room
Holmes
Gandy

TO   : Mr. Sullivan   DATE: 4/6/71

                                          1 - Mr. Sullivan
FROM   : A. Rosen   1 - Mr. Rosen
                                          1 - Mr. Malley
                                          1 - Mr. Scatterday

SUBJECT: IRWIN ALLEN GINSBERG
         ALSO KNOWN AS ALLEN GINSBERG   b1
         _____   b3
         NAME CHECK REQUEST
                          CLASSIFIED BY _____
                          DECLASSIFY ON: 25X ___ 3-22-2029

PURPOSE:
(S) _____
    _____ b1
                                                               b3

    BACKGROUND:
(S) _____ b1
    _____ b3

            Bufiles show Ginsberg is a "beatnik" poet who visited
    Cuba in 1965; has been associated with a pro-Castro front group;
    has demonstrated in favor of legalizing marijuana; has reportedly
    admitted being a narcotics user and homosexual; was formerly a
    patient in the New York State Psychiatric Institute for eight
    months; was active among the "Yippies" at the 1968 Democratic
    Convention in Chicago; was expelled from Czechoslovakia, primarily
    because of his admitted homosexual activities with young Czechs;
    and has supported anti-Vietnam war activities, including refusal
    to pay income taxes to support the war. Ginsberg has received
    considerable newspaper and magazine publicity concerning his
    activities. He has FBI Identification Record Number 713 322 B,
    showing arrests in 1949 for grand larceny and stolen auto, no
    disposition, and in 1954 for vagrancy, found not guilty.(U)

    OBSERVATION: FX-112   REC-65 105-13-7059-12
(S) _____ We do name checks _____   b1
                                             However, as a   b3
    cooperative measure, it is believed in this case we should furnish
    _____ (S)

    RECOMMENDATION: 1B APR 8 1971
            If approved, _____ will be furnished a summary of   b6
    Ginsberg's activities and a copy of his Identification Division b7C
    record.(U)
                                    Classified by 6080
                                    Exempt from GDS, Category
                                    Date of Declassification Indefinite
    CHS:cs (5)

                                    SECRET

Ernest Hemingway

IN THE YEARS AFTER completing *For Whom The Bell Tolls*, Ernest Hemingway relocated to Cuba, befriended a number of American diplomats, and began his foray into spycraft.

The now staple American author of *The Sun Also Rises*, *A Farewell to Arms*, and *The Old Man and the Sea* first came to the FBI's acquaintance via Spruille Braden, the Ambassador of Cuba along with other representatives of the U.S. embassy there. His relationship with the Bureau got off to a less-than-completely-affectionate start; the FBI Legal Attache who reported on the author to J. Edgar Hoover noted that he had previously been introduced by Hemingway as a "member of the Gestapo." However, the incident was written off as jest, and Hemingway began working in intelligence on behalf of the American Embassy in Havana in September 1942, soon assembling a team of over a dozen "barmen, waiters, and the like" for a program budgeted at $500 a month, roughly $7,500 in 2018 dollars.

Hemingway's activities reportedly included using his knowledge as a sailor familiar with the Cuban coast, under the pretext of "scientific investigations concerning the migration of Marlin on behalf of the Museum of Natural History, New York City." But Hoover's connection in Cuba, R.G. Leddy, was less than impressed with Hemingway's "so-called information," dismissing him as a "phony." Hoover himself called Hemingway the "last man ... to be used in any such capacity," while also recognizing that the author's close relationship with Ambassador Braden basically meant that there was nothing for the Bureau to do but humor the swarthy scribe's delusions of grandeur.

Hemingway's official Embassy operations were cut off on April 1st, 1943, though it seemed he carried on work for the Navy, as the FBI's interest in him was renewed shortly afterward.

Over the next decades, Hemingway published *The Old Man and the Sea*, won the Nobel Prize in Literature, and was challenged to a duel by a New Zealander journalist in Havana over some still-redacted insult. Hemingway declined the duel, to the Bureau's dismay, citing citing ill health and "a lot of writing to do."

In January 1961, the FBI received a letter about Hemingway's health, which was weak, both mentally and physically. That July, Hemingway passed away from a self-inflicted gun-shot wound. Three years later, Hoover received a letter from the journalist Quentin Reynolds, which contained an envelope bearing commemorative stamps of the author created by the Cuban government. The envelope had been given to Reynold's by Hemingway's widow, Mary, who feared it would be used to smear Hemingway was a closet Communist, and wanted the record set straight with the Bureau.

Considering his dislike for the man when he was alive, Hoover's handwritten response in reassurance doubles as an oddly sentimental epitaph — "Knowing Hemingway as I did, I doubt he had any Communist leanings. He was a rough, tough guy and always for the underdog."

CONFIDENTIAL

ALL INFORMATION CONTAINED
HEREIN IS UNCLASSIFIED
EXCEPT WHERE SHOWN
OTHERWISE

Havana, Cuba
October 8, 1942

Director,
Federal Bureau of Investigation,
Washington, D. C.

Re: ERNEST HEMINGWAY

Dear Sir:

DECLASSIFIED BY 6383 VET/AG
ON

The writer desires to acquaint the Bureau, in detail,
with a relationship that has developed under the direction of the
Ambassador with Mr. ERNEST HEMINGWAY.

As the Bureau is aware, HEMINGWAY has been resident in
Cuba almost continuously during the past two years, occupying his
private finca at San Francisco de Paula about 14 miles east of
Havana.

Mr. HEMINGWAY has been on friendly terms with Consul
KENNETH POTTER since the spring of 1941; recently he has become
very friendly with Mr. ROBERT P. JOYCE, Second Secretary of Embassy,
and through Mr. JOYCE has met the Ambassador on several occasions.
It is the writer's observation that the initiative in developing
these friendships has come from HEMINGWAY, but the opportunity of
association with him has been welcomed by Embassy officials.

At several conferences with the Ambassador and officers
of the Embassy late in August 1942, the topic of utilizing HEMINGWAY'S
services in intelligence activities was discussed. The Ambassador
pointed out that HEMINGWAY'S experiences during the Spanish Civil
War, his intimate acquaintances with Spanish Republican refugees
in Cuba, as well as his long experience on this island, seemed to
place him in a position of great usefulness to the Embassy's
intelligence program. While this program is inclusive of all
intelligence agencies and the Embassy's own sources of information,
the fact is that the Ambassador regards the Bureau representation
in the Embassy as the unit primarily concerned in this work. The
Ambassador further pointed out that HEMINGWAY had completed some
writing which had occupied him until that time, and was now ready
and anxious to be called upon.

RECORDED & INDEXED   64-23312-X

The writer pointed out at these conferences that any
information which could be secured concerning the operations of the
Spanish Falange in Cuba would be of material assistance in our work,
and that if HEMINGWAY was willing to devote his time and abilities
to the gathering of such information, the results would be most
welcome to us. It was pointed out to Mr. JOYCE, who is designated

FEDERAL BUREAU OF INVESTIGATION
OCT 16 1942
DEPARTMENT OF JUSTICE

CLASS. & EXT. BY SA
REASON - FCIM 11, 1-2.4.2 (B)
DATE OF REVIEW 10-24-89

-X JAN 4 1943

CONFIDENTIAL

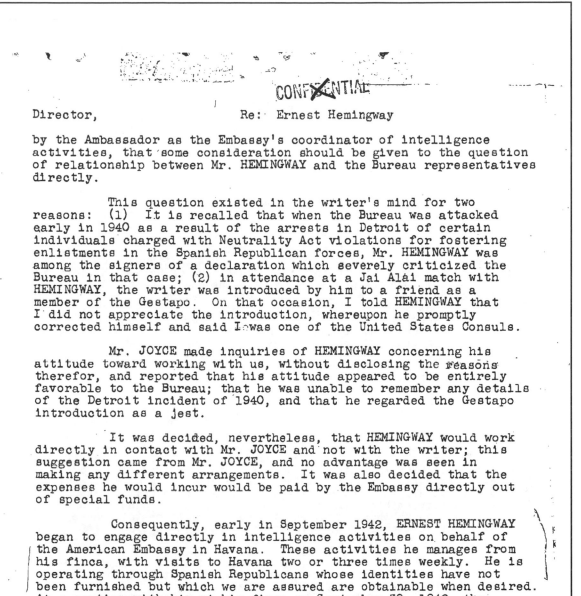

CONFIDENTIAL

Director,   Re: Ernest Hemingway

by the Ambassador as the Embassy's coordinator of intelligence
activities, that some consideration should be given to the question
of relationship between Mr. HEMINGWAY and the Bureau representatives
directly.

     This question existed in the writer's mind for two
reasons: (1) It is recalled that when the Bureau was attacked
early in 1940 as a result of the arrests in Detroit of certain
individuals charged with Neutrality Act violations for fostering
enlistments in the Spanish Republican forces, Mr. HEMINGWAY was
among the signers of a declaration which severely criticized the
Bureau in that case; (2) in attendance at a Jai Alai match with
HEMINGWAY, the writer was introduced by him to a friend as a
member of the Gestapo. On that occasion, I told HEMINGWAY that
I did not appreciate the introduction, whereupon he promptly
corrected himself and said I was one of the United States Consuls.

     Mr. JOYCE made inquiries of HEMINGWAY concerning his
attitude toward working with us, without disclosing the reasons
therefor, and reported that his attitude appeared to be entirely
favorable to the Bureau; that he was unable to remember any details
of the Detroit incident of 1940, and that he regarded the Gestapo
introduction as a jest.

     It was decided, nevertheless, that HEMINGWAY would work
directly in contact with Mr. JOYCE and not with the writer; this
suggestion came from Mr. JOYCE, and no advantage was seen in
making any different arrangements. It was also decided that the
expenses he would incur would be paid by the Embassy directly out
of special funds.

     Consequently, early in September 1942, ERNEST HEMINGWAY
began to engage directly in intelligence activities on behalf of
the American Embassy in Havana. These activities he manages from
his finca, with visits to Havana two or three times weekly. He is
operating through Spanish Republicans whose identities have not
been furnished but which we are assured are obtainable when desired.
At a meeting with him at his finca on September 30, 1942, the
writer was advised that he now has four men operating on a full
time basis, and 14 more whose positions are barmen, waiters, and
the like, operating on a part-time basis. The cost of this
program is approximately $500 a month. Reports are submitted to
HEMINGWAY, who dictates the material to a personal secretary and
furnishes duplicate copies to Mr. JOYCE, one being for the Embassy
and the other for our use. The material thus far submitted appears
to be carefully prepared and set out, and the Ambassador has noted

CONFIDENTIAL

- 2 -

CONFIDENTIAL

Director,   Re: Ernest Hemingway

on several memoranda that he likes HEMINGWAY'S approach, and wishes
to encourage him in the type of work that he is doing. HEMINGWAY
himself told me that he declined an offer from Hollywood to write
a script for a "March of Time" report on the "Flying Tigers" in
Burma, for which the compensation was to be $150,000, because he
considers the work he is now engaged in as of greater importance.

     One of the aspects of Mr. HEMINGWAY'S relationships with the
Embassy is the plan of the Naval Attache, Lieutenant Colonel
HAYNE D. BOYDEN, U.S.M.C., to utilize his services for certain
coastal patrol and investigative work on the south coast of Cuba.
HEMINGWAY, who has a wide reputation as a fisherman, knows the
coast line and waters of Cuba very intimately; he has also engaged
over a 12-year period in some scientific investigations concerning
the migration of Marlin on behalf of the Museum of Natural History,
New York City. On the pretext of continuing such investigations,
the Naval Attache has acceded to HEMINGWAY'S request for authorization to patrol certain areas where submarine activity has been
reported. Special permits have been secured for him, and an allotment of gasoline is now being obtained for his use. He has requested
that some firearms and depth charges be furnished him, which is also
being done, and he has secured from the Ambassador a promise that his
crew members will be recognized as war casualties for purposes of
indemnification in the event any loss of life results from this
operation.

     With specific reference to the conducting of intelligence
investigations on the island of Cuba by Mr. HEMINGWAY, the writer
wishes to state that his interest thus far has not been limited to
the Spanish Falange and Spanish activities, but that he has included
numerous German suspects. His reports are promptly furnished and he
assures Mr. JOYCE that his only desire is to be of assistance on a
cooperative basis, without compensation to himself, and that he will
be guided at all times by our wishes. So far, no conflict has
developed between his work and that which Bureau personnel is handling
in Havana; and HEMINGWAY told me that he wishes to be told where to
limit his investigations whenever this is thought desirable.

     The Bureau will be continuously advised of pertinent
developments in this situation. Meanwhile, if there is any information or instructions for the guidance of the writer, I would
appreciate being advised.

                              Very truly yours,

                              R. G. Leddy

                              R. G. LEDDY
RGL:RM   Legal Attache

- 3 -

Federal Bureau of Investigation

United States Department of Justice

Washington, D. C.

December 17, 1942

CHC:LL   ~~CONFIDENTIAL~~

DECLASSIFIED BY 5768 SLD/phn/
ON 2/25/86 appeal #. 80-1042

MEMORANDUM FOR THE DIRECTOR

Re: ERNEST HEMINGWAY

ALL INFORMATION CONTAINED
HEREIN IS UNCLASSIFIED
EXCEPT WHERE SHOWN
OTHERWISE

BACKGROUND

Mr. Ernest Hemingway, well-known American writer, recently has been acting as personal informant of Ambassador Spruille Braden in Havana, Cuba.

DETAILS

FBI Attache R. G. Leddy, stationed at the American Embassy in Havana, Cuba, has recently advised that Ernest Hemingway, well-known American writer, has been residing in Cuba, just outside Havana, for approximately two years. Hemingway, it will be recalled, engaged actively on the side of the Spanish Republic during the Spanish Civil War, and it is reported that he is very well acquainted with a large number of Spanish refugees in Cuba and elsewhere. Hemingway, it will be recalled, joined in attacking the Bureau early in 1940, at the time of the "general smear campaign" following the arrests of certain individuals in Detroit charged with violation of Federal statutes in connection with their participation in Spanish Civil War activities. It will be recalled that Hemingway signed a declaration, along with a number of other individuals, severely criticizing the Bureau in connection with the Detroit arrests. Hemingway has been accused of being of Communist sympathy, although we are advised that he has denied and does vigorously deny any Communist affiliation or sympathy. Hemingway is reported to be personally friendly with Ambassador Braden, and he is reported to enjoy the Ambassador's complete confidence. According to Agent Leddy, Hemingway is also on very friendly terms with United States Consul Kennett Potter, presently stationed in Cuba, and with Mr. Robert P. Joyce, Second Secretary of the American Embassy in Havana.

Mr. Leddy has advised that Hemingway has been acting as an informant of Ambassador Braden for the past several months and in this capacity has been dealing closely with Ambassador Braden and Second Secretary Joyce. Leddy stated that Ambassador Braden has made no secret of this connection, in so far as Agent Leddy is concerned, and, further, that the Ambassador has instructed that all of Hemingway's reports and any information furnished by him must be turned over to Mr. Leddy.

RECORDED & INDEXED   64-23312-X2

COPIES DESTROYED 10/24/79 BY SP-1 DSJ/

08 NOV 20 1961

CLASS. & EXT. 11. 1-2. 4. -85
REASON - FCIM 10-24-85
DATE OF REVIEW

70 FEB 10 1943

CONFIDENTIAL

FOR DEFENSE
BUY
UNITED
STATES
SAVINGS
BONDS
AND STAMPS

DO NOT FILE. RETURN AT ONCE TO SIS

Memorandum for the Director   CONFIDENTIAL   Page 2

        Mr. Leddy has advised that the original arrangement whereby
Mr. Hemingway would act as informant of Ambassador Braden was largely
concerned with certain political matters, particularly as to the connection or alleged connection of certain Cuban political leaders with the
Spanish Falange and the involvement of Cuban officials generally in
local graft and corruption within Cuba. Ambassador Braden, as you will
recall, is a very implusive individual and he apparently has had a
"bee in his bonnet" for some time concerning alleged graft and corruption
on the part of certain Cuban officials. Agent Leddy has stated that
Mr. Hemingway has apparently organized a number of informants among the
Spanish refugee group, whose identities are not known to Leddy, and,
according to the best of his information, their identities are not known
to anyone except Hemingway.

        Agent Leddy has advised that Hemingway's activities have
branched out and that he and his informants are now engaged in reporting
to the Embassy various types of information concerning subversive
activities generally. Mr. Leddy stated that he has become quite concerned with respect to Hemingway's activities and that they are undoubtedly going to be very embarrassing unless something is done to put
a stop to them. Mr. Leddy has advised that Hemingway is apparently under-
taking a rather involved investigation with regard to Cuban officials
prominently connected with the Cuban Government, including General
Manuel Benitez Valdes, head of the Cuban National Police; that he,
Agent Leddy, is sure that the Cubans are eventually going to find out
about this if Hemingway continues operating, and that serious trouble
may result.

        Mr. Leddy has advised that there is an individual attached
to the Embassy by the name of Gustavo Duran, who is of Spanish descent
and is employed by the Coordinator of Inter-American Affairs; that Duran
is a very close friend of Hemingway and is apparently consulting and
actually working with Hemingway in connection with the latter's
activities.

        This matter has been discussed at some length with Mr. Leddy,
and he was asked just what objection, if any, he has ever personally
or officially offered to the arrangement or whether he has discussed its
possible bad effects with the Ambassador.

        Leddy stated that he has not offered any objection whatsoever
to this proposition; that the Ambassador has advised Leddy quite frankly
and openly that Hemingway is the Ambassador's informant and that all information of any kind whatsoever furnished by Hemingway will be immediately

CONFIDENTIAL   CONFIDENTIAL

CONFIDENTIAL

Memorandum for the Director   CONFIDENTIAL   Page 3

turned over to Leddy, which, according to Leddy, is actually being
done. Leddy suggested that the Bureau take this matter up with Ambassador Braden while he is in the United States.

It was pointed out to Leddy that the Bureau certainly cannot
take the matter up with Ambassador Braden and protest to him unless
Leddy has first made the Bureau's position quite plain to the Ambassador
himself. It was pointed out to Mr. Leddy that the Ambassador would
undoubtedly resent any complaint or protest concerning the arrangement
from the Bureau direct, which complaint and protest could only be based
upon Leddy's recommendations and information, unless Leddy has himself
first discussed the matter with the Ambassador and pointed out the
Bureau's position, this being particularly true inasmuch as Ambassador
Braden has apparently been quite frank with Agent Leddy about the
arrangement and has insisted that all information furnished by Hemingway
be immediately furnished to Agent Leddy.

When the above was pointed out to Mr. Leddy, he stated that
he will, if the Bureau desires, approach the Ambassador and outline to
the latter just exactly how he feels about the situation. Leddy stated
that Hemingway's information is valueless; that our Agents in Cuba have,
of course, to check on it when it is submitted; that it is completely
unreliable information; that the time taken to investigate it and check
on it is purely wasted time and wasted effort; that Hemingway has not
actually interfered with any investigation that we might be conducting
to date, but that from the way he is branching out with his undercover
informants, he undoubtedly will. Mr. Leddy stated that he has a complete record of all the information submitted by Hemingway and can state
unequivocally that it is all completely unfounded and valueless and that
the time spent in investigating it by Bureau Agents has been completely
wasted.

Mr. Leddy stated that he can point out to the Ambassador that
he, Leddy, has not checked any reports from Hemingway concerning corruption
in the Cuban Government; that he does not feel that Bureau Agents should
become involved in any such investigations, it being entirely without our
jurisdiction and a matter in which the Cubans themselves alone are concerned and something that, if we get involved in it, is going to mean that
all of us will be thrown out of Cuba "bag and baggage."

Agent Leddy stated he can point out to the Ambassador the
extreme danger of having some informant like Hemingway given free rein
to stir up trouble such as that which will undoubtedly ensue if this
situation continues. Mr. Leddy stated that despite the fact the

CONFIDENTIAL

Memorandum for the Director   CONFIDENTIAL   Page 4

Ambassador likes Hemingway and apparently has confidence in him, he is
of the opinion that he, Leddy, can handle this situation with the Ambassador so that Hemingway's services as an informant will be completely discontinued. Mr. Leddy stated that he can point out to the
Ambassador that Hemingway is going further than just an informant;
that he is actually branching out into an investigative organization
of his own which is not subject to any control whatsoever.

RECOMMENDATION

        It is recommended that Agent Leddy take this matter up with
the Ambassador, along the lines outlined above, prior to any protest
being made by the Bureau at the Seat of Government. It is believed that
if not handled this way, the Ambassador will lose complete confidence in
Leddy, as well as other Bureau Agents operating in Cuba, this being
particularly true inasmuch as the Ambassador has apparently been quite
frank with Leddy about this matter.

        Mr. Leddy, if you approve, will be told to advise the Bureau
promptly and in detail as to the outcome of his negotiations with the
Ambassador concerning this matter, at which time we should, it is believed,
advise Mr. Berle for the Bureau's protection.

                                    Respectfully,

                                    D. M. Ladd

CONFIDENTIAL

CONFIDENTIAL

CONFIDENTIAL

MEMORANDUM

December 19, 1942

MEMORANDUM FOR MR. TAMM
                MR. LADD

ALL INFORMATION CONTAINED
HEREIN IS UNCLASSIFIED
EXCEPT WHERE SHOWN
OTHERWISE

64-23312-X2

        In regard to Mr. ___'s memorandum of the 17th instant
concerning the use of Ernest Hemingway by the United States Ambassador
to Cuba, I of course realize the complete undesirability of this sort
of a connection or relationship. Certainly Hemingway is the last man,
in my estimation, to be used in any such capacity. His judgment is
not of the best, and if his sobriety is the same as it was some years
ago, that is certainly questionable.

        However, I do not think there is anything we should do in
this matter, nor do I think our representative at Havana should do
anything about it with the Ambassador. The Ambassador is somewhat
hot-headed and I haven't the slightest doubt that he would immediately
tell Hemingway of the objections being raised by the FBI. Hemingway
has no particular love for the FBI and would no doubt embark upon a
campaign of vilification.

        In addition thereto, you will recall that in my conference
recently with the President, he indicated that some message had been
sent to him, the President, by Hemingway through a mutual friend, and
Hemingway was insisting that one-half million dollars be granted to
the Cuban authorities so that they could take care of internees.

        I do not see that it is a matter that directly affects our
relationship as long as Hemingway does not report directly to us or
we deal directly with him. Anything which he gives to the Ambassador
which the Ambassador in turn forwards to us, we can accept without any
impropriety.

Mr. Tolson _____
Mr. E. A. Tamm _____   I have no objection to Mr. Tamm informally talking with
Mr. Clegg _____ Mr. Berle about this matter, but impress Mr. Berle with the fact that
Mr. Glavin _____ we do not want to become involved in any controversies concerning the
Mr. Ladd _____
Mr. Nichols _____
Mr. Rosen _____   Very truly yours
Mr. Tracy _____   RECORDED & INDEXED
Mr. Carson _____
Mr. Coffey _____   John Edgar Hoover
Mr. Hendon _____   Director
Mr. Kramer _____
Mr. McGuire _____
Mr. Harbo _____
Mr. Quinn Tamm _____
Mr. Nease _____
Miss Gandy _____

FEB 5 1943

CONFIDENTIAL

Memorandum from
SIS #396
dated 12/8/42.

CONFIDENTIAL

ALL INFORMATION CONTAINED
HEREIN IS UNCLASSIFIED
EXCEPT WHERE SHOWN
OTHERWISE

December 17, 1942

CLASS. & EXT. BY
REASON - FCIM 11, 1.4.2
DATE OF REVIEW

THE DIRECTOR

RE: ERNEST HEMINGWAY

BACKGROUND   INFT. S. I. S. #396

_____, Havana,
Cuba, has advised that Ernest Hemingway, a well known writer, has been
employed by the American Embassy as a confidential informant.

FACTS

    Hemingway is on friendly terms with certain members of the Embassy
staff, especially with the United States Consul Kennett Potter and with Mr.
Robert P. Joyce, Second Secretary of the Embassy. Ambassador Braden is also
on very friendly terms with Hemingway and apparently is "sold" on him and
reposes complete confidence in him.

    It was thought that when Hemingway became an informant of the Embassy
that he probably could supply much information of value concerning the operations of the Spanish Falange. Mr. Hemingway has worked directly in contact
with Mr. Joyce and not with   INFT. S. I. S. #396

    It will be recalled that when the Bureau was attacked early in 1940
as a result of the arrests in Detroit of certain individuals charged with
neutrality act violations for fostering enlistments in the Spanish Republican
forces, Mr. Hemingway was among the signers of a declaration which severely
criticized the Bureau in that case. Hemingway has since stated that he has
forgotten that incident.

    Since Hemingway has become an Embassy informant he has organized a
group of operators whose identities are not known and who engage in investigative work. The reports of these operators' investigations are furnished to
the office of the Legal Attache. Hemingway and his staff have embarked on
investigations of all types and not merely on the Spanish Falange. One such
investigation has General Benitez as its subject.

    further advised that Hemingway has access to official
Embassy records a_____ stated that although he has insisted that
copies of Bureau reports should not be shown to anyone except a
limited number of Embassy officials, it is quite apparent that at
least the contents, if not the reports themselves, are known to
Mr. Hemingway. CLASSIFIED INFORMATION

CONFIDENTIAL

Memorandum for the Director   CONFIDENTIAL   ~~CONFIDENTIAL~~   -2-

An individual by the name of Gustavo Duran, who aids Hemingway in his investigations, is employed and paid by the State Department. Duran's operations and attitude, in direct relation with Mr. Joyce, assume proportions of domination and direction rather than assistance to the agencies properly engaged in investigating subversive activities. The organization operated by Hemingway is reported to be unknown for its reliability or trustworthiness. According to our information, data is transmitted to him without an official check being made on what happens to this information thereafter.

_____ advised that he has not as yet opposed Mr. Hemingway's services but had thought best to let the situation work itself out as long as no direct conflict with the Bureau's work occurred, in view of the friendly feeling and mutual understanding between the Embassy and Hemingway.   (b)u

ACTION

CONF. INFT. E. C. S. #396.

If you approve, _____ will be instructed to take up with Ambassador Braden the matter of Hemingway's employment as a confidential informant in relation to Hemingway's access to the Embassy files and his other investigative activities in Cuba. Attached is the proposed letter to   (c)u

_____ S. #396

Respectfully,

D. M. Ladd

CONFIDENTIAL

TWP:meb

CONFIDENTIAL   CONFIDENTIAL   'ALL INFORMATION CONTAINED
                                HEREIN IS UNCLASSIFIED
December 17, 1942   EXCEPT WHERE SHOWN
                                OTHERWISE

PERSONAL AND CONFIDENTIAL
VIA DIPLOMATIC AIR POUCH

CGRF

Havana, Cuba

RE: ERNEST HEMINGWAY

Dear Sir:

Reference is made to your memorandum dated December 8, 1942, regarding Ernest Hemingway's employment by the American Embassy as a confidential informant and his activities in relation thereto.

In view of the trust and friendship reposed in Hemingway by Embassy officials, you are instructed to discuss diplomatically with Ambassador Braden the disadvantages which you pointed out in your above referred to memorandum in relation to Hemingway's activities in Cuba. It should be stressed that because of the confidential nature contained in the Bureau's reports and the necessity of safeguarding its informants that it is unwise to allow anyone who is not a Government official to have access to the information contained in your files. In this connection it is pointed out that information is transmitted to you directly from the Bureau which was gained from confidential sources in the United States and elsewhere, and it is absolutely necessary that these sources of information be protected.

Any information which you may have relating to the unreliability of Ernest Hemingway as an informant may be discreetly brought to the attention of Ambassador Braden. In this respect it will be recalled that recently Hemingway gave information concerning the refueling of submarines in Caribbean waters which has proved unreliable.

I desire that you furnish me at an early date the results of your conversations with Ambassador Braden concerning Ernest Hemingway and his aides and their activities.

10/25/79
CLASS. & EXT. BY SA
REASON - FCIM 11, 1-2/4.2 (2)(3)
DATE OF REVIEW 10-25-79

Very truly yours,

CONFIDENTIAL

John Edgar Hoover
Director

ENCLOSURE

CC-287

JOHN EDGAR HOOVER
DIRECTOR

Federal Bureau of Investigation
United States Department of Justice
Washington, D. C.

CONFIDENTIAL   April 27, 1943

ALL INFORMATION CONTAINED
HEREIN IS UNCLASSIFIED
EXCEPT WHERE SHOWN
OTHERWISE

WHA:CSM:LNS

MEMORANDUM FOR THE DIRECTOR

RE: ERNEST HEMINGWAY

DECLASSIFIED BY 6383 UC/LASS
5-26-81

In accordance with your request, there is attached a memorandum which summarizes the information in our files regarding Ernest Hemingway, the author.

Mr. Hemingway, it will be noted, has been connected with various so-called Communist front organizations and was active in aiding the Loyalist cause in Spain. In the latter connection he spent sometime in Spain during the Spanish revolution and reported the events transpiring there for the North American Newspaper Alliance.

Despite Hemingway's activities, no information has been received which would definitely tie him with the Communist Party or which would indicate that he is or has been a Party member. His actions, however, have indicated that his views are "liberal" and that he may be inclined favorably to Communist political philosophies.

Hemingway is now in Havana, Cuba where he has resided for over two years. For sometime he acted as an under-cover informant for American Ambassador Spruille Braden, and apparently enjoyed the Ambassador's complete confidence. You will recall that on December 17, 1942, there were set forth in a memorandum for you, the details of Hemingway's activities in Cuba, as well as the details of his association with the American Ambassador.

Briefly, Hemingway established what was termed "an amateur information service" and gathered alleged intelligence data which he turned over to Mr. Braden. In this work Hemingway developed his own confidential informants and was said to be friendly with a number of Spanish refugees in Cuba. His relationship with the Ambassador was quite friendly, but the Ambassador was perfectly frank with the Bureau representatives in Havana regarding this relationship and made all of the information which Hemingway furnished to him, available to the Bureau. These data, however, were almost without fail valueless.

10-25-79
CLASS. & EXT. BY SPS/DSK/gm
REASON - FCIM 11, 1-2.2 (J)(3)
DATE OF REVIEW   10-25-89

RECORDED
64-23312-3

FOR VICTORY
BUY UNITED STATES SAVINGS BONDS AND STAMPS

75 JUN 18 1943

CONFIDENTIAL

MEMORANDUM FOR THE DIRECTOR

CONFIDENTIAL

- 2 -

C.I. S.I.S. # 396

██████████ the Bureau representative stationed at the American Embassy in Havana, Cuba has recently advised that the Ambassador discontinued Hemingway's services effective April 1, 1943. At the present time he is alleged to be performing a highly secret naval operation for the Navy Department. In this connection, the Navy Department is said to be paying the expenses for the operation of Hemingway's boat, furnishing him with arms and charting courses in the Cuban area. (E)U

The Bureau has conducted no investigation of Hemingway, but his name has been mentioned in connection with other Bureau investigations and various data concerning him have been submitted voluntarily by a number of different sources.

Respectfully,

D. M. Ladd

Enclosure

Naval information unclassified per their letter dated 2/9/87. So-5 cir/DAT 4/6/87.

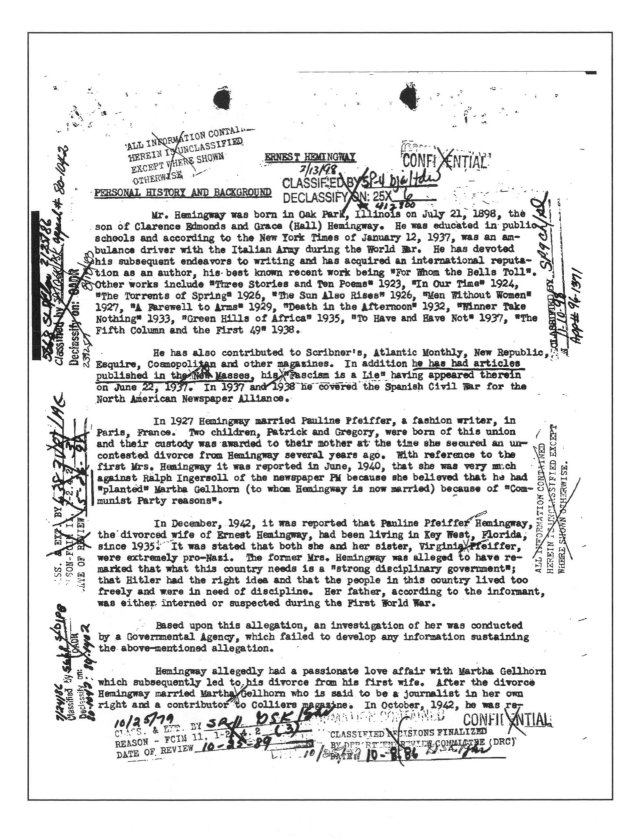

ERNEST HEMINGWAY
2/13/98

'CONFIDENTIAL'

CLASSIFIED BY SP-4
DECLASSIFY ON: 25X

'ALL INFORMATION CONTAIN...
HEREIN IS UNCLASSIFIED
EXCEPT WHERE SHOWN
OTHERWISE'

PERSONAL HISTORY AND BACKGROUND

Mr. Hemingway was born in Oak Park, Illinois on July 21, 1898, the son of Clarence Edmonds and Grace (Hall) Hemingway. He was educated in public schools and according to the New York Times of January 12, 1937, was an ambulance driver with the Italian Army during the World War. He has devoted his subsequent endeavors to writing and has acquired an international reputation as an author, his best known recent work being "For Whom the Bells Toll". Other works include "Three Stories and Ten Poems" 1923, "In Our Time" 1924, "The Torrents of Spring" 1926, "The Sun Also Rises" 1926, "Men Without Women" 1927, "A Farewell to Arms" 1929, "Death in the Afternoon" 1932, "Winner Take Nothing" 1933, "Green Hills of Africa" 1935, "To Have and Have Not" 1937, "The Fifth Column and the First 49" 1938.

He has also contributed to Scribner's, Atlantic Monthly, New Republic, Esquire, Cosmopolitan and other magazines. In addition he has had articles published in the New Masses, his "Fascism is a Lie" having appeared therein on June 22, 1937. In 1937 and 1938 he covered the Spanish Civil War for the North American Newspaper Alliance.

In 1927 Hemingway married Pauline Pfeiffer, a fashion writer, in Paris, France. Two children, Patrick and Gregory, were born of this union and their custody was awarded to their mother at the time she secured an uncontested divorce from Hemingway several years ago. With reference to the first Mrs. Hemingway it was reported in June, 1940, that she was very much against Ralph Ingersoll of the newspaper PM because she believed that he had "planted" Martha Gellhorn (to whom Hemingway is now married) because of "Communist Party reasons".

In December, 1942, it was reported that Pauline Pfeiffer Hemingway, the divorced wife of Ernest Hemingway, had been living in Key West, Florida, since 1935. It was stated that both she and her sister, Virginia Pfeiffer, were extremely pro-Nazi. The former Mrs. Hemingway was alleged to have remarked that what this country needs is a "strong disciplinary government"; that Hitler had the right idea and that the people in this country lived too freely and were in need of discipline. Her father, according to the informant, was either interned or suspected during the First World War.

Based upon this allegation, an investigation of her was conducted by a Governmental Agency, which failed to develop any information sustaining the above-mentioned allegation.

Hemingway allegedly had a passionate love affair with Martha Gellhorn which subsequently led to his divorce from his first wife. After the divorce Hemingway married Martha Gellhorn who is said to be a journalist in her own right and a contributor to Colliers magazine. In October, 1942, he was re-

'CONFIDENTIAL'

CLASS. & EXT. BY SP-1
REASON - FCIM 11, 1-2 & 2 (3)
DATE OF REVIEW 10-25-89

CLASSIFIED DECISIONS FINALIZED
BY DEPARTMENT REVIEW COMMITTEE (DRC)
DATE: 10-25-86

- 2 -

portedly living with her on a farm near Havana, Cuba which had been purchased
from Roger D'Orn. Martha Gellhorn apparently bought the farm before her marriage to Hemingway and after the marriage he moved there. Hemingway and Martha
Gellhorn were in Spain at the same time during the Spanish Revolution as an
article in the People's World for February 14, 1939, indicated that a person
recently back from Spain had remarked that he had met both Hemingway and
Martha Gellhorn in Madrid.

Hemingway is still residing in Havana, Cuba and on December 7, 1942,
was reportedly receiving his mail at the Ambos Mundos Hotel, Havana, Cuba, and
was said to be quite friendly with Manolo Asper, the manager of this hotel.

Hemingway is said to have a brother, Leicester Hemingway, who in
April, 1943, was reported to be working for the Office for Emergency Management
in Washington, D. C.

OFFICE OF THE LEGAL ATTACHE

ALL INFORMATION CONTAINED
HEREIN IS UNCLASSIFIED
EXCEPT WHERE SHOWN
OTHERWISE

EMBASSY OF THE
UNITED STATES OF AMERICA
HABANA, CUBA

June 26, 1943

Director,
Federal Bureau of Investigation,
Washington, D. C.

Re: ERNEST HEMINGWAY --
      INTELLIGENCE ACTIVITIES IN CUBA

Dear Sir:

        As of interest to the Bureau, the following matters
affecting general intelligence activities are set forth.

1) Communist Attack on Ernest Hemingway

        SIS #360 has submitted a memorandum concerning the
attack in the Communist newspaper "Hoy" of April 25, 1943,
against Ernest Hemingway. The article is entitled, "The Last
Position of the Traitor Hemingway," and is written by Raul
Gonzalez Tunon.

        The article attacks Hemingway on several grounds.
First, it condemns him as being one of the "war tourists" who
went to Spain, not to seek the popular and eternal Spain, but
to seek curious, "effeminate", queer characters. Not finding
such characters in the Loyalist zone, they made friends with
the most "delirious" adventurers infiltrated in the CNT and
with the individualists of the Trotskyist group of the POUM.
On Hemingway's return to America, he published a book that was
"so miserable, so slanderous", that it met with excellent reception among the Fascists, the Trotskyists and the Munichists.
This was "For Whom the Bell Tolls." "The attacks on Andre
Marty...constitute a repetition of known slanders whose origin
must be sought in the propaganda office of Dr. Goebbels."

        Now, the article states Hemingway is a champion of the
race theory, in reverse. He advocates in the United States a
campaign for the sterilization of all Germans as a means of pre-
serving peace. That is, he wants to make this a racial war
against Germany. He shakes hands with Goebbels, who, trying to
prevent the disaster of the German people, says that "the skin
of every German is at stake in this war." This idea of Hemingway's
is a Trotskyist idea at the service of Nazism.

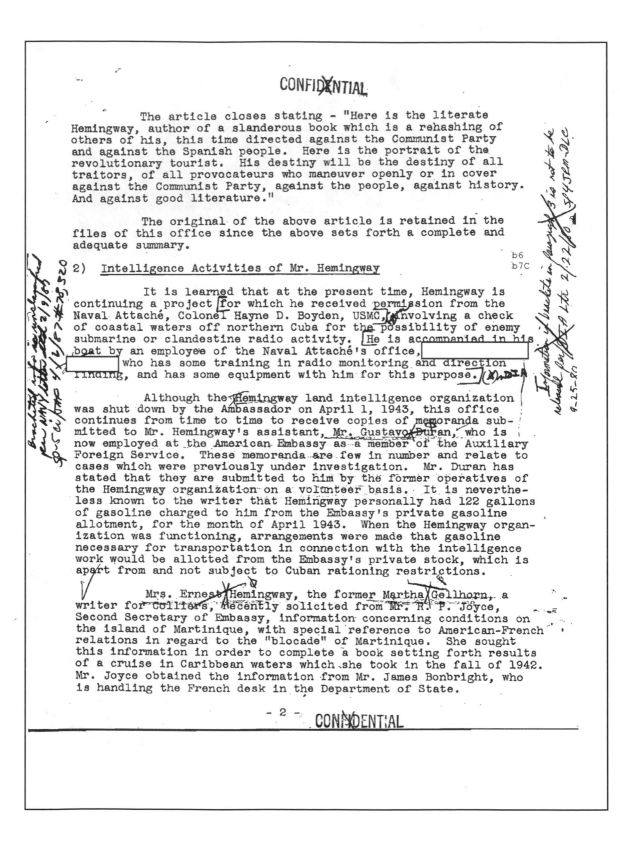

CONFIDENTIAL

The article closes stating - "Here is the literate Hemingway, author of a slanderous book which is a rehashing of others of his, this time directed against the Communist Party and against the Spanish people. Here is the portrait of the revolutionary tourist. His destiny will be the destiny of all traitors, of all provocateurs who maneuver openly or in cover against the Communist Party, against the people, against history. And against good literature."

The original of the above article is retained in the files of this office since the above sets forth a complete and adequate summary.

2)   Intelligence Activities of Mr. Hemingway

It is learned that at the present time, Hemingway is continuing a project for which he received permission from the Naval Attaché, Colonel Hayne D. Boyden, USMC, involving a check of coastal waters off northern Cuba for the possibility of enemy submarine or clandestine radio activity. He is accompanied in his boat by an employee of the Naval Attaché's office, _____ who has some training in radio monitoring and direction finding, and has some equipment with him for this purpose.

Although the Hemingway land intelligence organization was shut down by the Ambassador on April 1, 1943, this office continues from time to time to receive copies of memoranda submitted to Mr. Hemingway's assistant, Mr. Gustavo Duran, who is now employed at the American Embassy as a member of the Auxiliary Foreign Service. These memoranda are few in number and relate to cases which were previously under investigation. Mr. Duran has stated that they are submitted to him by the former operatives of the Hemingway organization on a volunteer basis. It is nevertheless known to the writer that Hemingway personally had 122 gallons of gasoline charged to him from the Embassy's private gasoline allotment, for the month of April 1943. When the Hemingway organization was functioning, arrangements were made that gasoline necessary for transportation in connection with the intelligence work would be allotted from the Embassy's private stock, which is apart from and not subject to Cuban rationing restrictions.

Mrs. Ernest Hemingway, the former Martha Gellhorn, a writer for Colliers, recently solicited from Mr. R. P. Joyce, Second Secretary of Embassy, information concerning conditions on the island of Martinique, with special reference to American-French relations in regard to the "blocade" of Martinique. She sought this information in order to complete a book setting forth results of a cruise in Caribbean waters which she took in the fall of 1942. Mr. Joyce obtained the information from Mr. James Bonbright, who is handling the French desk in the Department of State.

- 2 -   CONFIDENTIAL

CONFIDENTIAL

b6
b7C
b7D

3) Relations with Bureau Informants (S) u

[redacted] which has been actively
assisting this office, informed SIS #788 that under no conditions
did it wish its work known to anyone in the Embassy outside of this
office, because of their fear that their connections and activities
would thereby become known to Mr. Ernest Hemingway. [redacted]
stated that the Basques
resent the pro-Communist sympathies of Mr. Hemingway, who is well
acquainted with many members of the Basque Colony through his
interest in Jai Alai players; and also, being themselves a deeply
religious people, they feel offended by what they consider the
open anti-Catholic sentiments of Hemingway. (S)(M) u

On the other hand, Mr. Hemingway entertained Secretary
of the Treasury Henry Morgenthau at his finca during the visit
of this official to Habana in March of this year. Since that
time, correspondence has passed from the Secretary of the
Treasury to Mr. Hemingway through the State Department diplomatic
pouch.

Very truly yours,

#396 (S)u

Legal Attaché

RGL:RM

JOHN EDGAR HOOVER
DIRECTOR

CONFIDENTIAL

Federal Bureau of Investigation
United States Department of Justice
Washington, D. C.

RGL:mc   June 23, 1943

Mr. Tolson
Mr. E. A. Tamm
Mr. Clegg
Mr. Ladd
Mr. Nichols
Mr. Rosen
Mr. Tracy
Mr. Carson
Mr. Coffey
Mr. Hendon
Mr. Holloman
Mr. McGuire
Mr. Harbo
Mr. Quinn Tamm
Tele. Room
Mr. Nease
Miss Beahm
Miss Gandy

ALL INFORMATION CONTAINED
HEREIN IS UNCLASSIFIED
EXCEPT WHERE SHOWN
OTHERWISE

MEMORANDUM FOR MR. LADD

Re: Intelligence Activities of
Ernest Hemingway in Cuba

BACKGROUND

Mr. R. G. Leddy, Legal Attache at Havana, Cuba, submits
information concerning the intelligence activities of Ernest Hemingway
and his relations with the FBI.

DETAILS

Ernest Hemingway has resided almost continuously in Cuba on
a small country estate at San Francisco de Paula, outside Havana, during
the past two years. In this time he completed his latest book, a compilation of war stories, published in the fall of 1942.

Hemingway knows Cuba well and has lived on the island for
various periods during the past 12 years. He is well known as a sports-
man, engaging in deep sea fishing from his own fishing boat and maintaining
a pigeon shooting range on his own property. He is a well known figure at
jai alai matches and a back-slapping friend of the Basque jai alai players.
In Havana he frequents the Floridita and Basque Bar, two famous spots where
prominent Cubans and Americans gather at noon and in the evening.

During the current period of his residence in Cuba, Hemingway had
no contact with the American Embassy until August, 1942. He did, however,
cultivate the friendship of an American Consul on a personal basis before
this date. An Embassy employee and friend of this Consul remarked to the
Legal Attache that Hemingway's purpose appeared to have been some kind
of an "in" with American authorities at a time when he was only interested
in completing his book. In August, 1942, Hemingway was introduced to the
American Ambassador, Mr. Spruille Braden, and volunteered his services to
engage in intelligence work. The Ambassador inquired of the Legal Attache
whether Hemingway would be useful to investigate the Spanish Falange with the
aid of Spanish Republican refugees known to him. The Ambassador said
that he regarded Hemingway's experience in the Spanish Civil War and
his long-time acquaintance with Spain and the Spanish people as giving
him unique qualifications to investigate the Spanish Falange in Cuba
which the Ambassador regarded as an imminent danger.

FOR DEFENSE
BUY
UNITED
STATES
SAVINGS
BONDS
AND STAMPS

RETURN DIRECTLY TO [SIS] FILES

CONFIDENTIAL
CONFIDENTIAL

CONFIDENTIAL   CONFIDENTIAL

Memorandum for Mr. Ladd
Page 2

The Ambassador's inquiry was taken up by Mr. Joyce, Second
Secretary of the Embassy, with the Legal Attache and Mr. Joyce was advised that there was some question as to the attitude of Mr. Hemingway
to the FBI, with which organization he had presumably been requested to
work. This question existed, Mr. Joyce was advised, because of Hemingway's
action as a principal signer of the denounciation of the FBI in the
Detroit Communist-Spanish enlistment case in 1940 and also because of
Hemingway's remark on meeting the Legal Attache some weeks previously at
which time he referred to the FBI as "the American Gestapo." Mr. Joyce
volunteered to sound out Hemingway on his attitude toward the FBI, as
casually as possible, and returned with the advice that Hemingway had
paid no particular attention to the petition he signed in 1940 denouncing
the FBI and could now hardly remember what it said; Hemingway told Mr.
Joyce that people are always shoving petitions under his nose and like
many famous people he is inclined to sign them on the request of a friend
without full information as to their contents. Hemingway also dismissed
the reference to the FBI as "the American Gestapo" as a mere jest.

The American Ambassador, nevertheless, decided to engage Hemingway's
services under his own personal direction without any direct contact with the
Legal Attache. Arrangements were made whereby copies of Hemingway's reports
would be furnished to the Legal Attache in order that the latter might be
advised of developments in investigations conducted into the Spanish
Falange by Ernest Hemingway.

These reports began to be submitted in September, 1942. At
first they related principally to individuals singled out as pro-Falange
or pro-Franco regardless of nationality. The form of the report consisted
of the original Spanish dictation of Hemingway's operative to which a sheet
of comments was attached by Hemingway signed only "E. H." The information
submitted by the Spanish operative has almost always been of the denounciation
type characteristic of European police investigations. Thus, a Spanish or
Cuban merchant would be reported as "violently pro-Franco, filled with
Totalitarian ideas and opposed to the United States and the Democratic
Powers." Details of the subject's activity or statements on which the foregoing conclusions were based were almost always lacking. In one case a
subject was denounced as a Fascist because of the out-worn character and
obstinacy of his ideas ("Por la Antiguedad y Contumacia de sus Opiniones"),
although the informant's report stated that he had no other indication of
the character or sympathies of the subject. No follow ups of the subjects
were made.

The organization which Hemingway gathered for this work was composed exclusively of Spanish Republican refugees in Cuba. Their identity
was not disclosed in Hemingway's reports but they were designated by a
number. They grew from an original force of four full-time operatives,
alleged to be former members of the Spanish police force, and 12 part-time

CONFIDENTIAL

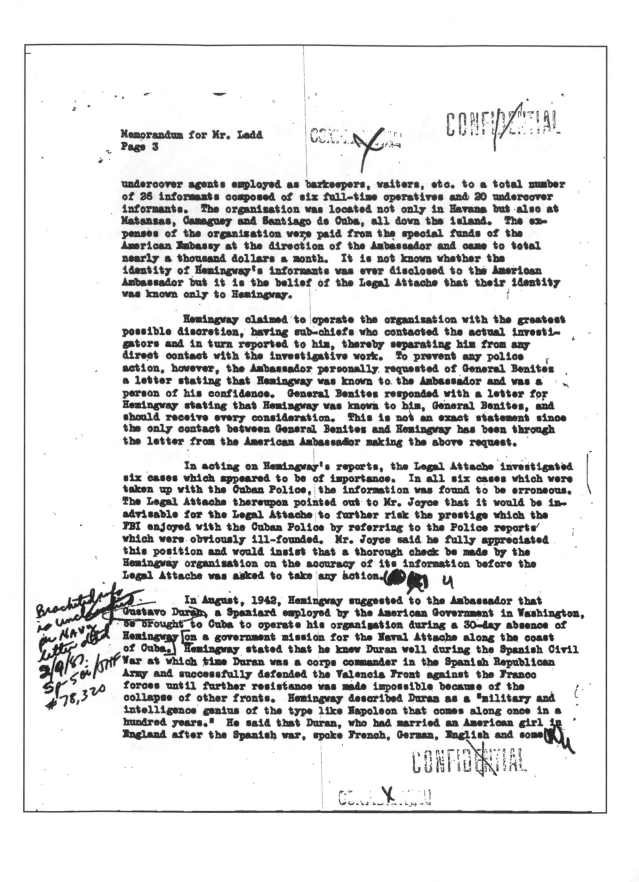

Memorandum for Mr. Ladd
Page 3

undercover agents employed as barkeepers, waiters, etc. to a total number
of 26 informants composed of six full-time operatives and 20 undercover
informants. The organization was located not only in Havana but also at
Matanzas, Camaguey and Santiago de Cuba, all down the island. The expenses of the organization were paid from the special funds of the
American Embassy at the direction of the Ambassador and came to total
nearly a thousand dollars a month. It is not known whether the
identity of Hemingway's informants was ever disclosed to the American
Ambassador but it is the belief of the Legal Attache that their identity
was known only to Hemingway.

     Hemingway claimed to operate the organization with the greatest
possible discretion, having sub-chiefs who contacted the actual investi-
gators and in turn reported to him, thereby separating him from any
direct contact with the investigative work. To prevent any police
action, however, the Ambassador personally requested of General Benitez
a letter stating that Hemingway was known to the Ambassador and was a
person of his confidence. General Benitez responded with a letter for
Hemingway stating that Hemingway was known to him, General Benitez, and
should receive every consideration. This is not an exact statement since
the only contact between General Benitez and Hemingway has been through
the letter from the American Ambassador making the above request.

     In acting on Hemingway's reports, the Legal Attache investigated
six cases which appeared to be of importance. In all six cases which were
taken up with the Cuban Police, the information was found to be erroneous.
The Legal Attache thereupon pointed out to Mr. Joyce that it would be in-
advisable for the Legal Attache to further risk the prestige which the
FBI enjoyed with the Cuban Police by referring to the Police reports
which were obviously ill-founded. Mr. Joyce said he fully appreciated
this position and would insist that a thorough check be made by the
Hemingway organization on the accuracy of its information before the
Legal Attache was asked to take any action.

     In August, 1942, Hemingway suggested to the Ambassador that
Gustavo Duran, a Spaniard employed by the American Government in Washington,
be brought to Cuba to operate his organization during a 30-day absence of
Hemingway on a government mission for the Naval Attache along the coast
of Cuba. Hemingway stated that he knew Duran well during the Spanish Civil
War at which time Duran was a corps commander in the Spanish Republican
Army and successfully defended the Valencia Front against the Franco
forces until further resistance was made impossible because of the
collapse of other fronts. Hemingway described Duran as a "military and
intelligence genius of the type like Napoleon that comes along once in a
hundred years." He said that Duran, who had married an American girl in
England after the Spanish war, spoke French, German, English and some

Memorandum for Mr. Ladd
Page 4

Russian; that he was pure Republican, not a Communist, and would get
to the bottom of the Falange in short order. Hemingway said that Duran
was wasting his time as an employee of the Division of Cultural Relations
in the Department of State and should be brought to Cuba to direct
Hemingway's intelligence organization at least for this limited period.
It was learned by the Legal Attache that Duran was actually an employee of
the Coordinator of Inter-American Affairs, for which reason it was pointed
out by the Legal Attache to the Ambassador that Duran's assignment in
connection with intelligence work in Cuba might raise jurisdictional questions
in Washington. The Ambassador took the position that Duran would be working
directly under the Embassy and in any event his assignment was only
temporary for a period of 30 days.

Mr. Duran arrived in Cuba early in November, 1942, and began
working with Hemingway. His work has not been of the same sensational
character as Hemingway's, as noted below, but has not been in any way
different or distinct from the type of reports which Hemingway had submitted.
These reports as mentioned above are of the type received by Bureau Field
Divisions from voluntary complainants, being unspecific and unverified
and showing no continuing investigation to establish a line of conduct or
suspicious activities by the subject.

The only innovation introduced by Mr. Duran was an attempted
partial coverage of public opinion in Cuba in relation to the war and the
United States submitted in reports entitled "The Voice of the Street."
These reports contain quotations from persons in cafes, bars and pool rooms
and claim to set out the opinion of the people regarding developments in
the war. They are, however, limited to the type of individual met in
such places and, in the opinion of the Legal Attache, do not represent a
fair cross section of general public opinion. Likewise, in the extent of
their coverage, these reports have not given the opinions of sufficient
persons to warrant the conclusion that they reflect the thoughts of even
this general class of Cuban individuals.

The American Ambassador, however, has been highly impressed with
this type of information and on his return from a trip to Washington in
December, 1942, remarked that the reports were very well thought of in
the Department of State.

Although Hemingway's services were engaged to investigate the
Spanish Falange in Cuba, he soon branched out to cover the entire field
of intelligence.

After reading an article in the New York Times about a new type
of oxygen-powered submarine used by the Germans, Hemingway instituted an
investigation of the supply and distribution of oxygen and oxygen tanks in

Memorandum for Mr. Ladd
Page 5

CONFIDENTIAL   CONFIDENTIAL

Cuba. He immediately advised that "at last with this development we
have come to the point after months of work where we are about to crack
the submarine refuelling problem." Shortly afterwards, his investigation
was referred to the Legal Attache by the Embassy and a check was made on
the supply and distribution of oxygen and oxygen tanks throughout Cuba
with the result that the available supplies were well-accounted for.
[The Naval Attache also participated in this investigation.] Nothing
further was heard from Hemingway about the subject.

Hemingway's investigations began to show a marked hostility
to the Cuban Police and in a lesser degree to the FBI.

About a week before the visit of President Batista to Washington,
Hemingway sent in a report, presumably prepared by him, alleging preparations by General Benitez to seize power in Cuba and make himself President
during Batista's absence from the country. This report stated that
Benitez had no such ideas until his own trip to Washington "which had been
so successful." The report alleged that Benitez was training a large
squadron of motor cycle police officers with patrol cars and that the
police force was being trained daily with rifles as a military unit.
The report said that it was Benitez's plan to take Cuba while Batista and
the American Ambassador, the two strongest individuals in Cuba, were absent
and that an investigation should be commenced at once to uncover the
preparations of Benitez in securing fire arms and steel protection shields
for the motor cycle and squad cars.

Mr. Joyce asked the Legal Attache to check on this report.
The Legal Attache pointed out that no such preparations as Hemingway
alleged were observed by FBI Agents working in daily contact at Police
headquarters and that the training of the Cuban Police force with rifles
is a practice which has gone on for years inasmuch as the Cuban National
Police is an integral part of the Cuban Army. The danger of alienating
police cooperation by this type of report was also pointed out to Mr.
Joyce inasmuch as, according to a well known maxim "there are no secrets
in Cuba."

In the case of Prince Camilo Ruspoli, Italian Fascist leader
interned by the Cuban authorities but confined to a clinic because of
illness, Hemingway reported that Ruspoli had paid off the Cuban Chief of
Police, General Benitez, and was not really ill, and inferred that the
Legal Attache had accepted the word of the police as to the guarding of
Ruspoli at the clinic without any investigation. Through Mr. Joyce,
Hemingway was requested by the Legal Attache to secure details as to the
actual state of health of Ruspoli. He promised to do so through an under-
cover operative employed as a male nurse at the particular clinic where
Ruspoli was confined. Nothing further was heard from Hemingway about
this phase of the investigation.

Bracketed
info is un-
classified per
NAVY letter
dtd 2/4/87.
Sq-Sec DNF
4/6/87.
78,320

CONFIDENTIAL

CONFIDENTIAL

Memorandum for Mr. Ladd   CONFIDENTIAL   CONFIDENTIAL
Page 6

        In December, 1942, however, Hemingway reported that Ruspoli
had attended a public luncheon in honor of the new Spanish Charge
d'Affaires, Pelayo Garcia Olay, at the Hotel Nacional. This report
greatly disturbed the Ambassador; there was an immediate check at the
Hotel Nacional by the Legal Attache and no substantiation of the public
luncheon or the presence of Ruspoli could be found either from the
hotel management and employees or from two of the guests alleged to have
been present. The Ambassador was so advised and later Hemingway wrote
a memorandum asking that his source, a waiter at the hotel, not be
"grilled" by the FBI as this would destroy his usefulness; he also asked
to see our proofs regarding the absence of Prince Ruspoli from this
public luncheon.

        Hemingway reported sighting a contact between a submarine
and the Spanish steamer SS Marques de Comillas at high noon on December 9,
1942, off the Cuban coast. Hemingway was ostensibly fishing with Winston
Guest and four Spaniards as crew members, but actually was on a confidential
mission for the Naval Attache. The report was referred to the Legal
Attache, both by the Embassy and by the Naval Attache with the request for
investigation. The Legal Attache's investigation consisted of interview,
with Cuban Police cooperation, of forty crew members and some fifty
passengers of the vessel, most of the latter known anti-Fascists re-
patriated from Spain. None of the persons interviewed would admit
sighting a submarine as Hemingway had from his 36-foot launch. The
negative results of this inquiry were reported. Thereupon Hemingway submitted a memorandum stating that it would be a tragedy if the submarine
were carrying saboteurs possibly let off the steamship at this point on
a mission to the United States and that the Legal Attache discounted
Hemingway's report because it had not come from an FBI Agent, thereby
permitting the saboteurs to land in the United States without advance
notice.

        In January, 1943, Mr. Joyce of the Embassy asked the assistance
of the Legal Attache in ascertaining the contents of a tightly wrapped
box left by a suspect at the Bar Basque under conditions suggesting
that the box contained espionage information. The box had been recovered
from the Bar Basque by an operative of Hemingway. The Legal Attache made
private arrangements for opening the box and returned the contents to
Hemingway through Mr. Joyce. The box contained only a cheap edition of
the "Life of St. Teresa." Hemingway was present and appeared irritated
that nothing more was produced and later told an Assistant Legal Attache
that he was sure that we had withdrawn the vital material and had shown
him something worthless. When this statement was challenged by the
Assistant Legal Attache, Hemingway jocularly said he was only joking but
that he thought something was funny about the whole business of the box.

                                        CONFIDENTIAL

                        CONFIDENTIAL

Bracketed
info in this
¶ [illegible]
per NAVy letter
[illegible] 2/4/87.
SP-54/JMF
4/6/87

CONFIDENTIAL

Memorandum for Mr. Ladd
Page 7

Hemingway's ill-disguised hostility to the FBI became more
evident in February, 1943 when the Ambassador received charges that
Special Agent Knoblaugh, just assigned to the Embassy as Assistant Legal
Attache, was a participant of the Franco movement in Spain and had
acted as a paid Franco propagandist. The Ambassador declined to disclose the source of these charges when they were promptly challenged
and proof demanded by the Legal Attache. The latter learned, however,
positively that the charges were given to the Ambassador by Ernest
Hemingway and Gustavo Duran, as ascertained from a highly reliable and
confidential source within the Embassy. The charges centered about a
book written by Special Agent Knoblaugh "Correspondent in Spain" upon
his return from assignment as Associated Press correspondent in Madrid
in 1938. Hemingway knew Special Agent Knoblaugh at that time and was
most friendly with him. He had met him in Havana immediately after
Special Agent Knoblaugh's arrival. Although ostensibly friendly,
Hemingway made no remark to Special Agent Knoblaugh concerning his book
or to the Legal Attache but took his complaint directly to the Ambassador.
The latter admitted that he had read only the first forty pages of the
book and after originally requesting the Legal Attache to have Mr.
Knoblaugh transferred to some other position where the Spanish Falange
was not the acute problem which the Ambassador believed it to be in Cuba,
the Ambassador dismissed the subject as "not as important as he had
originally thought."

In personal relations Hemingway has maintained a surface show
of friendship and interest with representatives of the FBI. Through
statements he has made to reliable contacts of the Legal Attache, however,
it is known that Hemingway and his assistant, Gustavo Duran, have a low
esteem for the work of the FBI which they consider to be methodical,
unimaginative and performed by persons of comparative youth without
experience in foreign countries and knowledge of international intrigue
and politics. Both Hemingway and Duran, it is also known, have personal
hostility to the FBI on an idealogical basis, especially Hemingway, as
he considers the FBI anti-Liberal, pro-Fascist and dangerous as developing into an American Gestapo.

Although Hemingway's opinions coincide with those of some
Communists in this regard, he has repeatedly asserted that he is anti-
Communist and that he was as much opposed to the Communist influence in
the Spanish war as he was to the Fascist.

As of April 1, 1943, however, Hemingway's activities as an
undercover informant for the American Ambassador were terminated. This
resulted from general dissatisfaction over the reports submitted, and the
strong position against these services taken by Mr. Albert Nufer, Commercial
Counsellor of the Embassy and a highly respected State Department official.
An additional factor in motivating the Ambassador's action was the

CONFIDENTIAL

CONFIDENTIAL

CONFIDENTIAL

Memorandum for Mr. Ladd
Page 8

inconsistency of continuing to employ an undercover organization operated
by Hemingway at a time when the Ambassador was discouraging and restricting
the employment of paid informants by the official attaches of the Embassy.

While the investigation of suspects as such is discontinued,
the Ambassador has requested Mr. Gustavo Duran to continue to turn in
reports on public opinion in Cuba as previously undertaken by him in
"The Voice of the Street." The Ambassador made this request of Mr.
Duran because he feels that these reports give him an "inside picture"
of what people are thinking in Cuba which he did not get in any other way;
further, on his trip to Washington in December, 1942, the Ambassador was
informed at the Department of State that these reports are received with
great interest and for this reason he is desirous of continuing to submit
them to Washington. A force of two or three Spanish agents will continue
to gather this material for Mr. Duran with expenses estimated at no more
than $200.00 per month. Mr. Duran is now employed at the American Embassy
at Havana on a permanent basis as a member of the Auxiliary Foreign
Service. His time is devoted to analyzing political comments and articles
in the Cuban press and assisting the Ambassador in the preparation of
speeches to be delivered in Spanish.

The Legal Attache has mentioned to the American Ambassador that
FBI representatives are prepared to gather and submit reports on public
opinion. The Ambassador has shown no desire to take advantage of the
investigative service of the FBI in this field. The Legal Attache at
Havana states that the Ambassador has always regarded the Hemingway
organization as a pet project of his own and in continuing a minor phase
of its work the Ambassador has given the Legal Attache the impression
that he is unwilling, not merely for Hemingway's sake but his own, to
order a complete dissolution of Hemingway's organization. Hemingway,
however, is not directly operating "The Voice of the Street" investigations
but has turned them over entirely to Mr. Gustavo Duran.

The action of the Ambassador was delicately handled, being based
on the position that Mr. Hemingway's organization had filled the breach
at a time when the FBI and Cuban Police were just beginning to organize
their services in Cuba but as all this was now done no further need existed
for the "excellent work" produced by Hemingway.

Regarding this work, the Legal Attache points out that while none
of it on checking has proved of value, it is nevertheless so extensive and
all inclusive regarding the reporting of suspects that at any time a real
espionage case may develop on a subject signaled by Hemingway. The Legal
Attache therefore points out that it is unwise to characterize Hemingway's
work in a derogatory manner as subsequent evidence may uncover a case
which he could claim originated from him.

CONFIDENTIAL

CONFIDENTIAL

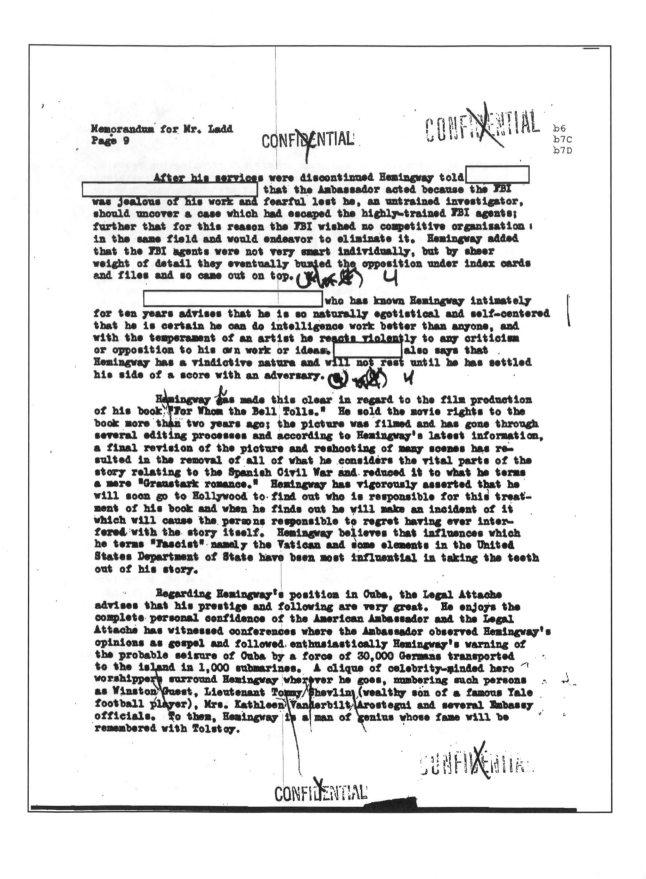

CONFIDENTIAL   CONFIDENTIAL

b6
b7C
b7D

After his services were discontinued Hemingway told ▮▮▮▮▮
▮▮▮▮▮▮▮▮▮▮▮▮ that the Ambassador acted because the FBI
was jealous of his work and fearful lest he, an untrained investigator,
should uncover a case which had escaped the highly-trained FBI agents;
further that for this reason the FBI wished no competitive organisation
in the same field and would endeavor to eliminate it. Hemingway added
that the FBI agents were not very smart individually, but by sheer
weight of detail they eventually buried the opposition under index cards
and files and so came out on top.

▮▮▮▮▮▮▮▮▮▮ who has known Hemingway intimately
for ten years advises that he is so naturally egotistical and self-centered
that he is certain he can do intelligence work better than anyone, and
with the temperament of an artist he reacts violently to any criticism
or opposition to his own work or ideas. ▮▮▮▮▮▮ also says that
Hemingway has a vindictive nature and will not rest until he has settled
his side of a score with an adversary.

Hemingway has made this clear in regard to the film production
of his book "For Whom the Bell Tolls." He sold the movie rights to the
book more than two years ago; the picture was filmed and has gone through
several editing processes and according to Hemingway's latest information,
a final revision of the picture and reshooting of many scenes has resulted in the removal of all of what he considers the vital parts of the
story relating to the Spanish Civil War and reduced it to what he terms
a mere "Granstark romance." Hemingway has vigorously asserted that he
will soon go to Hollywood to find out who is responsible for this treatment of his book and when he finds out he will make an incident of it
which will cause the persons responsible to regret having ever interfered with the story itself. Hemingway believes that influences which
he terms "Fascist" namely the Vatican and some elements in the United
States Department of State have been most influential in taking the teeth
out of his story.

Regarding Hemingway's position in Cuba, the Legal Attache
advises that his prestige and following are very great. He enjoys the
complete personal confidence of the American Ambassador and the Legal
Attache has witnessed conferences where the Ambassador observed Hemingway's
opinions as gospel and followed enthusiastically Hemingway's warning of
the probable seizure of Cuba by a force of 30,000 Germans transported
to the island in 1,000 submarines. A clique of celebrity-minded hero
worshippers surround Hemingway wherever he goes, numbering such persons
as Winston Guest, Lieutenant Tommy Shevlin (wealthy son of a famous Yale
football player), Mrs. Kathleen Vanderbilt Arostegui and several Embassy
officials. To them, Hemingway is a man of genius whose fame will be
remembered with Tolstoy.

CONFIDENTIAL   CONFIDENTIAL

Memorandum for Mr. Ladd
Page 10

~~CONFIDENTIAL~~   ~~CONFIDENTIAL~~

Hemingway claims great political influence and told an Assistant Legal Attache that the FBI had better get along with him because he carried a lot of weight in Washington. The principal political influence of Hemingway known to the Legal Attache is that Hemingway's wife, the former Martha Gelhorn, is a personal and literary friend of Mrs. Eleanor Roosevelt and has a standing invitation to stay at the White House when in Washington.

Hemingway is gathering material for a book at the present time. Although his intelligence activities have ended, he is on a special confidential assignment for the Naval Attache chasing submarines along the Cuban coast and keeping a careful observance on the movements of Spanish steamers which occasionally come to Cuba. This naval patrol work of Mr. Hemingway is regarded by him and the Naval Attache as extremely confidential and is known to the Legal Attache purely through unofficial sources.

These brackets unclassified per NAVY letter dtd 2/9/87. Sp Scipio 4/30/87

RECOMMENDATION

The Legal Attache at Havana expresses his belief that Hemingway is fundamentally hostile to the FBI and might readily endeavor at any time to cause trouble for us. Because of his peculiar nature, it is the belief of the Legal Attache that Hemingway would go to great lengths to embarrass the Bureau if an incident should arise. In view of his prestige as a literary man, accepted by large sections of public opinion in matters not related to writing, it is the recommendation of the Legal Attache at Havana that great discretion be exercised in avoiding an incident with Ernest Hemingway.

Respectfully,

C. H. Carson

Addendum: 6-21-43--I do not concur with the conclusion reached in this memorandum. The Bureau has by careful and impartial investigation from time to time disproved practically all of the so-called Hemingway information. I don't care what his contacts are or what his background is -- I see no reason why we should make any effort to avoid exposing him for the phoney that he is. I don't think we should go out of our way to do this but most certainly if in the protection of the Bureau's interest it is necessary to meet him head-on, I don't think we should try to avoid such an issue. I am also in strong disagreement with the statement contained in the last paragraph on page 8 of this memorandum. Since our investigation has disproved all of Hemingway's alleged facts, I see no reason why, if and when we are asked by persons entitled to a frank answer, that we should fail to so state. I think it is preposterous to take the position that we should not speak disparagingly of his information "because it might be of some value in the future". Such a premise is basically unsound.

CONFIDENTIAL   CONFIDENTIAL   *Edw. A. Tamm*

CONFIDENTIAL

ALL INFORMATION CONTAINED
HEREIN IS UNCLASSIFIED
EXCEPT WHERE SHOWN
OTHERWISE

Original cannot be located and is not on record. When original is received in Files Division it will be filed either with this copy or may be given a new serial.

June 21, 1943

MEMORANDUM FOR   MR. LADD

With regard to the attached memorandum which was prepared by Mr. Leddy, Legal Attache at Havana, Cuba, and with regard to Mr. Tamm's addendum thereof, I think it only fair to point out that the memorandum is probably misleading in so far as correctly or accurately expressing exactly what Mr. Leddy had in mind. In the first place I think that the report with regard to Leddy's dealings with Hemingway and Ambassador Braden in connection with Hemingway's organization more or less speaks for itself. Leddy has never at any time so far as we can tell at the Seat of Government shown the slightest inclination to sidestep any challange with regard to Hemingway wherever he felt that Bureau interests were involved to the slightest extent. It will be recalled that Mr. Leddy immediately after Ambassador Braden made his arrangements whereby Hemingway would carry on investigations through his so-called informants for the Embassy, sought Bureau permission to approach Ambassador Braden and point out that this would constitute a violation of the Bureau's jurisdiction. It will be recalled that the Bureau did not authorize Agent Leddy to take such action. I do know, however, that upon every occasion where opportunity presented itself for Hemingway and the quality of his work and his informants to be discussed with Braden arose, Leddy unhesitatingly pointed out to Mr. Braden exactly what the true situation and facts were to the knowledge of Leddy.

RECORDED   64-23312-6X1

During a conversation which I had with Robert Joyce of the Embassy at Havana, Joyce mentioned to me that Leddy, early in the scope of Hemingway's operations, convinced Joyce that the Hemingway setup was not propitious and was not altogether sound. Joyce is a professed personal friend of Hemingway and of Braden. Joyce told me that Leddy handled this entire matter both with Joyce and Ambassador Braden in a scrupulously fair, impartial and direct manner. I believe it quite pertinent to note that despite Ambassador Braden's and Joyce's protestations of friendship and admiration for Hemingway, the latter is no longer in any way connected with the American Embassy in Havana, which fact, is attributed to Leddy having furnished the true facts to Joyce and the Ambassador and also having utilized the opportunity of Ambassador Braden insisting upon knowing the identity of the Attache's informants by pointing out to the Ambassador the incongruity of having the Attaches required to furnish the identity of informants and Hemingway not similarly required.

It should be further recalled that in connection with the matter involving Special Agent Knoblaugh in Havana, Leddy handled this in a very

CLASS. & EXT.
REASON - FCIM A. 1-2. 4. 2 (3)
DATE OF REVIEW 10-26-89

CONFIDENTIAL

CONFIDENTIAL

Memorandum for Mr. Ladd   page 2

firm and uncompromising manner. He accepted the challenge and insisted that
the Ambassador produce substantiation with regard to the allegations that
Knoblaugh is a Falangist; this the Ambassador could not do; whereupon, Leddy
together with Knoblaugh pointed out to the Ambassador information which would
seem to completely explode any charges to the effect that Knoblaugh is Falangist.
This caused Ambassador Braden in so far as his dealings with Leddy are concerned,
to immediately backdown with regard to his request that Knoblaugh be removed from
Cuba.

With regard to the wording contained in the last paragraph of the
memorandum on page 8, it is believed that this is somewhat unfortunate in
setting out what Mr. Leddy actually had in mind. It is known to the writer
that Leddy has upon his own initiative whenever called upon to do so by the
Ambassador and by Joyce, advised these two unhesitatingly that the information
furnished by Hemingway and the latter's organization was completely unfounded
and unsubstantiated in every single instance. Leddy, of course, accomplished
this by furnishing the results of his, Leddy's, check as to the reports of
Hemingway. I am quite sure that what he intended to express in the unfortunately
worded paragraph is that he does not feel that information furnished by Hemingway
should be ignored and disregarded as having come from unreliable sources merely
because such information has in the past proved unsubstantiated. It is believed
that he is also seeking to point out what is true with regard to many informants,
professional in character, namely, that these individuals furnish information
in such a way and in such an all-inclusive nature with regard to conjecture,
probabilities, and vaguely worded allegations that it is impossible to definitely
establish that no truth whatsoever is contained in the allegations and information
furnished. It is believed that Mr. Leddy will agree with the Bureau if inquiry
should be made by persons entitled to know the truth, he respond by furnishing
the exact facts in so far as information furnished to the office of the Legal
Attache by Hemingway is concerned, that is that the information has been in no
way verified or substantiated by investigation.

                                    Respectfully,

                                    C. H. Carson

CONFIDENTIAL

CONFIDENTIAL   CONFIDENTIAL

OFFICE OF THE LEGAL ATTACHE

ALL INFORMATION CONTAINED
HEREIN IS UNCLASSIFIED
EXCEPT WHERE SHOWN
OTHERWISE

EMBASSY OF THE
UNITED STATES OF AMERICA
HABANA, CUBA

August 13, 1943

Director,
Federal Bureau of Investigation,
Washington, D. C.

CLASS. & EXT. BY _____
REASON FCIM II 4-2 _____
DATE OF REVIEW _____

Re: ERNEST HEMINGWAY

Dear Sir:

John Kelly

SIS #357 advises that Mr. Hemingway, of whose
intelligence activities under Ambassador Spruille Braden
the Bureau has been previously advised, is currently
engaged in writing a book based on his experiences in
that work. Hemingway states that all of the people
whom he has known during the last year in Cuba in connection with intelligence work will appear in his book,
including Ambassador Braden. We are not yet informed
as to what role the representatives of the FBI will
play, but in view of Hemingway's known sentiments, will
probably be portrayed as the dull, heavy-footed,
unimaginative professional policeman type. (X)u

[_____] has advised that in recent conversations with Hemingway, he has indicated that the
Federal Bureau of Investigation is only a mediocre
intelligence organization. He has also made reference
to the departure of SIS #788, with the statement that
he succeeded in having this Bureau Agent removed from
Cuba by use of his great personal influence with
Ambassador Spruille Braden.

b2
b6
b7C
b7D

RECORDED & INDEXED   64-23312-7XI

Very truly yours,

FEDERAL BUREAU OF INVESTIGATION
AUG 17 1943
U. S. DEPARTMENT OF JUSTICE

R. G. LEDDY
Legal Attaché

10/26/79
CLASS. & EXT. BY _____
REASON - FCIM 11, 1 4.2 _____
DATE OF REVIEW 10/26/89

RGL:RM   Classified by _____
              Declassify on: OADR
              239261

CONFIDENTIAL

77 AUG 27 1943

Blue memo for Mr. Ladd
8-21-43   A.R.A.

CONFIDENTIAL

ARA:FJS
Memo to Ladd fr. Carson dated 8/21/43
Memo for Director dated 9/20/43
CLASSIFIED DECISIONS FINALIZED
BY DEPARTMENT REVIEW COMMITTEE October 14, 1943
DATE:

In reply, please refer to
File No.   RECORDED

64-23312-7X2

[SIS #396]

PERSONAL AND CONFIDENTIAL
VIA DIPLOMATIC AIR COURIER POUCH

CLASS. & EXT. BY SR
REASON - FCIM 11, 1-   4.2 (2)(3)
DATE OF REVIEW   10/26/89

CLASS. & EXT. BY
REASON-FCIM 11.
DATE OF REVIEW

Re: Ernest Hemingway
     Latin American Matters

Dear Sir:

Classified by
Declassify on OADR

Reference is made to your radiogram dated September 18, 1943, concerning a book which had been previously reported to be under consideration by Ernest Hemingway, the subject matter to be based on his intelligence experiences in Cuba.

It is desired that you take steps to insure that Bureau personnel assigned to the Embassy and operating under cover be on the alert to report any information received that would indicate Ernest Hemingway's plans to include mention of the Bureau in any publication which he may be preparing or about to prepare.

It is further requested that the Bureau be kept advised as to the whereabouts of Ernest Hemingway and as to the date of his departure from Cuba for the United States.

It is suggested that this letter should be destroyed when it has served your purpose.

Classified by
Declassify on OADR

Very truly yours,

John Edgar Hoover
Director

COMMUNICATIONS SECTION
M A I L E D 7
★ OCT 14 1943 P.M.
FEDERAL BUREAU OF INVESTIGATION
U. S. DEPARTMENT OF JUSTICE

OCT 20 1943

CONFIDENTIAL

CONFIDENTIAL

ARA:HH
64-4461-247

DO-11

FEDERAL BUREAU OF INVESTIGATION
CONFIDENTIAL
DATE August 21, 1943

Mr. Tolson
Mr. E. A. Tamm
Mr. Clegg
Mr. Coffey
Mr. Glavin
Mr. Ladd
Mr. Nichols
Mr. Rosen
Mr. Tracy
Mr. Acers
Mr. Carson
Mr. Harbo
Mr. Hendon
Mr. Mumford
Mr. Starke
Mr. Quinn Tamm
Tele. Room
Mr. Nease
Miss Beahm
Miss Gandy

ALL INFORMATION CONTAINED
HEREIN IS UNCLASSIFIED
EXCEPT WHERE SHOWN
OTHERWISE

MEMORANDUM FOR MR. LADD

Re: Ernest Hemingway – Cuba

BACKGROUND

The following information is of interest in connection with the activities of Ernest Hemingway in Cuba and his attitude toward the Bureau representatives in that country. Information concerning the complete extent of Hemingway's intelligence activities under the personal direction of the American Ambassador in Cuba, has been previously brought to your attention.

DETAILS

Recently, Ernest Hemingway advised a Bureau undercover representative in Cuba concerning a book which Hemingway is currently writing, based on his experiences in intelligence activities under the American Ambassador. Hemingway stated that all of the people whom he has dealt with during the past year in Cuba in intelligence matters will be mentioned in the book, including Ambassador Braden. In this connection the Bureau legal attache at Havana states that no information has been received as to what extent FBI representatives will be mentioned in the book.

However, Hemingway's attitude toward the FBI is already known, as indicated by Hemingway's action in signing a petition castigating the Bureau in connection with the Detroit Spanish Enlistment Case in 1940, and more recently indicated in Hemingway's remark that the FBI is "the American Gestapo".

A confidential informant of the Bureau legal attache in Havana reports that in a recent conversation with Hemingway, the latter indicated that the FBI is but a mediocre intelligence organization. Hemingway also commented on the recent departure of Special Agent [   ] from Cuba.

INFORMATIVE MEMORANDUM - NOT TO BE SENT TO FILES SECTION

Mr. Ladd
Page 2

ACTION

No action is recommended in this matter at the present time, and the above information is being set out to supplement information previously called to your attention concerning Ernest Hemingway.

Respectfully,

C. H. Carson

We ought to try
& keep close to this
development.

OFFICE OF THE LEGAL ATTACHÉ

CONFIDENTIAL

'ALL INFORMATION CONTAINED
HEREIN IS UNCLASSIFIED
EXCEPT WHERE SHOWN
OTHERWISE

EMBASSY OF THE
UNITED STATES OF AMERICA
HABANA, CUBA

September 21, 1943

Director,
Federal Bureau of Investigation,
Washington, D. C.

DECLASSIFIED BY
ON

Re: ERNEST HEMINGWAY
     Cuba Latin American Matters

CLASS. & EXT. BY
REASON - FCIM 11,
DATE OF REVIEW

Dear Sir:

On September 13, 1943, SIS #213 accepted an invitation
to have lunch with Subject at his finca located in San Francisco
15 kilometers from Habana. There was no other person present.
Hemingway was quite talkative but kept away from controversial
subjects. He revealed that MARTHA GELLHORN HEMINGWAY, his present wife, left for the United States the first week in
September, and planned to talk with her publishers about the book
which she has been writing for the past few months. Hemingway
had previously informed the writer that he had proofread the
work of his wife, and was convinced that she had something worth
while. He further revealed that after conferring with her publishers, it was her intention to join the Allied Forces invading
Europe as a correspondent for Colliers. She is expected to be
gone for five or six months.

Hemingway stated that he is tired of being on land
with nothing to do and is anxious to return to his confidential
work (which, we are confidentially advised, is patrol duty in
the Caribbean waters on behalf of the U. S. Navy) On September 13,
1943, he stated that he expected to leave on or before the 20th,
but in conversation with him on September 20, he told the writer
that he would not be able to leave before September 22 or 23
due to delay in repairs to his boat. As in the past, he is to
be accompanied by WINSTON GUEST and a small crew. He explained
that the usual procedure is to patrol for twelve hours, ostensibly
fishing, and tie up at whatever dock is convenient every night.
This particular trip is expected to last approximately two
months. At the expiration of this trip, Hemingway plans to
spend from six to eight weeks in New York City and Long Island,
making the round of the night spots and duck shooting on Long
Island, as he expressed it.

RECORDED
&
INDEXED

64-23312-10

FEDERAL BUREAU OF INVESTIGATION
D- SEP 24 1943
U. S. DEPARTMENT

CONFIDENTIAL

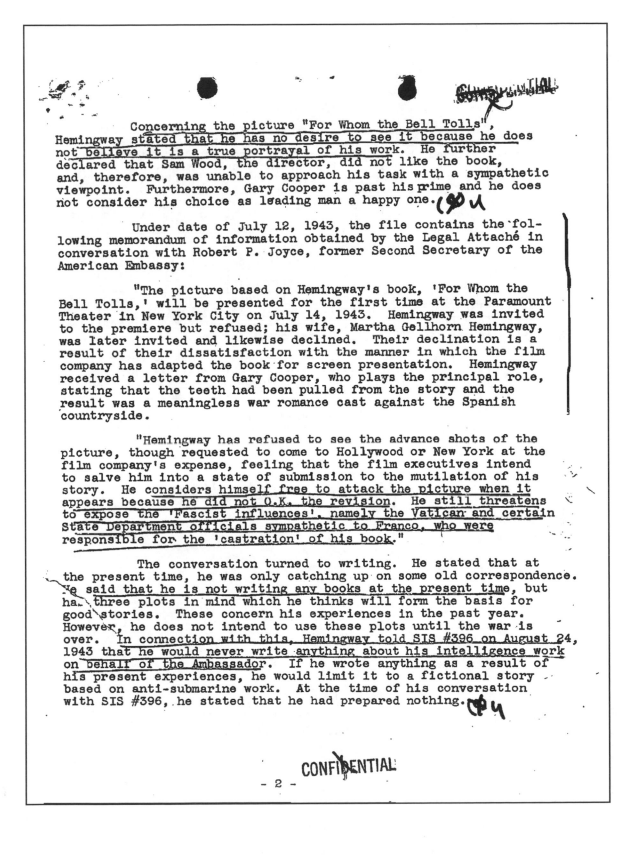

Concerning the picture "For Whom the Bell Tolls", Hemingway stated that he has no desire to see it because he does not believe it is a true portrayal of his work. He further declared that Sam Wood, the director, did not like the book, and, therefore, was unable to approach his task with a sympathetic viewpoint. Furthermore, Gary Cooper is past his prime and he does not consider his choice as leading man a happy one.

Under date of July 12, 1943, the file contains the following memorandum of information obtained by the Legal Attaché in conversation with Robert P. Joyce, former Second Secretary of the American Embassy:

"The picture based on Hemingway's book, 'For Whom the Bell Tolls,' will be presented for the first time at the Paramount Theater in New York City on July 14, 1943. Hemingway was invited to the premiere but refused; his wife, Martha Gellhorn Hemingway, was later invited and likewise declined. Their declination is a result of their dissatisfaction with the manner in which the film company has adapted the book for screen presentation. Hemingway received a letter from Gary Cooper, who plays the principal role, stating that the teeth had been pulled from the story and the result was a meaningless war romance cast against the Spanish countryside.

"Hemingway has refused to see the advance shots of the picture, though requested to come to Hollywood or New York at the film company's expense, feeling that the film executives intend to salve him into a state of submission to the mutilation of his story. He considers himself free to attack the picture when it appears because he did not O.K. the revision. He still threatens to expose the 'Fascist influences', namely the Vatican and certain State Department officials sympathetic to Franco, who were responsible for the 'castration' of his book."

The conversation turned to writing. He stated that at the present time, he was only catching up on some old correspondence. He said that he is not writing any books at the present time, but ha three plots in mind which he thinks will form the basis for good stories. These concern his experiences in the past year. However, he does not intend to use these plots until the war is over. In connection with this, Hemingway told SIS #396 on August 24, 1943 that he would never write anything about his intelligence work on behalf of the Ambassador. If he wrote anything as a result of his present experiences, he would limit it to a fictional story based on anti-submarine work. At the time of his conversation with SIS #396, he stated that he had prepared nothing.

CONFIDENTIAL

CONFIDENTIAL

        In a discussion of columnists, Hemingway stated that
DREW PEARSON is known to him only slightly. However, he has
always believed that in his search for sensational stories, he
frequently makes statements that are only half truths. As an
example of this tendency, he referred to an article that Pearson
had written in his column, "The Daily Washington Merry-Go-Round,"
in which Pearson stated that individuals who had fought in the
Abraham Lincoln Brigade in the Spanish Civil War were discriminated
against by U. S. Army authorities when they sought admission to
Officers' Training School. Although Hemingway thinks that members
of the Abraham Lincoln Brigade have been the subjects of discrimination, he stated that Pearson was unfortunate in his choice of
examples. According to Hemingway, each individual that Pearson
claimed was refused admission to Officers' Training School was
an out and out Communist, having attended a Communist Indoctrination
School located in the Catskill Mountains in New York State. In
these instances, Hemingway affirmed that the Army was perfectly
justified in the action which was taken.

        Regarding his work, Hemingway stated that he never
intended to find himself in any such line of activity. His
explanation for organizing an intelligence service which was in
operation until April 1, 1943, was that he did so when specifically
requested to do so by the Ambassador, who believed that he was
eminently qualified to aid the Embassy in gathering information
about the Spanish Falange because of his long association with
Spaniards.

                                Very truly yours,

                        [CONF. INFR. S. I. S. # 396]
                                Legal Attaché

RMD:RM

                    - 3 -   CONFIDENTIAL

ALL INFORMATION CONTAINED
HEREIN IS UNCLASSIFIED EXCEPT
WHERE SHOWN OTHERWISE

CONFIDENTIAL

CONFIDENTIAL

F.B.I. RADIOGRAM

ALL INFORMATION CONTAINED
HEREIN IS UNCLASSIFIED (U)
EXCEPT WHERE SHOWN
OTHERWISE

DECODED COPY

FROM HAVANA   9-18-43   NR 496   5:08 PM EWT
(U)   DECLASSIFIED BY 60324/BAW/DK/ntw
                             ON 11-04-2008

Mr. Tolson
Mr. E. A. Tamm
Mr. Clegg
Mr. Coffey
Mr. Glavin
Mr. Ladd
Mr. Nichols
Mr. Rosen
Mr. Tracy
Mr. Acers
Mr. Carson
Mr. Harbo
Mr. Hendon
Mr. Mumford
Mr. Starke
Mr. Quinn Tamm
Mr. Nease
Miss Gandy

RE ERNEST HEMINGWAY CUBA LATIN AMERICAN MATTERS. REFERENCE YOUR
RADIOGRAM NUMBER 328. HEMINGWAY SEPTEMBER 19 ON ANOTHER SUBMARINE
PATROL TRIP CARRIBEAN AREA AS DESCRIBED IN MY LETTER JUNE 26 PAGE 2.
EXPECTS TO BE GONE ABOUT 2 MONTHS AND IS ACCOMPANIED BY
ADVISED SIS NUMBER 213 THAT AFTER INSTANT TRIP HE WILL
PROCEED TO NEW YORK FOR VACATION FROM ONE MONTH TO SIX WEEKS DUR-
ATION. FURTHER STATED HE IS DOING NO WRITING WHATSOEVER AT PRESENT
TIME BUT HAS THREE GOOD PLOTS IN MIND FOR POST WAR BOOKS. DID NOT
INDICATE NATURE OF SUBJECT MATTER. NO FURTHER REFERENCE HAS BEEN
MADE BY HIM REGARDING PROPOSED BOOK REFERRED TO MY LETTER AUGUST
13. HIS WIFE, MARTHA GELLHORN HEMINGWAY NOW IN NEW YORK ARRANGING
FOR PUBLICATION OF HER BOOK REFERRED TO MY LETTER JUNE 26. SHE
IS PLANNING LATER TO ACCOMPANY AMERICAN INVASION TROOPS TO EUROPE
AS CORRESPONDENT FOR COLLIERS FOR FIVE OR SIX MONTHS. SUGGEST
NEWS ITEM REFERRED TO MAY BE BLIND PLANTED BY HEMINGWAY TO COVER
ACTIVITIES AND ABSENCE FROM CUBA, OR MAY REFER TO PREVIOUS TRIPS
OF SIMILAR NATURE. LEDDY.

b6
b7C

(U)   CONF. INFT. S. I. S. # 394
RECEIVED   X   [9-18-43]   5:17 PM EWT
                                           JCK
                                           DATE 06-01-2007
                                           CLASSIFIED BY 60324/BAW/JLF/cld
                                           DECLASSIFY ON: 25X 3.9(3)
NOTE: UNDERLINED PORTION OBTAINED FROM GARBLE.   06-01-2032

CLASSIFIED DECISIONS FINALIZED
BY DEPARTMENT REVIEW COMMITTEE (DRC)
DATE:

                                           Classified by
10/26/79   Declassify on: OADR
CLASS. & EXT. BY
REASON - FCIM 11
DATE OF REVIEW   10/26/89

                                           RECORDED &   64-23312-11
CLASS. & EXT. BY   INDEXED   F B I
REASON-FCIM II 1.2.4.2   31 OCT 6 1943
DATE OF REVIEW
        5-21-81

                             AAP # 96-1371
                             CLASSIFIED DECISIONS FINALIZED
                             BY DEPARTMENT REVIEW COMMITTEE (DRC)
                             DATE: 3-18-99
[9-20-43]
        If the intelligence contained in the above message is to be disseminated
        outside the Bureau, it is suggested that it be suitably paraphrased in
        order to protect the Bureau's cryptographic systems.

OCT 28 1943   CONFIDENTIAL
                                     CONFIDENTIAL

JOHN EDGAR HOOVER
DIRECTOR

Federal Bureau of Investigation
United States Department of Justice
Washington, D. C.

287   Mr. Tolson
Mr. E. A. Tamm
Mr. Clegg
Mr. Coffey
Mr. Glavin
Mr. Ladd
Mr. Nichols
Mr. Rosen
Mr. Tracy
Mr. Carson
Mr. Starke
Mr. Hendon
Mr. Mumford
Mr. Starke
Mr. Quinn Tamm
Tele. Room
Mr. Nease
Miss Beahm
Miss Gandy

ARA:rls   CONFIDENTIAL   September 20, 1943   CLASS. & EXT. BY
REASON-FCIM
DATE OF REVIEW

ALL INFORMATION CONTAINED
HEREIN IS UNCLASSIFIED
EXCEPT WHERE SHOWN
OTHERWISE

MEMORANDUM FOR THE DIRECTOR

RE: ERNEST HEMINGWAY

Background

You will recall that for a time Ernest Hemingway was
engaged in intelligence activities at the request of and under the
direct supervision of the American Ambassador in Havana, Cuba. As
of April 1, 1943, however, the Ambassador dispensed with the intelligence
services of Hemingway, and it was indicated that Hemingway's organization of
confidential informants in Cuba would no longer render reports on intelligence
matters. The Bureau Legal Attache in Havana has ascertained that Hemingway
has since April 1, 1943, continued operations in Cuba on behalf of the United
States Naval Attache; that is, operations consisting of cruising the waters
off the coast of Cuba in a small boat for the purpose of ascertaining the
extent of enemy submarine activities.

CLASS. & EXT. BY
REASON - FCIM
DATE OF REVIEW

Details

On August 13, 1943, the Bureau Legal Attache advised that Hemingway
recently told an undercover SIS Representative that he is currently writing
a book based on his experiences in intelligence activities in Cuba. Hemingway
indicated that his book would make mention of all persons whom he had contacted during the past year in Cuba concerning intelligence matters and that
he would mention Ambassador Braden among other persons. At that time the
undercover Agent was unable to ascertain to what extent FBI Representatives
would be mentioned in the forthcoming book by Hemingway. Of course,
Hemingway's attitude toward the Bureau has been expressed by Hemingway's
action in signing a petition criticizing the Bureau in connection with the
Detroit Spanish Enlistment Case, and not long ago Hemingway remarked that
the FBI is "the American Gestapo."

RECORDED
&
INDEXED

During the week of September 12, 1943, the New York columnist
Leonard Lyons stated in his column that Ernest Hemingway had departed
Cuba, without further elaboration.

The Bureau Legal Attache in Havana advises that Hemingway departed
from Cuba on September 19, 1943, on another submarine patrol trip in
the Caribbean area, accompanied by Winston Guest, and expects to be
gone for approximately two months, after which Hemingway stated he will

FOR VICTORY
BUY
UNITED
STATES
WAR
BONDS
AND
STAMPS

- 2 -   CONFIDENTIAL

would proceed to New York for a vacation of approximately six weeks. Prior
to his departure on this most recent patrol trip, Hemingway advised a SIS
Representative that he is doing no writing at the present time whatsoever
but is considering three plots for use in writing books during the post-
war period. Hemingway has made no further reference to the proposed book
that he was previously reported to be writing concerning his intelligence
experiences in Cuba.

     Martha Gellhorn Hemingway, wife of Ernest, is presently in New
York arranging for publication of a book which she has reportedly written
concerning conditions on the Island of Martinique, based in part upon
information which Martha Gellhorn obtained from the State Department
through the assistance of a United States official in Havana.

     There has been reported no change in the situation existing
between Hemingway and the American Embassy in Havana, and Hemingway
apparently enjoys the full confidence of Ambassador Spruille Braden and
is continuing his activities on behalf of the United States Naval Attache.
Despite the ostensible discontinuance of Hemingway's intelligence activities
for the Ambassador on April 1, 1943, the Bureau Legal Attache has ascertained
that Hemingway had a quantity of gasoline charged to him from the private
stock of the Ambassador for the month of April, 1943, indicating an actual
continuance of an arrangement which had been previously in effect for the
benefit of Hemingway's intelligence organization prior to April 1, 1943.
It is also known that Hemingway's assistant in intelligence activities,
Gustavo Duran, himself allegedly a member of the Communist Party and
presently under investigation on that account, is carrying on a part of
the intelligence program which Hemingway began on behalf of Ambassador
Braden.

Action

     It appears from the latest reports submitted by the Bureau
Legal Attache in Havana that Hemingway has made no further reference to
writing a book based on his intelligence experiences in Cuba, Hemingway
having stated on the contrary that he is doing no writing whatsoever at the
present time. However, it is proposed with your approval to instruct the
Bureau Legal Attache at Havana Cuba to insure that Bureau Agents assigned
to the Embassy and operating under cover be on the alert to report any
information received that would indicate Hemingway plans to include mention
of the Bureau in any publication, which he may be in the process of preparing.

                    Respectfully,

                    D. M. Ladd   CONFIDENTIAL

...ew York, 7, N. Y.

May 22, 1944

MR. HOOVER -

RE: ERNEST HEMINGWAY

Ernest is a great admirer of you
and the Bureau. In a conversation with an
Agent of this Office, he stated that he had
met several of the Bureau representatives
while in Havana, Cuba, and he thought that
they were of an unusually high type and,
further, that their work was most effective
there. He stated that he had been very
friendly with General Benitz, who was a
ranking political power in Cuba, and he
thought it was most amusing the General
should hold his present position inasmuch
as some years ago Benitz had acted in several
Hollywood pictures in which he played "Latin
lover" roles.

E. E. CONROY

ALL INFORMATION CONTAINED
HEREIN IS UNCLASSIFIED
DATE 10/26/79 BY SP-1

RECORDED
&
INDEXED

64-23312-13
F B I

32 JUN 7 1944

STANDARD FORM NO. 64

Office Memorandum • UNITED STATES GOVERNMENT

TO : MR. FLETCHER   CONFIDENTIAL   ALL INFORMATION CONTAINED   30, 1949
                                          HEREIN IS UNCLASSIFIED
FROM : V. P. KEAY   EXCEPT WHERE SHOWN
                                          OTHERWISE
SUBJECT: REQUEST FROM THE OFFICE OF THE SECRETARY
OF DEFENSE FOR NAME CHECK ON
ERNEST HEMINGWAY

Mr. Tolson
Mr. Clegg
Mr. Glavin
Mr. Ladd
Mr. Nichols
Mr. Rosen
Mr. Tracy
Mr. Egan
Mr. Gurnea
Mr. Harbo
Mr. Quinn Tamm
Tele. Room
Mr. Nease
Miss Holmes
Miss Gandy

        Attached hereto is a blind memorandum prepared in response to
a request from the Office of the Secretary of Defense for a check of
FBI files, to include a summary of any information which "would affect
clearance for access to highly classified material."

        In addition to the information set out in the blind memorandum
it is noted that Bureau files show that Ernest Hemingway operated an
intelligence organization for the American Ambassador in Havanna, Cuba from
August 1942 to April 1943. During this period Hemingway was in frequent
contact with the Office of the Legal Attache at Havanna, Cuba.

        The Legal Attache reported in June 1943 that in personal relations
Hemingway maintained a surface show of friendship and interest with
representatives of the FBI. Through statements he made to reliable contacts
of the Legal Attache, however, it was known that Hemingway and his assistant,
Gustavo Duran, had a low esteem for the work of the FBI which they considered
to be methodical, unimaginative, and performed by persons of comparative youth
without experience in foreign countries and knowledge of international
intrigue and politics. Both Hemingway and Duran, it was also known, had
personal hostility to the FBI on an ideological basis, especially Hemingway;
that he considered the FBI anti-Liberal, pro-Fascist, and dangerous of developing into an American Gestapo.

        It is noted that Ernest Hemingway was a principal signer of the
denunciation of the FBI in the Detroit Communist-Spanish Enlistment Case in
1940. In addition the Legal Attache advised that on meeting Hemingway some
weeks previously the latter had referred to the FBI as "The American Gestapo".
At the request of the Legal Attache Hemingway was sounded out by a representative of the Embassy at Havanna concerning these remarks. The Embassy
representative later returned with the advise that Hemingway stated he had
paid no particular attention to the petition he had signed in 1940 denouncing
the FBI and could now hardly remember what it said; Hemingway told the Embassy
representative that people were always shoving petitions under his nose and
like many famous people he was inclined to sign them on the request of a friend
without full information as to their contents. Hemingway also reportedly
dismissed the reference to the FBI as "The American Gestapo" as a mere jest.
(64-23312-6X)

CMN:skr

Attachment

RECORDED - 34

164-23312-15

de-indexed 3/11/58

CONFIDENTIAL

CONFIDENTIAL

In addition to the organizations mentioned in the attached blind memorandum, it is noted that Bureau files reflect Hemingway's past affiliation with such organizations as the Medical Bureau to Aid Spanish Democracy, American Relief Ship Mission for Spain, and the American Writers' Congress. None of these organizations are on the Attorney General's list and the Bureau has not established Hemingway's membership in these organizations by investigation.

ACTION:

It is recommended that the information developed concerning Hemingway during his service to the American Ambassador in Havana, Cuba, not be made available to the Office of the Secretary of Defense since this information is largely of an administrative nature and does not appear to be such as would affect clearance for access to highly classified material. It is also recommended that the information associating Hemingway with the organizations mentioned above not be made available to the requesting agency since these organizations are not on the Attorney General's list.

If the attached blind memorandum meets with your approval, it is recommended that it be returned to Room 7633 for transmittal to the Office of the Secretary of Defense.

- 2 -

CONFIDENTIAL

AIR POUCH
PRIORITY

OFFICIAL USE ONLY
(Security Classification)

DO NOT TYPE IN THIS SPACE

737.00/11-659

FOREIGN SERVICE DESPATCH

FROM :   Amembassy HABANA

682
DESP. NO.

November 6, 1959
DATE

TO   :   THE DEPARTMENT OF STATE, WASHINGTON.

REF   :

For Dept. Use Only	ACTION	DEPT.						
20	ARA-4	I N F O	RM/R-2 IRC-8 P-5 PPT-2 SY-2 SCA-3					5
REC'D 11/10		OTHER	CIA-10 USIA-10 OSD-4 Army-4 Navy-3 Air-1					

SUBJECT: Ernest HEMINGWAY Gives Views on Cuban Situation

BEGIN UNCLASSIFIED

ALL FBI INFORMATION CONTAINED
HEREIN IS UNCLASSIFIED
DATE 2/13/98 BY SP-4/c/l(w) #412800

For many years past, perhaps the most famous American resident in Cuba has been Ernest HEMINGWAY, who has a home in San Francisco de Paula, near Habana, where he spends a large part of his time. Hemingway generally lives a retired life there, together with his wife and frequent visitors.

Hemingway returned from a long visit in Spain on November 3, 1959. He was interviewed at the airport by Prensa Latina, and contrary to his usual custom, made several statements on the local situation and his reaction. Among other things, he said, as quoted by Prensa Latina:

1) His opinion of the Revolutionary Government was unchanged since January—he supported it and all its acts completely, and thought it was the best thing that had ever happened to Cuba.

2) He had not believed any of the information published abroad against Cuba. He sympathized with the Cuban Government, and all our difficulties.

3) Hemingway emphasized the our, and was asked about it. He said that he hoped Cubans would regard him not as a Yanqui (his word), but as another Cuban. With that, he kissed a Cuban flag which was nearby. He refused to repeat the gesture for photographers, saying that he "had kissed the flag with sincerity", implying that publicity would cheapen the act.

4) Hemingway said he knew nothing about any recent note from the U.S. Government to the Cuban Government on relations between the two countries. He said that he had come from New York, where they "knew nothing about Cuba or the world. There all they talk about is Van Doren and the scandal of the TV quiz shows".

64-23312-
NOT RECORDED
201 NOV 13 1959

(END UNCLASSIFIED) COPY TO THE FBI

BEGIN OFFICIAL USE ONLY

Comment: Hemingway's remarks have been strongly played by Prensa Latina, and given wide publicity locally. It is unfortunate that because of his position and

NOV 20 1959

NOV 16 1959
SY - LIAISON

DEPARTMENT OF STATE
NOV 13 1959
OFFICE OF SECURITY
NOT TO BE FILED

NAT. INV. SEC.

POL:

OFFICIAL USE ONLY
INFORMATION COPY
Retain in divisional files or destroy in accordance with security regulations

b6
b7C

THE ABOVE DISTRIBUTION APPLIES TO THE DEPARTMENT ONLY

FD-36 (Rev. 12-13-56)

F B I

Date: 1/13/61

Transmit the following in _____ PLAIN _____
(Type in plain text or code)

Via   AIRTEL _____
(Priority or Method of Mailing)

- -

TO: DIRECTOR, FBI   PERSONAL ATTENTION

FROM: SAC, MINNEAPOLIS

RE: ERNEST HEMINGWAY
         INFORMATION CONCERNING

b6
b7C

ERNEST HEMINGWAY, the author, has been a patient at Mayo
Clinic, Rochester, Minnesota, and is presently at St. Mary's
Hospital in that city. He has been at the Clinic for several
weeks, and is described as a problem. He is seriously ill,
both physically and mentally, and at one time the doctors
were considering giving him electro-shock therapy treatments.

[   ] Mayo Clinic, advised to
eliminate publicity and contacts by newsmen, the Clinic had
suggested that Mr. HEMINGWAY register under the alias GEORGE
SEVIER. [   ] stated that Mr. HEMINGWAY is now
worried about his registering under an assumed name, and is
concerned about an FBI investigation. [   ] stated that
inasmuch as this worry was interfering with the treatments
of Mr. HEMINGWAY, he desired authorization to tell HEMINGWAY
that the FBI was not concerned with his registering under
an assumed name. [   ] was advised that there was no
objection.

3 - Bureau
1 - Minneapolis
WHW:RSK
(4)
cc - DeLoach

64-23312-18

ALL INFORMATION CONTAINED
HEREIN IS UNCLASSIFIED
DATE 10/29/79 BY SP-1 DSK/gdn

11 JAN 24 1961

CRIME RESEARCH

52 JAN 31 1961

Approved: _____   Sent _____ M   Per _____
          Special Agent in Charge

QUENTIN REYNOLDS
201   SIX EAST 79TH STREET
NEW YORK 21, N.Y.

January 6, 1964

Dear Edgar:

Ernest Hemingway

I'm sure that this is a tempest in a teapot, but Mary
Hemingway is understandably disturbed that the enclosed
"commemorative" stamp might by implication hurt Ernest's
reputation. Toots and I knew Hemingway very well and we
both knew him as a non-political guy. He owned a house
in Cuba, and like most Americans in residence there he
hated Battista, and like millions, welcomed anyone who
could oust the dictator. He didn't know Castro well;
Mary says he met Castro at a fishing party and talked to
him for five minutes - period. He never met him again.

After Ernest's death Mary received word that Castro
was going to take over the house. Very smart, she made a
deal before this took place. She said the Cuban government
could have the house if she could have the unfinished
manuscripts in his safe there. The government agreed; they
have the house and land and she has the manuscripts.

They have made a sort of shrine out of the house, Mary
says. That, plus this stamp, is apt to persuade people that
Hemingway was a big Castro man, and again by association, a
fellow-traveler of some sort. This envelope was received by
Mary Saturday morning (January 4). It was sent from Havana
by Roberto Herrera who was a part-time secretary to Hemingway.
You'll notice that this envelope is stamped "Primer Dia" which
I suppose means first edition, first issue or first day. It
was hidden in a Christmas card Mary received from Herrera.
Mary and Ernest's son Gregory, who is an intern at the Jackson-
ville Hospital, Miami, Florida, asked me to have lunch with
them Saturday at Toots'. We talked it over with Toots and
all agreed to send the envelope to you. Mary is apprehensive
that the communists will try to make capital out of this.
The damn thing looks as if it had Ernest's sanction or Mary's
sanction, or for that matter, even Gregory's sanction. Of
course, it didn't.

- 2 -

Toots and I hate to bother you with something so trivial but of course it isn't trivial to Mary or her step-son. Mary just wanted someone in authority to know the facts in case some jerk columnist or some communist publication gets hold of it and uses it to help Castro. If you want one of your boys to talk to Mary she just moved to New York (27 East 65th St., Phone is AG 9-2017). I've just recently moved too and am now living at 201 East 79th St. (YU 8-2070).

I'm sorry about Clyde. Please give him my best when you see him next. And thanks so much for reading this dreary note about something that I'm sure won't amount to much.

Very sincerely,

Quent (Reynolds)

Mr. J. Edgar Hoover
Director
FBI
Washington, D.C.

P.S. If you don't need the envelope, could you please send it back to Mary or me. She has a large file of Ernest's letters, etc., and thinks this might belong there, but it really isn't important right now.

Return it. See that appropriate notation is made in our files. Knowing Hemingway as I did, I doubt he had any communist leanings. He was tough tough guy & always for the underdog.

64-23312-19

ENCLOSURE

January 9, 1964

REC-23 64 - 23312 - 19

Mr. Quentin Reynolds
101 East 79th Street
New York 21, New York

Dear Quent:

      Thank you for your letter of January 6th,
with enclosure. I can certainly understand Mary
Hemingway's concern as well as your own. You may be
certain this will be made a matter of official record.

      I will give Clyde your message and I know
it will cheer him to learn you were thinking of him.

      In accordance with your request the envelope
you sent is being returned.

      With every good wish,

      Sincerely,

      J. Edgar

MAILED 19
JAN 9 - 1964
COMM-FBI

Enclosure
1 - New York - Enclosures (2)
1 - Miami - Enclosures (2)
1 - Mr. Sullivan - Enclosures (2)

ALL INFORMATION CONTAINED
HEREIN IS UNCLASSIFIED
DATE 10/29/79 BY SP-1 BSK/gw

NOTE: Mr. Reynolds is on the Special Correspondents' List.

JH:sls
(6)

Tolson
Belmont
Mohr
Casper
Callahan
Conrad
DeLoach
Evans
Gale
Rosen
Sullivan
Tavel
Trotter
Tele. Room
Holmes
Gandy

TELETYPE UNIT

Aldous Huxley

A COMMITTED PACIFIST WITH a tendency for experimenting with hallucinogens, a man whose most famous book, *Brave New World*, depicts a nightmare vision of a future where individual freedom has been entirely eroded by state control, Aldous Huxley certainly had the background of somebody the FBI would be interested in. But while his views on technology's collision course with morality did raise a few eyebrows within the Bureau, those views weren't entirely unwelcome, leading to a FBI file that reads less like an investigation and more like a book report.

Huxley first appeared on the Bureau's radar in May 1958. Huxley, who had emigrated to the United States from England twenty years earlier, was interviewed by Mike Wallace as part of a television series financed by the Fund for the Republic, an anti-McCarthyist think tank that the FBI felt had ties to Moscow. With this as a literal metaphorical red flag, the Bureau reviewed what it had on Huxley to determine if he was a genuine subversive or just happened to have the wrong views.

Huxley had quite a few strikes against him — the aforementioned pacifism (in 1937, Huxley had written the *Encyclopedia of Pacifism*, which the FBI notes had been used by pro-peace groups to "promote their views"), membership in a few organizations the Bureau felt were at least insufficiently anti-Communist, if not full-blown pinko, and a son with alleged, but unproven Communist ties. All of which made Huxley suspect but didn't warrant an investigation.

Nevertheless, "for information purposes," the FBI assigned an agent to watch and annotate the interview, and what he saw was apparently interesting enough to make it to the desk of J. Edgar Hoover. A memo to the Director outlined Huxley's fears, expanded upon in *Brave New World*, that pharmacology and conditioning — facilitated by modern mass media — would make a mockery of democracy, leading to a public that would "accept a dictatorship willingly."

Hoover must have liked what he heard, because from this point on, the Bureau kept loose tabs on Huxley until his death. Along with a few newspaper clippings describing Huxley's warnings of subliminal influence, the FBI sent an agent to attend a symposium on "Human Values and the Scientific Revolution" at which Huxley was speaking. There, a somewhat more mellow Huxley urged the audience — including the incognito agent — to reject efficiency as the highest value, and instead embrace "love as an absolute necessity."

A heartwarming, optimistic note to end on, only slightly undercut by it being hidden in the secret police file of a man preaching peace.

STANDARD FORM NO. 64

Office Memorandum • UNITED STATES GOVERNMENT

TO   : Mr. L. V. Boardman   DATE: *May 23, 1958*

FROM : A. H. Belmont

SUBJECT: *FUND FOR THE REPUBLIC*
MIKE WALLACE TV INTERVIEW
PROGRAMS

ALL INFORMATION CONTAINED
HEREIN IS UNCLASSIFIED
DATE 11/6/84 ... BY 9145

FeIPA 25030

Tolson
Nichols
Boardman
Belmont
Mohr
Parsons
Rosen
Tamm
Trotter
Nease
Tele. Room
Holloman
Gandy

        The fourth program of the Fund-sponsored Mike Wallace TV series featured Mr. Aldous Huxley, British author and social critic, and was broadcast on May 18, 1958. The following is a summary of information contained in Bufiles regarding Aldous Huxley:

        Huxley has not been investigated by the FBI. He came to the United States in 1937 and was residing in Los Angeles, California, in 1953.

        Huxley was a delegate from England to the International Authors Congress for the Defense of Culture held in Paris, France, from June 21 to 25, 1935. Huxley was elected to the "praesidium" of the Congress. The "Daily Worker," an east coast communist newspaper which suspended publication on January 13, 1958, in its issue of November 5, 1944, reflected on page nine that a world congress of writers organized against fascism was held in Paris, France, in 1935 and a Paris publication attempted to expose the congress as a communist plot to take over France. This article mentioned that Huxley attended the congress.
        (100-72924-471; 100-336098-1)

        Huxley's book, "An Encyclopaedia of Pacifism," published in 1937 condemns all violence including communist and fascist violence and the use of violence to combat them. Huxley's words and publications have been used by pacifist groups to promote their own views.

        On May 23, 1951, testimony before the House Committee on Un-American Activities reflected that Huxley was one of a number of writers who worked in an organization called Friends of Intellectual Freedom. The purpose of the organization was to raise funds to help former communist writers rehabilitate themselves. (100-138754-926C page 596)

        Huxley's son, Mathew, was investigated by the Bureau in 1953 as an applicant for United Nations employment.

JJG:mje (5)

1 - Mr. Boardman
1 - Mr. Belmont
1 - Liaison Section
1 - Mr. Gaffney

REC- 51

EX - 123

23 MAY 27 1958

UNRECORDED COPY FILED IN:

Memo Belmont to Boardman
Re: FUND FOR THE REPUBLIC
*   MIKE WALLACE TV INTERVIEW*
*   PROGRAMS*

Investigation developed Mathew had some associates who were Communist Party (CP) members but there was no evidence of CP membership or sympathies on the part of Mathew Huxley. (138-1263)

The 11/7/52 issue of "Counterattack" reflected that a statement "recently" issued by the Authors' World Peace Appeal with headquarters in London, England, was signed by Huxley among others. According to the article, the statement advocated coexistence with Russia and condemned any writing liable to sharpen existing dangers and hatred. The Authors' World Peace Appeal was described as "assertedly non-Communist group of 950 writers. Many are definitely not pro-Communist." The signers of the statement were considered to have "fallen for one of Moscow's biggest lies." (100-350512-506)

ACTION:

None. For information and record purposes.

FBI

Date:

Transmit the following in _____
(Type in plain text or code)

Via ____AIRTEL_____ _____
(Priority or Method of Mailing)

NY 62-11998

　　　　HUXLEY claimed that one of the things that
will diminish our freedom is "overpopulation" and
to control an overpopulated world organization is
needed.

　　　　HUXLEY stated that technological devices that
are produced today can be used to persuade man against
his sense of reason or good judgment to accept
a dictatorship willingly. HUXLEY believes that this
persuasion can be accomplished through man's subconscious
and that such a development could make "nonsense of
the whole democratic procedure which is based on
conscious choice on rational ground."

　　　　HUXLEY stated that as was reflected in his
book "A Brave New World" (written 27 years ago) that
men might lose control of their minds from certain
"powerful mind-changing drugs." In addition,
HUXLEY felt the advertising agencies possible un-
principled use of television and other mass-media
could create the same effect. HUXLEY further stated
these methods used by advertising agencies could be
employed by evil individuals for political purposes
thus making us more receptive to ideas that are
totalitarian. HUXLEY mentioned subliminal advertising
as one example of these methods that could be used for
above purpose.

　　　　HUXLEY stated that our own technological
advances should be studied so that we are not caught
off guard by situations which we do not anticipate.

　　　　　　　　　　　　　　　　POWERS

- 2 -

Approved: _____   Sent _____ M   Per _____
　　　　Special Agent in Charge

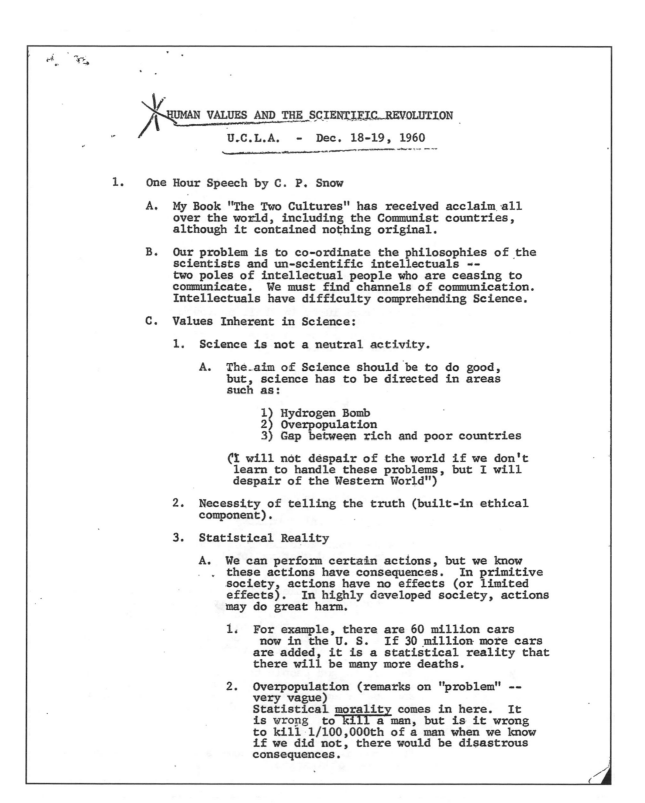

HUMAN VALUES AND THE SCIENTIFIC REVOLUTION
U.C.L.A.   -   Dec. 18-19, 1960

1.   One Hour Speech by C. P. Snow

   A.   My Book "The Two Cultures" has received acclaim all
     over the world, including the Communist countries,
     although it contained nothing original.

   B.   Our problem is to co-ordinate the philosophies of the
     scientists and un-scientific intellectuals --
     two poles of intellectual people who are ceasing to
     communicate. We must find channels of communication.
     Intellectuals have difficulty comprehending Science.

   C.   Values Inherent in Science:

      1.   Science is not a neutral activity.

         A.   The aim of Science should be to do good,
           but, science has to be directed in areas
           such as:

              1) Hydrogen Bomb
              2) Overpopulation
              3) Gap between rich and poor countries

         ("I will not despair of the world if we don't
          learn to handle these problems, but I will
          despair of the Western World")

      2.   Necessity of telling the truth (built-in ethical
         component).

      3.   Statistical Reality

         A.   We can perform certain actions, but we know
           these actions have consequences. In primitive
           society, actions have no effects (or limited
           effects). In highly developed society, actions
           may do great harm.

             1.   For example, there are 60 million cars
               now in the U. S. If 30 million more cars
               are added, it is a statistical reality that
               there will be many more deaths.

             2.   Overpopulation (remarks on "problem" --
               very vague)
               Statistical <u>morality</u> comes in here. It
               is wrong to kill a man, but is it wrong
               to kill 1/100,000th of a man when we know
               if we did not, there would be disastrous
               consequences.

-2-

3. Radiation -
It is a statistical reality that if we
play around with atomic and hydrogen
energy, the results will be that the
radiation will have harmful effects
some day on some people somewhere. We
cannot escape these consequences.

D. Conclusions

1. Unless we use our intelligence, we're damned and
doomed. Scientists must communicate the truth to
the intellectuals.

2. U. S. has been lucky in their achievements and
success in the industrial revolution -- our success
is not because of any virtue or hard work -- but due
only because we were lucky.

3. If any society has the moral responsibility to bridge
the gap between economic differences in the world
it is the U. S. This is part of the Scientific
Revolution. Unless we bridge this gap we shall fail --
and we shall deserve to fail.

II Panel Discussion

Sir C. P. Snow
Harold C. Urey
Aldous Huxley
Pamela Hansford Johnson (Lady Snow)

Huxley: (re Statistical Morality)

1. "One can form good ideas of what will happen in
the future and what rational policies we should
follow.

We have difficulties getting these policies across
in Democracies but it is easy in totalitarian
countries who have no trouble dictating these
rational policies which are to everyone's
advantage. In the long run they will be carried
out by force in every country."

2. We have to get people to vote for these rational
policies although it will upset the status quo
and cost them money and discomfort and get them
to implement these rational views.

Lady Snow:

1. "Our own interests must come second -- this is
our moral obligation."

-3-

2. "People choose their own kind of Truth, but Truth is determined on the base of all the indisputable facts we can find. If we don't like the Truth, we say it's untrue."

Dr. Urey:

1. We're confused about Science and Engineering.
   A. Science is to learn the Truth. Science doesn't hurt or benefit
   B. The application to practical things is what leads to trouble.

2. Concerning statistical morality, this is nothing new. We send some men into battle to be killed because in the long run fewer men will be killed.

   Sir Snow's statement that an increase in autos will cause an increase in deaths is not justified statistically because the number of casualties have not increased in proportion to the number of autos. And Sir Snow made no mention of the number of lives that have been saved by automobiles-- taking people to doctors, etc,

3. We should not think of this in a moral way -- actually, I'm not impressed with so-called "statistical morality".

Sir Snow: (Confused and backed down)

1. "I don't put any value on statistical morality either -- it just came to my mind as I was speaking."

2. The real problem is that we find it hard to be future directed.

Huxley:

1. We are lacking in a serious attempt to see the future.

2. If people in the 19th century had known about the horrible factory system that developed, they would have avoided the extreme hardships and penalties of the factories.

3. We must apply science to human need - this is a moral imperative in scientific enterprise.

Sir Snow:

-4-

Sir Snow:

1. Within 5 - 10 years, 10 countries will have
   nuclear weapons which will be a nuisance and
   will increase the chances of a nuclear disaster
   to the world, either by accident, madness or
   design. The world can't take more than 2 or
   3 of these nuclear disasters. This is not a
   risk but a certainty -- this is our moral
   imperative.

2. Overpopulation is another moral imperative.

Huxley:

1. In applied science, there is a built-in
   imperative -- efficiency.

2. Efficiency is not the prime value.

3. The main question is how do we maintain our
   human values.

Question to panel: "How does the intrinsic value of Science
lead scientists to engage in the creation of the atomic bomb?"

Sir Snow:

1. You've got to remember history -- it was a
   "battle" between the Pacifists against the
   others.

2. I took the others' side--to fight as long as
   we could.

Urey:

Scientists vary like others in population.

1. Some are Pacifists.

2. Others put all their efforts into
   protecting the country we hold dear.

Lady Snow: (disagrees very much with Urey)

1. Scientists can't be like the rest of society
   because they're dealing with matters of such
   great size and importance.

2. The responsibility is on the Scientist ---
   he can't be an ordinary person.

-5-

Huxley:

1. "Scientists and non-Scientists are prisoners
   of their culture. This is a horrible fact."

2. We all know there must be one world but how do
   we get this idea implemented--by consent or by
   force?

   (Riot here - student in first row stood up to
   oppose Huxley. Campus police took him out,
   kicking him, and with much struggle. People
   in first 5 rows (reserved) all stood up,
   and demanded the student be allowed to stay and
   speak, but he was taken out.)

Urey:

1. Most of my friends think the atomic bomb is one
   of the greatest problems, but we should not be
   discouraged.

2. But I am discouraged when the Scientists make
   the decisions and, in actuality, represent such a
   small percentage of the people.

Lady Snow:

1. "I have felt the problem of the people of
   India in my bones. We have to _experience_
   Science to bridge the gap."

   (Lady Snow writes books - novels, etc. to
   bridge this gap. She admitted, and rather bragged,
   that she was "mathematically blind" and knows
   nothing about science but she "feels it in her
   bones" and is able to communicate Science to the
   intellectuals.)

Huxley:

It is astonishingly difficult to bridge this gap.

Lady Snow:

It can't be deliberately done, but the mere
understanding that the problem exists helps.

Urey:

1. You don't have to understand everything that
   happens,

   For example, when we push the doorbell and a
   sound is heard in the kitchen, we don't have

-6-

to understand everything that made this
possible-- it isn't really necessary to
understand.

2. But what worries me is when people are proud
that they don't understand the facts.

Sir Snow: (no indication of change in subject)

1. My 2 essays on Culture have been well received
in the U.S.S.R.

2. The Russians have the advantage
   a) of knowing the importance of science
   b) of having high school education very
   much better than that in England or
   the U.S.

Urey:

1. I have made 2 trips to the U.S.S.R. -- one
just last week.

2. I am not impressed with the "advantages"
Sir Snow states the Russians have. I saw
no such advantages.

3. I was impressed that the Scientists will talk
no politics or public affairs.

4. I was impressed that I could see no Russian
Scientist in a private conversation.

5. The problem of communication between the two
cultures is, indeed, very important.
   a) I think scientists can do better in
   bridging this gap than non-scientists.
   b) But I'm also interested in politics and
   economics (indicated he wasn't sure we
   could, or should, bridge this gap.)

Problem presented to panel: Moral Imperative of Science vs
the Moral Imperative of Religion.

Sir Snow:

1. I'm a pious agnostic.

2. Morality is not connected with religion and
a lot of religion is not moral.

3. Morality exists apart from religion. The
best people I've met are not religious.

4. I see little evidence that the formally
religious societies are any more moral than

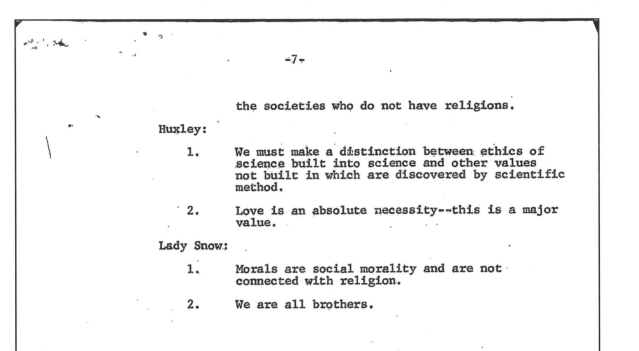

-7-

the societies who do not have religions.

Huxley:

1.   We must make a distinction between ethics of
science built into science and other values
not built in which are discovered by scientific
method.

2.   Love is an absolute necessity--this is a major
value.

Lady Snow:

1.   Morals are social morality and are not
connected with religion.

2.   We are all brothers.

Ken Kesey

COUNTERCULTURAL ICON KEN KESEY is perhaps equally famous for traversing the country in a technicolor bus, throwing LSD-fueled parties as one of the "Merry Pranksters," as he is as the author of *One Flew Over the Cuckoo's Nest*. But for one summer in 1966, Kesey was one thing and one thing only to the FBI: a fugitive.

Despite a long history of experimentation with psychoactive drugs — including a stint as a paid lab rat in a series of clinical studies later revealed to have been financed as part of the CIA's infamous MKULTRA program — Kesey finally ran afoul of the authorities in 1965 when he was arrested for marijuana possession in California. To escape imprisonment, Kesey, with help of the Pranksters, faked his death and fled to Mexico. Unfortunately for Kesey, nobody believed his overly-ornate suicide note, and by crossing state lines, the case ended up getting kicked up to the Bureau.

The FBI received several reports of Kesey sightings in Mexico, some of rather dubious nature — at one point, Kesey was supposedly staying in "Marijuana City," which is apparently 12 miles from Puerto Vallarta and also appears not to exist. The Bureau had even less luck questioning Kesey's "beatnik" friends; they were, to put it mildly, extremely uncooperative. His family was a different story; Kesey's dad, Fred, told the interviewing special agent that he would do anything to get his son turned in so he might be "straightened out," but fortunately for the younger Kesey, his father was unable to provide any useful leads.

Five months into the hunt, the FBI received a rather unusual — and no doubt frustrating — tip: the *San Francisco Chronicle* ran a front-page story, headlined "LSD Fugitive's Strange Story." Not only was Kesey was back in the States, but he was now actively mocking the Bureau's attempts to apprehend him. The investigation moved back up north, where the *Chronicle* reporters proved as reticent as the beatniks before them.

A couple weeks later, FBI special agents from the San Francisco Field Office had a lucky break — they ran into Kesey's truck at a red light. Kesey tried to drive away, but he was pursued by the special agents and was eventually forced to flee on foot. The agents caught him, and eight months after Kesey had first fled the country, he did his time: six months at an experimental work camp. Very few who ended up on the Bureau's bad side could claim to be so lucky.

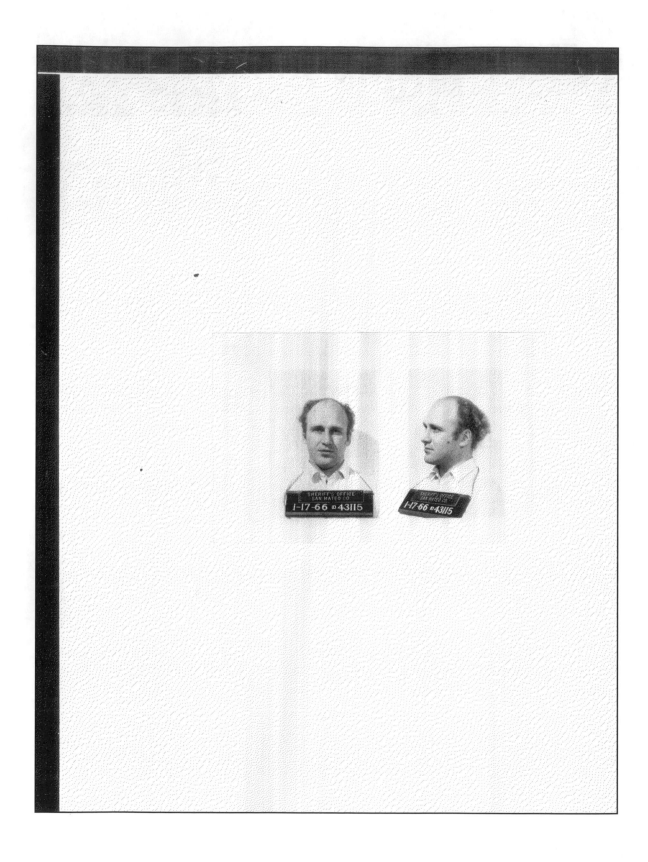

FD-65 (Rev. 3-25-63)
OPTIONAL FORM NO. 10
MAY 1962 EDITION
GSA GEN. REG. NO. 27

8010-106

UNITED STATES GOVERNMENT

Memorandum

TO   : Director, FBI   (Att.: Special Investigative Division)

FROM   : SAC, SAN FRANCISCO (88-10038)

SUBJECT: KEN ELTON KESEY - FUGITIVE
UFAP - POSSESSION OF MARIJUANA

DATE: 3/11/66
Office of
Origin: San Francisco

O.O. File No. _____
(If other than submitting office)

In order that a fugitive index card may be prepared without delay, the following information is furnished:

☐ Probation violator's warrant issued by USDC for District of _____

_____ , (date) _____

☒ Warrant issued by ☒ U. S. Commissioner ☐ Clerk, USDC at San Francisco, Calif.

_____ , (date) 3/11/66

Date probation violator or bond default case referred to office _____

Name and Aliases:	FBI #
KEN ELTON KESEY	Other Identifying # CII #2713297

Offense Charged: _____ UFAP - Possession of Marijuana

Title ___18___ , U. S. Code, Section _____1073

If an indictment or information is outstanding specify which, giving date and place of issuance: _____

_____

Description

Sex	Race	Complexion	Age	Birth date	Birthplace
☒ Male ☐ Female	White	Fair	30	7/17/35	La Junta, Colorado

Height	Weight	Build	Hair	Eyes	Residence
6'	190	Medium	Red	Blue	

Nationality	Marital status	Caution statement (where applicable)

Scars, marks and other identifying remarks

Mole on left cheek
FPC - 20 O 31 W MOM 20
       I 26 R OIM 20   ST-101

37196 —

MAR 14 1966

Occupation

57 MAR 17 1966

1-Bureau
2-San Francisco
FJC:ab

3/11/66

CODE

CABLEGRAM   URGENT

TO   LEGAT MEXICO CITY

FROM DIRECTOR FBI

KEN ELTON KESEY, FUGITIVE, UFAP DASH POSSESSION OF

MARIJUANA, OO: SAN FRANCISCO.

SAN FRANCISCO ADVISES SUBJECT, AUTHOR OF BEST SELLER BOOK

"ONE FLEW OVER THE CUCKOO'S NEST," IS WANTED BY SAN MATEO AND

SAN FRANCISCO AUTHORITIES FOR POSSESSION OF MARIJUANA. DISTRICT

ATTORNEY, SAN FRANCISCO REQUESTED UFAP PROCESS MARCH TEN, LAST.

AUSA JERROLD M. LADAR, SAN FRANCISCO, AUTHORIZED COMPLAINT

MARCH TEN, LAST, FILED BY SA FRANCIS J. COLLOPY BEFORE USC

RICHARD S. GOLDSMITH, MARCH ELEVEN INSTANT, CHARGING VIOLATION

T. EIGHTEEN, USC, S. ONE ZERO SEVEN THREE, UFAP DASH POSSESSION

OF MARIJUANA, AND WARRANT ISSUED, BOND RECOMMEND FIVE THOUSAND

DOLLARS.

INFORMATION RECEIVED FROM INFORMANTS INDICATING KESEY AS OF

APPROXIMATELY MARCH TWO, LAST, WAS IN PUERTO VALLARTA, MEXICO.

ADDITIONAL DETAILS WILL BE FURNISHED UNDER SEPARATE COVER.

REC-14

1 - Foreign Liaison (detached)

CWH:jcz
   (4)

VIA CABLEGRAM
MAR 11 1966

EX 105

NR.
ENC.
CK.
APPROVED BY
TYPED BY
LOGGED BY

MAIL ROOM ☐ TELETYPE UNIT ☑

3/13/66

CODE

CABLEGRAM   URGENT

TO LEGAT MEXICO CITY

FROM DIRECTOR FBI

    KEN ELTON KESEY - FUGITIVE - UFAP - POSSESSION MARIJUANA;

OO - SAN FRANCISCO.

    REURCAB MARCH TWELVE LAST.

    SUBJECT DESCRIBED AS FOLLOWS: RACE, WHITE; SEX, MALE;

BORN, JULY SEVENTEEN, THIRTYFIVE AT LA JUNTA, COLORADO; HEIGHT,

SIX FEET; WEIGHT, ONE NINETY LBS.; COMPLEXION, FAIR; BUILD,

MEDIUM; HAIR, RED (NOW CUT SHORT-BALDING); EYES, BLUE; SCARS

OR MARKS, MOLE ON LEFT CHEEK; FINGERPRINT CLASSIFICATION, TWO

ZERO ZERO THREE ONE W MOM TWO ZERO OVER TWO SIX R OIM TWO ZERO;

    METHOD OF TRAVEL UNKNOWN.

    SECURE BUREAU INTERESTS.   PHOTOGRAPH FOLLOWS.   MAR 14 1966

b6
b7C

1 - San Francisco (88-10038)
1 - Portland
1 - Foreign Liaison Unit (Route through for review)

CPH:jm
(5)

Tolson
DeLoach
Mohr
Wick
Casper
Callahan
Conrad
Felt
Gale
Rosen
Sullivan
Tavel
Trotter
Tele. Room
Holmes
Gandy

VIA CABLEGRAM
MAR 13 1966

NR
ENC.
CK.
APPROVED BY
TYPED BY
LOGGED BY

MAIL ROOM ☐   TELETYPE UNIT ☑

UNITED STATES DEPARTMENT OF JUSTICE

FEDERAL BUREAU OF INVESTIGATION

San Francisco, California

March 11, 1966

In Reply, Please Refer to
File No.

KEN ELTON KESEY

KESEY is the author of the best seller book entitled
"One Flew Over The Cuckoo's Nest." He is wanted by the San
Mateo County, California, Superior Court for failure to appear
at a hearing as to why his bond and probation should not be
revoked. At the time he was free on a stay of execution
granted by the court for his appeal on conviction for possession
of marijuana on January 17, 1966. At that time he was admitted
to probation for three years with the condition that he serve
six months of this three years in custody. During the time
KESEY was free pending this appeal he was arrested by the San
Francisco Police Department on January 19, 1966, for the same
charge, possession of marijuana. The District Attorney's Office
at San Francisco conferred with the District Attorney, San Mateo,
and decided to initiate Unlawful Flight proceedings out of San
Francisco.

On March 10, 1966, a complaint was authorized by
Assistant U. S. Attorney Jerrold M. Ladar, San Francisco, charging
subject with violation of Title 18, U. S. Code, Section 1073,
Unlawful Flight to Avoid Prosecution - Possession of Marijuana.
This complaint was filed by Special Agent Francis J. Collopy, Jr.,
before U. S. Commissioner Richard S. Goldsmith, San Francisco,
on March 11, 1966, and a warrant was issued; bond recommended
$5,000.

The San Mateo County Sheriff's Office on March 9, 1966,
received information from reliable informant that he had seen
KESEY on the beach at Puerto Vallarta, Mexico, approximately
seven days prior (March 2, 1966). This informant also advised
that KESEY was also frequenting a place, probably a coffee house,
in or near that city known as "Palapa."

88-37176-8

ENCLOSURE

RE: KEN ELTON KESEY

        KESEY is described as follows:

Race:	White
Sex:	Male
Born:	7/17/35 at La Junta, Colorado
Height:	6'
Weight:	190 lbs.
Complexion:	Fair
Build:	Medium
Hair:	Red (now cut short)
Eyes:	Blue
Scars or marks:	Mole on left cheek
Fingerprint	
Classification:	20 O 31 W MOM 20
	I 26 R OIM 20

b6
b7C

Driver's License:	Oregon #87504
California Bureau of Criminal	
Identification and Investigation	
Number:	2713297

2

4-3 (Rev. 1-27-66)

DECODED COPY

☐ **AIRGRAM**   xxx **CABLEGRAM**   ☐ **RADIO**   ☐ **TELETYPE**

STATE-01

URGENT 3-15-66

TO DIRECTOR

FROM LEGAT MEXICO CITY   NO. 812

KEN ELTON KESEY-FUGITIVE-UFAP POSSESSION MARIJUANA.

REBUCAB MARCH 13, LAST.

CHECK OF REGISTRY OF ALL PRIVATE PLANES AND OF PASSENGER

LISTS OF COMMERCIAL AIRLINES REFLECTS NO RECORDS OF ARRIVAL

OF SUBJECT AT PUERTO VALLARTA, JALISCO. ALL HOTELS AND

MOTELS AT PUERTO VALLARTA AND NEARBY AREAS CHECKED MARCH 13

LAST, WITH NEGATIVE RESULTS. INVESTIGATION CONTINUING.

SAN FRANCISCO REQUESTED TO FURNISH PHOTO OF SUBJECT AND

ANY INFORMATION KNOWN CONCERNING HOTEL OR MOTEL WHERE SUBJECT

HAS RESIDED IN PAST.   REC 25   88- 1196- 9

SUCAB.

MAR 16 1966

NATHAN L. FERRIS

RECEIVED: 4:49 PM RPT

RD CC MR. BRENNAN

UNITED STATES DEPARTMENT OF JUSTICE

FEDERAL BUREAU OF INVESTIGATION

San Francisco, California

April 4, 1966

In Reply, Please Refer to
File No.

<u>KEN ELTON KESEY</u>

Information has been received to the effect that
KESEY was seen twice recently at Puerto Vallarta. According
to information, KESEY is staying in a place called Marijuana
City located approximately 12 miles from Puerto Vallarta.
KESEY supposedly owned two buses, one of which was recovered
in northern California and the other, a Volkswagen bus, was
supposedly seen recently at Oceanside, California. Information
is being obtained regarding description and license number of
vehicles owned by KESEY.

ENCLOSURE *88 3 71 96 - 12*

OPTIONAL FORM NO. 10
MAY 1962 EDITION
GSA GEN. REG. NO. 27   5010-106-03

UNITED STATES GOVERNMENT

Memorandum

TO   :   **Director, FBI (88-37196)**   DATE: 5/13/66

FROM   :   **Legat, Mexico (88-534) (RUC)**

SUBJECT: **KEN ELTON KESEY - FUGITIVE**
              UFAP - POSSESSION OF MARIJUANA

Remycab, 3/15/66; San Francisco LHMs, 3/11/66 and
4/4/66.

protect, who has furnished reliable informa-
tion in the past, advised by written report received 4/30/66
of the following investigation conducted on 4/27,28/66:

At Yelapa, Jalisco, source determined that the
only coffee shop in this area is the restaurant of the Hotel
Lagunitas. This is the place where all of the tourists visiting this area gather and is known as a hangout for beatniks
and marijuana smokers.

ROBERTO PALLARES, Manager of the Hotel Lagunitas,
was exhibited a photograph of the subject and stated he could
not identify him as being a person who had been in this area.
He stated he was familiar with most of the people who have
visited in this area and does not recall anyone resembling
the subject as being here. He stated that inasmuch as Yelapa
can only be reached by boat from Puerto Villarta, there are
few visitors to this area that he does not know.

At Puerto Villarta, Jalisco, source exhibited a
photograph of the subject to employees at all hotels and
other logical rooming houses without effecting an identification.

A search of the registers of all hotels since 1/1/66
to 4/28/66 failed to reflect any information relating to the
subject.

Inasmuch as logical investigation has been
conducted in Mexico without identifying the subject, no further
investigation is being contemplated at this time.

5 - Bureau
  (1 - Liaison Section)
  (2 - San Francisco)
1 - Mexico City
RJO:cms
  (6)

1
88-10038
PJH:das

The following investigation was conducted by SA ▮▮▮▮▮

b6
b7C

▮▮▮▮ CALIFORNIA

On April 7, 1966, ▮▮▮▮▮▮▮▮ advised that ▮▮▮▮▮▮ and that the last time that she saw him was ▮▮▮▮▮ She stated that ▮▮▮▮▮

▮▮▮▮▮ to the effect that he had ▮▮▮▮ and that he would ▮▮▮▮ She stated that ▮▮▮

▮▮▮▮ and she presumed that this is where he was going. She stated that this was the first time that ▮▮▮

b6
b7C
b7D

She advised that she is currently residing ▮▮▮ stating that ▮▮▮

▮▮▮ advised that ▮▮▮ and that she has ▮▮▮ It was ▮▮▮ opinion that ▮▮▮ stating that ▮▮▮ She continued by stating that ▮▮▮

▮▮▮ only knows the Subject on an artistic basis and not a personal one. She advised that

3

2
SF 88-10038
PJH:das

███
██████████████████████ and that at the time ███
███
██ She stated that ██████████████████████████████
███
███

████████ stated that ███████████████████████████
█████████████████████ at the time ██████████████
stating that ██████ formerly resided with ██████
█████████████ She stated that ██████████████████
██████████████████████████████ She stated that ██
███
██████████████████ She stated that it was the ███
███
█████████████████████████████ stated she
doubts very much ████████████ would have any knowledge regarding Subject's whereabouts. She further advised that ████
██
███████████ She advised that ███████████████
███████ but doubted too if he would have any knowledge concerning his whereabouts.
      It was ███████████ personal opinion that ████████
███
███████ stating that ██████████████████████████
███

b6
b7C
b7D

4

SF 88-10038
FJC:law

b6
b7C

        On April 28, 1966, Mrs. ANITA BABBS and JIM MC ELROY,
3125 Soquel Drive, Soquel, California, were interviewed.
They stated that Mrs. KEN KESEY has returned to the Oregon
area with her children and are living there with the Subject's
parents, as far as they knew. They advised that Mrs. KESEY
writes very infrequently and as a consequence she knows little
of her plans. Mrs. Babbs stated that she is separated from
her husband, who is travelling with the "Intrepid Trips"
and is somewhere back East. Mrs. BABBS was very evasive in
her answers and is a "beatnik:.

PD 88-4619
JRM:gmj
2

suspicion because it was hot-wired.   b6
had been found   b7C

At that time FRED
KESEY, subject's father, had been contacted by the Lane County
Sheriff's Office, concerning the vehicle. He had said he
had no idea where subject might be located and requested
the vehicle be towed to Orick and the bill sent to him.

FRED KESEY, manager of the Eugene Farmers Creamery,
568 Olive Street, stated he has absolutely no idea where
subject, his son, is located. He said he is completely
bewildered at his son's alleged conduct, subject having been
given what his parents considered careful parental guidance
and he had never been known by his parents to indulge in any
dissipation of any kind, he on the contrary to be devoted
to physical culture and at one time was an outstanding varsity
wrestler at the University of Oregon. He stated his son
probably has no financial problems as he has received
considerable money from his best selling books. He stated
subject's wife, FAY KESEY, and their three children, ages 2,
5 and 6, recently arrived from California and for the present
are visiting with her in-laws, the FRED KESEYs, at 2243 Debra
Drive in Springfield. He said he is sure subject's wife has
no information concerning his location.

He stated he last saw subject when he came to
Eugene during the Christmas holidays, 1965. At that time
he came with a GEORGE WALKER, formerly of Eugene, who was
driving a Lotus Elans automobile. He said he had no
information concerning the identity of subject's friends in
California. He pointed out that he had once, in 1965, gone to
subject's home at Lahonda, California, and had found 50 or 60
people, mostly beatniks, milling about. Subject had stated
he did not, himself, know many of them; that his residence
was an open house for faculty people from Berkeley and Palo
Alto and for students from those schools. KESEY stated he
will do anything to cause subject's apprehension in order

PD 88-4619
JRM:gmj
3

that he might be "straightened out" and will immediately advise
the FBI if he gains any information of possible pertinence
to this investigation. He stated subject has no sister and

DATE: MARCH 17, 1966
AT:
NAME: SA

b6
b7C

and has heard nothing from him since that
time. She said that

She said she had

She stated that

b6
b7C
b7D

She said
she had no idea where GEORGE WALKER, friend of subject's,
might be located and that FREDERICK T. ADAMS of Los Altos,
California, is unknown to her. She stated that

4-3 (Rev. 1-27-66)

DECODED COPY

☐ AIRGRAM   ☒ CABLEGRAM   ☐ RADIO   ☐ TELETYPE

STATE 003

URGENT 10-7-66

TO DIRECTOR (88-37196)

FROM LEGAT MEXICO CITY NO. 202

KEN ELTON KESEY, AKA;-FUGITIVE; UFAP-POSSESSION OF MARIJUANA.

REBUCAB OCTOBER 7 INSTANT.

[   ] ADVISED TODAY THAT CURRENT INQUIRY IN MANZANILLO,

COLIMA OCTOBER 7 INSTANT INDICATES SUBJECT SNEAKED AWAY FROM

HOUSE HE OCCUPIED THERE IN MIDDLE OF NIGHT SEPTEMBER 17 LAST

LEAVING HOUSE IN SHAMBLES AND CONSIDERABLE DAMAGE AND RENT

UNPAID. NO INDICATION OF DESTINATION BUT SUBJECT NOT SEEN

SINCE IN MANZANILLO AREA. INQUIRIES BY INFORMANT AND OTHER

SOURCES CONTINUING AND ADDITIONAL FACTS WILL BE FURNISHED TO

BUREAU ON EXPEDITE BASIS.

RECEIVED: 10:39 PM RAK

88-37196-20

REC-3

OCT 11 1966

b7D

SSD CC MR. BRENNAN

OCT 14 1966

October 7, 1966
· SPECIAL INVESTIGATIVE DIVISION

This relates to K᠌ ᠌y, white
aged 31, a "beatnik" author and
narcotics addict who is being
sought as an unlawful flight subject
on the basis of local warrants at
San Mateo and San Francisco,
California, charging possession of
marijuana. One of Kesey's books
is "One Flew Over the Cuckoo's
Nest", a book relating to the
experiences of an individual
confined to a mental institution.

sources, determined that individual
believed to be Kesey, using an alias,
had been associating with several
marijuana addicts at Tepic, Mexico.
Attached teletype relates to
Kesey's alleged presence in San
Francisco where he talked to
reporters of San Francisco Chronicle
on 10-5 at a private party. San
Francisco has taken matter up with
U. S. Attorney. Investigation continuing.

JBE/

b7D

WA -02-   3:54 PDT   SRH

URGENT 10-6-66 BLM

TO DIRECTOR (88-37196)

FROM SAN FRANCISCO (88-10038

also known as   Unlawful Flight to Avoid Prosecution

KEN ELTON KESEY, AKA - FUGITIVE, UFAP - POSSESSION OF MARIJUANA.

SAN FRANCISCO CHRONICLE, OCTOBER SIX INSTANT, CARRIED A FRONT

PAGE STORY HEADLINED "LSD FUGITIVE'S STRANGE STORY." ARTICLE ALLEGED

SUBJECT IN SAN FRANCISCO OCTOBER FIVE LAST WHERE HE APPEARED AT PRIVATE

PARTY AT SAN FRANCISCO RESIDENCE AND INTIMATING SUBJECT TALKED WITH

CHRONICLE REPORTERS.

, CONFIDENTIALLY

ADVISED SAC OCTOBER SIX INSTANT THAT

b6
b7C
b7D

United States Attorney

USA CECIL F. POOLE, SAN FRANCISCO, ADVISED CHRONICLE STORY DID

NOT CONSTITUTE VIOLATION HARBORING STATUTE AS NO INDICATION AID AND

COMFORT HAD BEEN GIVEN TO SUBJECT. NO FURTHER EFFORTS BEING MADE

TO CONTACT REPORTERS AT THIS TIME.

END OF PAGE ONE

REC 5   88-37196-21

EX 106.

5 OCT 12 1966

OPTIONAL FORM NO. 10
MAY 1962 EDITION
GS\ GEN. REG. NO. 27   5010—106

UNITED STATES C ERNMENT

Memorandum

TO   : Mr. Gale   DATE: October 20, 1966

FROM : A. B. Eddy

SUBJECT: KEN ELTON KESEY
         FUGITIVE
         UFAP - POSSESSION OF MARIJUANA
         OO: SAN FRANCISCO

At 11:02 P.M. 10-20-66, Supervisor Richard Luebben of the San Francisco Office telephonically contacted the Bureau and spoke with SA [   ] night supervisor, Special Investigative Division.

Luebben stated that captioned fugitive was apprehended this evening by Special Agents of the San Francisco Office and was incarcerated in the San Francisco City Jail.

Apprehension occurred when SA Frances J. Collopy, Jr., Supervisor [   ] and Supervisor Glenn Harter of the San Francisco Office who were riding home in their personally owned automobile at 6:20 P.M. this evening when they spotted two individuals in a vehicle on the San Francisco Freeway. Vehicle was a panel truck driven by a beatnik-type individual and other occupant wearing dark glasses but observed to resemble captioned fugitive. After checking the photograph Agent Collopy had in his pocket, it was established that subject was in car. Efforts to get vehicle to pull over by showing credentials failed and a high speed chase ensued. Agents maneuvered car in front of fugitive's vehicle slowing it down eventually causing it to stop. Fugitive ran from truck and climbed fence with Agents pursuing. Agents apprehended subject without further incident.

b6
b7C

Subject is author of best seller "One Who Flew Over the Cuckoo's Nest" which is about the experiences of an inmate in a mental institution. A Federal complaint was filed 3-11-66 charging subject with unlawful flight as he was wanted by San Mateo and San Francisco, California, authorities for possession of marijuana. Subject fled to Mexico to avoid apprehension. San Francisco "Chronicle" on 10-6-66 carried front-page

1 - Mr. DeLoach
1 - Mr. Wick
1 - Mr. Gale
1 - Mr. Eddy
1 - Mr. [   ]
GWS:mtsm
(6)

REC- 129

EX-108

88 - 3116 - 23

3 OCT 24 1966
continued - over

61 NOV 9

Memorandum to Mr. Gale
Re: Ken Elton Kesey

headline "LSD Fugitive's Strange Story." This article alleged subject in
San Francisco on 10-5-66 where he appeared at a private party at a
San Francisco residence.

ACTION:

San Francisco is making a local press release due to the
anticipated press interest in this case.

Supervisor Thomas Bishop, Crime Records Division,
was advised of the above apprehension.

San Francisco was instructed to immediately submit a
teletype summary of the apprehension as it occurred along with the SAC's
recommendations for commendation.

- 2 -

October 21, 1966

PERSONAL

Mr. William M. Whelan, Jr.
Director of Special Services
Medical Review and Advisory Board
California Medical Association
993 Sutter Street
San Francisco, California 94102

Dear Whelan:

I have learned of the assistance you

rendered to my associates in the San Francisco Office

in connection with the arrest of Ken Elton Kesey on

October 20th. Your helpfulness in this matter is

indeed appreciated and I did not want the occasion

to pass without expressing my thanks.

Sincerely,

J. Edgar Hoover

REC 26

1 - San Francisco (88-10038)
    Reurtel 10-20-66
NOTE: SAC San Francisco recommends this letter and the
Special Investigative Division concurs. Mr. Whelan is on the
Special Correspondents' List. He is a former SAC who EOD 1-21-41 and resigned
3-5-58.
PDW:car
   (4)

Tolson
DeLoach
Mohr
Wick
Casper
Callahan
Conrad
Felt
Gale
Rosen
Sullivan
Tavel
Trotter
Tele. Room
Holmes
Gandy

MAIL ROOM ☐   TELETYPE UNIT ☐

FD-302 (Rev. 4-15-64)

FEDERAL BUREAU OF INVESTIGATION

Date_____ 10/26/66 _____

1

At approximately 6:20 p.m., Agents HARTER, ⬚ ⬚ and COLLOPY were proceeding south on the Peninsula Freeway enroute to their respective homes in an automobile driven by SA HARTER.

As the automobile approached the Army Street Off Ramp, an individual resembling KEN KESEY was observed in a red pickup truck, bearing California license CLS 220. A photograph of KESEY was observed by all Agents, and all agreed that the individual in the passenger side of the truck bore a striking resemblance to the Subject. It was decided that the truck would be flagged down and that this individual would be checked to determine if he was indeed identical.

SA HARTER maneuvered his automobile alongside the truck and honked his horn. Agents ⬚ and COLLOPY exhibited credentials to the driver. He refused to stop and continued down the freeway at a greater rate of speed. Agents followed until no off ramps would be available to the truck and then proceeded to cut in front of this vehicle, gradually slowing to a stop. Because of the press of traffic, the truck, too, had to stop. As it did so, the individual resembling KESEY was observed to jump from the truck and disappear into the trees located along the freeway. SAs COLLOPY and ⬚ jumped from HARTER's vehicle and chased this individual down the steep embankment, over a cyclone fence, and for approximately five blocks.

At the end of this run, the individual, who identified himself as KESEY, surrendered to Agents. He was returned to the freeway where Agents ⬚ HARTER and ⬚ were questioning ⬚ driver and owner of the vehicle.

Highway Patrolman ⬚ had arrived on the scene and drove SAs ⬚ and COLLOPY, with Subject KESEY, to the San Francisco City Jail. He was booked enroute U.S. Marshal.

- 2 -

On___10/20/66___ at __San Francisco, California__ File #__SF 88-10038__

SAs ⬚ __GLENN A. HARTER,__

by___and __FRANCIS J. COLLOPY, JR./vhk_____ Date dictated___10/25/66___

This document contains neither recommendations nor conclusions of the FBI. It is the property of the FBI and is loaned to your agency; it and its contents are not to be distributed outside your agency.

TRUE COPY

Dear Sir:

I am a student at **Fallbrook High School** and am currently involved in a term (**research**) paper about author Ken Kesey. It has come to my attention that Mr. Kesey was apprehended by the **FBI** and convicted as a felon.

Information about this author is scarce, especially in the area of Mr. Kesey's criminal record. For example, what crime he committed, how long he was in prison, where he was tried, etc. Any information about his childhood would also be appreciated. Please rush this information if possible. Paper is due in two weeks.

Thank you.

TRUE COPY

*Office of the Director
Federal Bureau of Investigation*

Washington, D.C.

REC-85

88-37196-33

June 2, 1970

b6
b7C

Dear

Your letter was received on May 28th. I am unable
to answer all of the questions you raised since information in our
files must be maintained as confidential in accordance with regulations of the Department of Justice. I can tell you, however, that
Ken Elton Kesey was apprehended by Special Agents of this Bureau
on October 20, 1966, near San Francisco, California. Kesey was a
fugitive charged with unlawful flight to avoid prosecution as he was
wanted by the San Mateo and San Francisco, California, law enforcement authorities for possession of marijuana. After his apprehension,
he was turned over to the San Francisco, California, law enforcement
authorities.

MAILED 11
JUN - 2 1970
COMM-FBI

Sincerely yours,

J. Edgar Hoover
John Edgar Hoover
Director

NOTE: Bufiles contain no record of correspondent. Kesey is the author
of a best-selling book entitled "One Who Flew Over The Cuckoo's Nest."
A Federal complaint was filed 3/11/66 charging him with Unlawful
Flight as he was wanted by San Mateo and San Francisco, California,
authorities for possession of marijuana. He fled to Mexico to avoid
apprehension. He returned to the United States and was apprehended
when Special Agents of the FBI, who were riding home in their personally
owned automobile, spotted Kesey on the San Francisco Freeway. After
a high-speed chase, Bureau Agents managed to stop the vehicle in which
Kesey was riding and apprehended him. He was turned over to the San
Francisco, California, authorities on 10/20/66. (Bufile 88-37196)

Tolson
DeLoach
Walters
Mohr
Bishop
Casper
Callahan
Conrad
Felt
Gale
Rosen
Sullivan
Tavel
Soyars
Tele. Room
Holmes
Gandy

51 JUN 9 mb 1970

MAIL ROOM ☐   TELETYPE UNIT ☐

Director of Information
Federal Bureau of Investigation
Washington, D.C.

Dear Sir,

I am attempting to get in touch with a man named Ken Kesey.
I do not know him personally, but he has been brought to my attention
by his presence in Tom Wolfe's Electric Kool-Aid Acid Test, and
I would like to communicate with him concerning certain characters
in the book and other matters. I assure you that I have neither
a criminal record nor criminal intents. I believe Mr. Kesey was
arrested and convicted for possession of marijuana in California
in the middle Sixties. I would appreciate your telling me either
his whereabouts or how I can locate him. Thank you.

Sincerely,

b6
b7C

EX-111
REC-5 88-37196-34

6 FEB   971

CORRESPONDENCE

February 1, 1971

EX-111
REC-54   88-37196-34

Dear

    Your letter was received on January 27th. I am
unable to furnish the information you requested since data in our
files must be maintained as confidential in accordance with the
regulations of the Department of Justice. I regret I cannot be of
help in this instance.

                Sincerely yours,

                J. Edgar Hoover

                John Edgar Hoover
                Director

MAILED 11
FEB 1 - 1971
COMM-FBI

NOTE: Bufiles contain no record of correspondent. Kesey is the author
of a best-selling book entitled "One Who Flew Over the Cuckoo's Nest."
A Federal complaint was filed 3-11-66 charging him with Unlawful Flight
as he was wanted by San Mateo and San Francisco, California, authorities
for possession of marijuana. He fled to Mexico to avoid apprehension.
He returned to the United States and was apprehended when Special Agents
of the FBI, who were riding home in their personally owned automobile,
spotted Kesey on the San Francisco Freeway. After a high-speed chase,
Bureau Agents managed to stop the vehicle in which Kesey was riding
and apprehended him. He was turned over to the San Francisco,
California, authorities on 10-20-66. (Bufile 88-37196).

Tolson
Sullivan
Mohr
Bishop
Brennan, C.D.
Callahan
Casper
Conrad
Felt
Gale
Rosen
Tavel
Walters
Soyars
Tele. Room

EFT:gar (3)

62 FEB 10 1971   MAIL ROOM ☐   TELETYPE UNIT ☐

Norman Mailer

NORMAN MAILER LAUNCHED INTO the literary spotlight with his WWII novel *The Naked and the Dead*, which sat for over a year on the New York Time best seller list. In the mid-'50s, amid a run of books less successful than his first, he helped to found the *Village Voice*, which would become a leader in alternative journalism. During that decade, he penned a series of essays meditating on "American existentialism" and infamously stabbed his wife with a knife at a party. But none of that would be enough to start the FBI's inquiry into the notoriously egotistical author. It wasn't until 1962 that they perked their ears at the sound of the Mailer on stage at Carnegie Hall where he delivered a pithy critique of the men in black: "The F.B.I. has done more damage to America than the Communist party."

Less than a month later, he criticized Hoover directly: "The worst celebrity in America is of course J. Edgar Hoover; the worst play would be the he most enjoyed — was it J.B." Theodore Roethke provided back-up in the piece, captioning an image of the head Fed with "J. Edgar Hoover, head of our thought police — a martinet, a preposterous figure, but not funny." A review of Mailer's previous agency criticisms was conducted.

Louis Budenz, a former Communist turned FBI informant, claimed that Mailer was a member of the party, though other reports refuted such a classification, even suggesting that known Communists found Mailer distasteful. For the next decade, the Feds tracked Mailer's travels and residences.

On January 1969 review of Mailer's *Miami and the Siege of Chicago*, Hoover scrawled, "Let me have a memo on Mailer."

However, given that Mailer had not planned travel to Cuba, there were no immediate concerns, as far as the New York Office was concerned. Interest flared up again a few years later, when Lloyd Shearer, a gossip columnist, contacted a former FBI Special Agent to let them know that Mailer was making some serious insinuations about the FBI's role in the death of starlet Marilyn Monroe. And though they considered options for removing the allegations from the piece, they were ultimately unsuccessful and dropped their interest in the writer.

OPTIONAL FORM NO. 10

UNITED STATES

Memora

TO   Mr. W. C. Sullivan   DATE: June 29, 1962

FROM   Mr. J. F. Bland

                                      1–Mr. Belmont
                                      1–Mr. Sullivan
                                      1–Mr. DeLoach
                                      1–Mr. Bland
                                      1 – Mr. Haack
                                      1–Mr. Kitchens

SUBJECT: NORMAN KINGSLEY MAILER
         SECURITY MATTER - C

Tolson _____
Belmont _____
Mohr _____
Callahan _____
Conrad _____
DeLoach _____
Evans _____
Malone _____
Rosen _____
Sullivan _____
Tavel _____
Trotter _____
Tele. Room _____
Holmes _____
Gandy _____

George Sokolsky in his column 6-29-62 criticizes Norman Mailer for writing an "Esquire" magazine article on Jacqueline Kennedy which he states drools on and on in a "vein of slight ridicule and colossal impudence." The Director requested a memorandum on Mailer.

Mailer, 39, resides New York City and is in Section A of the Reserve Index. He is author of the novel "The Naked and the Dead," a best seller. In November, 1960, he received much notoriety for the stabbing of his wife for which he received a three-year suspended sentence. Mailer has been characterized as an "off-beat crusader for peace." In March, 1960, he appeared on a radio panel show and admitted being a "leftist." He charged the FBI with being a secret police organization and said it should be abolished. On a television show on 8-8-61 he said that no one is happier than the FBI to see communism and Castro succeed in Cuba since it gives the FBI something to do.

Louis Budenz, former managing editor of the "Daily Worker," who broke with the Communist Party in 1945, advised on 6-30-50 that Mailer was a concealed communist and that until at least 1945 he was closely connected with the Communist Party. During the period 1948-1950 subject was a member of a citizens committee to elect Simon W. Gerson, communist and American Labor Party candidate, to the City Council of New York City; was active in the campaign of Henry Wallace, Progressive Party candidate for President in 1948; and was a sponsor of the Freedom Crusade of the Civil Rights Congress to be held in Washington, D. C., the day after the trial of the communist leaders opened in Federal court in New York City. The "Daily Worker" issue of 3-28-49 reported that Mailer made the statement, "So long as there is capitalism, there is going to be war." Mailer received an invitation to attend a reception to be held on 7-22-53 at the Polish Consulate in New York City but the source did not know whether he attended it. In 1956 Mailer was listed as a member of the National Committee of the Kutcher Civil Rights Committee, which had been organized to fight the dismissal on loyalty charges of James Kutcher, a legless veteran, from his position with the Veterans Administration.

ACTION: For your information.

REC 138   100-370923-46

11 JUL 11 1962

ALL INFORMATION CONTAINED
HEREIN IS UNCLASSIFIED
DATE 3-23-88 BY SP2mackel

UNITED STATES DEPARTMENT OF JUSTICE

FEDERAL BUREAU OF INVESTIGATION

New York, New York
September 13, 1962

DECLASSIFIED BY 60324 UC BAW/RS/VCF
ON 09-25-2008

In Reply, Please Refer to
File No.

Bufile 100-370923
NYfile 100-93909

Re: Norman Kingsley Mailer
    Security Matter - C

On September 7, 1962, [   ]
[   ] Court of General Sessions, 100 Centre Street, New
York City, furnished the following information to Special
Agent [   ]

b6
b7C

On August 27, 1962, Mailer advised [   ] that
he had attended a Writers' Conference in Edinburgh, Scotland,
leaving New York on August 21, 1962, and returning on August
24, 1962. [   ] was unable to furnish any further
information concerning travel by the subject.

Norman Mailer resides at 142 Columbia Heights,
Brooklyn, New York, and is a self-employed writer from his
residence.

A confidential source, who has furnished reliable
information in the past, advised on June 30, 1950, that Norman
Mailer was a "concealed" Communist. The source stated that
a "concealed" Communist is one who does not want himself known
as a Communist and would deny membership in the Party.

A second confidential source, who has furnished
reliable information in the past, advised on April 6, 1960,
that Norman Mailer, author of "The Naked and the Dead"
apparently is known by many individuals within the Communist
Party (CP). The informant reported that from general
conversations with individuals within the CP, it may be assumed
that Mailer at the present time is anti-Communist and that
apparently CP members do not like him personally or approve
of his writing. According to the source, Communists have
indicated that his writing is considered "disruptive" in
nature.

b2

AGENCY [   ]

REQ. REC'D

DATE FORW. 9/21/62

HOW FORW.

DECLASSIFIED 12-10-76
4417 50

This document contains neither
recommendations nor conclusions
of the FBI. It is the property
of the FBI, and is loaned to
your agency; it and its contents
are not to be distributed outside your agency. This is in
answer to your request for a
check of FBI files.

CONFIDENTIAL

49

ENCLOSURE

CONFIDENTIAL

Re Norman Kingsley Mailer   CONFIDENTIAL   CONFIDENTIAL

The following is a description of Norman Mailer:

Sex	Male
Race	White
Date of birth	January 31, 1923
Place of birth	Long Branch, New Jersey
Height	Five feet eight inches
Weight	145 pounds
Build	Medium
Hair	Brown
Eyes	Blue

CONFIDENTIAL

CONFIDENTIAL

-2-

CONFIDENTIAL

SECRET

NY 100-98909

B. Marital Status B. APPROX. *1937* *Mailer*

The "New York Times", a daily newspaper
published in New York City, in an article on May 18,
1962, reflected that NORMAN MAILER confirmed on May 17,
1962, that he and Lady JEAN CAMPBELL, 33 year old
daughter of Britain's Duke of Argyle, had been secretly
married. The bride first mentioned the marriage in
a column she wrote for the "London Evening Standard"
a newspaper owned by her grandfather. *England, N.Y.*

Mr. MAILER said he and Lady JEAN had been married
"for some time", and plan to live in Brooklyn. [MAILER]
declined to give the exact date or place of the wedding.

C. Status of Health

The "New York Post" edition of November 22,
1960, page 1, carried an article concerning the subject's arrest for stabbing his wife at their residence
on November 21, 1960. In the article it was noted
that the New York City Police Department quoted the
subject's wife as saying that her husband had "homicidal
tendencies", and that his family had been trying to
induce him to see a psychiatrist. The newspaper article
additionally quoted the New York City Police Department
as stating that the subject's sister, Mrs. BARBARA ALSON, *Mailer*
stated "she has been trying to get him to see a psychiatrist".

D. Arrest Record

Division of Supervision, Probation Department, Court of
General Sessions, 100 Centre Street, New York City, on
September 15, 1961, advised SA [   ] that
the subject is currently under deferred sentence supervision
in the Court of General Sessions, New York City, awaiting
sentencing on November 13, 19   after pleading guilty on
March 9, 1961, to third degree assault
[   ] on November 21, 1960; [   ] in
New York City *Mailer*

b6
b7C

- 2 -

SECRET

~~SECRET~~

NY 100-98909

The November 14, 1961 edition of the "New York Times" on page 45, carried an article reporting that NORMAN MAILER had received a suspended sentence on November 13, 1961, on his plea of guilty to the stabbing of his wife, ADELE, last year. The suspended sentence was given by General Sessions Judge, MITCHELL D. SCHWEITZER who continued the subject on probation for a period not to exceed three years.

The Identification Division, Federal Bureau of Investigation, Washington, D.C. in August, 1961, furnished the following arrest record for NORMAN MAILER under Federal Bureau of Investigation number 218795B:

CONTRIBUTOR OF FINGERPRINTS	NAME AND NUMBER	ARRESTED OR RECEIVED	CHARGE	DISPOSITION
Army	NORMAN K. MAILER #42 127 367	3-27-44 Camp Upton NY.		
PD NY NY	NORMAN MAILER #B-471516	11-21-60	felonious aslt (knife) 240 PL	
Prob Dept Crt of Gen Sess NY NY	NORMAN MAILER #84276	11-21-60	aslt 3rd deg	PG

The following descriptive information was included in the identification record:

Residence   250 West 94th Street New York City in 1960 (as on prt #84276)

Fingerprint   I 32 W OIM 14
Classification   I 28 W IMI

- 3 -

~~SECRET~~

OPTIONAL FORM NO. 10

ALL INFORMATION CONTAINED
HEREIN IS UNCLASSIFIED
DATE 07-11-2008 BY 60324 UC BAW/RS/VCF

UNITED STATES GOVERNMENT

Memorandum

TO : Mr. DeLoach   DATE: 6-4-63

FROM : M. A. Jones

SUBJECT: NORMAN KINGSLEY MAILER
CRIMINAL OF BUREAU DURING LECTURE
AT CARNEGIE HALL, 5-31-63

Tolson _____
Belmont _____
Mohr _____
Casper _____
Callahan _____
Conrad _____
DeLoach _____
Evans _____
Gale _____
Rosen _____
Sullivan _____
Tavel _____
Trotter _____
Tele. Room _____
Holmes _____
Gandy _____

"The New York Times" of 6-2-63, carried an article concerning a
lecture by Mailer at Carnegie Hall on 5-31-63, in which Mailer was critical of
the Bureau. This article, written by Brian O'Doherty, not identifiable in Bufiles,
treats Mailer's comments in a caustic manner, stating that since Mailer had become
famous through his novel, "The Naked and the Dead," he has spent his time "putting
himself on display."

The article states that Mailer, in commenting on various aspects
of the national scene, bemoaned the lack of a "hero in government and the F.B.I.
and the implacable facelessness of capitalism and communism." He also made the
comment that "The F.B.I. has done more damage to America than the Communist
Party." The article contains no additional pertinent reference to the FBI.

The writer pokes fun at Mailer throughout the article and rather
effectively blunts the sharp edge of Mailer's criticism against the FBI.

INFORMATION IN BUFILES: EX-117   REG- 57   100- 370923-53

Mailer, a well-known author in his early 40's, is probably best
known for his post World War II best seller, "The Naked and the Dead." He was
described by Louis Budenz as an adherent of the Communist Party and as being
closely associated with the Party until 1945. Investigation conducted as a result
of this information disclosed that Mailer has been active in various communist
fronts since the late 1940's.   13 JUN 12 1963

Mailer, a New York City resident, received a great deal of notoriety
in early 1961 when he stabbed his wife after a party. He was committed to Bellevue
on that occasion for observation and his condition was described as acute paranoia
with homicidal-suicidal tendencies. Mailer subsequently received a suspended
sentence for stabbing his wife and was placed on probation for a period of three years.
He is currently listed on the Reserve Index.

1 - Mr. DeLoach
1 - Mr. Belmont   100-370923
1 - Mr. Sullivan   434   JUN 17 1963
ELR:ear   (8)

ENCLOSURE

M.A.Jones to DeLoach Memo
RE: Norman Kingsley Mailer

       On 3-20-60, Mailer made extremely critical statements concerning the FBI during his appearance on a Chicago television program. He claimed that the FBI was a secret police organization and should be abolished. During this program he admitted to being a "leftist" but denied Communist Party membership. Mailer was also critical of the FBI on 8-8-61, while appearing on a New York City television program as a guest panelist. He stated in substance that the FBI liked to tell people what to do and that we were happy to see communism and Castro succeed in Cuba since that gave us something to do. He also implied that communism was no longer a menace in the United States. Both these television appearances were made the subjects of memoranda submitted by the Crime Records Division.

RECOMMENDATION:

       For information.

- 2 -

ALL INFORMATION CONTAINED
HEREIN IS UNCLASSIFIED
DATE 07-11-2008 BY 60324 UC_BAW/RS/VCF

b6
b7C

TRUE COPY

Mr. Edgar Hoover
Director F.B.I.
Washington, D. C.

Dear Sir:

    The novel "The Naked and The Dead" by
Norman Mailer, is on the reading list for our high school
students. May I have your opinion as to the suitability
and advisability of students reading this book. Also may I
have your permission to show your reply to our local School Board.

    Thank you so very much for your consideration.

          Sincerely,

March 12, 1964

1 TC 3-17-64 jog

ack 3-18-64 RR/car

ALL INFORMATION CONTAINED
HEREIN IS UNCLASSIFIED
DATE 07-11-2008 BY 60324 UC BAW/RS/VCF

b6
b7C

100-370733-54

March 18, 1964

REC-3

Dear

I have received your letter of March 12th.

Although I would like to be of service, the FBI being
an investigative agency of the Federal Government, neither makes
evaluations nor draws conclusions as to the character or integrity
of any organization, publication or individual. Also, it has been
my policy over the years not to comment on any material not
prepared by the FBI or me. In view of the foregoing, I am sure
you will understand why it is not possible for me to comment
in the manner you requested concerning the novel, "The Naked
and The Dead," by Norman Mailer.

Sincerely yours,

E. Edgar Hoover

John Edgar Hoover
Director

MAILED 19
MAR 18 1964
COMM-FBI

NOTE: Correspondent is not identifiable in Bufiles. The novel, "The Naked
and The Dead," was a best-selling book concerning World War II. The author,
Norman Mailer, is well known to the Bureau and has been highly critical
of the Bureau in the past. He was committed to Bellevue Hospital, New York,
after stabbing his wife. Hospital authorities diagnosed his problem as
acute paranoia, homicidal-suicidal tendencies.

Tolson _____
Belmont _____
Mohr _____
Casper _____
Callahan _____
Conrad _____
DeLoach _____
Evans _____
Gale _____
Rosen _____
Sullivan _____
Tavel _____
Trotter _____
Tele. Room _____
Holmes _____
Gandy _____

RR:cai
(3)

MAIL ROOM ☐   TELETYPE UNIT ☐

OPTIONAL FORM NO. 10

UNITED STATES GOVERNMENT

Memorandum

ALL INFORMATION CONTAINED
HEREIN IS UNCLASSIFIED
DATE 07-11-2008 BY 60324 UC BAW/RS/VCF

TO   : Mr. DeLoach   DATE: 8-6-63

FROM   : M. A. Jones

SUBJECT: NORMAN KINGSLEY MAILER
         CRITICISM OF THE DIRECTOR
         DISSENT MAGAZINE

BACKGROUND:

Captioned individual's introduction to his "The Presidential Papers" appears
in the Summer, 1963, issue of "Dissent." According to a footnote, the book is to be
published by Putnam this September. Mailer styles himself as a "special self-appointed
Presidential advisor" and states that his book will contain a discussion of "all the topics
a President ought to consider and rarely does, and some of all the topics he considers
every day, but rarely in a fashion which is fresh." One of Mailer's complaints, in the
introduction, is that the President has a wealth of statistical information at his fingertips,
such as "the number of FBI men in the American Communist Party," but he is guilty of
doing nothing to remedy "a total and depressing lack of attention for that vast heart of
political matter which is utterly resistant to categorization, calculation, or statistic."
He avers that no President "can save America from a descent into totalitarianism without
shifting the mind of the American politician to existential styles of political thought."
Mailer states one must read his book for an explanation of "existential styles of political
thought;" however, he will give a clue to its definition. He then states that it has long been
his thesis that the FBI has done more damage to America than the American Communist
Party, through putting a sense of inhibition into the popular arts and the popular mind. He
alleges this has happened because of the lack of an heroic man as its leader. Mailer claims
the FBI has a leader, but not a hero and alleges the Director is a man who embodies his
time but is not superior to it. He cites Franklin D. Roosevelt as a hero of his description
and lists as merely leaders, Calvin Coolidge, Herbert Hoover and Dwight Eisenhower.
The gist of his remarks concerning the FBI is that the organization would prosper with an
heroic leader, and it would deserve to prosper because existential politics is rooted in
the concept of the hero who enriches whatever corner of the world he finds himself by
using his imagination, strength, timing, wit and bravery.

INFORMATION IN BUFILES:

100- 3 70923
NOT RECORDED
184 AUG 28 1963

"Dissent" is a self-styled "quarterly of socialist opinion."

Mailer, a well-known author in his early 40's, is probably best known for
his post World War II best seller, "The Naked and the Dead." He was described by

1 - Mr. DeLoach
1 - Mr. Sullivan
1 - Mr. Belmont
HHA:cc (6)

SENT DIRECTOR

M. A. Jones to Mr. DeLoach Memo
RE: NORMAN KINGSLEY MAILER

Louis Budenz as an adherent of the Communist Party and as being closely associated with the Party until 1945. Investigation conducted as a result of this information disclosed that Mailer has been active in various communist fronts since the late 1940's. He is currently listed on the Reserve Index.

Mailer, a New York City resident, received a great deal of notoriety in early 1961 when he stabbed his wife after a party. He was committed to Bellevue on that occasion for observation and his condition was described as acute paranoia with homicidal-suicidal tendencies. Mailer subsequently received a suspended sentence for stabbing his wife and was placed on probation for a period of three years.

On 3-20-60, Mailer made extremely critical statements concerning the FBI during his appearance on a Chicago television program. He claimed that the FBI was a secret police organization and should be abolished. During this program he admitted to being a "leftist" but denied Communist Party membership. Mailer was also critical of the FBI on 8-8-61, while appearing on a New York City television program as a guest panelist. He stated in substance that the FBI liked to tell people what to do and that we were happy to see communism and Castro succeed in Cuba since that gave us something to do.

During a lecture in Carnegie Hall on 5-31-63, Mailer stated, "The FBI has done more damage to America than the Communist Party." A critical account of Mailer's lecture appeared in "The New York Times" on 6-2-63 in which he was described as a person who has "put himself on display" after writing a successful novel.

RECOMMENDATION:

None. For information.

- 2 -

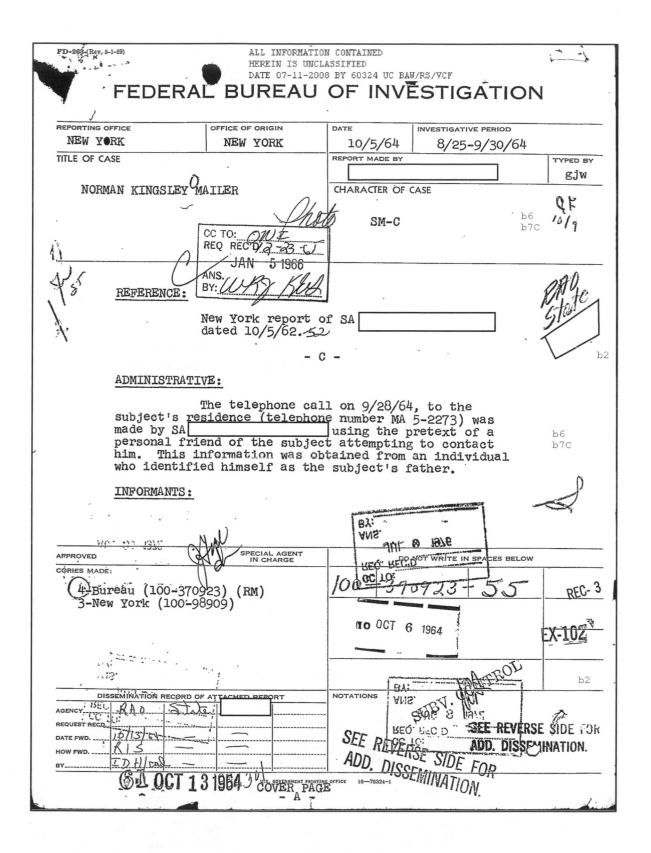

FD-263 (Rev. 5-1-59)

ALL INFORMATION CONTAINED
HEREIN IS UNCLASSIFIED
DATE 07-11-2008 BY 60324 UC BAW/RS/VCF

FEDERAL BUREAU OF INVESTIGATION

REPORTING OFFICE	OFFICE OF ORIGIN	DATE	INVESTIGATIVE PERIOD
NEW YORK	NEW YORK	10/5/64	8/25-9/30/64

TITLE OF CASE	REPORT MADE BY	TYPED BY
NORMAN KINGSLEY MAILER		gjw

CHARACTER OF CASE

SM-C

b6
b7C

CC TO: ONE
REQ REC'D 2-23-6?
JAN 5 1966
ANS.
BY:

REFERENCE:

New York report of SA
dated 10/5/62.

- C -

b2

ADMINISTRATIVE:

The telephone call on 9/28/64, to the
subject's residence (telephone number MA 5-2273) was
made by SA _____ using the pretext of a
personal friend of the subject attempting to contact
him. This information was obtained from an individual
who identified himself as the subject's father.

b6
b7C

INFORMANTS:

APPROVED	SPECIAL AGENT IN CHARGE	DO NOT WRITE IN SPACES BELOW

COPIES MADE:

4-Bureau (100-370923) (RM)
3-New York (100-98909)

100-370923-55   REC-3

OCT 6 1964   EX-102

b2

DISSEMINATION RECORD OF ATTACHED REPORT

				NOTATIONS
AGENCY	RAD State			
REQUEST RECD				
DATE FWD.	10/13/64			
HOW FWD.	RIS			
BY	IDH/cal			

SEE REVERSE SIDE FOR
ADD. DISSEMINATION.

OCT 13 1964   COVER PAGE
- A -

U.S. GOVERNMENT PRINTING OFFICE   16—76324-1

ALL INFORMATION CONTAINED
HEREIN IS UNCLASSIFIED EXCEPT
WHERE SHOWN OTHERWISE

UNITED STATES DEPARTMENT OF JUSTICE

FEDERAL BUREAU OF INVESTIGATION
Washington, D. C. 20535
February 1, 1968

*In Reply, Please Refer to
File No.*

EXEMPTED FROM AUTOMATIC
DECLASSIFICATION
AUTHORITY DERIVED FROM:
FBI AUTOMATIC DECLASSIFICATION GUIDE
EXEMPTION CODE 25X(1, 6)
DATE 07-15-2008

NO FOREIGN DISSEMINATION

~~SECRET~~

(S)   NORMAN KINGSLEY MAILER

b1

(S)

On December 14, 1967, according to a confidential
informant who has furnished reliable information in the past,

On October 30, 1967, "The New York Post"
advised that author Norman Mailer had appealed
his conviction for disorderly conduct in the
October 21, 1967 anti-war march on the Pentagon."

NO FOREIGN DISSEMINATION

~~SECRET~~

~~GROUP 1
Excluded from automatic
downgrading and
declassification~~

100-370923-66

ENCLOSURE

OPTIONAL FORM NO. 10
MAY 1962 EDITION
GSA GEN. REG. NO. 27

5010-106

UNITED STATES GOVERNMENT

Memorandum

TO   : Mr. W. C. Sullivan   DATE: January 10, 1969

FROM   : C. D. Brennan

SUBJECT: BOOK REVIEW
"MIAMI AND THE SIEGE OF CHICAGO"
BY NORMAN MAILER
INTERNAL SECURITY - NEW LEFT MATTER

Tolson
DeLoach
Mohr
Bishop
Casper
Callahan
Conrad
Felt
Gale
Rosen
Sullivan
Tavel
Trotter
Tele. Room
Holmes
Gandy

        This memorandum presents a review of captioned book,
which is being retained in the Communist Infiltrated and New
Left Groups Unit, Internal Security Section, Domestic Intelligence
Division.

SYNOPSIS: Mailer, a well known author and self-admitted "leftist,"
is on "Section A," Reserve Index, New York Office. Captioned book
called by author, who was present at both conventions, "an informal
history of the Republican and Democratic Conventions of 1968," but
actually more of study of Mailer's innermost reactions to the two
conventions, individual candidates, and their supporters, in relation
to his own philosophy. It is written in his usual obscene and bitter
style. He vacillates greatly in his thinking--first deciding he must
have become a "closet Republican" because of sympathy with that Party
when they spoke on need to return to individual human effort; then
deciding he felt great weariness in listening to "black" cries of
"black superiority," which definitely was not in line with his
previous concepts and writings; but in long run emerging at end of
book calling Yippies and like groups his "troops and his "children,"
all left-wing "blacks" his "polemical associates," and asserting his
determination to vote for no one, unless for Eldridge Cleaver. Book
contains reference to Senator McCarthy's statement that he would
replace Director, if elected, and other uncomplimentary statements
of type that might be expected from Mailer regarding the FBI and
the Director.

ACTION: None. For information.

100-370923

1 - Mr. DeLoach   1 - Mr. Shackelford
1 - Mr. Sullivan   1 -
1 - Mr. C. D. Brennan
1 -   1 - 62-46855 (Book
                               Review File)
LMc:lm
(8)

JAN 22 1969

REC 91 100-370923-70

b6
b7C

DETAILS - Page Two

Memorandum for Mr. W. C. Sullivan
BOOK REVIEW
"MIAMI AND THE SIEGE OF CHICAGO"
BY NORMAN MAILER
100-370923

DETAILS:

The Author

      Mailer is a well known author in his middle 40's and
is probably best known for his post World War II best seller
"The Naked and the Dead." He is currently listed on "Section A"
of the Reserve Index of the New York Office and is a self-admitted
"leftist." He has been highly critical of this Bureau and U. S.
Government policies. He was described by Louis Budenz as an
adherent of the Communist Party and as being closely associated
with the Party until 1945. Investigation conducted as a result
of this information disclosed that Mailer has been active in
various communist fronts since the late 1940's. He received a
great deal of notoriety in early 1951 when he stabbed his wife
after a party. He was committed to Bellevue Hospital, New York
City, on that occasion for observation and his condition was
described as acute paranoia with homicidal-suicidal tendencies.

      Mailer was arrested for disorderly conduct in the
10/21/67 antiwar march on the Pentagon. During the Democratic
National Convention, he was one of several speakers on 8/28/68
in Grant Park, Chicago, Illinois.

FBI and Mr. Hoover Mentioned

      References to the FBI or Mr. Hoover appear as follows
in captioned book:

Page 107: With reference to President Johnson's ability to comprehend the higher game of what Mailer called "international politics-
is-property," Mailer declared him about as well-equipped as
William F. Buckley, Eleanor Roosevelt, Barry Goldwater, George
Patton, J. Edgar Hoover, Ronald Reagan, and Averill Harriman.
"Politics-is-property" was defined by Mailer as never giving
something away for nothing.

Page 122: Mailer quoted Senator McCarthy as having stated, in a
session at the Democratic Convention: "They say I was impersonal.
I want you to know that I am the only candidate who said he would
get rid of J. Edgar Hoover and that is a person."

-2-

Memorandum for Mr. W. C. Sullivan
BOOK REVIEW
"MIAMI AND THE SIEGE OF CHICAGO"
BY NORMAN MAILER
100-370923

Page 130: In an interview with Senator McCarthy, Mailer told
the Senator that he would have made "a perfect chief for the
F.B.I.," to which McCarthy allegedly replied: "Of course,
you're absolutely right."

Page 146: Mailer stated he had gone to Humphrey's private headquarters one night very late during the Democratic Convention
where there was nobody to receive him "but six or eight young
Secret Servicemen or F. B. I. with bullet-faces, crew-cuts, and
an absurd tension at the recognition of his name."

Page 158: Mailer predicted that years of sabotage are ahead and
said they would be giving engineering students tests in loyalty
before they were done and that the F.B.I. would come to question
whoever took a mail order course in radio.

Page 214: With reference to the "establishment," Mailer classified
its members as "all the bad cops, U. S. marshals, generals,
corporation executives, high government bureaucrats, rednecks,
insane Black militants, half crazy provocateurs, Right-wing
faggots, Right-wing high-strung geniuses, J. Edgar Hoover, and
the worst of the rich surrounding every seat of Establishment
in America."

Book Review

        Captioned book, published in October, 1968, is called
by the author, who was present at both conventions, "an informal
history of the Republican and Democratic Conventions of 1968,"
but is actually more of a study of Mailer's innermost reactions
to the two conventions, the individual candidates, and their
supporters, in relation to his own philosophy. It is written in
his usual obscene and bitter style.

        The first section of the book is devoted to the
Republican Convention and is entitled "Nixon in Miami." Mailer
states he has disliked Nixon intimately ever since his Checkers
speech in 1952 and has never written anything nice about him,
but listening to Nixon's speeches during the Republican Convention
he finds himself believing that Nixon has changed from the
"Tricky Dick" of old. Mailer decides he must have become a
"closet Republican" because of his sympathy with the Republican

-3-

Memorandum for Mr. W. C. Sullivan
BOOK REVIEW
"MIAMI AND THE SIEGE OF CHICAGO"
BY NORMAN MAILER
100-370923

Party when Nixon emphasized the need to return to individual human effort; however, this section of the book ends with Mailer being indecisive about Nixon, not knowing whether he was ready to like the candidate or detested him for his "resolutely non-poetic binary system, his computer's brain, did not know if the candidate were real as a man, or whole as a machine, lonely in his sad eminence or megalomaniacal, humble enough to feel the real wounds of the country or sufficiently narcissistic to dream the tyrant's dream."

Because the reporters were kept waiting at a press conference with Ralph D. Abernathy during the Republican Convention, Mailer decided he was getting tired of Negroes and their rights and was weary to the bone of listening to Black cries of Black superiority, which definitely was not in line with his previous concepts and writings; however, he emerges at the end of the book calling all left-wing "blacks" his "polemical associates" and asserting his determination to vote for no one, unless for Eldridge Cleaver.

The second section of the book is entitled "The Siege of Chicago." Mailer expresses his belief that President Johnson, using Mayor Daly as his instrument, deliberately plotted to crack his Party in two because that Party had been willing to let him go. He claimed that President Johnson completely controlled the Democratic Convention, although he never appeared there in person to speak, and intimated that the police brutality exhibited during the demonstrations was at the President's express command.

Mailer chastises himself throughout the second section of the book for not joining the demonstrators during the first days of the convention. Although he knows he belongs with them, he rationalizes that he cannot afford to be injured or jailed because he has a book to write and must cover the Convention; however, he is haunted by the fact that the real reason may be that he is afraid. When he finally spoke at a meeting of the demonstrators on August 28, 1968, after fortifying himself with several drinks, he was so pleased with himself that he felt there was no rank in any Army suitable for him below the level of General. He stated, "It was something to discover the secret source of the river of one's own good guts or lack of them. And booze was no bad canoe."

-4-

Memorandum for Mr. W. C. Sullivan
BOOK REVIEW
"MIAMI AND THE SIEGE OF CHICAGO"
BY NORMAN MAILER
100-370923

Before allying himself with the demonstrators, Mailer
was watching the conflict between the police and the demonstrators
from the 19th floor window of his hotel. He stated he could then
understand how Mussolini's son-in-law had been able to find
the bombs he dropped from his airplane beautiful as they burst
because as he watched the clubbing, gassing, and chaos below
him he felt a sense of calm and beauty. He stated it was as if
the war had finally begun, and this, therefore, was a great and
solemn moment.

Mailer vacillates greatly in his thinking, making this
book difficult to read and impossible at times to comprehend.
While he calls himself a revolutionary and states he belongs in
England, where one's radicalism might never be tested, he loathes
the thought of living anywhere but in America where he has been
allowed to write and earn a good income. At the same time, he
calls the Yippies and like groups his "troops" and his "children."

OP ONAL FORM NO. 10
1962 EDITION
GEN. REG. NO. 27   5010-106

UNITED STATES GOVERNMENT

Memorandum

ALL INFORMATION CONTAINED
HEREIN IS UNCLASSIFIED
DATE 07-15-2008 BY 60324 UC BAW/RS/VCF

TO   : Mr. Bishop   DATE: 12-5-69

FROM   : M. A. Jones

SUBJECT: ARTICLE TITLED "THE INVISIBLE POLICE,"
IN 12-8-69 ISSUE OF "THE NATION" MAGAZINE
BY JOSEPH R. LUNDY, LEGISLATIVE ASSISTANT
TO CONGRESSMAN ABNER J. MIKVA
(D) ILLINOIS (94-64216)

This is a four page article dealing with the "increasing use of police spies and undercover agents" which author Lundy feels "may have put us on the way to America's first experience with 'political police.'" He states that in the conspiracy trial of the Chicago 8, the government is relying almost entirely on evidence gathered by police undercover agents. He says that Louis Salsberg, a newspaper photographer who, "The New York Times" stated, "had become a regular fixture at radical gatherings in New York City," revealed that he had been a paid informer of the FBI since 1967. Author Lundy stated that Herbert Philbrick, the FBI's best-known undercover operative, produced "I Led Three Lives," which was a best seller during the 1950's. He discusses police informers and pertinent Supreme Court decisions such as the Hoffa case. On page 631 he says application of the Fourth Amendment to secret agents who move into political groups would not ban their use elsewhere.

At the bottom of page 631 author refers to former SA Turner and quotes Turner at the top of page 632 on the types of intelligence squads found in police agencies. Lundy completes his article by quoting Norman Mailer who stated "the infiltration of political groups by police secret agents had become, in 1963, a chronic joke." But the author feels that in a country which continues to pride itself on unfettered political exchange, it is not a very funny joke.

BUFILES:

Nothing on author Joseph R. Lundy. References on Congressman Abner J. Mikva (D) of Illinois show he has had the support of Communist Party in past because of his "liberal" views regarding racial equality and civil liberties. At one time he was a member of the National Lawyers Guild, a cited communist front organization. As a newly elected Congressman, Inspector [   ] saw Congressman Mikva on 1-31-69. Mikva was most cordial and he greatly appreciated having a Bureau representative contact him. He said he admired the Director, was interested in perfecting stringent gun control laws and had studied Director's views on this subject. (94-64216-1, 2)

RECOMMENDATION:
For information.

1 - Mr. DeLoach   1 - Mr. Bishop   1 - M. A. Jones

OPTIONAL FORM NO. 10
MAY 1962 EDITION
GSA FPMR (41 CFR) 101-11.6

UNITED STATES GOVERNMENT

Memorandum

ALL INFORMATION CONTAINED
HEREIN IS UNCLASSIFIED
DATE 07-15-2008 BY 60324 UC BAW/RS/VCF

TO   :   ACTING DIRECTOR, FBI   DATE: 7/6/73

FROM :   ADIC, LOS ANGELES (66-1700)

SUBJECT: LLOYD SHEARER, Editor
              "Parade" Magazine;
              NORMAN MAILER
              INFORMATION CONCERNING

Mr. WILLIAM G. SIMON, former SAC, called the office 7/5/73, with the following information.

Mr. SIMON stated that he had a call from LLOYD SHEARER, editor of "Parade" Magazine. SHEARER wanted to know if SIMON was, in fact, SAC of the Los Angeles Office in 1962. SIMON told him he was. SHEARER then stated that NORMAN MAILER has written a book on the life of MARILYN MONROE which is going to carry a price list of $20.00 per copy and hopefully, be on the Book-of-The-Month within a few months. There is an allegation in the book to the effect that in 1962, FBI Agents in Los Angeles went to the telephone company in Santa Monica, California, and removed a "paper tape" of MARILYN's calls, some of which were presumably calls to the White House or White House Staff on the night of her death. Mr. SHEARER said there was some further suggestion that the FBI was either providing her some protection or providing the White House Staff with some protection.

SHEARER asked Mr. SIMON if he knew anything about this and Mr. SIMON told SHEARER that he had absolutely no recollection of any such events. SHEARER asked if he, SIMON, should not have known about this if he was Agent in Charge and SIMON reiterated that he should have known about such activity but that he had no recollection of any such events.

Mr. SIMON stated that SHEARER did not press the issue further and he does not know how far SHEARER intends to carry his inquiry but he wanted this office and the Bureau to know of SHEARER's inquiry and of this reference to the FBI in the forthcoming book if it had not already been brought to the Bureau's attention.

REC-57 100-370923-74

(2)- Bureau
3 - Los Angeles
      (1cc 100-30576) EX-109
      (1cc 62-7251)
(5)-

WFBI XEROX   17 JUL 27 1973

AUG 9 1973

PERS. REG. UNIT

Buy U.S. Savings Bonds Regularly on the Payroll Savings Plan

COPY RETAINED IN PERSONNEL RECORDS

UNRECORDED COPY FILED IN 62-86111-1

5010-108

Mr. SIMON stated that he was being very truthful with SHEARER and he did not have any recollection of any such events or any such allegations occurring in 1962 or associated with MARILYN MONROE's death.

A number of individuals in the Los Angeles Office recall hearing stories and gossip outside the Bureau at the time of MARILYN MONROE's death to the effect that she had made some calls to BOBBY KENNEDY shortly before her death, but that discreet inquiry in this office and a review of our indices revealed no confirming facts and certainly no indication of any Bureau involvement as alleged by MAILER.

In view of MAILER's alleged allegation concerning the FBI, the Bureau may desire to explore what avenues might possibly be utilized which would result in the allegation being removed from MAILER's book.

- 2 -

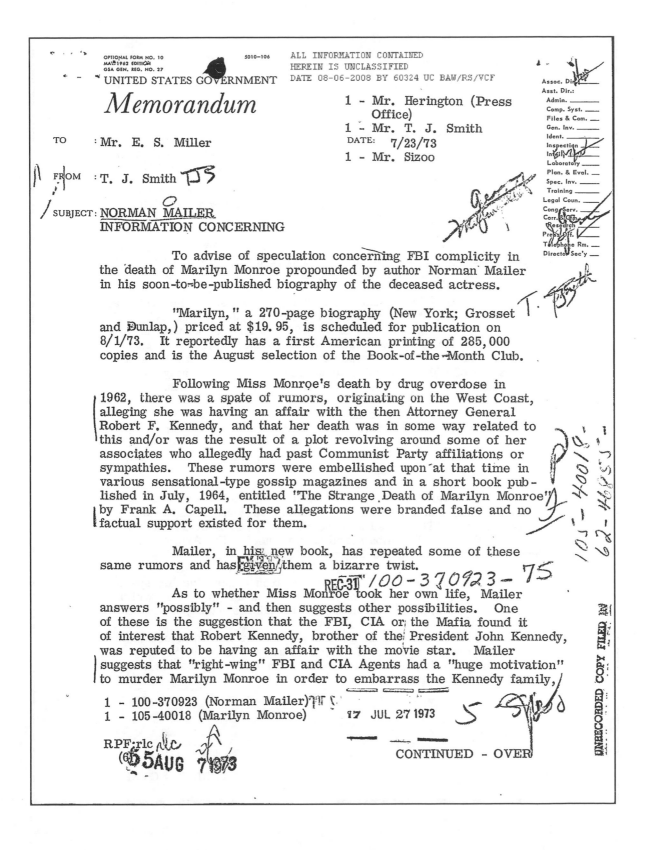

OPTIONAL FORM NO. 10
MAY 1962 EDITION
GSA GEN. REG. NO. 27   5010—106

UNITED STATES GOVERNMENT

Memorandum

TO   : Mr. E. S. Miller

FROM   : T. J. Smith

SUBJECT: NORMAN MAILER
INFORMATION CONCERNING

1 - Mr. Herington (Press Office)
1 - Mr. T. J. Smith
DATE: 7/23/73
1 - Mr. Sizoo

Assoc. Dir.
Asst. Dir.:
Admin.
Comp. Syst.
Files & Com.
Gen. Inv.
Ident.
Inspection
Intell.
Laboratory
Plan. & Eval.
Spec. Inv.
Training
Legal Coun.
Cong. Serv.
Corr. & Com.
Research
Press Off.
Telephone Rm.
Director Sec'y

To advise of speculation concerning FBI complicity in the death of Marilyn Monroe propounded by author Norman Mailer in his soon-to-be-published biography of the deceased actress.

"Marilyn," a 270-page biography (New York; Grosset and Dunlap,) priced at $19.95, is scheduled for publication on 8/1/73. It reportedly has a first American printing of 285,000 copies and is the August selection of the Book-of-the-Month Club.

Following Miss Monroe's death by drug overdose in 1962, there was a spate of rumors, originating on the West Coast, alleging she was having an affair with the then Attorney General Robert F. Kennedy, and that her death was in some way related to this and/or was the result of a plot revolving around some of her associates who allegedly had past Communist Party affiliations or sympathies. These rumors were embellished upon at that time in various sensational-type gossip magazines and in a short book published in July, 1964, entitled "The Strange Death of Marilyn Monroe" by Frank A. Capell. These allegations were branded false and no factual support existed for them.

Mailer, in his new book, has repeated some of these same rumors and has given them a bizarre twist.

As to whether Miss Monroe took her own life, Mailer answers "possibly" - and then suggests other possibilities. One of these is the suggestion that the FBI, CIA or the Mafia found it of interest that Robert Kennedy, brother of the President John Kennedy, was reputed to be having an affair with the movie star. Mailer suggests that "right-wing" FBI and CIA Agents had a "huge motivation" to murder Marilyn Monroe in order to embarrass the Kennedy family,

REC-31 100-370923-75

1 - 100-370923 (Norman Mailer)
1 - 105-40018 (Marilyn Monroe)   17 JUL 27 1973

RPF:rlc
5 AUG 1973

CONTINUED - OVER

UNRECORDED COPY FILED IN

Memorandum to Mr. E. S. Miller
Re: Norman Mailer

claiming the FBI and CIA were furious with the Kennedys because following the Bay of Pigs invasion President Kennedy was moving to limit the power of these agencies.

Mailer has admitted in recent press interviews concerning his book that he has no evidence to support his theory and that it is based on his "writer's instinct" and on speculation.

A second allegation purportedly contained in the book was recently brought to the attention of the Los Angeles Office by Lloyd Shearer, editor of Parade Magazine. This allegation is that in 1962 FBI Agents in Los Angeles went to the telephone company in Santa Monica, California, and removed a "paper tape" of Marilyn Monroe's telephone calls, some of which according to Mailer, were presumably to the White House or White House staff on the night of her death.

This is false and neither the files of the Los Angeles Office nor FBI Headquarters indicate the existence of any such tapes. This again appears to be a variation of a spurious charge contained in Capell's 1964 book in which he alleged that such tapes were in the custody of the Los Angeles Police Department.

Norman Mailer is an eccentric but well-known author, who in the past has won a Pulitzer Prize and a National Book Award. He is the author of "The Naked and the Dead," "The Deer Park," "An American Dream," "Cannibals and Christians," "The Armies of the Night," and "Miami and the Siege of Chicago."

He admits to little or no research concerning his speculation about Marilyn Monroe's death. He states his motive in writing the book is his dire need for money. He admits having no evidence to support his theory of FBI or CIA involvement and uses it to sensationalize his book and to gain publicity. Mailer has even coined a new word which describes some of his speculative writing in "Marilyn." The "factoid" he defines as "an event which has no existence other than it has appeared in print."

- 2 -   CONTINUED - OVER

Memorandum to Mr. E. S. Miller
Re: Norman Mailer

　　　　A review in Time Magazine on 7/16/73, a Mike Wallace
television interview, a 7/22/73 New York Times book review by Pauline
Kael, and a Washington Post article dated 7/20/73 by Stephen Isaacs,
are all critical of Mailer for his unsubstantiated theorizing and for
engaging in "yellow" journalism.

ACTION:

　　　　For information only. No action is recommended regarding
Mailer's allegations. Any public statements by the FBI would merely
serve to feed the fires of publicity which Mailer is attempting to stoke.

- 3 -

Ayn Rand

ONE OF THE MOST ardently anti-Communist intellectuals of the 20th century, Ayn Rand seems like a perfect compliment to one of the most ardently anti-Communist organizations of the 20th century, J. Edgar Hoover's FBI. And, indeed, Rand's file shows that for decades, the two appeared to have a strong mutual admiration for each other — until Rand overstepped Hoover's strict boundaries.

Rand's file begins in 1947 with, appropriately enough, a book review. Hoover wanted a compilation of information on various Hollywood figures testifying at the House Un-American Activities Commission, which counted Rand among the friendly witnesses. Special agent A. Jones notes that while the Bureau hadn't anything of value on Rand, her first major novel, *The Fountainhead*, had been released a few years earlier to literary and public acclaim.

The next year, the head of the Bureau's Los Angeles office notified Hoover that Rand had apparently volunteered herself in the FBI's fight against "Communist infiltration of the literary field," sending the office clippings of books she felt contained subversive messages — including a children's book about forest creatures that learn how to share.

Rand's proactive goodwill towards the Bureau appears to have paid off. In 1961, Hoover received a concerned letter calling for a "subversive activities investigation" into Rand for her vocal atheism and "odious philosophy" of objectivism. Hoover curtly responded by noting that Rand was not a Communist, which ended the matter as far as he was concerned.

Five years later, Rand wrote to Hoover directly. A *Saturday Evening Post* article quoted the Director describing himself as "objectivist," and Rand wished to know if that was indeed a reference to her philosophy. Beyond bragging rights for having such a high-profile practitioner, there was a practical element to Rand's questioning; she had a "personal-political problem" she wanted to discuss with Hoover.

With characteristic brusqueness, Hoover scrawled a note proclaiming that he had "never said he was an objectivist — whatever that is" and immediately launched an inquiry to find out whatever "objectivism" is. The Bureau went only so far into Rand's philosophy as to subscribe to her newsletter, and a clipping from the *Saturday Evening Post* confirmed that Hoover had used the term in the specific context of his professed apoliticism and nothing else.

Hoover, famously loath to meet with favor-seekers, wrote back to decline Rand's request for meeting and made it clear that if she did come calling, she'd be talking to one of his assistants. That was the last formal communication between Rand and the Director, though a few years later the Bureau did investigate a series of harassing letters from a man who saw himself as the successor to Rand's Objectivist legacy.

Hoover's attitude towards Rand is perhaps best summed up by his reaction to an unsolicited copy of Rand's *For the New Intellectual* received from an anonymous contact. That copy ended up in Rand's own file — presumably never having been read.

STANDARD FORM NO. 64

Office Memorandum • UNITED STATES GOVERNMENT

ECK:GO

TO   : Mr. Nichols   DATE: 10-24-47

FROM   : M. A. Jones

SUBJECT: Ayn Rand
          Information Concerning

FOIPA 230629

ALL INFORMATION CONTAINED
HEREIN IS UNCLASSIFIED
DATE 3/23/83 BY SP1 GS/c

Mr. Tolson
Mr. E. A. Tamm
Mr. Clegg
Mr. Coffey
Mr. Glavin
Mr. Ladd
Mr. Nichols
Mr. Rosen
Mr. Tracy
Mr. Carson
Mr. Egan
Mr. Hendon
Mr. Pennington
Mr. Quinn Tamm
Tele. Room
Mr. Nease
Miss Beahm
Miss Gandy

          There is no information of value in our files
concerning this individual.

          Miss Rand is the author of the book "The Fountainhead."
This book is the dramatic story of three men and one woman told
against the backdrop of New York's architectural sky line. It
is a love story revolving around a young architect and his
ego. The book was published in 1943 and received enthusiastic
support in literary circles as well as with the general public.

4 SE 21   62-85631-1

RECORDED

INDEXED 29 DEC 16 1947

60 JAN 15 1948   EX-43   5

- 374

3

Federal Bureau of Investigation
United States Department of Justice

Los Angeles, California
October 17, 1947

IN REPLY, PLEASE REFER TO

FILE NO. _____ __ _____

Director, FBI   PERSONAL AND ~~CONFIDENTIAL~~

Re: COMMUNIST INFILTRATION OF THE MOTION
     PICTURE INDUSTRY
     INTERNAL SECURITY - C

Dear Sir:

        It has come to the attention of this office that some of the
individuals within the motion picture industry who are to be subpoenaed
to Washington as witnesses in the House Un-American Activities Committee
hearing later this month desire to meet the Director, if possible, and to
take a tour of the Bureau. They may call you while in Washington.

        Specifically, [   ] have made requests to meet the Director.

                          Very truly yours,

                          R. B. HOOD, SAC

LFW:KH
100-15732

STANDARD FORM No. 64

Office Memorandum • UNITED STATES GOVERNMENT

TO : Director, FBI   DATE: March 1 1948

FROM : SAC Los Angeles

SUBJECT: COMMUNIST INFILTRATION INTO THE LITERARY FIELD INTERNAL SECURITY (C)   STRICTLY CONFIDENTIAL

AYN RAND, 10000 Tampa Street, Chatsworth, California, is a well-known novelist who testified before the House Un-American Activities hearings in Washington during October 1947.

INTERNAL SECURITY (C)," Los Angeles File 100-15732, Bureau File 100-138754.

b7E

RAND frequently reads numerous book reviews and clips newspaper and periodical articles dealing with these reviews where she thinks they contain attempts to inject Communist philosophy either directly or indirectly.

DEFERRED RECORDING

There are being enclosed herewith to the Bureau and New York several photostatic copies of articles identified below, which all fall within the above category. The possible Communist indoctrination has been pencil-marked [ ] Also enclosed is photostatic copy of an article appearing in the October 22, 1947 issue of "The Nation," which deals with one of RAND's books, a ninety-eight page novel entitled, "Anthem".

These clippings are forwarded for information purposes only and need not be returned to this office. They may be retained or destroyed at the discretion of the Bureau and the New York Office.

"Rumor in the Forest" by MADELEINE COUPPEY, published by SCRIBNER - "New York Times," July 13, 1947; "Chicago Sunday Tribune," July 13, 1947; "New York Herald Tribune," August 31, 1947; "Time" magazine, July 14, 1947.

ENCL ATTACHED

[ ] also mentioned that a novel entitled "Albert Sean" by MILLEN BRAND, published by SIMON & SCHUSTER, New York, deals with racial discrimination as exemplified by certain real estate restrictive covenants. [ ] thought this book might be of interest to the Bureau.

Enclosure
cc New York - Enclosure
LFW:MEH
100-0

DECLASSIFIED BY 1-2-5-9
ON 9/28/78

RECORDED 162-85631—3
INDEXED 33 MAR 8 1948

52 MAR 25 1948

November 5, 1961

Director
Subversive Activities Investigation
F.B.I.
Washington 25, D.C.

Dear Sir :

I feel that your department should be informed of the type
of information which is apparently gaining some measure of
importance with the public. The article to which my enclosed
letter refers is The Curious Cult of Ayn Rand; it may be
found in the Nov. 11, 1961 issue of the Post.

I am sure that your department is already aware of the
importance of this woman and her odious philosophy to the
freedom and welfare of the general public, I only hope that
I have helped in some way by attempting to give voice to
my opinion and conclusions.

If I may be of any aid to you in your working against these
difficulties, please let me know.

Sincerely,

S E Chaney

S.E.Chaney

1747 Bel Aire Dr.
Glendale 1, California

P.S. I'd like to know what comes of all this.

Thanks
SEC

REC- 91   62-85631-4

22 NOV 14 1961

Ack.
w/encs.
11-13-61
RDS/blw.

ENCLOSURE

REC- 91

Nov 13   4 33 PM '61
REC'D-READING ROOM
BI

1 - Mr. Simpson

November 13, 1961

Mr. S. E. Chaney
1747 Bel Aire Drive
Glendale 1, California

Dear Mr. Chaney:

I have received your letter dated November 5,
1961, with its enclosure, and your interest in furnishing
this information and affording me the benefit of your
observations is indeed appreciated.

It is not possible for me to advise you of the
results of any inquiry which this Bureau may conduct. A
regulation of the Department of Justice prohibits the disclosure of such information to other than appropriate
agencies in the executive branch of the Federal Government.

There are enclosed several items of literature
available for distribution by the FBI concerning the menace
of communism which you may like to read.

Sincerely yours,

J. Edgar Hoover

John Edgar Hoover
Director

Enclosures - 4

RDS:blw
(3)

SEE NOTE ON YELLOW PAGE TWO

MAILED 20
NOV 13 1961
COMM-FBI

Belmont

room

MAIL ROOM ☐   TELETYPE UNIT ☐

Mr. S. E. Chaney

NOTE ON YELLOW:

Bufiles contain no identifiable data concerning the correspondent. The enclosure to correspondent's letter was a copy of a letter he has written to the "Saturday Evening Post" objecting to an article in that magazine concerning Ayn Rand.

The article mentioned by correspondent concerning Ayn Rand which appeared in the "Saturday Evening Post" has been reviewed and does not appear to be communist propaganda. The article indicates she is an atheist and discusses her cult of objectivism based upon her theory that "Money is the root of all good."

Bufiles indicate that

b7E

The following items of literature were sent to the correspondent.

1. "The Communist Party Line"

2. "The Deadly Contest"

3. "Faith in God -- Our Answer To Communism"

4. Director's statement re Internal Security 4-17-61.

- 2 -

November 5, 1961

Editor
Saturday Evening Post
Curtis Publishing Company
Independence Square
Philadelphia 5, Pa.

Dear Sir:

Just recently I've become sensitive to what is called, "logic tight compartments"; Miss Rand's Objectivism is one such.

In attempting to object to her "militant atheism" on grounds of faith, the attacker would find himself on shaky logical ground because faith is founded on subjective phenomena assumed to be valid on an individual but not on any universal or even communicable basis. Faith in this respect is abstract, and attempting to dislodge the concrete with the abstract proves quite difficult, so I've decided to attack on altogether different bases.

(1) Miss Rand's extrovertive espousal of arch-capitalism evidenced by her statement, "Money is the root of all good.", seems to place her in a definite anti-communist position - or so she would have us believe. To further color her stand in this wise she comments of Bolshevism, "I knew it was evil", and complains of "having a thin time of it because the communist influence there (Hollywood) was too strong." These phrases paint a seemingly positive background against which we find her central idea - that of Objectivism.

(2) "Whatever exists exists independent of any perceiver; man can perceive and understand reality, but only through reason - intuition, emotion, faith have no validity as paths to knowledge." From the article I find that Atlas Shrugged combines Ideas 1 and 2 in such overwhelming complexity that an extremely intelligent reader would be sorely vexed in attempting even a cursory analytical critique.

If an individual accepts this block of hardened logic in the form of ideas 1 plus 2 he takes a side with capitalism (he thinks) and admits to himself that all reality is external or objective. Now so far this doesn't seem too bad, but let's analyze what happens if we disagree.

(a) To disagree with the idea, "Money is the root of all good." makes a sensitive, self conscious person think that he is anti-capitalism or even just slightly pink, especially if money is to be equated with or accepted to be the symbol of capitalism.

(b) To disagree with the idea that man can perceive reality causes an individual to doubt;he questions his own values and becomes insecure about his own mental ability.

In other words - if you do not accept the tenets of the doctrine you begin to have serious trouble with your mental attitudes and thinking. This should be the first clue to you that there is something inherently wrong with it.

※※※   ※※※   ※※※   ※※※   ※※※   ※※※   ※※※   ※※※

Now, let's clarify this dubious philosophy.

62-85631—

ENCLOSURE

2.

Point 1:

Money is a medium of exchange; it is crystallized services or goods. Its use simplifies trade and relieves man of the burden of the bulky barter system by creating a value which is universally recognized and is easier to transport by virtue of its smaller mass. At the present level of development of industrial civilization in the world money is a necessity. It is not, repeat not to be understood as a symbol for anything.

Point 2:

Perception is a thought process; thoughts are subjective and internal not objective and external. If you define your reality as being only that which you perceive through your senses then you are denying your own internal existence and denying the existence of thought because thought is not perceived it is subjectively understood. All of your perceptions are internal and subjective and your thoughts about these things constitute your reality.

Miss Rand's <u>Objectivism</u> is an excellent example of classical doubletalk. It cannot be accepted in whole or in part without very troublesome mental inconsistencies for a free thinking individual because it is against the grain of free human nature.

Mr. Karl Marx, history's greatest professional sorehead, complained until he composed a dirge similar in many respects to Rand's double symphony. Her verbal harmony seems to sell well, but if you buy her records and listen because you think you need it you'll soon be dancing to her tune. Her projection is a penetrating prose and she is quite obviously well disciplined - these things interest those who are in need of strong leadership (this applies largely to the young) and stimuli (this applies to almost everyone). If Miss Rand's <u>rational self-interest</u> can cause you to believe intellectually that all reality is external and perceived then denial of your non-perceivable self will be quite logical. The step from this to that oB being a completely altruistic, thought slave, worker of the "people's republic" with complete denial of individuality is an easy one.

If Miss Rand is not a communist as she says she is not, then she has been led down the rosy path and is guilty of very incomplete thinking, because a careful reader can see the suds still clinging to the brain.

--- --- --- --- --- ---

Freedom is the right of the individual to react to his perceptions without being restricted to a particular view or a particular reaction.

Physical freedom is impossible without mental freedom.

Objectivism and communism are both mental and physical slavery because they restrict the individual to a particular view.

My regards to Mr. Kobler for a clear and understandable article. I'm quite elated that I didn't find Rand in your "people on their way up" department.

Sincerely,

S.E.Chaney
1747 Bel Aire Dr.
Glendale 1, California

P.S. I've sent copies to the F.B.I. and my congressman - they should read this also.

THE OBJECTIVIST NEWSLETTER INC.

120 East 34th Street / New York 16, N.Y. / LExington 2-5787

Ayn Rand and Nathaniel Branden
Editors and Publishers

January 8, 1966

Mr. J. Edgar Hoover
Federal Bureau of Investigation
Washington, D. C.

ALL INFORMATION CONTAINED
HEREIN IS UNCLASSIFIED
DATE 3/23/83 BY SPGSK/94
230,029

Dear Mr. Hoover:

In the article "Hoover of the FBI," in the September 25, 1965 issue of The Saturday Evening Post, there appears the sentence (page 32): "Hoover disavows the ultraconservative political label, terms himself an 'objectivist,' etc..."

I would like very much to know whether you meant that you agree with my philosophy of Objectivism - or whether you used that term in some different meaning. Forgive me for attaching any sort of even provisional credence to that article, which I regard as extremely unfair, in a magazine for which I have no respect at all. I would like to know the truth for obvious reasons - since an Objectivist such as yourself would be more than welcome.

Regardless of your answer, that is, without presuming that that statement is necessarily true, I should like very much to meet you - to discuss a personal-political problem. If you find it possible to give me an appointment, I would come to Washington at any time at your convenience.

Sincerely yours,

Ayn Rand

Ayn Rand

AR:dk

ENCLOSURE

I have never said I was an "objectivist" whatever that is

REC 57
62 85631

JAN 17 1966

JAN 17 1966

OPTIONAL FORM NO. 10
MAY 1962 EDITION
GSA GEN. REG. NO. 27

5010–106

UNITED STATES GOVERNMENT

Memorandum

TO   :   Mr. Wick   DATE: 1-13-66

FROM :   D. C. Morrell

SUBJECT: **REQUEST TO MEET THE DIRECTOR**
AYN RAND
NEW YORK, NEW YORK

Tolson _____
DeLoach _____
Mohr _____
Casper _____
Callahan _____
Conrad _____
Felt _____
Gale _____
Rosen _____
Sullivan _____
Tavel _____
Trotter _____
Tele. Room _____
Holmes _____
Gandy _____

By letter dated January 8th to the Director, captioned individual referred to the September, 1965, issue of "The Saturday Evening Post" wherein the article on the Director contains the statement to the effect that he terms himself an "objectivist."

(Captioned individual requests to be informed whether the Director meant that he agrees with her philosophy of Objectivism or whether he used the term in a different meaning. She states that she would like to know since an Objectivist such as the Director would be more than welcome. The Director has noted "I have never said I was an "objectivist" whatever that is. H")

Captioned individual states that she would like to meet the Director to discuss a personal political problem and that she would come to Washington at any time at the Director's convenience, if he would give her an appointment.

Captioned individual is a well-known writer and lecturer and her books include such publications as "The Fountainhead" and "Atlas Shrugged." The publication "Who's Who of American Women" describes her as an exponent of the philosophy objectivism. She was born in Russia in 1905 and attended private schools including the University of Leningrad.

b7E

REC-35   62-25631-6

Enclosure   1-14-66

ST-124   JAN 25 1966

1 - Miss Holmes - Enclosures
1 - Mr. Wick - Enclosures
1 - Mr. Jones - Enclosures
1 - Tour Room - Enclosures

ALL INFORMATION CONTAINED
HEREIN IS UNCLASSIFIED
DATE 3/23/93 BY SP GSK/BJ
FOIPA # 230,029

CONTINUED - OVER

DFC:jms (6)

60 JAN 28 1966

Recently the FBI has been keeping a close eye on the ultraright Minutemen. Although Hoover is a towering hero to much of the right, the founder of the Minutemen, Robert DePugh, flatly refused to furnish the FBI with a list of his membership. "It could serve as an assassination list for the Communists when they take over," says DePugh, who believes that the "take-over" is inevitable, Hoover or no Hoover. Despite the tendency of many liberals to lump Hoover with his far-right admirers, Hoover disavows the ultraconservative political label, terms himself an "objectivist," and has publicly declared that he "has no respect" for the extremist notions of Robert Welch, founder of the John Birch Society. "I know Mr. Hoover says that about Mr. Welch," says Birch public-relations director John Rousselot sadly. "But *we* still have high regard for him and the FBI."

Excerpt from the article "Hoover of the FBI,"
9-25-65 issue of "The Saturday Evening Post."

ALL INFORMATION CONTAINED
HEREIN IS UNCLASSIFIED
DATE 3/23/83 BY SP/45K/glt

62-85631-5.

ENCLOSURE

Morrell to Wick memo

RE: REQUEST TO MEET THE DIRECTOR
     AYN RAND
     NEW YORK, NEW YORK

        In 1947, captioned individual testified before the House Committee on Un-American Activities regarding communist infiltration of the motion picture industry. She is self-admittedly an anti-communist.

        In 1957, Bennett Cerf sent the Director a copy of Ayn Rand's book "Atlas Shrugged."

        (Bufiles contain no information on the philosophy of objectivism other than references to individuals who subscribe to the "Objectivist Newsletter" by Ayn Rand.)

        As indicated in the attached excerpt from "The Saturday Evening Post" article to which captioned individual refers, it is noted that it does contain the statement that the Director terms himself an "objectivist." It is felt, however, that in this instance it means that the Director maintains an open-minded outlook uncolored by any preconceived conclusions.

        It is not felt that the Director would want to take time from his busy schedule to see captioned individual, and she will be advised that the Director's commitments preclude his making an appointment. She will also be advised that, if she desires to come to FBI Headquarters to speak to one of the Director's Assistants, to contact you (Mr. Wick). She will also be advised that the Director has never stated that he is an "objectivist" but has always tried to maintain a balanced perspective uncolored by preconceived notions.

RECOMMENDATIONS:

        (1) That the Director not take time from his busy schedule to see captioned individual.

        (2) That the attached letter go forward expressing the Director's regrets and advising her to contact you (Mr. Wick) if she desires to come to FBI Headquarters.

- 2 -

REC- 57 62-85631-5   January 13, 1966

Miss Ayn Rand
The Objectivist Newsletter, Inc.
120 East 34th Street
New York, New York 10016

**ALL INFORMATION CONTAINED
HEREIN IS UNCLASSIFIED**
DATE 3/23/83 BY SP1GSK/pl
FOIPA 230,029

Dear Miss Rand:

I received your letter of January 8th and want to thank
you for the interest in writing.

I have never stated that I am an objectivist; however,
I have always made every effort to maintain an impartial, balanced
perspective and judge matters in the light of the facts rather than
preconceived notions.

With respect to your request, I regret that the pressure
of my official schedule precludes my making an appointment to see you.
If you wish to speak to one of my Assistants when you are in Washington,
please feel free to communicate with Assistant Director Robert E. Wick,
either by letter addressed to him directly here at FBI Headquarters,
Ninth Street and Pennsylvania Avenue, N. W., Washington, D. C. 20535,
or telephonically at EXecutive 3-7100, extension 691. He will be glad to
render whatever assistance he can. If I am in my office at the time of
your visit, you may be sure it will be a pleasure to talk to you.

MAILED 7
JAN 14 1966
COMM-FBI

Sincerely yours,

J. Edgar Hoover

1 - New York - Enclosure
1 - Miss Holmes - Enclosure (sent with cover memo)
1 - Mr. Wick - Enclosure (sent with cover memo)
1 - Mr. Jones - Enclosure (sent with cover memo)
1 - Tour Room - Enclosure (sent with cover memo)
NOTE: See D. C. Morrell to Mr. Wick memorandum dated 1-13-66 captioned
"Request to Meet the Director, Ayn Rand, New York, New York."
DFC:kcf (8)
79 JAN 19 1966

Tolson
DeLoach
Mohr
Casper
Callahan
Conrad
Felt
Gale
Rosen
Sullivan
Tavel
Trotter
Wick
Tele. Room
Holmes
Gandy

MAIL ROOM ☐ TELETYPE UNIT ☐

DO-6

OFFICE OF DIRECTOR
FEDERAL BUREAU OF INVESTIGATION
UNITED STATES DEPARTMENT OF JUSTICE

*RWT
16*

July 13, 1970

The attached copy of the paperback
book "For the New Intellectual" by
Ayn Rand is inscribed to the
Director as follows:

"To J. E. Hoover
from

There was no return address on
the envelope and the postmark is
not clear.

nm

MR. TOLSON _____
MR. DELOACH _____
MR. WALTERS _____
MR. MOHR _____
MR. BISHOP _____
MR. CASPER _____
MR. CALLAHAN _____
MR. CONRAD _____
MR. FELT _____
MR. GALE _____
MR. ROSEN _____
MR. SULLIVAN _____
MR. TAVEL _____
MR. SOYARS _____
MR. JONES _____
TELE. ROOM _____ b6
MISS HOLMES _____ b7C
MRS. METCALF _____
MISS GANDY _____

*INFORMATION CONTAINED
IS UNCLASSIFIED
DATE 3/23/88 BY
FOIPA 230,029*

UI

*Bufiles. No ack
since address was
not furnished.*

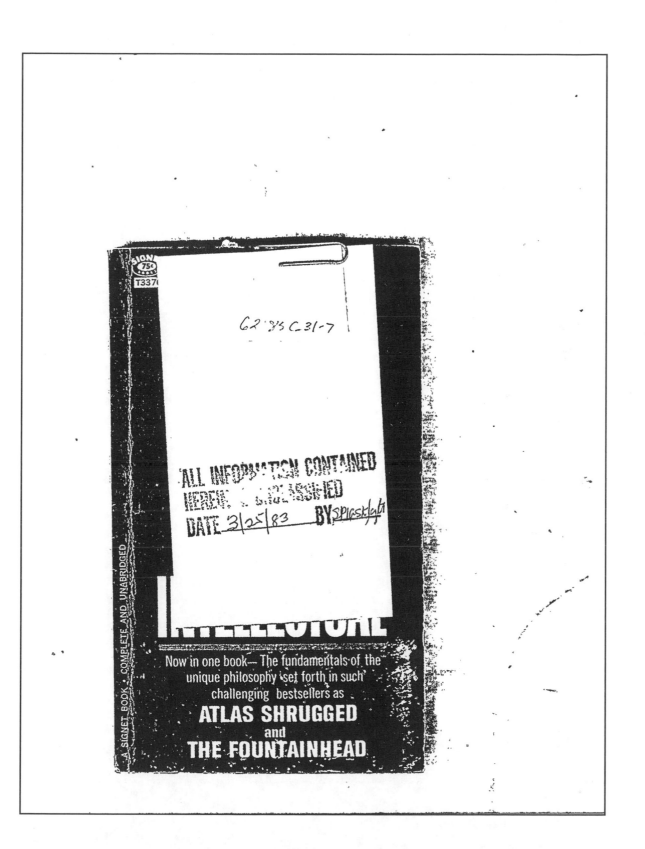

Susan Sontag

AS A PROLIFIC SOCIAL critic covering topics from AIDS to American interventionism, Susan Sontag seemed almost fated to run afoul of the Bureau. Although her association with the "New Left" of the '60s first put her on the FBI's radar, it was her writing in opposition to the Vietnam war that earned her her own investigation and the personal attention of no less than Director J. Edgar Hoover.

Sontag's file begins in early 1968. By this point Sontag had already participated in several antiwar demonstrations, including a 1966 "Read-in for Peace" alongside several other New York authors and a three-day protest of a Selective Service station in 1967 that ended in her arrest for "Disorderly Conduct," none of which escaped the attention of the Bureau, who noted these activities in a "Security Matter" file categorized as "miscellaneous." Through infiltrators and informants within the antiwar movement, the FBI received a tip that Sontag had visited Hanoi at the invitation of the North Vietnamese government — a violation of her passport's restriction on visiting communist countries — but lacking evidence, the special agent in charge of the New York Field Office recommended no further investigation unless advised contrary.

A few months later, they were advised contrary and then some. The New York Field Office was told to have a full report on Sontag's travel in two weeks, with Hoover himself demanding that the case be given immediate attention. What had happened in the meantime to warrant this sudden interest in Sontag?

The Bureau had received credible evidence regarding Sontag's trip to Hanoi — a feature in *Esquire* describing her experiences talking to leading figures of the North Vietnamese government, including Prime Minister Pham Van Dong, that would later be adapted into the book *Trip to Hanoi*.

Though the New York office did produce a comprehensive report on the origins of the article and all of Sontag's previous antiwar activity (citing a total of nine informants, whose names remain redacted) within the two week deadline, the investigation into Sontag stretched on for another two years. A 1971 memo from the Department of State confirmed that Sontag hadn't sought or received permission for her travel to North Vietnam, and another memo from what appears to be French intelligence was passed on from the CIA.

A final report dated in March of 1972 upgrades Sontag's "Security Matter" to full-blown "Subversive," and offers two conclusions. First, it was not recommended that the Bureau interview Sontagon, on account of her "status as a writer" which "could result in embarrassment. Second, her activities, though indeed subversive, were not enough to qualify for her inclusion into the ADEX, the FBI's "Administrative Index," of people "considered to be a threat to the security of the country." Similar to Allen Ginsberg, Sontag was deemed more of an irritant than a danger, and for the second time in four years her file was closed. Hoover's death a little over a month later ensured it would stay closed.

OPTIONAL FORM NO. 10
MAY 1962 EDITION
GSA FPMR (41 CFR) 101-11.6

DECLASSIFICATION AUTHORITY DERIVED FROM:
FBI AUTOMATIC DECLASSIFICATION GUIDE
DATE 04-25-2014 By J89J28T90

UNITED STATES GOVERNMENT

Memorandum

TO   DIRECTOR, FBI   DATE: 4/19/68   b6
                                                                              b7C
FROM   SAC, NEW YORK (100-162314)(C)

SUBJECT: SUSAN SONTAG
          SECURITY MATTER - MISCELLANEOUS
          (OO:NY)

        ReBUairtel to AL, 11/6/67, captioned"INVESTIGATION
OF THE NEW LEFT."

        Enclosed herewith are the original and 8 copies
of a letterhead memorandum reflecting anti-Vietnam activities
of the subject.

        The source utilized in the LHM is [   ]   b7D

        The LHM is classified "Confidential" because of
information furnished by the above source. If the identity
of this source was disclosed it could be injurious to the
national defense.

        Records of the Credit Bureau of Greater New York
as reviewed on 3/4/68, by IC [   ], reflected a 1965   b6
report on Miss SUSAN SONTAG, 82 Washington Place, NYC,   b7C
formerly of 350 West End Avenue, NYC, self-employed as a
writer from her residence.

        Records of [   ] as reviewed on 3/11/68, by SA   b6
[   ] reflected subject was born on 1/16/33,   b7C
resides at 346 Riverside Drive, NYC, and is employed as a   b7D
writer. She is under a direct payment plan certificate #
11 239 467.

        The following [   ] informants were contacted concerning
the subject, with negative results: 100-450066-X   b6
                                                                 b7C
                                                                 b7D

2-Bureau (Enc. 9)(RM)
1-New York
                          REC-19
                                    12 APR 23 1968   b6
   (3)   Buy U.S. Savings Bonds Regularly on the Payroll Savings Plan   b7C

5010-108

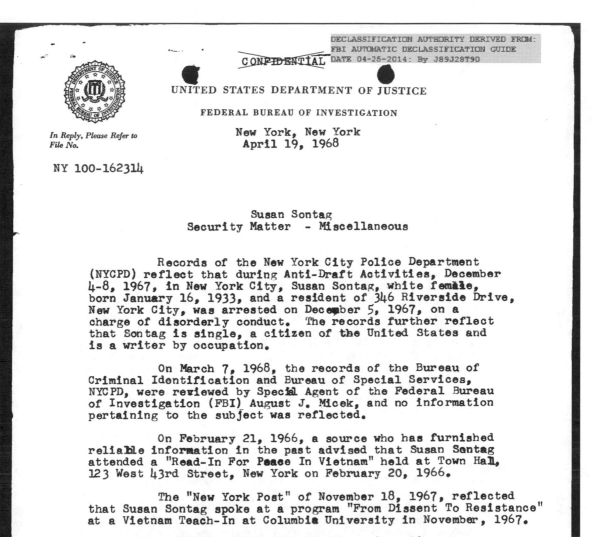

CONFIDENTIAL

UNITED STATES DEPARTMENT OF JUSTICE

FEDERAL BUREAU OF INVESTIGATION

New York, New York
April 19, 1968

*In Reply, Please Refer to
File No.*

NY 100-162314

Susan Sontag
Security Matter   -   Miscellaneous

Records of the New York City Police Department
(NYCPD) reflect that during Anti-Draft Activities, December
4-8, 1967, in New York City, Susan Sontag, white female,
born January 16, 1933, and a resident of 346 Riverside Drive,
New York City, was arrested on December 5, 1967, on a
charge of disorderly conduct. The records further reflect
that Sontag is single, a citizen of the United States and
is a writer by occupation.

On March 7, 1968, the records of the Bureau of
Criminal Identification and Bureau of Special Services,
NYCPD, were reviewed by Special Agent of the Federal Bureau
of Investigation (FBI) August J. Micek, and no information
pertaining to the subject was reflected.

On February 21, 1966, a source who has furnished
reliable information in the past advised that Susan Sontag
attended a "Read-In For Peace In Vietnam" held at Town Hall,
123 West 43rd Street, New York on February 20, 1966.

The "New York Post" of November 18, 1967, reflected
that Susan Sontag spoke at a program "From Dissent To Resistance"
at a Vietnam Teach-In at Columbia University in November, 1967.

The "Village Voice" of January 18, 1968 on page 11,
column 1 reflected that Susan Sontag signed a scroll pledging
to counsel, aid and abet any young man who wished to refuse
the draft.

This document contains neither recommendations
nor conclusions of the Federal Bureau of Investigation. It
is the property of the Federal Bureau of Investigation and
is loaned to your agency; it and its contents are not to be
distributed outside your agency.

COPIES DESTROYED

342   JUN   8   1971

CONFIDENTIAL
GROUP   1
Excluded from automatic
downgrading and
declassification

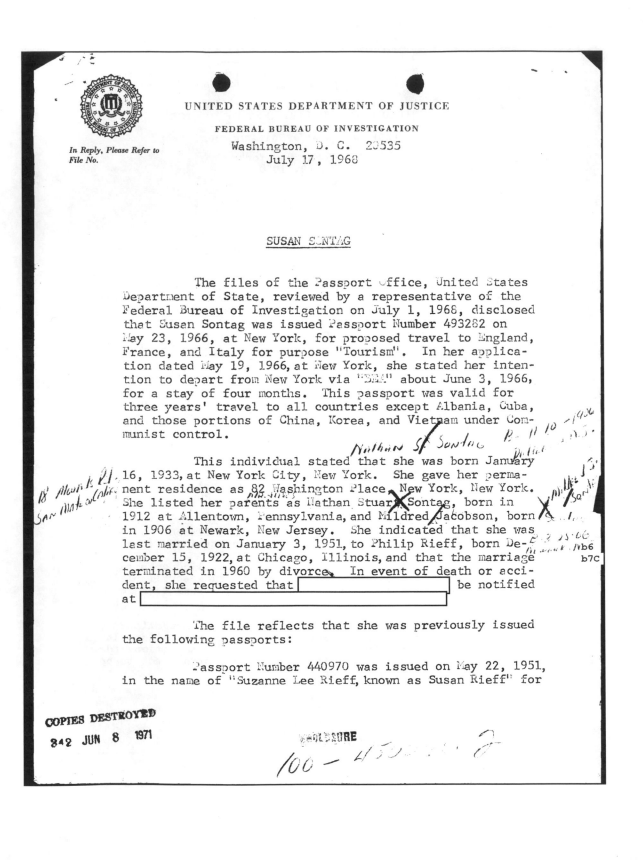

UNITED STATES DEPARTMENT OF JUSTICE

FEDERAL BUREAU OF INVESTIGATION

Washington, D. C. 20535
July 17, 1968

*In Reply, Please Refer to
File No.*

SUSAN SONTAG

The files of the Passport Office, United States
Department of State, reviewed by a representative of the
Federal Bureau of Investigation on July 1, 1968, disclosed
that Susan Sontag was issued Passport Number 493282 on
May 23, 1966, at New York, for proposed travel to England,
France, and Italy for purpose "Tourism". In her application dated May 19, 1966, at New York, she stated her intention to depart from New York via "BOAC" about June 3, 1966,
for a stay of four months. This passport was valid for
three years' travel to all countries except Albania, Cuba,
and those portions of China, Korea, and Vietnam under Communist control.

This individual stated that she was born January
16, 1933, at New York City, New York. She gave her permanent residence as 82 Washington Place, New York, New York.
She listed her parents as Nathan Stuart Sontag, born in
1912 at Allentown, Pennsylvania, and Mildred Jacobson, born
in 1906 at Newark, New Jersey. She indicated that she was
last married on January 3, 1951, to Philip Rieff, born December 15, 1922, at Chicago, Illinois, and that the marriage
terminated in 1960 by divorce. In event of death or accident, she requested that [   ] be notified
at [   ]

b6
b7C

The file reflects that she was previously issued
the following passports:

Passport Number 440970 was issued on May 22, 1951,
in the name of "Suzanne Lee Rieff, known as Susan Rieff" for

COPIES DESTROYED

842 JUN 8 1971

ENCLOSURE

CONFIDENTIAL

Susan Sontag

The December 4, 1967 issue of "Diamondback",
student paper of the University of Maryland, on page three,
reflected that the subject read verbatim her argument on
"The Aesthetics of Silence" to an audience of over three
hundred on November 29. The article pointed out that "after
graduating from North Hollywood High School at the age of
fifteen, Miss Sontag received her bachelors degree from the
University of Chicago at eighteen. While a teaching fellow
of philosophy at Harvard, she completed all the requirements
for her doctorate except the dissertation, which she plans
to finish within the next year. Miss Sontag was the recipient
of a Rockefeller Foundation Grant in 1964, a Merrill Foundation Grant in 1965 and a Guggenheim Fellowship in 1966-67".

A third source who has furnished reliable information in the past advised on April 8, 1968, that at a
meeting of the Socialist Workers Party-New York Local, (SWP-NYL)
held on March 7, 1968 at 873 Broadway, New York City, it was
announced that one Susan Sontag, among others, attended the
SWP's first lecture class.

A characterization of the SWP-NYL
is attached hereto.

On May 11, 1968, Special Agents (SAS) of the FBI
determined that a meeting was held by the National Mobilization
Committee to End the War in Vietnam (NMC) at St. Stephens'
Church, Newton Street, North West, at 16th Street, Washington
D.C., from 12:00 noon to 5:00 PM. It was stated at this
meeting that the subject was presently in Hanoi, North Vietnam.

The June 15, 1968 issue of "WIN", the semi-monthly
magazine of the War Resisters League, on page five, carried
a photograph of the subject and others, at the "Me Kong
Workshop", cave, Hoa Binh, North Vietnam.

CONFIDENTIAL

-2-

DECLASSIFICATION AUTHORITY DERIVED FROM:
FBI AUTOMATIC DECLASSIFICATION GUIDE
DATE 05-19-2014 F38M26K32

OPTIONAL FORM NO. 10
MAY 1962 EDITION
GSA FPMR (41 CFR) 101-11.6

UNITED STATES GOVERNMENT

Memorandum

TO   : DIRECTOR, FBI (100-450066)   DATE: 8/13/68

FROM   : SAC, NEW YORK (100-162314) (C)

SUBJECT : SUSAN SONTAG aka
           SM-C
           (OO:NY)

Re WFO letter 7/17/68, and NY letter 4/19/68.

Enclosed herewith for the Bureau are the original
and five copies of a LHM concerning the subject.

Sources utilized in the LHM are as follows:

Files of the NYO do not contain any identifiable
references to the subject's parents or stepfather.

The enclosed LHM is classified "Confidential"
because of information furnished by the above sources. If
the identity of these sources was disclosed, it could be
injurious to the national defense.

A review of subject's file in the NYO reflects her
activities do not warrant further investigation or recommendations of any kind at this time. UACB no report is being
prepared at this time.

REC 82 100-450066-3

EX-100   AUG 16 1968

-Bureau (Encls. 6) ENCLOSURE
-New York
(3)

57 AUG 26 1968

Buy U.S. Savings Bonds Regularly on the Payroll Savings Plan

b6
b7C

b7D

b6
b7C

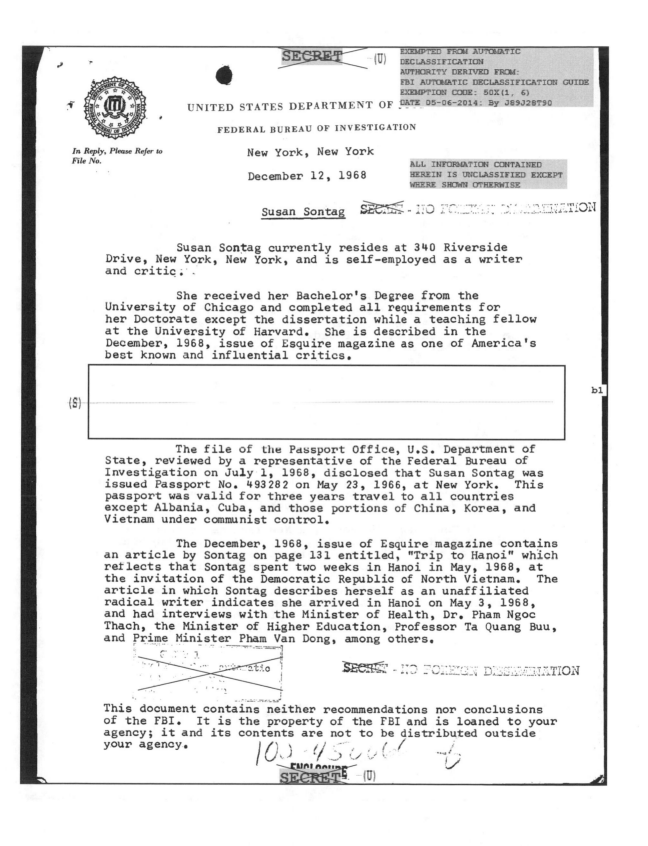

~~SECRET~~ (U)

UNITED STATES DEPARTMENT OF ~~JUSTICE~~

FEDERAL BUREAU OF INVESTIGATION

In Reply, Please Refer to
File No.

New York, New York

December 12, 1968

<u>Susan Sontag</u> ~~SECRET - NO FOREIGN DISSEMINATION~~

Susan Sontag currently resides at 340 Riverside Drive, New York, New York, and is self-employed as a writer and critic.

She received her Bachelor's Degree from the University of Chicago and completed all requirements for her Doctorate except the dissertation while a teaching fellow at the University of Harvard. She is described in the December, 1968, issue of Esquire magazine as one of America's best known and influential critics.

(S) b1

The file of the Passport Office, U.S. Department of State, reviewed by a representative of the Federal Bureau of Investigation on July 1, 1968, disclosed that Susan Sontag was issued Passport No. 493282 on May 23, 1966, at New York. This passport was valid for three years travel to all countries except Albania, Cuba, and those portions of China, Korea, and Vietnam under communist control.

The December, 1968, issue of Esquire magazine contains an article by Sontag on page 131 entitled, "Trip to Hanoi" which reflects that Sontag spent two weeks in Hanoi in May, 1968, at the invitation of the Democratic Republic of North Vietnam. The article in which Sontag describes herself as an unaffiliated radical writer indicates she arrived in Hanoi on May 3, 1968, and had interviews with the Minister of Health, Dr. Pham Ngoc Thach, the Minister of Higher Education, Professor Ta Quang Buu, and Prime Minister Pham Van Dong, among others.

~~SECRET - NO FOREIGN DISSEMINATION~~

This document contains neither recommendations nor conclusions of the FBI. It is the property of the FBI and is loaned to your agency; it and its contents are not to be distributed outside your agency.

~~ENCLOSURE~~

~~SECRET~~ (U)

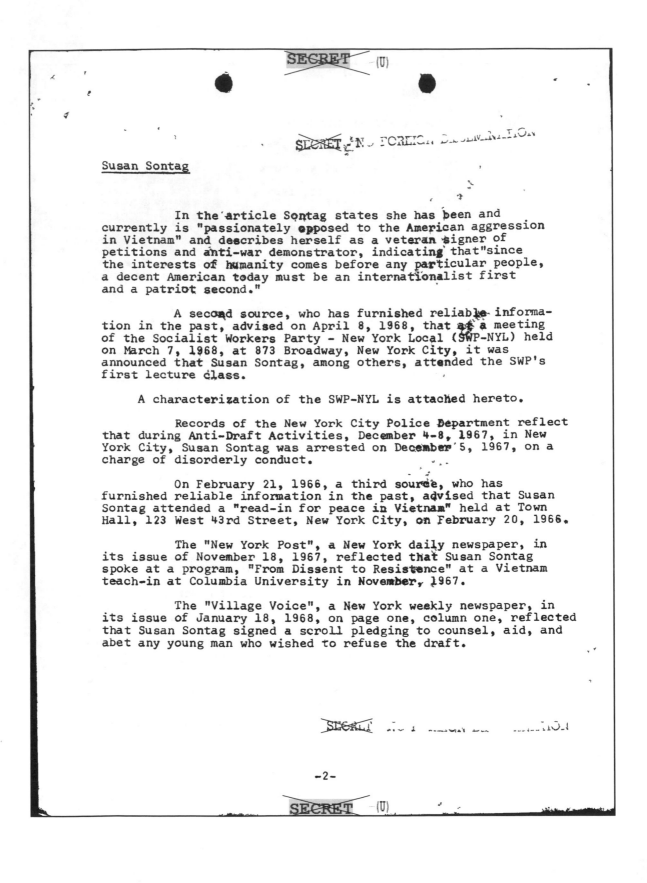

SECRET   (U)

SECRET - NO FOREIGN DISSEMINATION

Susan Sontag

      In the article Sontag states she has been and
currently is "passionately opposed to the American aggression
in Vietnam" and describes herself as a veteran signer of
petitions and anti-war demonstrator, indicating that "since
the interests of humanity comes before any particular people,
a decent American today must be an internationalist first
and a patriot second."

      A second source, who has furnished reliable informa-
tion in the past, advised on April 8, 1968, that at a meeting
of the Socialist Workers Party - New York Local (SWP-NYL) held
on March 7, 1968, at 873 Broadway, New York City, it was
announced that Susan Sontag, among others, attended the SWP's
first lecture class.

      A characterization of the SWP-NYL is attached hereto.

      Records of the New York City Police Department reflect
that during Anti-Draft Activities, December 4-8, 1967, in New
York City, Susan Sontag was arrested on December 5, 1967, on a
charge of disorderly conduct.

      On February 21, 1966, a third source, who has
furnished reliable information in the past, advised that Susan
Sontag attended a "read-in for peace in Vietnam" held at Town
Hall, 123 West 43rd Street, New York City, on February 20, 1966.

      The "New York Post", a New York daily newspaper, in
its issue of November 18, 1967, reflected that Susan Sontag
spoke at a program, "From Dissent to Resistance" at a Vietnam
teach-in at Columbia University in November, 1967.

      The "Village Voice", a New York weekly newspaper, in
its issue of January 18, 1968, on page one, column one, reflected
that Susan Sontag signed a scroll pledging to counsel, aid, and
abet any young man who wished to refuse the draft.

SECRET - NO FOREIGN DISSEMINATION

-2-

SECRET   (U)

~~SECRET~~   (U)

NY 100-162314

        The "New York Post" a New York daily evening news-
paper in its issue of November 18, 1967, reflected that SUSAN
SONTAG spoke at a program "From Dissent to Resistance" at a
Vietnam teach-in at Columbia University, New York City, in November,
1967.

        The "Village Voice", a New York City newspaper, in its
issue of January 18, 1968, on page 1, column 1, reflected that
SUSAN SONTAG signed a scroll pledging to counsel, aid, and abet
any young man who wished to refuse the draft.

        On February 6, 1968, JOHN R. Mc DONOUGH, Assistant
Deputy Attorney General, turned over to Special Agents of the
FBI a huge scroll approximately 50 feet long and three feet wide
left abandoned in the Andretta Room of the Justice Building,
Washington, DC by a five-man delegation of clergy and laymen
following a meeting with departmental officials on February 6, 1968.

        The scroll, dated January, 1968, bore the names and
addresses of numerous individuals including that of the subject
signifying that they would counsel draft refusal "to any young
man who will not, because of conscience, serve as a soldier in
this criminal war." The scroll states that the undersigned "will
aid and abet him and make his welfare (their) concern until the
war ends."

        Also turned over to the Agents were envelopes bearing the
names and addresses of the subject among many others indicating
that they had contributed $1 "in support of a draft resister".
"I wanted to aid and abet young men who refuse the draft. This
war is illegitimate and our actions are legitimate."

        The "Village Voice", a New York weekly newspaper, in its
issue of March 14, 1968, page 27, column 1, reflects that SUSAN
SONTAG would appear at a benefit for DAVID MITCHELL" on March 17,
1968, at Saint Clement's Church, 432 West 46th Street. FF N P/ (U)

_____ who was convicted on March
16, 1966, in United States District Court, Hartford, Connecticut,   b6
for failure to report for and submit to induction into the Armed   b7C
Forces and sentenced to a five year prison term, had been ordered
to surrender himself at the Office of the United States Marshal,
United States Post Office building, 141 Church Street, New Haven,
Connecticut, on February 6, 1967, to begin his prison term. (U)

-6-

~~SECRET~~   (U)

~~SECRET~~   (U)

NY 100-162314

On February 6, 1967, Deputy United States Marshal, [   ] stated [   ] would be transported to the Lewisburg Federal Penitentiary, Lewisburg, Pennsylvania to serve his term. (u)

The March 21, 1967 late city edition of the New York Times carries the information that on March 20, 1967, the Supreme Court of the United States declined without comment to review MITCHELL's appeal of a five year prison sentence. u

The December, 1968 issue of Esquire magazine contains an article authored by the subject on page 131 entitled "Trip to Hanoi" which reflects that she spent two weeks in Hanoi in May, 1968 at the invitation of the Democratic Republic of North Vietnam. The article reflects that the subject considers herself an un-affiliated radical American writer "passionately opposed to the American aggression in Vietnam", and feels that the war has given radical Americans "a clear cut moral issue on which to mobilize discontent and expose the camouflaged contradictions in the system."

The subject states that her patriotism is the well spring of her opposition to American foreign policy and the interests of humanity demand that "a decent American today must be an internationalist first and patriot second." According to the subject, current American patriotism since World War II has been synonymous with bigotry, provincialism, and selfishness.

The article concerning her trip to Hanoi states that the subject, for the first half of her stay, experienced difficulty reaching a rapport with the Vietnamese; the differences of culture, manners, philosophy of life, as well as being guided around the country "by skilled bureaucrats specializing in relations with foreigners" was preventing her from taking a true picture, but in the second half of her trip, the subject states she began to understand Vietnamese behavior which "reflects the Confucian idea that both body politic and an individual's well-being depend on cultivating the rules of appropriate and just behavior."

-7-

~~SECRET~~   (U)

NY 100-162314

The subject states the Vietnamese believe their
country is and always has been democratic and they have a great
respect for America, consider the American people their friends,
but hold the present American Government as their enemy.

According to the subject, the adversities of the war
have united the Vietnamese as never before. It has improved the
moral level of the people, it has further democratized their
society by limiting the material goods and restricting the social
space available to them. It has deepened their love of country,
However, she stated Vietnam is not the model of a just state citing
the persecution of the Trotskyites in 1946, forcible collect-
ivization of agriculture in 1956, and recent brutalities and in-
justices committed by high officials.

Referral/Consul

The October 24, 1968 issue of "Village Voice" contained
an advertisement supporting DAVE MC REYNOLDS, Peace and Freedom
Party candidate for Congress in the 19th Congressional District,
New York City sponsored by the Citizens Committee For MC REYNOLDS
for Congress of which SUSAN SONTAG is a member.

"WRL News" in the September-October, 1968 edition of the
self described official publication of the War Resisters League
(WRL), 5 Beekman Street, New York 10038, a branch of the War
Resisters International and self characterized as a Pacifist organ-
ization with affiliates in 53 countries identified DAVID ERNEST
MC REYNOLDS as the WRL Field Secretary.

-8-

SECRET   (U)

NY 100-162314

IV. FOREIGN TRAVEL

(S)   NY T-1

The December, 1968 Esquire article authored by the subject reflects that the subject was in Cuba for a three month stay
in 1960.

The Esquire magazine article reflects that in mid April,
1968 SUSAN SONTAG was invited by the Democratic Republic of North
Vietnam to go to Hanoi for a period of two weeks.

According to SONTAG, she met in Cambodia in late April,
1968 with two other Americans, ANDREW KOPKIND, a Journalist, and
                                                   now working full
time for the anti-war movement "with whom she made the trip to
Hanoi .

On April 23, 1968, NY T-7, who has furnished reliable
information in the past, advised that ROBERT GREENBLATT is the
National Coordinator of the National Mobilization Committee. to
end the war in Vietnam.

According to SONTAG, because of delay and missed connections including a four day layover in Vientiane, Laos it took
ten days to go from New York to Paris and Phnom Penh to Hanoi.

She arrived at Gia Lam airport, Hanoi from Vientiane
via a small International Control Commission Plane on the
"evening" of May 3, 1968.

They were met at the airport by four members of the
Peace Committee;

          the   year old leader of the group and one of
the leading composers in North Vietnam;
before working full time for the Peace Committee;
and

While in Hanoi they stayed at the Thong Nhat (Reunification)
Hotel. She departed Hanoi the evening of May 17, 1968 for
Vientiane.

-9-

SECRET   (U)

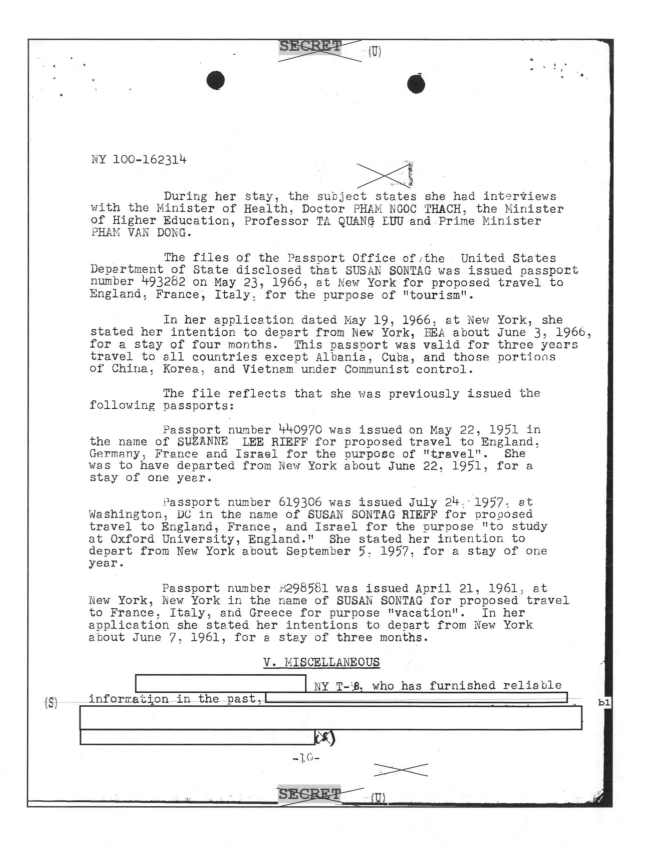

SECRET   (U)

NY 100-162314

During her stay, the subject states she had interviews
with the Minister of Health, Doctor PHAM NGOC THACH, the Minister
of Higher Education, Professor TA QUANG LUU and Prime Minister
PHAM VAN DONG.

The files of the Passport Office of the United States
Department of State disclosed that SUSAN SONTAG was issued passport
number 493282 on May 23, 1966, at New York for proposed travel to
England, France, Italy, for the purpose of "tourism".

In her application dated May 19, 1966, at New York, she
stated her intention to depart from New York, BEA about June 3, 1966,
for a stay of four months. This passport was valid for three years
travel to all countries except Albania, Cuba, and those portions
of China, Korea, and Vietnam under Communist control.

The file reflects that she was previously issued the
following passports:

Passport number 440970 was issued on May 22, 1951 in
the name of SUZANNE LEE RIEFF for proposed travel to England,
Germany, France and Israel for the purpose of "travel". She
was to have departed from New York about June 22, 1951, for a
stay of one year.

Passport number 619306 was issued July 24, 1957, at
Washington, DC in the name of SUSAN SONTAG RIEFF for proposed
travel to England, France, and Israel for the purpose "to study
at Oxford University, England." She stated her intention to
depart from New York about September 5, 1957, for a stay of one
year.

Passport number B298581 was issued April 21, 1961, at
New York, New York in the name of SUSAN SONTAG for proposed travel
to France, Italy, and Greece for purpose "vacation". In her
application she stated her intentions to depart from New York
about June 7, 1961, for a stay of three months.

V. MISCELLANEOUS

NY T-8, who has furnished reliable
(S)   information in the past,   b1

(S)

-10-

SECRET   (U)

NY 100-162314

(S)

(K)

(U)   On January 17, 1968, NY T-9?, who has furnished reliable
information in the past, advised that SUSAN SONTAG was sent an
invitation to attend a reception for NIKOLAIT. FEDORENKO, a former
permanent representative of the Soviet Union to the United Nations,
who departed the United States on January 25, 1968. (S)

          Confidential informants, who are aware of Communist
activities in the New York area, were contacted during December,
1968 and they had no information to furnish concerning the subject.

          The following physical description is set forth con-
cerning the subject:

Name	SUSAN SONTAG aka Mrs. Philip Rieff, Suszanne Lee Rieff, nee Susan Rosenblatt, Suszanne Lee Rosenblatt
Sex	Female
Race	White
Date of Birth	January 16, 1933
Place of Birth	New York, New York
Height	5 feet 10 inches
Hair	Black
Eyes	Brown

-11-

1 - Mr. N. P. Callahan

SAC, New York (100-97235)
    Attention: Liaison Section   2/14/69

Director, FBI (62-46855)   1 -
                                            1 -
                                            1 -

PURCHASE OF BOOKS
BOOK REVIEWS

        You are authorized to obtain discreetly one copy
each of the following books for the use of the Bureau. Mark
books to the attention of the Research-Satellite Section,
Domestic Intelligence Division.

        1. "Trip to Hanoi" by Susan Sontag,
            Noonday Press (branch of Farrar, Straus,
            Giroux), 19 Union Square W., New York,
            New York 10003, paperback, $1.45

        2. "No More Vietnams: The War and the
            Future of American Foreign Policy"
            edited by Richard M. Pfeffer,
            Harper and Row, New York,
            New York 10016, $5.95

1 - Nationalities Intelligence (Route through for review)
1 - Mr. M. F. Row (6221 I.B.)

(10)

NOTE:

        Books requested for review by SA H. D. Clough, Jr.,
NIS, Domestic Intelligence Division. Books will be filed
in Bureau Library where not now available. In the interest
of economy, the paperback edition of #1 is requested.

MAILED 4
FEB 14 1969
COMM-FBI

100-450066

NOT RECORDED
FEB 19 1969

TELETYPE UNIT

FD-204 (Rev. 3-3-59)

~~SECRET~~ - (U)

~~SECRET~~ - NO FOREIGN DISSEMINATION

UNITED STATES DEPARTMENT OF JUSTICE
FEDERAL BUREAU OF INVESTIGATION

Copy to:

Report of: **Office:** New York, New York   b6
Date: 3/6/72   b7C

Field Office File #:   100-162314   **Bureau File #:**   100-450066

Title: SUSAN SONTAG

Character: SECURITY MATTER - SUBVERSIVE

Synopsis:
        Subject resides at 340 Riverside Drive, NY, NY, and
        is self-employed as a writer. Subject has permitted
the use of her name in connection with fund raising activities
of the PCPJ and has travelled in Cuba. In addition, subject is
reported to be on the Steering Committee of Resist.

                                -C-

DETAILS:

        I. BACKGROUND

Residence and Employment

        On March 2, 1972,
                              New York, New York, advised that the   b6
subject maintains her residence in Penthouse A at the above   b7C
address and that she is engaged as a writer, selling her work
where she can to various publications.

                    ~~SECRET~~ - NO FOREIGN DISSEMINATION
                    GROUP I
                    Excluded from automatic
                    downgrading and
                    declassification.

                        ~~SECRET~~   U.S. GOVERNMENT PRINTING OFFICE: 1969 O - 351-076

SECRET   (U)

NY 100-162314

No interview of the subject is contemplated in view of her activities as a writer. It is felt that in view of her minimal activity and her status as a writer, an attempt to interview her could result in embarrassment to the Bureau, which would not be compensated by the information obtainable, if she were cooperative.

No recommendation is being made to include the subject in ADEX. It is felt that her activities as reflected in instant report and referenced report do not qualify her for inclusion on ADEX.

INFORMANTS

Identity of Source	File Number Where Located
NY T-1	100-162314-45
NY T-2	
NY T-3	100-162314-30

(S)

b1
b7D

Referred to in instant report is information contained in CIAlet, dated 2/14/72, and is located in NYfile 100-162134-60.

The other informants mentioned in instant report as having no information concerning captioned subject are as follows:

b7D

-B*-
COVER PAGE

SECRET   (U)

SECRET (U)

FD-263 (Rev. 12-19-67)

FEDERAL BUREAU OF INVE

REPORTING OFFICE	OFFICE OF ORIGIN	DATE	INVESTIGATIVE PERIOD	
NEW YORK	NEW YORK	3/6/72	11/30/71 - 3/6/72	

TITLE OF CASE	REPORT MADE BY	TYPED BY
SUSAN SONTAG, aka		b6 b7C

CHARACTER OF CASE

SM - SUBVERSIVE

REFERENCE

        Summary report of SA KENNETH J. HUNNEMEDER, dated
12/20/68, at New York.

                        -C-

ADMINISTRATIVE

        This report is being ~~classified~~ "~~Secret~~ - No
Foreign Dissemination" because the information received from
CIA was so ~~classified~~ and because the information concerning
the subject's travel abroad was likewise so ~~classified~~.

        A suitable photograph of the subject is available.

ACCOMPLISHMENTS CLAIMED					☐ NONE	ACQUIT-TALS	CASE HAS BEEN:		
CONVIC.	AUTO.	FUG.	FINES	SAVINGS	RECOVERIES		PENDING OVER ONE YEAR ☐YES ☐NO		
							PENDING PROSECUTION OVER SIX MONTHS ☐YES ☐NO		

APPROVED	SPECIAL AGENT IN CHARGE	DO NOT WRITE IN SPACES BELOW

COPIES MADE:

        5 - Bureau (100-450066) (RM)
        1 - New York (100-162314)

REC-13

MAR 16 1972

Dissemination Record of Attached Report

Agency	
Request Recd.	
Date Fwd.	3-27-72 3/9/7
How Fwd.	R/s
By	

Notations

70 MAR 29 1972

b6
b7C

-A-
COVER PAGE

SECRET (U)

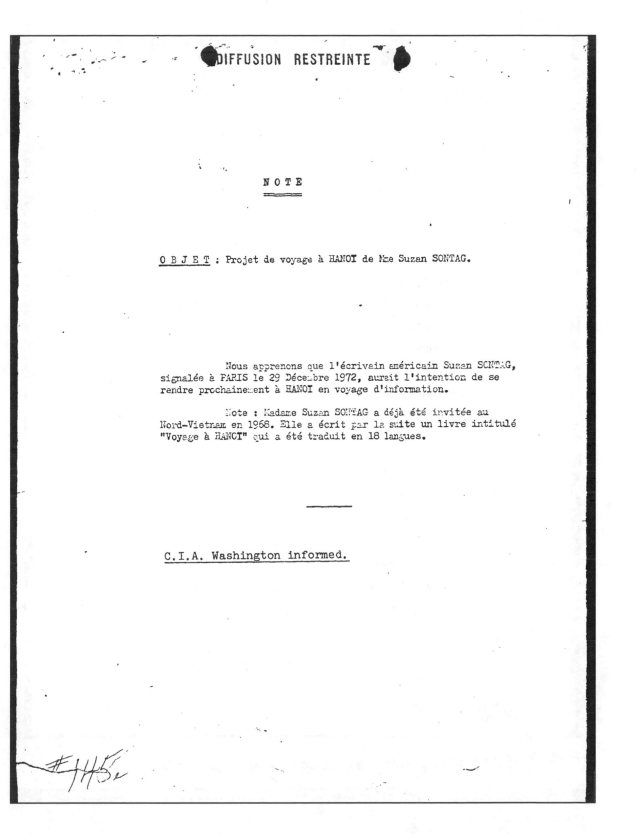

DIFFUSION RESTREINTE

N O T E

O B J E T : Projet de voyage à HANOI de Mme Suzan SONTAG.

Nous apprenons que l'écrivain américain Suzan SONTAG, signalée à PARIS le 29 Décembre 1972, aurait l'intention de se rendre prochainement à HANOI en voyage d'information.

Note : Madame Suzan SONTAG a déjà été invitée au Nord-Vietnam en 1968. Elle a écrit par la suite un livre intitulé "Voyage à HANOI" qui a été traduit en 18 langues.

C.I.A. Washington informed.

UNCLASSIFIED U.S. Department of State Case No. F-2014-10333 Doc No. C05623077 Date: 08/21/2014

RELEASED IN PART,
FOIA B6

DEPARTMENT OF STATE

Washington, D.C. 20520

May 11, 1971

FBI LIAISON: FOR INFORMATION ONLY

RE: SONTAG, SUSAN

DATE OF BIRTH: Jan. 16, 1933

PLACE OF BIRTH: New York, New York

RESIDENCE: 340 Riverside Drive
                                    New York, New York 10025

BUREAU FILE NUMBER: ~~UNKNOWN~~   100-450066

WASHINGTON FIELD OFFICE: UNKNOWN

PASSPORT NUMBER: B 911273

DATE OF ISSUE: May 3, 1971

PLACE OF ISSUE: New York

SOCIAL SECURITY NUMBER: [   ]   FOIA B6

PROPOSED TRAVEL PLANS

DATE OF DEPARTURE: May 9, 1971   NOT RECORDED
                                                        2 MAY 25 1971
PURPOSE OF TRIP: Vacation

LENGTH OF STAY: 4 months

MEANS OF TRANSPORTATION: Air

COUNTRIES TO BE VISITED: France, England, Italy

REVIEW AUTHORITY: Richard Zorn, Senior
Reviewer

                                                        PASSPORT OFFICE
                                                        ROBERT D. JOHNSON
PT/L-25
5-70
58 MAY 27 1971

FOIA # 1246083, 100-HQ-450066, Section 1, Serial 14, Pg. 71

UNCLASSIFIED U.S. Department of State Case No. F-2014-10333 Doc No. C05623077 Date: 08/21/2014

Terry Southern

TERRY SOUTHERN IS BETTER known for his prolific work as a Hollywood screen-writer than he is as a novelist, penning countercultural hits such as *Barbarella* and *Easy Rider* and transforming the script for the straight-laced Cold War thrilled *Red Alert* into the satirical masterpiece *Dr. Strangelove*. Though the latter film certainly appeared to raise a few eyebrows in the Bureau for its "controversial" nature, it was a different kind of strange love that finally earned Southern the FBI's attention.

The file begins and ends in the early months of 1965. In February, Director J. Edgar Hoover received a priority air mail from the special agent in charge of the Los Angeles Field Office. As part of an ongoing investigation involving the Charlotte and Albuquerque Field Offices, Los Angeles had discovered that millions of copies of Southern's novel *Candy* were already hitting the newsstands, "pure pornography" according to an informant, who also added that the publisher, anticipating legal difficulties, had sought counsel to fight attempts to bar the book.

Seemingly unknown to the Bureau, *Candy* had already undergone its share of legal difficulties. Originally written by Southern and collaborator Mason Hoffenberg as a combination literary exercise and cash grab, *Candy* was first published in 1958 under a pseudonym; following Southern's rise to prominence in the '60s, the publisher, Olympia Press, decided to re-publish the book in 1964 under the authors' real names to great financial and literary success — and Southern and Hoffenberg's great dismay.

By 1965, the two had managed to work out a royalty deal, and the book had become a surprise hit — none of which interested the Bureau. Its only concerns were determining if *Candy* was indeed irredeemable filth and following up on the informant's lead that Southern was in possession of "one of the finest collections of pornographic films ever made" — allegedly including some material formerly belonging to the late King Farouk of Egypt — which he would screen for visitors to his Connecticut home.

To address the former concern, the FBI's Indianapolis field office acquired a copy of *Candy* through Indiana's chapter of Citizens for Decent Literature, which they offered to the FBI laboratory for testing. Possibly embarrassed, the lab declined the offer. For the latter interest, the FBI's New Haven field office interviewed a Connecticut State Police officer in Canaan, where Southern lived, who informed the agent that though Southern often had "beatnik" guests, he had no arrest record; the officer had never heard anything about him owning a collection of pornographic films, world's finest or otherwise.

Shortly thereafter, Assistant Attorney General Herbert J. Miller — who would later go on to help secure an unconditional pardon for Richard Nixon after the Watergate scandal — weighed in: by merit of having any critical reception, *Candy* had proven some redeeming value and was therefore not pornography. Hoover quietly informed all branches to drop the investigation. *Candy* became one of the biggest-selling novels of the '60s.

FD-36 (Rev.,5-22-64)

F B I

Date: **2/15/65**

Transmit the following in _____
                                        (Type in plaintext or code)

Via ___ **AIR TEL** _____   **AIR MAIL**
                                              (Priority)

- -

TO: DIRECTOR, FBI

FROM: SAC, LOS ANGELES (145-698) (RUC)

RE: TERRY SOUTHERN
           (Screen Writer)
           ITOM
           OO: New Haven

     Reference is made to BuAirtel to SACS Houston and Los Angeles 2/11/65 in the case entitled: RICHARD ARNO YERXA, Aka, et al; dba REED ENTERPRISES, INC., San Diego, California, ITOM, OO: Houston (HO 145-130) Bufile 145-2846 which communication advises that the Bureau is in receipt of the paperback book entitled "CANDY" from both the Charlotte Office and Albuquerque Office.

     Reference is also made to the report of SA [ ] Los Angeles, 2/5/65 wherein the interview of [ ] of Palm Springs, California is set forth in the RICHARD ARNO YERXA investigation. During the course of the interview, [ ] advised he had 1½ million copies of "CANDY" printed and distributed as Greenleaf Classics, that he was also aware that [ ] of New York had printed and distributed this book and was suing his concern in the State of New York. [ ] also advised that LANCER and BRANDON HOUSE had published this same story.

     In an interview of [ ] at North Hollywood, California on 2/5/65, [ ] advised he was aware that about "5 million copies of CANDY are presently on the newsstands" and "it is laying an egg".

     For the information of all offices, [ ] also advised that he had indemnified the 700 outlets of Kable News Company against prosecution for the sale and distribution of "CANDY", that he expects trouble with this book and has retained the services of attorney STANLEY FLEISHMAN of Hollywood to take care of any legal difficulties.

     On 2/1/65 [ ] Columbia Broadcasting System, TV-City, Hollywood was interviewed by SA LESLIE F. WARREN on another matter at which time [ ] furnished the following information, strictly on a confidential basis:

b6
b7C

b6
b7C
b7D

③ Bureau
1 – Albuquerque (145-195) (Info)
1 – Charlotte (145-289) (Info)
1 – Houston (145-130) (Info)
1 – New York
1 – Los Angeles (145-698) (1cc 145-582)
HEY:
(9)
        Special Agent in Charge
        C C • Wick

Approved _____   M   Per _____

REC/104   145-3225-1

FEB 26 1965

LA 145-698

b6
b7C
b7D

(It is further pointed out that [ ] is an established source [ ] and his identity must be concealed to any outside agency.)

About three months ago [ ] had lunch with one [ ]. [ ] said that TERRY SOUTHERN, who received screen credit for the controversial film "Dr. STRANGELOVE", written in conjunction with others, had written one of the current best sellers, "CANDY", which, in the opinion of [ ] "is pure pornography".

[ ] also advised that TERRY SOUTHERN has one of the finest collections of pornographic films in the country. [ ] explained that this is not the ordinary type of pornographic film but is high quality, the best made, including some made for KING FAROUK.

No further information was available from [ ] other than that set forth above.

On 2/1/65 SA WARREN contacted [ ] (an established source) who advised that as of May 1963, TERRY SOUTHERN resided at RFD E, Canaan, Connecticut and could be reached in care of Sterling Lad Agency, 75 East 55th Street, New York, New York. SOUTHERN received joint screen play credit for "DR. STRANGELOVE" along with STANLEY KUBRICK, Producer-Director, and PETER GEORGE, who wrote the book. Columbia Pictures Corp., released the film. SOUTHERN has no local address, past or present, in Los Angeles, and is a member of the Writers Guild of America East, New York.

In view of the fact prior ITOM investigations pertaining to paperback books has included the identifying of the author, knowing of his credit and criminal background and, in most cases, interviewing the author as to his contractual relationships with the publisher, this is set forth for informational purposes for all offices receiving copies of this communication.

However, it is believed that the Bureau should furnish the investigative direction of this particular individual as to whether he should be directly interviewed as to any work he has done on the book "CANDY", which of the publishing houses employed him to do such work, if any.

With reference to the pornographic library of films which SOUTHERN allegedly has in his possession, it is not known to this office whether it is a local violation in Connecticut to display films to "guests" and it is therefore left to the discretion of the Bureau as to whether such information should be made available, strictly on a confidential basis, to a local law enforcement agency covering SOUTHERN'S place of residence.

- 2 -

SAC, New Haven   2/26/65

Director, FBI 145- 3225-1   1 - Mr. Conley

TERRY SOUTHERN
(SCREEN WRITER)
ITOM
OO: NEW HAVEN

        ReLAairtel 2/15/65 indicating New Haven as OO,
but no copy designated for that office. Two copies of
reairtel are enclosed for the New Haven Office.

        For the further information of the New Haven Office,
the Bureau has forwarded to the Criminal Division of the
Department a copy of the paperback book entitled "Candy,"
and asked that same be reviewed for an opinion as to whether
this book will be a suitable vehicle for prosecution under
the ITOM statutes. Accordingly, New Haven is instructed
only to review its indices, conduct credit and criminal
checks concerning Southern and advise Bureau and interested
offices results of same. No interview is to be conducted
with Southern concerning this matter.

        With regard to the information furnished to the
Los Angeles Office by [   ] New Haven is instructed   b6
to make this information concerning Southern and his alleged   b7C
collection of pornographic films available to the ranking   b7D
officer of the appropriate law enforcement agency covering
Southern's Connecticut residence, providing such officer is
considered reliable and trustworthy. It should be noted
Los Angeles has pointed out [   ] identity must be concealed
and not furnished to local authorities. It must be stressed
that the reliability of the information cannot be attested
to by the FBI and is furnished solely as a matter of information.

        Los Angeles score form error for not designating
airtel to New Haven Office.

Enclosures (2)

2 - Los Angeles (145-698)
1 - Albuquerque (145-105)
1 - Charlotte (145-289)
1 - Houston (145-130)
1 - New York

JAC:ekh

Tolson _____
Belmont _____
Mohr _____
DeLoach _____
Casper _____
Callahan _____
Conrad _____
Felt _____
Gale _____
Rosen _____
Sullivan _____
Tavel _____
Trotter _____
Tele. Room _____
Holmes _____
Gandy _____

MAIL ROOM   TELETYPE UNIT

(SEE NOTE PAGE 2)

MAILED 25
FEB 26 1965
COMM-FBI

b6
b7C
b7D

NOTE: Los Angeles received information from source ⬚
who claimed he had a recent conversation with ⬚
"New York Times" correspondent in California who claimed Terry
Southern, Canaan, Connecticut, had written one of the current
best sellers "Candy". "New York Times" representative also
alleges Southern has "one of the finest collections of
pornographic films in the country," including some made of
for King Farouk. Los Angeles advises Southern received
joint screen play credit for motion picture "Dr. Strangelove."
Los Angeles suggested Bureau might desire Southern be
interviewed concerning book "Candy" and leaving to Bureau's
discretion whether information concerning movie film should
be given to local authorities. No identifiable record in
Bureau indices concerning Southern.

OPTIONAL FORM NO. 10
MAY 1962 EDITION
GSA GEN. REG. NO. 27

5010–107

UNITED STATES GOVERNMENT

Memorandum

TO   :   DIRECTOR, FBI   DATE: March 23, 1965

FROM :   SAC, NEW HAVEN (145-279) (P)

SUBJECT: TERRY SOUTHERN
            (SCREEN WRITER)
            ITOM
            (OO: NEW HAVEN)

Re Bureau letter to New Haven 2/26/65.

New Haven indices negative regarding subject SOUTHERN.

On March 10, 1965, Lieutenant CLEVELAND FUESSENICH,
Connecticut State Police, Canaan, Connecticut, advised
that the subject has no arrest record at Canaan,
Connecticut. FUESSENICH advised that the subject
resides on Lower Road, North Canaan, Connecticut, and
has resided there for the past three or four years.
FUESSENICH advised that he has heard the subject is
a writer and has done work in the movies, however, he
has no personal knowledge regarding the subject or
his activities. FUESSENICH advised that he purchased
an old house and in recent months has completely re-
finished the house, inside and out. FUESSENICH stated
that the subject has a lot of visitors with New York
license plates, however, he did not know the purpose.
FUESSENICH advised that he has seen the [   ]
on a few occasions and she gives the appearance of a
"beatnick", in that, she is sloppy and extremely dirty.

b6
b7C

Lieutenant FUESSENICH was advised by SA [   ]
[   ] regarding SOUTHERN and his alleged
collection of pornographic films. FUESSENICH advised
that he had heard nothing in this regard and had no
information regarding obscene films.

3 - Bureau
1 - Albuquerque (145-105) (info)
1 - Charlotte (145-289) (info)
1 - Houston (145-130) (info)
1 - Los Angeles (145-698) (info)
1 - New York (info)
1 - New Haven
WBZ/kjb
(9)

REC 37

12 MAR 24 1965

EX-101

58 APR 13 1965

Buy U.S. Savings Bonds Regularly on the Payroll Savings Plan

NH 145-279

On March 15, 1965, [redacted],
Litchfield County Credit Rating Bureau, Inc.,
Torrington, Connecticut, advised the subject and
[redacted] had been on file with his Bureau
only since March 4, 1965. [redacted] advised that
the subject resides RFD, North Canaan, Connecticut,
and is alleged to be a writer, however, his employment has not been verified. [redacted] advised that
the subject has one child and is supposed to have
lived at his present address for the past four years.
[redacted] advised that due to the limited trade
experience for the subject they could not rate his
credit position.

b6
b7C

For the information of the Bureau, the following
information was taken from an article captioned
"Candy' Scarce in Hartford", which appeared in the
"Waterbury Republican" (daily newspaper) on March
16, 1965, dateline Hartford, Connecticut (AP).

"Candy' is going to be scarce in Hartford. Distributors
of the controversial book written by Mason Hoffenberg
and Terry Southern are being asked by police to
remove 'Candy' from their stands. The request stems
from a meeting of Police Chief John J. Kerrigan and
Attorney George I. Silvester, Jr., Chief Prosecutor
of Circuit Court 14. Kerrigan announced Monday that
the book is considered obscene and that distributors
were being asked by the Vice Squad to take the book
out of circulation. 'If any books are found on
newsstands after these requests are made,' said
Kerrigan, 'arrests will be made.'"

2.

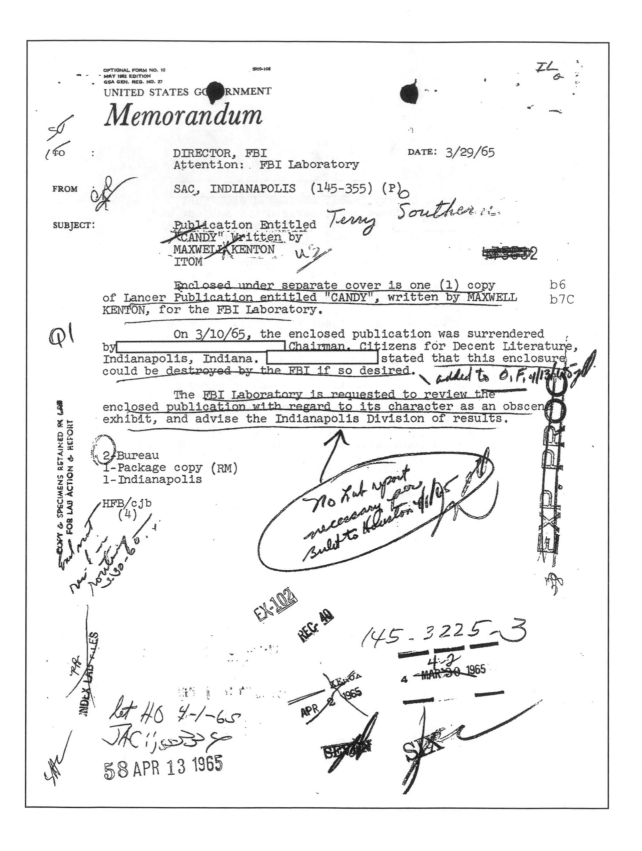

OPTIONAL FORM NO. 10
MAY 1962 EDITION
GSA GEN. REG. NO. 27

UNITED STATES GOVERNMENT

Memorandum

TO   :   DIRECTOR, FBI   DATE: 3/29/65
             Attention: FBI Laboratory

FROM   :   SAC, INDIANAPOLIS (145-355) (P)

SUBJECT :   Publication Entitled
             "CANDY" Written by
             MAXWELL KENTON
             ITOM

             Enclosed under separate cover is one (1) copy   b6
        of Lancer Publication entitled "CANDY", written by MAXWELL   b7C
        KENTON, for the FBI Laboratory.

             On 3/10/65, the enclosed publication was surrendered
        by _____ Chairman. Citizens for Decent Literature,
        Indianapolis, Indiana. _____ stated that this enclosure
        could be destroyed by the FBI if so desired.

             The FBI Laboratory is requested to review the
        enclosed publication with regard to its character as an obscene
        exhibit, and advise the Indianapolis Division of results.

        2-Bureau
        1-Package copy (RM)
        1-Indianapolis

        HFB/cjb
        (4)

Director, Federal Bureau of Investigation   March 23, 1965

                                                    HJM:TK:mtg
                                                    97-38-21
Herbert J. Miller, Jr., Assistant
Attorney General, Criminal Division   *Terry Southern*

Suitability of the novel "Candy" for prosecutive action
under 18 U.S.C. 1462

         We have reviewed the paperback book entitled "Candy,"
as you requested in your memorandum of February 12, 1965.
In our judgment the work is not a suitable vehicle for
prosecution.

         "Candy," for all its sexual descriptions and foul language,
is primarily a satirical parody of the pornographic books which
currently flood our newsstands. Whatever erotic impact or
prurient appeal it has is thoroughly diluted by the utter
absurdity and improbability of the situations described.

         The jacket of the hardcover Putman edition claims the
endorsement of Dwight MacDonald, Nelson Algren, James Jones
and other literary figures. The book has been seriously
reviewed in Newsweek (May 18, 1964), The New York Times Book
Review Section (May 17, 1964), The New York Review (May 14,
1964), and other literary magazines and supplements. The
reviewers, while not uniformly praising "Candy," have
generally recognized it as an effective and amusing lampoon
of "dirty" books.

         This sort of critical judgment serves to reaffirm our
convictions that "Candy" is not a work which is "utterly
without social importance." In the recent words of the
Supreme Court, "/M 7aterial dealing with sex in a manner
that advocates ideas * * * or that has any literary . . .
value . . ., may not be branded as obscenity and denied the
constitutional protection. Jacobellis v. Ohio, 378 U.S.
184, 191. We feel that this statement settles the question
of "Candy's" suitability for prosecutive action.

                                        145-3325-
                                        NOT RECORDED
                                        170 APR 5 1965

58 APR 13 1965

OPTIONAL FORM NO. 10
5010-104

UNITED STATES GOVERNMENT

Memorandum

TO   :   DIRECTOR, FBI (145-2846)   DATE: 4/20/65

145-3225

FROM :   SAC, NEW HAVEN (145-279)(C)

SUBJECT: TERRY SOUTHERN
           (SCREEN WRITER)
           ITOM

           OO: NEW HAVEN

145-2846-1

Re Bureau letter to Houston 4/1/65 captioned, "RICHARD
ARNO YEEXA, aka ETAL, d/b/a Reed Enterprises, Inc., San
Diego, California, ITOM, OO: Houston".

In view of the Department's ruling that "Candy" was not
a suitable vehicle for prosecution, no further investigation
is being conducted by the New Haven Division.

2 - Bureau
1 - New Haven
WBZ/hmg
   (3)

REC- 24   145- 3225 - 4

EX 109   3 APR 21 1965

6 4 APR 26 1965

Hunter S. Thompson

ACCORDING TO THE FBI, some of their records on Hunter S. Thompson, countercul-ture journalist and Gonzo investigator, may have been destroyed in purges in 1994 and 1998; the rest were sent over to the National Archives and Records Administration, vault of historically-relevant materials from federal agencies across the government. What remains in the available 58 pages reveal that the agency's interest in the drug-toting Doctor began before his hit *Fear and Loathing in Las Vegas*, starting with his coverage of the Hell's Angels motorcycle gang.

Thompson first came across the Bureau's radar around the time of the 1967 publication of his book about riding along with the Hell's Angels motorcycle gang. The collection revved up with Thompson's 1970 entry into the Pitkin County, Colorado sheriff's race — "despite the natural horror of seeing myself as the main pig." The inquiry involved on-the-ground interviews, including with the local liquor store clerk.

Confidential informants in Colorado provided additional background for the agency, and a note from one of Thompson's Kentucky-based childhood acquaintances labeled him as "the bad boy of our neighborhood."

There also appear a few of the Aspen Wall Posters he used for his campaign, highlighting version No. 4 and its critique of law enforcement, including a swastika in place of the "x" in then-President Richard Nixon's name.

However, the Bureau didn't go so far as to cover Thompson's death, seemingly a suicide conducted at the man's kitchen table, the moment at which his FBI file became subject to public disclosure.

Identification Record Request
FD-9 (Rev. 4-28-65)

INSTRUCTIONS

1. *This form may be submitted in legible hand printing.*

2. *Use separate form for each individual on whom record is requested.*

3. *Make effort to furnish FBI identification number, law enforcement identification number, or military service number.*

4. *Furnish descriptive data and fingerprint classification only when FBI number not available.*

5. *Indicate office for reply in lower right corner only. Also list in lower right corner all offices which should receive copies of available records. Include carbon of FD-9 for each office receiving copies and forward with original to Bureau.*

6. *Do not fill in block in lower left corner.*

To: DIRECTOR, FBI Attention: Identification Division	Date 11/3/70

Re

RESIDENT AGENCY
GRAND JUNCTION, COLORADO

Field File No. 66-1377

Furnish The Known Identification Record of the Following:

Name				FBI No.	
HUNTER STOCTON THOMPSON				Other No.	

Aliases

Hunter S. Thompson

Sex	Race	Birth Date	Birthplace	Residence
Male	White	7/18/37	--	Aspen, Colorado

Height	Weight	Build	Hair	Eyes	Complexion	Age
6'3"	190		Brown	Brown		

Fingerprint Classification	Scars, marks and tattoos

Also Furnish:

☐ Photo

☐ Fingerprints

☐ Handwriting Specimens

Identification Division's Reply

☑ On basis of information furnished, unable to identify:

☑ Criminal Files	☐ Civil Files	☐ All Files

☐ Record Attached

☐ Photo Attached

☐ Photo Not Available

☐ Fingerprints Attached

☐ Handwriting Specimen Attached

Return Reply to:

DENVER

Send Copies To:

100-9353-11
66-1377

SEARCHED ___ INDEXED ___
SERIALIZED _X_ FILED ___
NOV 12 1970
FBI — DENVER

OPTIONAL FORM NO. 10
5010-104

UNITED STATES GOVERNMENT

Memorandum

TO : SAC, DENVER   DATE: 1/27/67

FROM : SAC, SAN FRANCISCO (100-56017)(P)

SUBJECT: HUNTER S. THOMPSON
SM - C

[FOIA(b)7 - (D)] on November 5, 1965, furnished information that a subscription to the People's World was maintained in the name of HUNTER THOMPSON, 318 Parnassus Avenue, San Francisco, This subscription was a new yearly subscription that was due to expire on November 6, 1966.

[FOIA(b)7 - (D)] on December 12, 1966, furnished information that the yearly subscription which was due to expire on November 6, 1967, in the name of HUNTER THOMPSON was changed from 318 Parnassus Avenue, San Francisco, to Woody Creek, Colorado. The 1964-65 San Francisco Polk's Directory listed HUNTER S. THOMPSON and SANDRA D. THOMPSON as residing at 318 Parnassus Avenue. The wife's name was set forth as SANDRA D. THOMPSON. A route postman which covers 318 Parnassus advised in December, 1965, that HUNTER THOMPSON and his wife have resided at that location for approximately 9 to 11 months. Further that THOMPSON is approximately 28 to 32 years of age and white. The postman advised that the mails gave no hint as to the occupation of THOMPSON, but that he did receive a lot of quality magazines and was receiving the People's World.

San Francisco Polk's Directory for 1966 listed HUNTER S. THOMPSON and wife SANDRA D. THOMPSON as residing at 318 Parnassus Avenue, San Francisco. The Registry of Voters for the city and county of San Francisco contained no record that HUNTER THOMPSON had registered to vote. However, a Mrs. SANDRA DAWN THOMPSON of 230 Grattan Street, San Francisco, who formerly resided at 318 Parnassus Avenue, registered to vote in July, 1966. She registered her intent to affiliate in one of the major parties. She set forth her occupation as housewife, that she was born in New York and was 5'5".

2 - Denver (RM)
2 - San Francisco
JD:vlh
(4)

SEARCHED___INDEXED
SERIALIZED___FILED
FEB 1 1967
FBI—DENVER

NW 6524 DocId:59161781 Page 2

SF 100-56017
JD:vlh

FOIA(b)7 - (D) San Francisco, California,
advised on January 20, 1967, that HUNTER THOMPSON, 230 Grattan,
changed his address, effective September 10, 1966, to Owl House,
Woody Creek, Colorado.

The People's World is a West Coast
newspaper published weekly in San Francisco.

LEAD:

DENVER

AT WOODY CREEK, COLORADO. Will attempt to
verify the residence of HUNTER S. THOMPSON at the Owl House,
Woody Creek, Colorado.

2

GC Photo   Fee Pd   Examiner or Clerk

COLORADO   SEE REVERSE SIDE FOR CORRECTIONS
DRIVERS LICENSE   PITKIN 57
COUNTY

HUNTER STOCKTON THOMPSON
OWL HOUSE GEN. DEL.
WOODY CREEK COLO 81656

DATE OF ISSUE   OCT 19, 1966

OPERATOR

X 332338

EXPIRES ON YOUR
BIRTHDATE. RENEW   1969
WITHIN 90 DAYS PRIOR

| M | 190 | 6-3 | BRN | BRN |
| SEX | WEIGHT | HEIGHT | HAIR | EYES |

DATE OF BIRTH   PREVIOUS LICENSE
JULY 18, 1937   CALIF

CORRECTIVE LENS   SIGNAL LIGHTS

LEFT SIDE R.V. MIRROR   AUTOMATIC TRANS.

OTHER RESTRICTIONS

X _Hunter S. Thompson_

ISSUED PURSUANT TO CHAPTER 13 C. R. S. 1963 AS AMENDED

DIRECTOR OF
REVENUE

MASTER FILES ORIGINAL

RIGHT
INDEX FINGER

5. DO YOU HAVE HEART TROUBLE, EPILEPSY, DIABETES, PARALYSIS, SEIZURES, CONVULSIONS, LAPSES OF CONSCIOUSNESS OR ANY OTHER PHYSICAL HANDICAP OR DISABILITY?   YES ☐ NO ☑

I DO UNDERSTAND THAT ANY FALSE INFORMATION GIVEN ABOVE WOULD BE CAUSE FOR CANCELLATION OF THIS LICENSE.

SIGNATURE OF APPLICANT _Hunter S. Thompson_

DO NOT WRITE IN THIS SPACE   FOR EXAMINERS USE ONLY

WRITTEN: SERIES _New_ GRADE _98_ ROAD SIGNS PASSED ☐ 100

VISION: WITHOUT CORRECTION: R.20/ 20 L.20/ 20 Both 20/ 20

CORRECTIVE GLASSES: R.20/____ L.20/____ Both 20/____

CONTACT LENS: R.20/____ L.20/____ Both 20/____

COLOR BLIND: YES ☐ NO ☒ HEARING GOOD ☒ H OF H ☐ DEAF ☐

RESTRICTIONS AND REMARKS: _____

INST. PERMIT ☐   NO DRIVE ☒   DRIVE ☐

SUBSCRIBED AND SWORN TO BEFORE ME THIS DATE _Oct 18 1966_

SIGNATURE OF EXAMINER _H.J. Cullin_

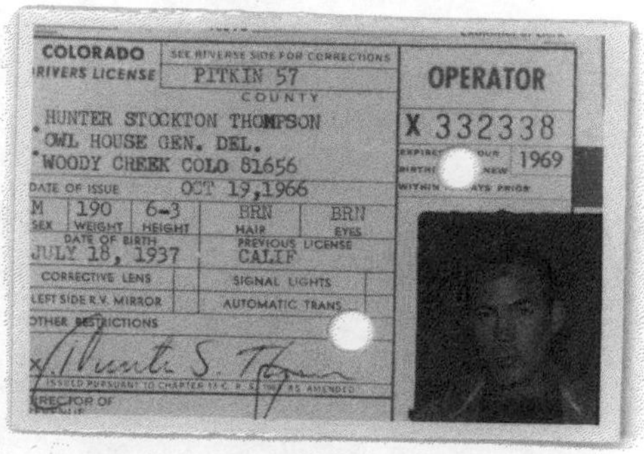

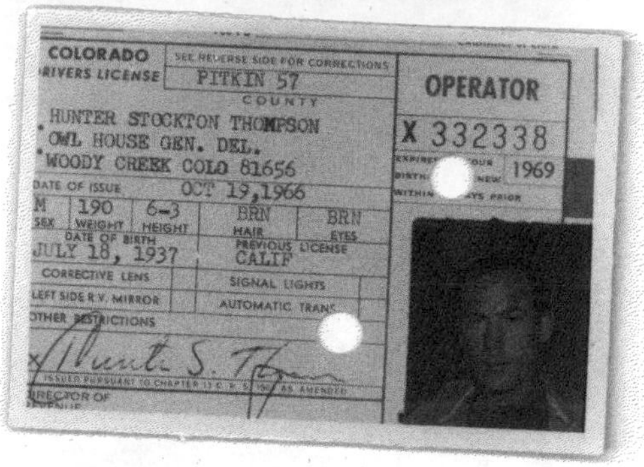

NW 6524 DocId:59161781 Page 12

SAC, SAN FRANCISCO (100-56017)   3/30/67

SAC, DENVER (100-9353) (P)

HUNTER S. THOMPSON
SM - C

    Re San Francisco letter to Denver dated 1/27/67.

    For information San Francisco, Denver indices negative
regarding subject.

    The following investigation was conducted by SA
VINCENT R. JONES:

    On 3/16/67 Mrs. [FOIA(b)7 - (D)] (protect identity),
[FOIA(b)7 - (D)] and store operator at Woody Creek, Colorado,
advised that HUNTER S. THOMPSON, with wife SANDRA, and son,
presently are renting a house on a ranch located about five
miles east of Woody Creek.

    Mrs [FOIA(b)7 - (D)] advised that THOMPSON and his wife had
mentioned to her that THOMPSON had lived with the Hell's
Angels for one and a half years and had then written a book
about them. They indicated that he recently appeared on
national TV programs, the "Today" show and "I've Got a Secret".

    Mrs [FOIA(b)7 - (D)] stated she understood that THOMPSON and
his wife are going to have to give up their rental house soon
and will be moving. She stated she did not know where they
would be moving to.

    Mrs [FOIA(b)7 - (D)] stated that Mr. THOMPSON mentioned that in
the past he had lived in South America as a roving reporter.

    Mrs [FOIA(b)7 - (D)] advised that two or three days earlier, Mr.
THOMPSON had gotten home from a trip and indicated that he had
been to Canada, where he had appeared on a TV program.

    Mrs [FOIA(b)7 - (D)] advised that the THOMPSONs previously lived
in the area for about one year, ending around January, 1965,
and that they recently returned to the Woody Creek area.

2- San Francisco (RM)
3- Denver
VRJ:mdd
(5)

Serialized
Indexed
Filed

100-9353-2

NW 6524   DocId:59161781   Page 18

DN 100-9353

Mrs FOIA(b)7 - (D) tated that she has observed some very obscene publications come through the mail to THOMPSON from unknown publishing company in New York.

LEADS:

DENVER DIVISION

AT WOODY CREEK, COLORADO

Will recontact the [FOIA(b)7 - (D)] and determine when subject THOMPSON and his wife move, and to what location.

AT DENVER, COLORADO

Will check the records of the State Driver's License and Motor Vehicle Registration Offices relative to subject HUSTER S. THOMPSON and his wife SANDRA D. THOMPSON.

Attempt to obtain photographs of each of them and in the event operator's licenses located, secure a photocopy of the application bearing a fingerprint, so that this may be submitted to the Identification Division in an effort to check for an Identification Record.

Will check with informants in the Denver Division to determine whether subject is known to them.

2

OPTIONAL FORM NO. 10
MAY 1962 EDITION
GSA FPMR (41 CFR) 101-11.6

UNITED STATES GOVERNMENT

Memorandum

TO   :   SAC, DENVER (100-9353)   DATE: April 19, 1967

FROM :   SA ELMER A. SAMSON

SUBJECT:

       HUNTER S. THOMPSON
       SM - C

     IC DONALD L. RAY, on April 6, 1967, obtained driver's license photographs and Xerox copies of driver's license information on subject and his wife which have been placed in the 1-A section of the file. HUNTER S. THOMPSON had a clear driving record, however, his wife SANDRA D. THOMPSON, had an accident January 13, 1963.

     THOMPSON has registered to him a 1957 two-door sedan, which had 1966 Colorado License ZG 3028. This license was issued to THOMPSON at the following address.

       Owl House
       Woody Creek, Colorado

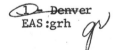 were contacted by SA ELMER A. SAMSON and SA JOSEPH C. LEARNED and these informants had no information concerning subject or his wife.

     Subject is apparently identical with the author of the current best seller "Hell's Angels," published by Random House.

1 - Denver
EAS:grh

SEARCHED _____ INDEXED _____
SERIALIZED _____ FILED _____
APR 1 9 1967
FBI — DENVER
V. JONES

Buy U.S. Savings Bonds Regularly on the Payroll Savings Plan

5010-108-01

NW 6524   DocId:59161781   Page 21

OPTIONAL FORM NO. 10
MAY 1962 EDITION
GSA GEN. REG. NO. 27

5010-107-02

UNITED STATES GOVERNMENT

Memorandum

TO   : SAC DENVER (62-0   DATE: 6-23-70

FROM   : SA VINCENT R. JONES

SUBJECT : ASPEN WALL POSTER;
           JOHN T. TRACY; LIONEL OLAY;
           TOM BENTON; HUNTER THOMPSON;
           GENE JOHNSON; JOHN G. CLANCY;
           BOB KRUEGER;
           MISCELANEOUS INFORMATION CONCERNING

    Attached is Aspen Wall Poster #4, which is a publication
being printed at Aspen, Colo.

    In view of the comments regarding law enforcement and the
Director, I thought would be a good idea to submit a copy and to
index the names of person connected with the publication.

    HUNTER THOMPSON was a member of the Calif. motorcycle gang and
wrote a book about it. He apparently plans to run on the independent
ticket for sheriff at Aspen.

    Under the black ink near the top on the front page, in red ink,
are words which appear to be "Impeach Nixon", only they use a
awastika in place of the "x". (It is necessary to hold the paper up to
a strong light to read this.)

    VRJ

100-9353-8

SEARCHED_____ INDEXED_____
SERIALIZED_____ FILED_____
JUN 24 1970
FBI — DENVER

Buy U.S. Savings Bonds Regularly on the Payroll Savings Plan

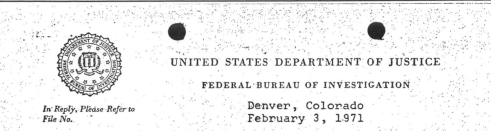

UNITED STATES DEPARTMENT OF JUSTICE

FEDERAL BUREAU OF INVESTIGATION

Denver, Colorado
February 3, 1971

In Reply, Please Refer to
File No.

C̶O̶N̶F̶I̶D̶E̶N̶T̶I̶A̶L̶

HUNTER STOCKTON THOMPSON

On November 5, 1965, a source, who has furnished reliable information in the past, advised that Hunter Thompson of 318 Parnassus Avenue, San Francisco, California, was a subscriber to the "People's World." Subsequently, Hunter Thompson changed his address from 138 Parnassus Avenue, San Francisco, to Woody Creek, Colorado.

According to the 1966 San Francisco Polk's City Directory, the wife of Thompson was listed as Sandra D. Thompson.

On April 6, 1967, a second source, who has furnished reliable information in the past, advised the subscription of Hunter Thompson to the "People's World" was cancelled.

"People's World" is a west coast communist newspaper published weekly in San Francisco.

On April 6, 1967, records of the Colorado Department of Motor Vehicles, Denver, Colorado, disclosed the Colorado driver's license of Hunter Stockton Thompson indicates he was a white male, born July 18, 1937, 6'3" in height, 190 pounds, with brown hair and brown eyes.

On March 16, 1967, a third source, who has furnished reliable information in the past, reported that Hunter S. Thompson and his wife, Sandra, and son were renting a house on a ranch located about five miles east of Woody Creek in Pitkin County, Colorado. Thompson claimed to have lived with the "Hell's Angels" for about one and a half years and to have written a book about them.

C̶O̶N̶F̶I̶D̶E̶N̶T̶I̶A̶L̶

VRJ:mf
(7)
100-9353

GROUP 1
Excluded from automatic
downgrading and
declassification

Searched 100-9353 15
Serialized
Indexed
Filed

NW 6524 DocId:39161782 Page 46

C O N F I D E N T I A L

HUNTER STOCKTON THOMPSON

According to the third source, Thompson may be
identical with the author of the current best seller (1967)
"Hell's Angels," published by Random House.

"The Aspen Wallposter," No. 4, published June, 1970,
listed as a bimonthly publication of the Meat Possum Press,
Inc., Box K-3, Aspen, Colorado, listed Chairman Emeritus,
John T. Tracy; Executive Editor, Lionel Olay; Editors, Tom
Benton, Hunter Thompson; General Manager, Gene Johnston;
Senior Corporation Counsel, John G. Clancy; and Photography,
Bob Krueger.

"The Aspen Wallposter," No. 4, contained derogatory
information concerning law enforcement in general and,
specifically, concerning the sheriff at Aspen, Colorado.

Under the black ink near the top on the front page
in red ink appeared the words "Impeach Nixon," only it appeared that a swastika had been used in place of the "x" in
the word "Nixon."

The outside cover of "The Aspen Wallposter," No. 4,
appeared to depict a telescopic sight centered on a human
brain.

The "Rocky Mountain News," a daily newspaper
published at Denver, Colorado, edition of October 18, 1970,
contained an article with the caption "Aspen sheriff's job
eyed by 'outlaw journalist.'" Part of the story reads as
follows:

"ASPEN--Hunter S. Thompson says he's a 'foul-
mouthed outlaw journalist,' but he's also deadly
serious about becoming sheriff of Pitkin County
and this booming ski town.

"And that's 'despite the natural horror of
seeing myself as the main pig.'

"Under the apolitical slogan of 'Freak Power,'
Thompson says his success depends on 'how many
freaks, heads, criminals, anarchists, beatniks,

C O N F I D E N T I A L

- 2 -

NW 6524 DocId:59161781 Page 47

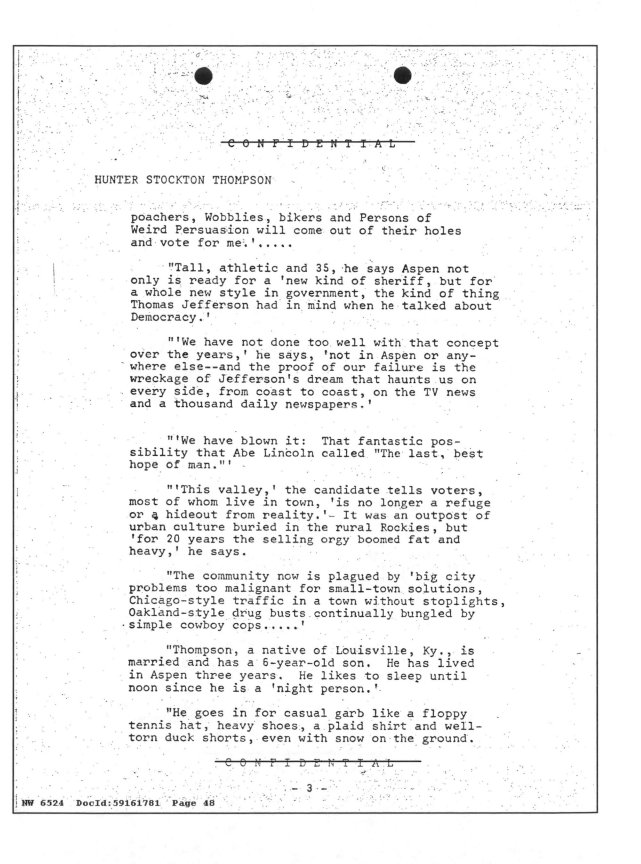

HUNTER STOCKTON THOMPSON

poachers, Wobblies, bikers and Persons of
Weird Persuasion will come out of their holes
and vote for me.'.....

"Tall, athletic and 35, he says Aspen not
only is ready for a 'new kind of sheriff, but for
a whole new style in government, the kind of thing
Thomas Jefferson had in mind when he talked about
Democracy.'

"'We have not done too well with that concept
over the years,' he says, 'not in Aspen or anywhere else--and the proof of our failure is the
wreckage of Jefferson's dream that haunts us on
every side, from coast to coast, on the TV news
and a thousand daily newspapers.'

"'We have blown it: That fantastic possibility that Abe Lincoln called "The last, best
hope of man."'

"'This valley,' the candidate tells voters,
most of whom live in town, 'is no longer a refuge
or a hideout from reality.'- It was an outpost of
urban culture buried in the rural Rockies, but
'for 20 years the selling orgy boomed fat and
heavy,' he says.

"The community now is plagued by 'big city
problems too malignant for small-town solutions,
Chicago-style traffic in a town without stoplights,
Oakland-style drug busts continually bungled by
simple cowboy cops.....'

"Thompson, a native of Louisville, Ky., is
married and has a 6-year-old son. He has lived
in Aspen three years. He likes to sleep until
noon since he is a 'night person.'

"He goes in for casual garb like a floppy
tennis hat, heavy shoes, a plaid shirt and well-
torn duck shorts, even with snow on the ground.

- 3 -

C O N F I D E N T I A L

HUNTER STOCKTON THOMPSON

"Thompson said he writes for various underground publications and published a book called
'Hell's Angels,' dealing with his experiences
with a motorcycle gang. He says some of them
beat him up.

"Thompson at various times attended the
University of Kentucky, Florida State University
and Columbia."

An article from the "Rocky Mountain News," Denver,
under date of October 25, 1970, contains a photograph of
Hunter S. Thompson and his manager, Paul Katzoff, looking at
a campaign poster which showed a badge with a red, double-
thumbed fist clutching a green peyote button. The article
contained in part the following:

"Thompson, who is expecting to be swept into
office on a tide of 'freak power,' has a well-
publicized program.

"He wants to:

"Sod the streets at once, ripping up the
pavement with jackhammers and using the 'junkasphalt'
to build a parking lot out of town and out of sight;

"Change the name 'Aspen' by referendum to
'Fat City,' in order to prevent 'greedheads, land-
rapers and other human jackals' from exploiting
Aspen's overdeveloped image;

"Erect stocks on the courthouse lawn in order
to punish 'dishonest dope dealers in a proper public
fashion.' To Thompson, a dishonest dealer is anyone
who makes a profit on a drug transaction. 'Non-
profit sales will be viewed as borderline cases, and
judged on their merits.'

"Forbid hunting and fishing to nonresidents,
except for those who can get a resident's personal
endorsement.

C O N F I D E N T I A L

- 4 -

HUNTER STOCKTON THOMPSON

"Disarm the sheriff and his deputies. He
explains that every recent urban riot has been
set off by some trigger-happy cop in a fear
frenzy. To pacify the violence-prone Thompson
would rely on a pistol-grip Mace-bomb....."

"The Washington Post" newspaper, Washington, D. C.,
edition of October 18, 1970, contained an article captioned
"Hippies May Elect Sheriff." Contained therein were the
following passages:

"ASPEN, Colo.--He was a littly shaky, Hunter
Thompson admitted. He had just tripped all night   -
on mescaline and now he stood on Mill Street,
ever-present beer can in his hand, sun hat covering
his bald head (which he had shaved to cover the
American Legion convention in Portland, Ore., for
Scanlan's magazine), contemplating with a sense of
disbelief the coming ordeal....."

"The Aspen Wallposter," No. 7, dated January, 1971,
shows Editors as Tom Benton and Hunter Thompson. It contains
a photograph of Hunter S. Thompson and comments concerning
his having lost the election for sheriff of Pitkin County,
Colorado. It contains considerable profanity and shows a
photograph of President Nixon which depicts blood running out
of his mouth and onto his collar.

Following are quotations from "The Aspen Wallposter,"
No. 7:

"THE RAPE OF NUMBER SIX

"As usual, we owe an apology to our many loyal
subscribers! Wallposter No. 5 - the Peyote-fist
campaign issue - should actually have been number
Six. But the original No. 5 (see cover, above)
proved to be absolutely unprintable - not only in
Aspen, but everywhere else in this country. After
two months of haggling with printers in Boulder,
San Francisco, Secaucus and the Antelope Valley, we

- 5 -

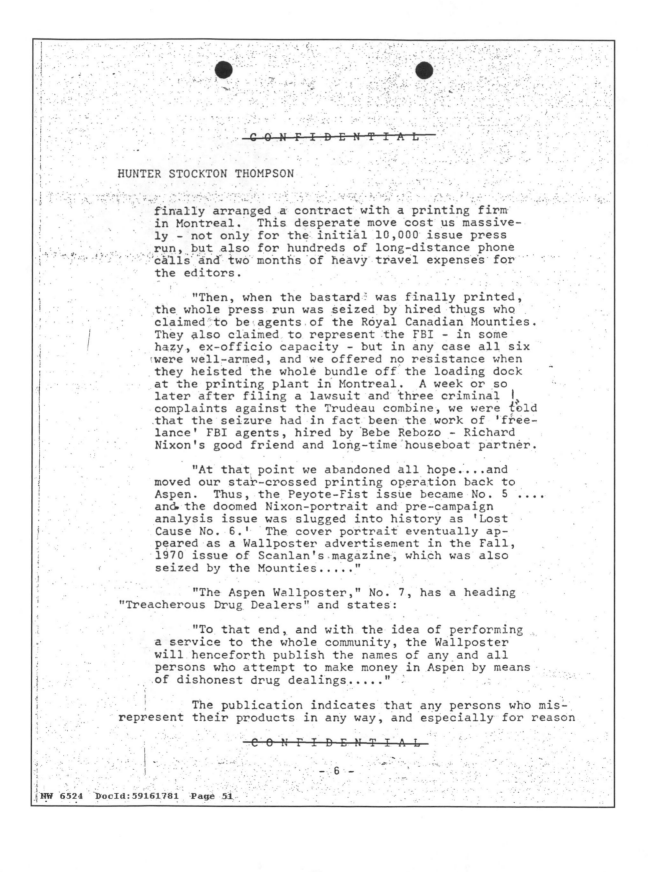

C O N F I D E N T I A L

HUNTER STOCKTON THOMPSON

finally arranged a contract with a printing firm
in Montreal. This desperate move cost us massive-
ly - not only for the initial 10,000 issue press
run, but also for hundreds of long-distance phone
calls and two months of heavy travel expenses for
the editors.

"Then, when the bastard was finally printed,
the whole press run was seized by hired thugs who
claimed to be agents of the Royal Canadian Mounties.
They also claimed to represent the FBI - in some
hazy, ex-officio capacity - but in any case all six
were well-armed, and we offered no resistance when
they heisted the whole bundle off the loading dock
at the printing plant in Montreal. A week or so
later after filing a lawsuit and three criminal
complaints against the Trudeau combine, we were told
that the seizure had in fact been the work of 'free-
lance' FBI agents, hired by Bebe Rebozo - Richard
Nixon's good friend and long-time houseboat partner.

"At that point we abandoned all hope.....and
moved our star-crossed printing operation back to
Aspen. Thus, the Peyote-Fist issue became No. 5 ....
and the doomed Nixon-portrait and pre-campaign
analysis issue was slugged into history as 'Lost
Cause No. 6.' The cover portrait eventually appeared as a Wallposter advertisement in the Fall,
1970 issue of Scanlan's magazine, which was also
seized by the Mounties....."

"The Aspen Wallposter," No. 7, has a heading
"Treacherous Drug Dealers" and states:

"To that end, and with the idea of performing
a service to the whole community, the Wallposter
will henceforth publish the names of any and all
persons who attempt to make money in Aspen by means
of dishonest drug dealings....."

The publication indicates that any persons who mis-
represent their products in any way, and especially for reason

C O N F I D E N T I A L

- 6 -

HUNTER STOCKTON THOMPSON

of profit, will be subject to public exposure. It indicates
the editors of the Wallposter will carefully investigate all
complaints against any person accused of selling drugs dis-
honestly and if they find the complaints to be justified, the
offender's name will be published.

The following is a quotation from "The Aspen
Wallposter," No. 7:

"The point, after all, is not to hassle
careless drug-sellers, but to expose the handful
of rotten bastards who sell things like Grass full
of oregano & alfalfa, 'organic mescaline' cut with
nutmeg, 'Acid' laced with speed, arsenic and
strychnine, or 'Hash' made of Kansas marijuana/mush
mixed with powdered Bennies and molasses. Any
question of 'illegality' in these sales is completely beside our point. That is a problem for the local
law enforcement officials to grapple with - in their
own special style & with their own atavistic finesse.
Our concern is entirely beyond the clumsy, archaic
laws that pretend to relate to the local drug
culture; We will focus only on complaints involving
proven Consumer Fraud....."

On January 26, 1971, Agent Stanley Belitz, U. S.
Secret Service office, Denver, Colorado, was advised of "The
Aspen Wallposter", No. 7, and its photograph of the President.

On January 25, 1971, Sheriff Carrol Whitmire,
Aspen, Colorado, advised that Hunter Stockton Thompson has
been in the Aspen area for approximately six years. He apparently is employed as a free-lance writer and is an editor
of "The Aspen Wallposter."

Sheriff Whitmire advised his office has no arrest
record concerning Thompson but he is believed to be a user
of narcotics and dangerous drugs.

Sheriff Whitmire advised that since the recent
election when he (Whitmire) successfully defeated Hunter

- 7 -

C O N F I D E N T I A L

HUNTER STOCKTON THOMPSON

Thompson as a candidate for sheriff of Pitkin County, an
investigation was conducted in an effort to discredit Whitmire.

Sheriff Whitmire advised that his former wife was
contacted by Court Freeman with the "Rocky Mountain News" in
Denver who told her he was investigating Sheriff Whitmire
because he was alleged to have two prior felony convictions,
according to Hunter Thompson.

Sheriff Whitmire stated he (Whitmire) did not have
any felony convictions.

This document contains neither recommendations nor
conclusions of the FBI. It is the property of the
FBI and is loaned to your agency; it and its contents
are not to be distributed outside your agency.

C O N F I D E N T I A L

- 8* -

OPTIONAL FORM NO. 10
MAY 1962 EDITION
GSA FPMR (41 CFR) 101-11.6

UNITED STATES GOVERNMENT

Memorandum

TO   :   SAC (100-9353)   DATE: 3/17/71

FROM   :   ASAC MORLEY

SUBJECT: HUNTER STOCKTON THOMPSON, aka
                 SM - MISCELLANEOUS

        Attached is an anonymous letter which was received
by GLEN RICKS, Aspen, Colorado, and was forwarded to this
office by SA JONES who received it from RICKS.

        Letter contains information concerning THOMPSON
which may be of value in the future. The envelope which
contained the letter was postmarked in Aspen but did not
contain a return address.

*Consolidated
21 August 1979
Rmf*

100-9353-18

SEARCHED
SE
MAR 17 197

1 - Denver
JFM:jt
(1)

Buy U.S. Savings Bonds Regularly on the Payroll Savings Plan

5010-108-01

NW 6524 DocId:59161781 Page 57

Louisville, Ky
Oct. 19, 1970

Dear Mr. Ricks:

    I think but do not know that Hunter
Thompson has a police record in Louisville.
He was _the_ bad boy of our neighborhood
when he was high school and college age.
It would probably have been around
1954-, 1955- 6 or 7.   At that time,
he lived on Ransdell Ave.

    I would sign my name but am
afraid I might be sued.   I am
interested in good government.

Gore Vidal

OF ALL THE WRITERS featured in this volume, Gore Vidal's mutually antagonistic relationship with the FBI — in particular, Director J. Edgar Hoover — is perhaps the most personal, even more so than that of James Baldwin. Unlike Baldwin, where the Bureau's interest was roughly equally divided between his literary output and his social criticism, the FBI seemed largely uninterested in Vidal's books. The file mentions one, *The City and the Pillar* (which is pithily summarized as "the physical adventures of a male homosexual"), and even then in the context of it having been reviewed in the Communist Party newspaper *The Daily Worker*. Instead, the file focuses almost entirely on cataloging Vidal's vocal criticism of the Director and his Bureau and the various ways the FBI considered revenge, from the petty to the deadly serious.

The file begins in 1961 with a memo to Deke DeLoach, the number three man in Bureau. A review of Vidal's new play, *The Best Man*, noted that there was a line containing an "unfair jibe" at Hoover, so the FBI's New York Field Office resolved to send an agent to see the play in person and evaluate its subversiveness. The agent attended a showing later that same day; after determining that the joke "fell very flat" and the large number audience walkouts during intermission meant the play wouldn't last very long, the New York Field Office recommended no action. It's unclear if Hoover was ever notified of the incident, but as he was at the height of his powers at the time, it's unlikely it escaped his attention.

Vidal had officially been made an enemy of the Bureau, and for the next decade they monitored his articles and television appearances closely. Hoover personally received several letters from concerned citizens drawing attention to Vidal's harsh remarks, which he responded to politely, clarifying that the FBI was strictly an investigative agency and didn't concern itself with such things. Not quite two years after one such letter, the New York Field Office was again taking it upon themselves to defend Hoover's honor. Late one night, an agent happened to be watching a talk show on WPIX-TV that featured Vidal as a guest; the FBI's poor handling of civil rights cases in the South was discussed in detail. In response, agents at the field office organized a campaign to call the station demanding the show's cancellation, taking care "not to identify themselves with the Bureau."

The rivalry took a more serious turn in 1968, when Hoover himself got involved. After Vidal had made comments urging students not to go to Vietnam if drafted, Hoover sent a memo to the New York field office asking them to open a preliminary investigation into whether such comments violated the Selective Service Act. While nothing in the file indicated that the investigation went anywhere beyond that initial inquiry, it's a worrying indication of Hoover's willingness to silence the critics.

OPTIONAL FORM NO. 10

UNITED STATES GOVERNMENT

Memorandum

TO   : Mr. DeLoach   DATE: April 1, 1960

FROM : M. A. Jones

SUBJECT: "THE BEST MAN"
LEGITIMATE PLAY
NEW YORK CITY, NEW YORK

Tolson
Mohr
Parsons
Belmont
Callahan
DeLoach
Malone
McGuire
Rosen
Tamm
Trotter
W.C. Sullivan
Tele. Room
Ingram
Gandy

b6
b7C

    ASAC Alton M. Bryant telephonically contacted the Bureau
Headquarters this afternoon and advised Wick that in a review by Louis Sobel
which appeared in the "New York Journal American" concerned comments
about the season's newest play, "The Best Man," by Gore Vidal. Sobel's
column states, "But there was one jarring note to this reporter--and that was
an unnecessary, quite unfunny and certainly unfair jibe at J. Edgar Hoover.
Some among the audience expressed their displeasure in loud 'boos!'" Bryant
advised no Agents were in attendance at this play. A Special Agent will attend
this performance tonight and the New York Office will advise the results of
this review tomorrow.

    Bufiles reflect Gore Vidal was mentioned in the January 20,
1948, issue of the "Daily Worker" in a review of his book,"The City and The
Pillar." This book dealt with the physical adventures of a male homosexual.
Vidal was also associated with two individuals who were the subject of security-
type investigations in 1954 and 1956.

RECOMMENDATION:

    None. For information.
Addendum:REW:4-2-60: Supervisor Tom Ring of the New York Office saw this play
4-1-60. The only reference to the Director is when one play character (presumably Vice President Nixon) says to another (presumably Harry Truman) "J. Edgar
Hoover considers you to be one of the most moral and religious men ever to be
in the White House." The man addressed replies with a sarcastic inflection: "I'll
reserve my opinion of J. Edgar Hoover for a posthumous
memoir." This is apparently where the audience booed,
3-31-60. Agent Ring says the crack came out fast and fell
very flat in the 4-1-60 performance. He says several people
filed out in the middle of the second act. Ring was told to
take no action.

1 - Mr. DeLoach

JMR:paw
(3)

REC- 26
EX- 105

62-107665-

18 APR 7 1960

51 APR 13 1960
MAR 1 1962

CRIME REC.

OPT..NAL FORM NO. 10

UNITED STATES GOVERNMENT

Memorandum

TO   : Mr. DeLoach   DATE: 7-28-61

FROM : M. A. Jones

b6
b7C

SUBJECT: ARTICLE ENTITLED "COMMENT"
BY GORE VIDAL IN
AUGUST, 1961, ISSUE OF
ESQUIRE MAGAZINE

The August, 1961, issue of captioned magazine carried an article on page 120 entitled "Comment" by Gore Vidal which generally points out that President Kennedy and various other people have been telling citizens of the United States what to do to improve our society. Vidal seeks to add his advice in this matter and states that he feels there are many problems to solve in our own society, ranging from the abolition of capital punishment to school integration. He then makes the statement that the citizen can be useful in social and moral legislation where much work is needed, and he must be vigilant regarding civil liberties or he might one day find himself living, if not in a police state, at least in a police city.

Vidal then related an incident which he had reportedly witnessed in Washington, D. C., in the Spring of 1961, wherein he alleged he saw four policemen beat up two unresisting persons on a public street for absolutely no cause. He stated he had called a local newspaper to report the incident; however, nothing has happened since.

Vidal then related that when he got back to New York, he read an editorial of a southern editor attacking the John Birch Society. The editor allegedly quoted the FBI as saying that the "Birchers were 'irresponsible.'" Vidal then related (the editor) that some hours before the editorial was published, two FBI Agents visited him and inquired as to his authority on the "irresponsible" quotation. It turned out that the editor's sources were unreliable; however, when the editor inquired how the FBI knew of his editorial in advance, he got no answer.

INFORMATION IN BUREAU FILES

The "editorial" referred to by Vidal is possibly an article which appeared in the 3-19-61 issue of "The Nashville Tennessean," which stated in part, "An FBI spokesman in Washington said last week the FBI...would characterize the society (John Birch Society) as 'irresponsible but not subversive.'" Numerous inquiries were received by the Bureau regarding this article, which were answered by informing them of the fact that no FBI official in Washington had publicly characterized

RLR:dgs
(4)

ENCLOSURE

REC- 42
62-107665-XI
AUG 2 1961

CRIME RESEARCH

518 Perugia Avenue
Coral Gables, Fla.

The F.B.I.
Washington, D.C.

Dear Sirs;

Enclosed is an article in an old (Aug.)"ESQUIRE" magazine that I and several friends of mine have only just read. I think that ESQUIRE enjoys a good reputation and therefore we were astounded at what Gore Vidal (I think Mrs. J. Kennedy's step-brother) has to say about the F.B.I. You will find this toward the end of the article; the first example about the detectives of the Washington police force I suppose is no business of yours....but the F.B.I. protecting the John Birch Society? Is this true? Why would almost a member of the first family desire to attack the F.B.I. if it is not true? I await your reply anxiously as do the others I have shown the article to, in the hopes that it may not be true. Also I certainly would appreciate it if you would return the clipping. Thank you.

Sincerely,

Mrs. Mario Nuñez de la Vega
Mrs. Mario Nuñez de la Vega

REC- 29

62_107665

b6
b7C

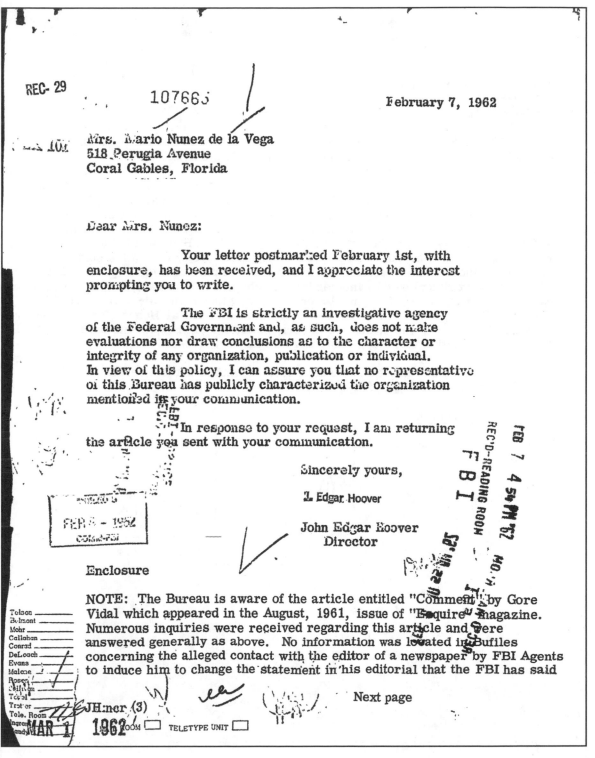

REC- 29   107665   February 7, 1962

Mrs. Mario Nunez de la Vega
518 Perugia Avenue
Coral Gables, Florida

Dear Mrs. Nunez:

        Your letter postmarked February 1st, with
enclosure, has been received, and I appreciate the interest
prompting you to write.

        The FBI is strictly an investigative agency
of the Federal Government and, as such, does not make
evaluations nor draw conclusions as to the character or
integrity of any organization, publication or individual.
In view of this policy, I can assure you that no representative
of this Bureau has publicly characterized the organization
mentioned in your communication.

        In response to your request, I am returning
the article you sent with your communication.

                            Sincerely yours,

                            J. Edgar Hoover

                            John Edgar Hoover
                            Director

Enclosure

NOTE: The Bureau is aware of the article entitled "Comment" by Gore
Vidal which appeared in the August, 1961, issue of "Esquire" magazine.
Numerous inquiries were received regarding this article and were
answered generally as above. No information was located in Bufiles
concerning the alleged contact with the editor of a newspaper by FBI Agents
to induce him to change the statement in his editorial that the FBI has said

Tolson
Belmont
Mohr
Callahan
Conrad
DeLoach
Evans
Malone
Rosen
Sullivan
Tavel
Trotter
Tele. Room
Ingram
Gandy

GJH:mcr (3)

                                                 Next page

MAR 1 1962 ROOM ☐   TELETYPE UNIT ☐

Jones to DeLoach Memo
RE: Article "Comment"
By Gore Vidal

the John Birch Society. No information could be located in Bufiles regarding the alleged contact with the editor as related by Vidal in his article.

Bufiles reflect that Vidal was mentioned in the 1-20-48 issue of the "Daily Worker" in a review of his book, "The City and The Pillar." The book dealt with the physical adventures of a male homosexual. Vidal was an associate of two individuals who were the subjects of security-type investigations conducted in 1954 and 1956. He was also the author of a play entitled "The Best Man" which opened in New York City on 3-31-60. The play was a political-type drama which contained one small reference to the Director to the effect that one play character (presumably Vice President Nixon) said to another (presumably Harry Truman), "J. Edgar Hoover considers you to be one of the most moral and religious men ever to be in the White House." The reply was, "I'll reserve my opinion of J. Edgar Hoover for a posthumous memoir." An Agent who monitored the play stated the exchange came out fast and fell very flat. No action was taken regarding this matter. (62-0-59489)

Files reflect that we have enjoyed limited cordial relations with Esquire, Inc., since 1947. (94-3-4-350)

RECOMMENDATION:

For information.

b6
b7C

- 2 -

NOTE: continued

the "Birchers were irresponsible." Vidal was mentioned in the 1-20-48
issue of the "Daily Worker" in a review of his book, "The City and the
Pillar" dealing with the physical adventures of a male homosexual. Vidal
was also associated with two individuals who were subjects of security-
type investigations by the Bureau in 1954 and 1956. In April, 1960,
his play, "The Best Man," opened on Broadway and contained an
unnecessary and unfair remark about the Director which the audience
booed. The Bureau has not investigated Vidal. Correspondent cannot
be identified in Bufiles.

- 2 -

OPTIONAL FORM NO. 10
5010—104

UNITED STATES GOVERNMENT

Memorandum

TO   :   DIRECTOR, FBI   DATE: 10-23-62

FROM   :   SAC, BOSTON   ATTEN: CRIME RECORDS

SUBJECT: DEBATE BETWEEN GORE VIDAL AND
             WILLIAM F. BUCKLEY, JR.
             MODERATOR DAVID SUSSKIND

Mr. Tolson
Mr. Belmont
Mr. Mohr
Mr. Gaspar
Mr. Callahan
Mr. Conrad
Miss DeLoach
Mr. Evans
Mr. Gale
Mr. Rosen
Mr. Sullivan
Mr. Tavel
Mr. Trotter
Tele. Room
Miss Holmes
Miss Gandy

b6
b7C

          On 10/21/62 a debate between ~~one captioned in~~
dividuals was telecast over WGBH (Channel 2), the educational
channel in the Boston area. This program was viewed by
SA JOHN L. FAHERTY and he indicates that the comments between
BUCKLEY and VIDAL were quite caustic and vitriolic. SA
Faherty states that during one discussion concerning Civil
Rights, VIDAL mentioned that the Director had indicated
that there were about 22,000 known Communists in the United
States. VIDAL added that if the Director did not have a
complete dosier on these 22,000, "he is not doing his job.
VIDAL then said that there must be at least 22,000 FBI age

          On another occasion while discussing Civil Rights
BUCKLEY made the remark, "I wouldn't awaken an individual
at 3 o'clock in the morning for an interview either."
SA FAHERTY stated that the above were the only references
made to the FBI.

          The foregoing is furnished to the Bureau for
its information.

EJF:maw
(3)

REC- 35

62-107665-3
30

13 OCT 25 1962

54 NOV 9 1962

cc 100-3-95

EXP. PROC.

UNRECORDED COPY FILE IN

34   OCT 25 1962

34

b6
b7C

OPTIONAL FORM NO. 10
MAY 1962 EDITION
GSA GEN. REG. NO. 27   5010—106

UNITED STATES GOVERNMENT

Memorandum

TO   :   Mr. Mohr   DATE: June 24, 1964

FROM   :   C. D. DeLoach

SUBJECT: CRITICAL PROGRAM - CIVIL RIGHTS
            STATION WPIX-TV
            NEW YORK CITY

Reaction
Belmont
Mohr
Casper
Callahan
Conrad
DeLoach
Evans
Gale
Rosen
Sullivan
Tavel
Trotter
Tele. Room _____ b6
Holmes _____ b7C
Gandy

        Assistant Director Malone called at 10:20 a.m. today and advised that one of
the Agents in the office had just handed him a memorandum concerning a program which
appeared last night over the above-entitled station.

        Mr. Malone explained that WPIX is an independent station in New York City
and is not a member of one of the networks. He said that at 11:15 p.m. last night the
Agent was looking at the station and a program appeared called "Hot Line."

        This was a panel type show where the panelists take telephone calls from the
public and answer their questions. On the program were David Susskind; Gore Vidal (who
Malone described as being on the pink side); Reverend William Coffin, chaplain at Yale
University; and Dorothy Kilgallen.

        The first half of the program was extremely critical of the Director and the
FBI in the handling of civil rights cases and bombing cases in the South. One statement
was made that the Director should retire as he did not desire to carry out the law of the
land as far as civil rights cases are concerned. Susskind said the FBI had utterly failed
in the bombing cases in the South. There were, of course, other items taken up on the
program; however, at the conclusion Susskind said that this was the first of its kind and
was sort of a test pilot. He urged that listeners write in if they would like to have a program
of this type continued in the fall season of 1964.

NOT RECORDED

        Malone said that due to the late hour very few people saw the program and
the only comment he has had so far is from this one Agent who had accidentally tuned in
on it. He said that nevertheless some of the New York employees were going to write to
the station and say that the program stunk, was factually incorrect, and do not think the
program should be continued next fall. He said, of course, they would not identify themselves with the Bureau.

RECOMMENDATION: For information.

1 - Mr. Rosen
1 - Mr. Evans
1 - Mr. Jones
ECK:amr (5)

18 JUL 1964

CC TO: State (Cutbes)
REQ. REC'D. 3/24/66
APR   966
ANS.
BY: abs (nej)

January 6, 1965

GORE VIDAL
Born: October 3, 1925
Westport, New York

The FBI has conducted no independent investigation
concerning the subject of your name check inquiry. However,
files of this Bureau do disclose that Gore Vidal was
mentioned in the January 20, 1948, issue of the "Daily Worker"
in a review of his book, "The City And The Pillar." The
book dealt with the physical adventures of a male homosexual.
Vidal was an associate of two individuals who were the
subjects of security-type investigations conducted by the
FBI in 1954 and 1956.
(62-107665)
       "The National Guardian" dated November 13, 1961,
carried an article stating that Gore Vidal was to be among
the speakers for a Wednesday evening December 6, 1961,
meeting at Manhattan Center, New York City which was to be
a rally to abolish the House Un-American Activities Committee.
(61-7582-A)
       The July 17, 1961, issue of the "New York Herald
Tribune" carried a column by Gore Vidal who was substituting
for John Crosby who was on vacation. The column dealt with
the House Un-American Activities Committee and was critical
of this committee's activities.
62-10885-X1)
       A confidential informant who has furnished reliable
information in the past furnished on May 21 and May 22, 1961,

b7D

                     Located among this material was the
name Gore Vidal, Edgewater, Barrytown, New York.
(97-4196-34-38)
       The files of the FBI contain no further information
pertinent to the subject of your name check inquiry.
Original & 1-USIA
Request Received-12/8/64
TDW:ded
   (4)

REC 20   62-107665-   4

58 JAN 13 1965   21 JAN 8 1965

OPTIONAL FORM NO. 10
MAY 1962 EDITION
GSA GEN. REG. NO. 27

5010-106

UNITED STATES GOVERNMENT

Memorandum

1 - DeLoach
1 - Wick
1 - M.A.Jones

TO   :   MR. DeLOACH

DATE: May 4, 1967

FROM   :   STERLING B. DONAHOE

SUBJECT: GORE VIDAL
            WHITE HOUSE NAME CHECK REQUEST

Tolson
DeLoach
Mohr
Wick
Casper
Callahan
Conrad
Felt
Gale
Rosen
Sullivan
Tavel
Trotter
Tele. Room
Holmes
Gandy

b6
b7C

Mrs. Mildred Stegall called from the White House this morning. She advised that we had given them the results of a name check on Vidal in 1964 and she requested that this name check be brought up to date with as much information as possible about Vidal.

Apparently Vidal appeared on the "Today" show this morning and made some vicious remarks. No active investigation is desired but as previously indicated, as much detailed data as is available regarding him should be furnished. If necessary the office covering his place of residence should be contacted to determine whether that office has any additional data and we should be particularly alert to any public statements he has made.

ACTION:

For handling by Crime Records Division.

SBD:hmm
(4)

Handled by outgoing letter to mrs Stegall 5/8/67 JCF:KSF

REC-107   62-107655-5

5 MAY 12 1967

CRIME RECORDS

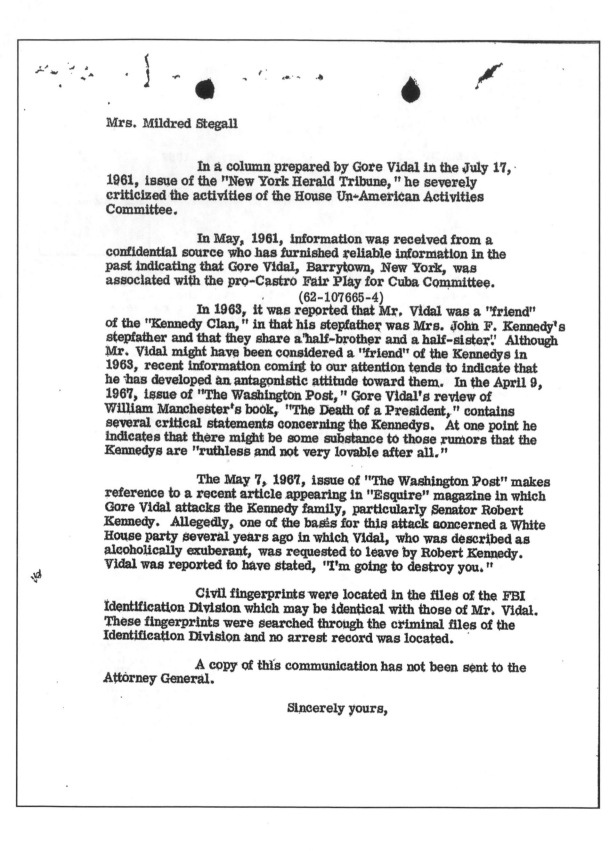

Mrs. Mildred Stegall

In a column prepared by Gore Vidal in the July 17, 1961, issue of the "New York Herald Tribune," he severely criticized the activities of the House Un-American Activities Committee.

In May, 1961, information was received from a confidential source who has furnished reliable information in the past indicating that Gore Vidal, Barrytown, New York, was associated with the pro-Castro Fair Play for Cuba Committee.
(62-107665-4)
In 1963, it was reported that Mr. Vidal was a "friend" of the "Kennedy Clan," in that his stepfather was Mrs. John F. Kennedy's stepfather and that they share a "half-brother and a half-sister." Although Mr. Vidal might have been considered a "friend" of the Kennedys in 1963, recent information coming to our attention tends to indicate that he has developed an antagonistic attitude toward them. In the April 9, 1967, issue of "The Washington Post," Gore Vidal's review of William Manchester's book, "The Death of a President," contains several critical statements concerning the Kennedys. At one point he indicates that there might be some substance to those rumors that the Kennedys are "ruthless and not very lovable after all."

The May 7, 1967, issue of "The Washington Post" makes reference to a recent article appearing in "Esquire" magazine in which Gore Vidal attacks the Kennedy family, particularly Senator Robert Kennedy. Allegedly, one of the bases for this attack concerned a White House party several years ago in which Vidal, who was described as alcoholically exuberant, was requested to leave by Robert Kennedy. Vidal was reported to have stated, "I'm going to destroy you."

Civil fingerprints were located in the files of the FBI Identification Division which may be identical with those of Mr. Vidal. These fingerprints were searched through the criminal files of the Identification Division and no arrest record was located.

A copy of this communication has not been sent to the Attorney General.

Sincerely yours,

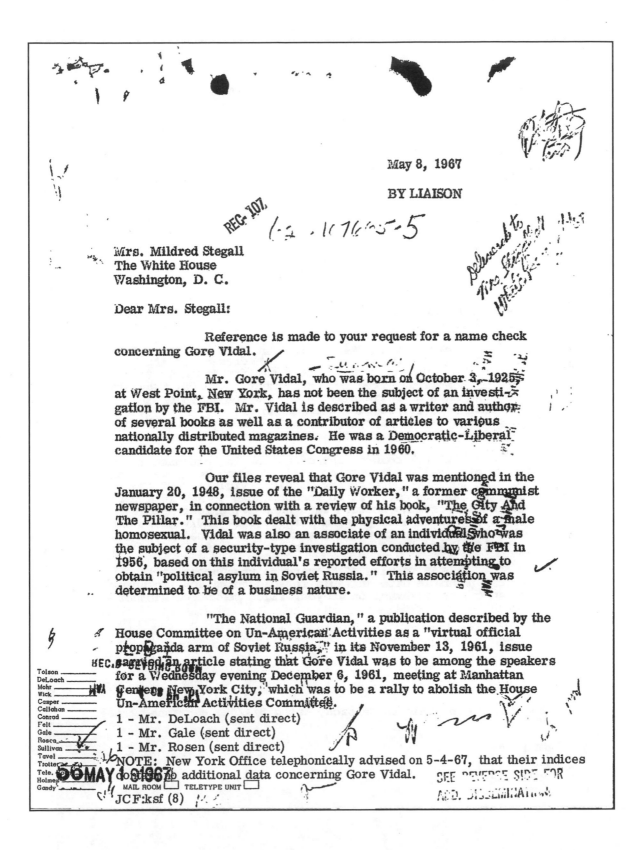

May 8, 1967

BY LIAISON

REG. 107

Mrs. Mildred Stegall
The White House
Washington, D. C.

Dear Mrs. Stegall:

Reference is made to your request for a name check concerning Gore Vidal.

Mr. Gore Vidal, who was born on October 3, 1925, at West Point, New York, has not been the subject of an investigation by the FBI. Mr. Vidal is described as a writer and author of several books as well as a contributor of articles to various nationally distributed magazines. He was a Democratic-Liberal candidate for the United States Congress in 1960.

Our files reveal that Gore Vidal was mentioned in the January 20, 1948, issue of the "Daily Worker," a former communist newspaper, in connection with a review of his book, "The City And The Pillar." This book dealt with the physical adventures of a male homosexual. Vidal was also an associate of an individual who was the subject of a security-type investigation conducted by the FBI in 1956, based on this individual's reported efforts in attempting to obtain "political asylum in Soviet Russia." This association was determined to be of a business nature.

"The National Guardian," a publication described by the House Committee on Un-American Activities as a "virtual official propaganda arm of Soviet Russia," in its November 13, 1961, issue carried an article stating that Gore Vidal was to be among the speakers for a Wednesday evening December 6, 1961, meeting at Manhattan Center, New York City, which was to be a rally to abolish the House Un-American Activities Committee.

Tolson _____
DeLoach _____
Mohr _____
Wick _____
Casper _____
Callahan _____
Conrad _____
Felt _____
Gale _____
Rosen _____
Sullivan _____
Tavel _____
Trotter _____
Tele. _____
Holmes _____
Gandy _____

1 - Mr. DeLoach (sent direct)
1 - Mr. Gale (sent direct)
1 - Mr. Rosen (sent direct)

NOTE: New York Office telephonically advised on 5-4-67, that their indices contain no additional data concerning Gore Vidal.   SEE REVERSE SIDE FOR ADD. DISSEMINATION

MAIL ROOM ☐   TELETYPE UNIT ☐

JCF:ksf (8)

5/2/68

Airtel   62-107665

To: SAC, New York	1 - Mr. DeLoach
	1 - Mr. Bishop
	1 - Mr. Gale
	1 - Mr. Eddy
From: Director, FBI (25-NEW)	1 - Mr. Moore

GORE VIDAL
SSA - COUNSELING

b6
b7C

There is enclosed for the New York Office, a true
copy of a letter from ⬛⬛⬛⬛⬛ addressed to the
Department of Justice. This letter was furnished to the
Bureau by memorandum from the Department, 4/26/68, requesting
the Bureau make a preliminary investigation to determine what
Vidal said on a TV program referred to in ⬛⬛⬛ letter.
This program was on WNEW-TV, Channel 5, New York, Saturday,
4/13/68, at 10:30 p.m., entitled "Is Liberalism Dead."

New York conduct investigation to determine the
content of Vidal's comments so that they may be reviewed to
determine whether there is any possible violation of the
Selective Service Act. If no reason known to New York Office
which would preclude contact with WNEW-TV, effort should be
made to obtain film of program for review. Individuals contacted should be advised the investigation is being conducted
at specific request of the Department of Justice.

Submit results of inquiry to the Bureau at the
earliest possible date suitable for dissemination including
any background information in your files regarding subject.

Enc.

1 - 62-107665

See cover memo Gale to DeLoach, dated 5/1/68, captioned same,
MHH:tdm.

MHH:tdm
66 MAY 14 1968

Oct. 15, 1970

Mr. J. Edgar Hoover
Director
Federal Bureau of Investigation
Washington D.C.

Dear Sir:

I was dismayed over a statement permitted to be broadcast
today over NBC national television network during the David
Frost Show--a statement by Gore Vidal, a sensationalist writer.

Among Mr. Vidal's seemingly unsolicited remarks, were scornful
statements about the vice president of the United States,
spilling from his mouth before he even seated himself, and
in which he rather obviously tried to solicite a rubber-stamp
of his position from Mr. Frost. Mr. Frost, while not dis-
associating himself with the remarks, fell short of endorsing
them.

Yet, Mr. Vidal pursued his opening vituperation with a
remarkable statement that in order for us to battle the
"sytem" (political), we could "blow up the capitol AND Mr.
Agnew!"

Would you please explain to me, why, in the name of freedom
of speech, we allow such dangerous statements to be broadcast
over the entire nation?

Advocacy of violence is intolerable, even masquerading as
smart-aleck entertainment. It does not go unmarked during
these troubled times for our country. We in California have
seen some of our government officials indeed "blown up".
We certainly don't take kindly to NBC's sponsorship of men
of Vidal's ilk.

I am wondering, too, at the rather curious position of Mr.
Frost. Is he a citizen of this country in which he finds so
much to question? I wonder what Mr. Frost's reaction would
be to an American entertainer on BBC, sponsoring, without
verbal disassociation, statements that the Prime Minister of
England or the Queen should be "blown up"? Or Parliament?
Would he bridle or giggle?

Sincerely,

EX 106

REC-73 63-107665-6

October 23, 1970

b6
b7C

Dear

       Your letter of October 15th has been received and I
can understand the concern which prompted you to write and furnish
me your views. The FBI is strictly an investigative agency of the
Federal Government and, as such, has no control over who appears
on television or other mass media.

                   Sincerely yours,

                   J. Edgar Hoover

b6
b7C

NOTE: Correspondent is not identifiable in Bufiles.

REK:jfh (3)

MAILED 21
OCT 23 1970
COMM-FBI

OCT 30 1970

Tolson
Sullivan
Mohr
Bishop
Brennan, C.D.
Callahan
Casper
Conrad
Felt
Gale
Rosen
Tavel
Walters
Soyars
Telo. Room
Holmes
Gandy

MAIL ROOM ☐   TELETYPE UNIT ☐

UNRECORDED COPY FILED IN

Afterword

J. EDGAR HOOVER DIED in office in 1972. In life, he would never face the reckoning he and his agency had long deserved for his nearly 50 year reign of surveillance-filled terror that ensnared well-known and unknown American dissidents alike. After his death, though, Congress's Church Committee — along with strengthening of the Freedom of Information Act, some dogged work by reporters, and brave acts of whistleblowing — would rip off the mask of Hoover's FBI, the secret files, and the surveillance apparatus system he created.

In the decades that followed, the Bureau — sometimes tacitly and sometimes explicitly — would be forced to condemn Hoover's spying apparatus, and FBI advocates now spend their days defending the agency by claiming "it is not J. Edgar Hoover's FBI." Former FBI director James Comey even professed to keeping the original letter authorizing surveillance of Martin Luther King Jr on his desk to remind him about the dangers of government overreach.

Yet, the FBI headquarters is still named after Hoover, and it's more than his ghost that still haunts its halls.

The FBI's approach to surveillance is no doubt different; it's now couched in legal advice and internal procedures meant to bestow a veneer of due process. Gone are the days of FBI agents shadowing the likes of Ernest Hemingway or James Baldwin (at least mostly). But in some ways, the modern incarnation of the FBI's spying machine is even more dangerous than the collection of files of embarrassing information on famous government critics that was the hallmark of Hoover.

The proliferation of technology has allowed the FBI to conduct electronic surveillance on a massive scale. The FBI now has tools at its disposal that Hoover could scarcely dream of in the 1950s and 60s.

To be sure, the FBI still follows people with informants. In fact, the Intercept reported in 2018 that "The FBI now has 15,000 informants, mostly tasked with surveilling the Muslim community — up from 1,500 when Congress began its hearings on COINTELPRO in 1974."

The FBI's current informant machine has lasered in on America's Muslim community, relentlessly attempting to use leverage and the threat of prosecution or deportation to persuade ever more people to inform on their community. These informants are often directed to stir up potential terrorist plots conceived entirely by the agency itself for the sole purpose of arresting and jailing poor and uneducated members of society. They are often tricked and cajoled into agreeing to do something extremely stupid in exchange for money, activity they'd have no means or ability to accomplish on their own.

Black Lives Matter organizers, environmental activists, and even journalists — as part of the FBI's ever-growing number of anti-leak investigations — also still count among the agency's targets.

But it is its technological force that is truly unprecedented. Aided by large tech and telecommunications companies and lax legal restrictions, the FBI sits at the helm of what many have called "the golden age of surveillance."

Cell phones — the stuff of science fiction in the 1950s — are now in the pocket of virtually every single American. They can track the location, sometimes within a few feet, of everywhere a person goes twenty four hours a day, seven days a week. The FBI once needed an entire team of people to follow a suspect around the clock. One agent now follows countless individuals with a few clicks of a button.

The FBI still needs a warrant to collect the content of purely domestic conversations between two Americans, but the agency argues it has the legal ability to collect virtually all other information with little court oversight — and in the case of "National Security Letters," sometimes no court oversight at all. Data points on who you talk to, when, where, and for how long, are considered "metadata" by the FBI and many courts, allowing the Bureau far more latitude to collect such information on a massive scale.

The FBI is a key partner of the NSA and its massive surveillance program that vacuums up an untold number of emails of Americans talking to people overseas. Wiretapping international phone calls and emails, considered illegal in the mid 20th century — although done anyways — has now been all but legalized by the FISA Amendments Act passed under the Bush administration after 9/11. One government document suggests the FBI accesses NSA data on Americans so much that it cannot possibly count how many times they've done so.

In addition, the FBI has access to surveillance technology of its own: surveillance drones, Stingrays (fake cell phone towers that can lock onto cell phones), license plate readers, and a facial recognition database that has grown to millions of people with little oversight or public scrutiny.

No longer is there a filing cabinet in the FBI Director's office containing a prominent writer's deepest darkest secrets. Instead, these files have been replaced with a thousand data points in faceless servers scattered in countless corners of the country, bits that can be pieced together and pulled up when an FBI agent hits a few commands and can then be scattered back into a thousand different parts after the fact.

That doesn't mean the FBI doesn't ever open up investigations on famous writers and dissidents anymore in clear violation of their rights. Oscar award-winning documentarian Laura Poitras has fought a years long legal battle with the FBI, DHS and other intelligence agencies to get access to her own files after being stopped and interrogated while traveling dozens of times during the Bush and Obama administrations. Award-winning writer William Vollmann told a harrowing story in Harper's Magazine in 2013 about discovering his own extensive FBI file showing he had been followed for years by agents — after a tip from a reader who didn't like one of his books.

Both Poitras and Vollmann only learned of this surveillance because they were able to use the Freedom of Information Act (FOIA) to access it.

FOIA is, in many ways, an imperfect tool. In some ways it is badly broken. It is full of exemptions that the government can lean on to keep all kinds of information secret indefinitely, and FOIA offices inside government agencies are often underfunded and overworked, creating giant backlogs that can leave people without documents for years.

And, yet, FOIA is one of the most powerful tools for transparency ever created in our democracy. At its core, it gives citizens the power to demand information from their government that they attempt to keep hidden from the public. It is the reason we now have so many files that make up this important book.

FOIA should, of course, be celebrated. But it also needs to be fought for and defended at every turn. Every year one government agency or another tries to insert another exemption into all kinds of unrelated bills. It has been under attack since before it ever became law, signed and then strengthened decades ago by presidents who privately condemned it.

Even after the Snowden revelations and leaks that followed it, we still know far too little about how the modern FBI operates and who exactly it is surveilling. The very existence of this book, and the stories of surveillance it tells, are a testament to the dangers of over-reach by government intelligence agencies. The only remedy is more transparency — and the accountability it provides. Whether that transparency comes through lawsuits or leaks, it is the only way we prevent our current generation of writers from ever seeing their names in this type of book in the future.

TREVOR TIMM